ISBN 0-8373-1060-1

C-1060 CAREER EXAMINATION SERIES

This is your PASSBOOK® for...

Special Agent FBI

Test Preparation Study Guide

Questions & Answers

NLC

NATIONAL LEARNING CORPORATION

National Learning Corporation

212 Michael Drive, Syosset, New York 11791

(516) 921-8888
(800) 645-6337
FAX: (516) 921-8743
www.passbooks.com
sales @ passbooks.com
info @ passbooks.com

PRINTED IN THE UNITED STATES OF AMERICA

PASSBOOK®

NOTICE

This book is SOLELY intended for, is sold ONLY to, and its use is RESTRICTED to *individual*, bona fide applicants or candidates who qualify by virtue of having seriously filed applications for appropriate license, certificate, professional and/or promotional advancement, higher school matriculation, scholarship, or other legitimate requirements of educational and/or governmental authorities.

This book is NOT intended for use, class instruction, tutoring, training, duplication, copying, reprinting, excerption, or adaptation, etc., by:

(1) Other publishers

(2) Proprietors and/or Instructors of "Coaching" and/or Preparatory Courses

(3) Personnel and/or Training Divisions of commercial, industrial, and governmental organizations

(4) Schools, colleges, or universities and/or their departments and staffs, including teachers and other personnel

(5) Testing Agencies or Bureaus

(6) Study groups which seek by the purchase of a single volume to copy and/or duplicate and/or adapt this material for use by the group as a whole without having purchased individual volumes for each of the members of the group

(7) Et al.

Such persons would be in violation of appropriate Federal and State statutes.

PROVISION OF LICENSING AGREEMENTS. — Recognized educational commercial, industrial, and governmental institutions and organizations, and others legitimately engaged in educational pursuits, including training, testing, and measurement activities, may address a request for a licensing agreement to the copyright owners, who will determine whether, and under what conditions, including fees and charges, the materials in this book may be used by them. In other words, a licensing facility exists for the legitimate use of the material in this book on other than an individual basis. However, it is asseverated and affirmed here that the material in this book *CANNOT* be used without the receipt of the express permission of such a licensing agreement from the Publishers.

NATIONAL LEARNING CORPORATION
212 Michael Drive
Syosset, New York 11791

Inquiries re licensing agreements should be addressed to:
The President
National Learning Corporation
212 Michael Drive
Syosset, New York 11791

PASSBOOK SERIES®

THE *PASSBOOK SERIES®* has been created to prepare applicants and cand dates for the ultimate academic battlefield – the examination room.

At some time in our lives, each and every one of us may be required to take an examination – for validation, matriculation, admission, qualification, registration, certification, or licensure.

Based on the assumption that every applicant or candidate has met the basic formal educational standards, has taken the required number of courses, and read the necessary texts, the *PASSBOOK SERIES®* furnishes the one special preparation which may assure passing with confidence, instead of failing with insecurity. Examination questions – together with answers – are furnished as the basic vehicle for study so that the mysteries of the examination and its compounding difficulties may be eliminated or diminished by a sure method.

This book is meant to help you pass your examination provided that you qualify and are serious in your objective.

The entire field is reviewed through the huge store of content information which is succinctly presented through a provocative and challenging approach – the question-and-answer method.

A climate of success is established by furnishing the correct answers at the end of each test.

You soon learn to recognize types of questions, forms of questions, and patterns of questioning. You may even begin to anticipate expected outcomes.

You perceive that many questions are repeated or adapted so that you can gain acute insights, which may enable you to score many sure points.

You learn how to confront new questions, or types of questions, and to attack them confidently and work out the correct answers.

You note objectives and emphases, and recognize pitfalls and dangers, so that you may make positive educational adjustments.

Moreover, you are kept fully informed in relation to new concepts, methods, practices, and directions in the field.

You discover that you are actually taking the examination all the time: you are preparing for the examination by "taking" an examination, not by reading extraneous and/or supererogatory textbooks.

In short, this PASSBOOK®, used directedly, should be an important factor in helping you to pass your test.

SPECIAL AGENT FBI

DUTIES AND RESPONSIBILITIES

As the primary investigative arm of the federal government, the FBI is responsible for protecting the United States by preventing future terrorist attacks, conducting sensitive national security investigations, and enforcing over 260 federal statutes.

The FBI's top ten investigative priorities are:

1. Protect the United States from terrorist attack
2. Protect the United States against foreign intelligence operations and espionage
3. Protect the United States against cyber-based attacks and high-technology crimes
4. Combat public corruption at all levels
5. Protect civil rights
6. Combat transnational and national criminal organizations and enterprises
7. Combat major white-collar crime
8. Combat significant violent crime
9. Support federal, state, county, municipal and international partners
10. Upgrade technology to successfully perform the FBI's mission

While the FBI remains committed to other important national security and law enforcement responsibilities, the prevention of terrorism takes precedence in investigations.

The FBI also works with other federal, state and local law enforcement agencies in investigating matters of joint interest and in training law enforcement officers from around the world.

When you join the FBI, you join a united effort against crime. It's a rewarding career for anyone who has the ability and desire to contribute to the proud history and bright future of today's FBI.

To ensure that FBI Special Agents (SA) are fully prepared to meet their responsibilities as leaders in the law enforcement community, applicants must pass a standardized Physical Fitness Test (PFT). The test consists of the following four mandatory events: 1) one minute sit-ups; 2) a 300-meter sprint; 3) maximum push-ups; and 4) a 1.5-mile run. SA Applicants must pass the PFT in order to be eligible for admission into a New Agent Training (NAT) class.

The FBI Academy at Quantico, VA

Each new Agent serves a two-year probationary period upon entering on duty with the FBI. However, preference eligible veterans serve a one year probationary period. At the FBI Academy, you will join a class of Special Agent trainees for slightly over 18 weeks of intensive training at one of the world's finest law enforcement training facilities.

Your classroom hours will be spent studying a wide variety of academic and investigative subjects. The FBI Academy curriculum also includes intensive training in physical fitness, defensive tactics, practical application exercises, and the use of firearms. Several tests will be administered in all of these areas to monitor your progress.

Upon successful completion of Academy training, you will graduate and receive the credentials of an FBI Special Agent.

Your First Assignment

As a newly appointed Special Agent, you will be assigned to one of the FBI's field offices based on the current staffing and/or critical specialty needs. New Agents are permitted to make known their preference for assignment and consideration is given to your desires; however, assignment will be based upon the staffing needs of the FBI.

Your first months will be guided by a veteran Special Agent who will help you apply the lessons learned at the FBI Academy.

Advancement

Throughout your career with the FBI, you can qualify for additional training and promotion to a variety of administrative and supervisory positions.

Special Agents enter as GS 10 employees on the law enforcement government pay scale and can advance to the GS 13 grade level in field non-supervisory assignments. Promotions to supervisory, management, and executive positions are available in grades GS 14 and GS 15 as well as in the Senior Executive Service. All Special Agents may qualify for availability pay, which is an additional premium compensation for unscheduled duty equaling 25 percent of the Agent's base salary.

As an FBI employee, you will be entitled to a variety of benefits, including group health and life insurance programs, vacation and sick pay, and a full retirement plan.

QUALIFICATION REQUIREMENTS

Entry Requirements

To carry out its mission, the FBI needs men and women who can fill a variety of demanding positions. To qualify as an FBI Special Agent, you must be a U.S. citizen, or a citizen of the Northern Mariana Islands, at least age 23 and not have reached your 37th birthday on appointment. Candidates must be completely available for assignment anywhere in the FBI's jurisdiction. Candidates need to have at least 20/20 vision in one eye and not worse than 20/40 vision in the other eye. If an individual has a satisfactory history of soft contact lens wear and is able to meet correction to 20/20 in one eye and no worse than 20/40 in the other eye, safety concerns are considered mitigated and applicant processing may continue. In addition, policy for color vision allows continuation of applicant processing if those who fail initial color vision screening are able to successfully complete the Farnsworth D-15 color vision test.

If an applicant has had laser eye corrective surgery, a six month waiting period is required with evidence of complete healing by ophthalmology clinical evaluation

Special Agent applicants also must meet hearing standards by audiometer test. No applicant will be considered who exceeds the following: a) average hearing loss of 25 decibels (ANSI) at 1000, 2000, and 3000 Hertz; b) single reading of 35 decibels at 1000, 2000, and 3000 Hertz; c) single reading of 35 decibels at 500 Hertz; and d) single reading of 45 decibels at 4000 Hertz.

Candidates must possess a valid driver's license, and be in excellent physical condition with no defects which would interfere in firearm use, raids, or defensive tactics.

Applicants must possess a four-year degree from a college or university accredited by one of the regional or national institutional associations recognized by the United States Secretary of Education.

Critical Skill Needs

Candidates who otherwise meet entry requirements and possess one or more of the following critical skills are currently deemed essential to address our increasingly complex responsibilities and will be prioritized in the hiring process.

1. Accounting
2. Computer Science and other Information Technology specialties
3. Engineering
4. Foreign Language proficiency (Arabic, Farsi, Pashtu, Urdu, Chinese [all dialects], Japanese, Korean, Russian, Spanish and Vietnamese)
5. Intelligence Experience
6. Law Experience
7. Law Enforcement or other Investigative Experience
8. Military Experience
9. Physical Sciences (Physics, Chemistry, Biology, etc.)

Although the above listing includes the most critical investigative skill needs, the FBI continues to be a diverse agency with employees possessing various experiences. Candidates who possess skills and experience such as accounting, law, business, education, and health care are also encouraged to apply.

Entry Programs

LAW

To qualify under the Law Program, you must have a JD degree from a resident law school.

ACCOUNTING/FINANCE

Any applicant who wishes to be considered for the Accounting Program may qualify when he/she either: 1) Has been certified as a CPA; OR 2) Possesses a four-year business degree with a major in accounting, or related business degree that included or was supplemented by 24 hours of accounting courses and an additional six semester hours of business law or other elective business courses, and two years of progressively responsible accounting work in a professional accounting firm or comparable public setting, such as a state comptroller or the General Accounting Office, the last which would be in a management, team leader or other type of position which would provide experiences in a variety of areas (banking, insurance, problem solving, etc.) and allow for exposure and experiences dealing with higher level organizational entities, i.e., partners and directors.

LANGUAGE

To qualify under the Language Program, you must have a BS or BA degree in any discipline and be proficient in a language that meets the needs of the FBI. Candidates will be expected to pass a Language Proficiency Test.

COMPUTER SCIENCE/INFORMATION TECHNOLOGY (CS/IT)

To qualify under the CS/IT Special Entry Program, the applicant must have a computer- or information technology-related degree, a degree in Electrical Engineering, a Cisco Certified Network Professional (CCNP) certification, or a Cisco Certified Internetworking Expert (CCIE) certification.

DIVERSIFIED

To qualify under the Diversified Program, you must have a BS or BA degree in any discipline, plus three years of full-time work experience, or an advanced degree accompanied by two years of full-time work experience.

Competitive candidates will complete a battery of written tests and, in some cases, specialized testing in your field of expertise. If you pass these tests, you may be eligible for an interview based upon your overall qualifications, your competitiveness among other candidates, and the needs of the FBI.

Successful completion of the written test and an interview will be followed by a thorough background investigation that will include: credit and arrest checks; interviews of associates; contacts with personal and business references, past employers and neighbors; and verification of educational achievements.

Just as some things can qualify you for a career as a Special Agent, some things can disqualify you. These may include: conviction of a felony or major misdemeanor; use of illegal drugs; or failure to pass a drug-screening test. All candidates will be given a polygraph examination to determine the veracity of information provided in the application for employment to include the extent of any illegal drug usage and issues surrounding security concerns.

Applicants must be U.S. citizens and consent to a complete background investigation, urinalysis, and polygraph. Only those candidates determined to be best qualified will be contacted to proceed in the selection process.

The FBI welcomes and encourages applications from persons with physical and mental disabilities and will reasonably accommodate the needs of those persons. The decision on granting reasonable accommodation will be on a case-by-case basis. The FBI is firmly committed to satisfying its affirmative obligations under the Rehabilitation Act of 1973, to ensure that persons with disabilities have every opportunity to be hired and advanced on the basis of merit within the FBI. The Federal Bureau of Investigation is an Equal Opportunity Employer. All qualified applicants will receive consideration for this vacancy. Except where otherwise provided by law, selection will be made without regard to, and there will be no discrimination because of race, religion, color, national origin, sex, political affiliations, marital status, non-disqualifying physical or mental disability, age, sexual orientation, membership or non-membership in an employee organization, or on the basis of personal favoritism or other non-merit factors.

SPECIAL AGENT FBI

APPLICANT INFORMATION
FBI SPECIAL AGENT SELECTION PROCESS

TABLE OF CONTENTS

SPECIAL AGENT FBI

SECTION I: FBI SPECIAL AGENT APPLICATION AND SELECTION PROCESS

General Information

The Special Agent Selection Process consists of a variety of steps, and two sets of tests: Phase 1 and Phase 2 tests. The tests that will be administered as part of the selection process were developed to provide an assessment of critical skills and abilities that are required upon entry to the FBI Special Agent position. These critical skills and abilities on which Special Agent applicants will be assessed include:

A. Ability to Write Effectively
B. Ability to Communicate Orally
C. Ability to Organize, Plan, and Prioritize
D. Ability to Relate Effectively with Others
E. Ability to Maintain a Positive Image
F. Ability to Attend to Detail
G. Ability to Evaluate Information and Make Judgment Decisions
H. Initiative and Motivation
I. Ability to Adapt to Changing Situations
J. Physical Requirements

This section presents information on qualifications for the Special Agent position and describes general information about the application and selection process. Section II presents general information about the testing process. Then, Section III describes the tests included in Phase 1, while Section IV describes the tests included in Phase 2.

Qualifications for the Special Agent Position

Special Agent candidates must:

1. be a United States citizen or a citizen of the Northern Mariana Islands

2. be completely available for assignment anywhere in the Bureau's jurisdiction

3. have reached his/her 23rd but not his/her 37th birthday

4. have uncorrected vision not less than 20/200 (Snellen) and corrected 20/20 in one eye and at least 20/40 in the other eye. All applicants must pass a color vision test.

5. meet following hearing standards by audiometer test. No applicant will be considered who exceeds the following: (a) average hearing loss of 25 decibels (ANSI) at 1000, 2000, and 3000 Hertz; (b) single reading of 35 decibels at 1000, 2000, or 3000 Hertz; (c) single reading of 35 decibels at 500 Hertz; (d) single reading of 45 decibels at 4000 Hertz.

6. possess a valid driver's license

7. be physically able to engage in firearm use, raids, or defensive tactics

8. all candidates must possess a four-year degree from a resident college or university which is certified by one of the six Regional Accreditation Associations

Special Agent candidates must qualify under one or more of the following entrance programs:

LAW - law school graduates with two years of undergraduate work.

ACCOUNTING - graduate of a four-year college or university with a degree in accounting or degree in another discipline, preferably economics, business or finance, with a major in accounting. An applicant must also have passed the Uniform Certified Public Accountant examination or provide certification from the school at which the accounting degree or major was earned that he/she is academically eligible to sit for the above examination.

LANGUAGE - four-year college degree plus fluency in a foreign language(s) for which the Bureau has a current need.

DIVERSIFIED - four-year college degree plus three years of fulltit.1e work experience. Those individuals possessing an advanced degree need only two years work experience.

The following are automatic disqualifiers for the Special Agent position:

1. felony conviction

2. student loan in default (insured by U.S. Government)

FBI Employment Drug Policy

The Federal Bureau of Investigation is firmly committed to a drug-free society and workplace. Therefore, the unlawful use of drugs by FBI employees will not be tolerated. Furthermore, applicants for employment with the FBI who currently are using illega drugs will be found unsuitable for employment. The FBI does not condone any prior unlawful drug use by applicants. The FBI realizes, however, some otherwise qualified applicants may have used drugs at some point in their past. The following policy sets forth the criteria for determining whether an applicant's prior use makes her/him unsuitable for employment, balanc ng the needs of the FBI to maintain a drug-free workplace and the public integrity necessary to accomplish its law enforcement mission, with the desirability of affording the opportunity of employment to the broadest segment of society consistent with those needs.

CRITERIA

1. An applicant who has illegally used any drug while employed in any law enforcement or prosecutorial position, or while employed in a position which carries with it a high level of responsibility or public trust, will be found unsuitable for employment.

2. An applicant who is discovered to have deliberately misrepresented her/his drug history in connection with her/his application will be found unsuitable for employment.

3. An applicant who has sold any illegal drug will be found unsuitable for employment.

4. An applicant who has illegally used any drug, other than experimental use of cannabis, within the past ten years will be found unsuitable for employment, absent compelling mitigating circumstances. Experimental use of drugs other than cannabis, which occurred more than ten years prior to the application for employment will be evaluated based upon the general factors specified below.

5. An applicant who has used cannabis within the past three years will be found unsuitable for employment. Experimental use of cannabis which occurred more than three years prior to the application for employment will be evaluated based upon the general factors specified below.

GENERAL FACTORS

1. The kind of position for which the person is applying, including the degree of public trust or risk in the position;
2. The nature and seriousness of the conduct;
3. The circumstances surrounding the conduct;
4. The decency of the conduct;
5. The age of the applicant at the time of the conduct;
6. Contributing societal conditions; and
7. The absence or presence of rehabilitation or efforts toward rehabilitation.

Special Agent Transfer Policy

The Director of the FBI maintains the authority to transfer any FBI employee when it is in the best interest of the United States Government. All Special Agents are subject to transfer at any time to meet the organizational and program needs of the FBI.FBI Special Agents accept the possibility of transfer as a condition of their employment. Special Agents may be transferred where and when the needs of the FBI may dictate. In this regard the overall needs of the Bureau, to include the assurance that investigatory experience levels are appropriately represented in all field offices, along with budgetary considerations, take precedence. The personal needs and preferences of the Agents are considered wherever possible in carrying out the transfer policy.

Special Agent Firearms Policy

In 1934, Congress authorized Special Agents of the Federal Bureau of Investigation to carry firearms under Title 18, USC, Section 3052. Special Agents are initially trained at the FBI Academy, Quantico, Virginia, for all aspects of the use and maintenance of firearms and related equipment under their control.

Special Agents must be armed or have immediate access to a firearm at all times when on official duty unless good judgment dictates otherwise. Special Agents may be required to utilize deadly force should circumstances dictate.

<u>Special Agent Application and Selection Components</u>

There are five main components to the selection process:

- <u>INITIAL APPLICATION</u>. All applicants will be required to complete a short form application titled, PRELIMINARY APPLICATION FOR SPECIAL AGENT POSITION (FD-646) and the Applicant Background Survey (FD-804). When complete, the initial application and Applicant Background Survey should be sent to the Applicant Coordinator at the FBI Field Office nearest to where you live.

  Applicants will be screened using this Initial Application to determine whether or not they meet the minimum qualifications outlined above. All applicants will be informed of their standing upon review of their applications. Those who are selected for further processing will be notified of this in advance by the Applicant Coordinator from the FBI Field Office nearest to them. They will be scheduled at a particular date, time, and location to take the Phase 1 tests.

- <u>PHASE 1 TESTS</u>. The first phase testing process consists of a battery of three tests, including: Biodata Inventory, Cognitive Ability Test, and Situational Judgment Test. These are all paper-and-pencil tests, and they are described in more detail in Section III. Individuals will be notified in writing whether they have passed or failed the first phase tests within 30 days. Those passing the first phase tests will be invited to submit the more lengthy application described next

- <u>SUBMISSION OF APPLICATION FOR EMPLOYMENT (FD-140)</u>. Applicants who pass the Phase 1 tests will be notified by letter and asked to submit this application by a specific date. This application is titled, APPLICATION FOR EMPLOYMENT (FD-140). Applicants will again be informed of their standing at this point in the selection process. Those positively reviewed will be scheduled for the Phase 2 tests described below. Individuals will be notified of this by the Applicant Coordinator at the nearest FBI Field Office to them. They will be scheduled at a particular date, time, and location to take the Phase 2 tests.

- <u>PHASE 2 TESTS</u>. The second phase testing process consists of a Structured Selection Interview and a written exercise. Performance on these tests will be evaluated by FBI Special Agents, who will serve as assessors. Those who pass the second phase of tests will be sent a conditional offer of employment letter. However, final employment will be contingent on successful completion of the steps listed belowcation described next.

- <u>FINAL APPLICANT SCREENING PROCESS</u>. The final applicant screening process is comprised of several steps, including polygraph examination, full background investigation, drug test and pre employment physical examination. Each of these is described briefly.

- <u>POLYGRAPH EXAMINATION</u>. All applicants will be given a polygraph examination to determine the veracity of information contained in the APPLICATION FOR EMPLOYMENT (FD-140) to include the extent of any illegal drug usage and any issues regarding security concerns.

- BACKGROUND INVESTIGATION. All applicants will be afforded a full field background investigation that includes credit and criminal checks; interviews of associates; contacts with personal and business references; interviews of past employers and neighbors; and verification of educational achievements.

- DRUG TESTING. All applicants will be given a urine analysis to screen for drug usage.

- PREEMPLOYMENT PHYSICAL EXAMINATION. All applicants will be afforded a physical examination to determine physical suitability for the Special Agent position.

Retesting

All applicants who fail the Special Agent Written Test (Phase 1) are eligible to retest one year after the date of taking the test for the first time. Those applicants who pass the Special Agent Written Test (Phase 1) are eligible to proceed to the Structured Interview and writing sample (Phase 2); these applicants will only be allowed to take Phase 2 tests once.

SECTION II: TESTING PROCESS

Logistics and Procedures

When and Where. Phase 1 and Phase 2 tests will be administered at various locations throughout the United States. Applicant Coordinators at each FBI Field Office will coordinate the testing and inform applicants of the date, time, and location of their testing sessions.

How Long. It will take each candidate four hours to complete the Phase 1 tests and approximately three hours to complete the Phase 2 tests.

Travel Arrangements. Candidates will be required to make their own arrangements to travel to the testing location.

Scheduling. Applicants will generally be given a30 day notice of their scheduled testing date, time, and location.

Only under exceptional circumstances will testing appointments be rescheduled. Since applicants will be notified of their scheduled date in advance, every effort should be made to be available at the scheduled time. If applicants have an important conflict with their scheduled appointment, they should notify the FBI Applicant Coordinator whose name will be provided on correspondence immediately to schedule an alternative date.

Tardiness. It is an applicant's responsibility to arrive on time for the scheduled appointment. If candidates are tardy, they will not be permitted to participate in the testing process, since the testing will be run on a strict time schedule.

What To Bring. Candidates must bring a driver's license to Phase 1 and Phase 2 testing. Applicants will not be permitted to participate in the testing process without proper identification. Applicants who have prior military service may also bring their Form DD 214, Certificate of Release or Discharge from Active Duty, to Phase 1 testing, if applicable. Applicants who carry firearms (i.e., who are in law enforcement positions) must NOT bring their firearm into FBI space or the testing facility.

Do not bring any of the following:

- This book
- Reference materials (dictionaries, textbooks, etc.)
- Pens or pencils (These will be provided)
- Reading materials (books, magazines, newspapers)
- Work-related materials
- Beepers/pagers (alarms on watches must be turned off)
- Papers (notification letter, notes, blank paper)
- Tape-recorder, cassette, or compact disc player, radio, calculator, camera
- Cellular telephones

What to Wear.

- Phase 1 Testing. Candidates are encouraged to dress in comfortable clothing.
- Phase 2 Testing. Candidates should dress in a professional manner. Business attire would be appropriate.

Rules

Restroom Use. Applicants may use the restrooms during breaks and not during administration of the tests.

Eating/Drinking. Eating and drinking will not be permitted during the testing, but will be allowed during breaks. Chewing gum or tobacco is discouraged during the interview, since oral communication skills will be evaluated as part of this exercise.

Phone Use. Candidates will not be permitted to use the telephone during the testing process. Do not bring beepers.

Leaving the Premises. Candidates will not be permitted to leave the testing premises during the testing. All breaks will be relatively short.

Talking. Once the orientation period has begun, applicants will not be permitted to talk with other applicants at any time during testing.

Discussing the Tests. Applicants should not discuss the examinations with anyone during or after the testing process. Discussing the tests may give others unfair advantages or disadvantages in the selection process.

Smoking. Smoking will not be permitted during the testing.

Time Limits. The time limits which have been set for the various tests will be strictly enforced. When time is called, applicants must immediately stop what they are doing and await further instructions.

FAILURE TO COMPLY WITH THESE RULES MAY RESULT IN DISQUALIFICATION.

SECTION III: PHASE 1 TESTS

Introduction to the Phase 1 Tests

When applicants arrive for the testing process, they will be checked in and asked to provide their driver's license. The license will be held by the Test Administrator until the testing is complete. A trained FBI employee will run the testing session. Three paper and-pencil multiple choice tests comprise the Phase 1 testing process. These are:

- Biodata (Biographical Data) Inventory
- Logical Reasoning Test
- Situational Judgment Test

When the testing process begins, applicants will be given one machine scan able answer sheet on which responses to all of the tests will be recorded. Different sections of the answer sheet are labeled for recording responses to each of the different tests.

On the answer sheet, applicants will be asked to print their last names, first names, and middle initials and then sign the form in a signature block. Applicants will also be asked to record their complete street address, city, state, and zip code on the answer sheet. The date and each applicant's Social Security Number will also be recorded on the answer form.

All information on the machine scan able forms must be filled in accurately, using only a #2 pencil that will be provided. Scratch paper will also be provided by test administrators. The answer ovals on the form must be filled in completely with dark, black marks. Any mistakes or stray marks must be completely erased. Failure to fill out the machine scan able forms properly may preclude the tests from being scored properly.

Once the general information on the answer form has been completed, each test will be administered in turn. The Test Administrator will distribute numbered test booklets, read instructions for the test, and answer any questions. Each test will begin when the Test Administrator indicates that timing for the test has started. When the time limit for the test has been reached, the administrator will call time. All applicants must cease working on their tests at that time and close their test booklets.

On the following pages, more information is provided about each test. Specifically, we provide a copy of the directions for each test and also the critical skills and abilities being measured. A manual has been prepared by the FBI to help applicants prepare for taking the Logical Reasoning Test. This Special Agent Exam Preparation Manual is free of charge and available through the FBI Applicant Coordinators.

Note: There are different versions of each test, only one of which you will receive. The tests look similar on the surface but are not. Therefore, any information regarding the tests that you obtain from others may be misleading and could harm your performance.

Tips for Taking the Phase 1 Tests:

- Read each question carefully.
- The time limits established for the Bidet Inventory and Situational Judgment Test should allow applicants to finish those tests without being rushed. However, you should work through the items efficiently.
- Work as quickly and as accurately as you can to complete as many items as possible. You should not spend too much time on anyone item.
- You will not be penalized for guessing answers on any of the tests.
- For the Biodata Inventory, it is very important that you answer the questions honestly. Do not choose what you think are the best answers; just describe yourself accurately. Doing otherwise will distort your test score and negatively affect your performance.

Scoring

Scoring. Scores on the Logical Reasoning Test, Biodata Inventory, and Situational Judgment Test will be combined to arrive at a final test score. The Biodata and Situational Judgment Test will be weighted twice as much as the Logical Reasoning Test in arriving at the final Phase 1 score. This is because the Biodata and Situational Judgment Test provide an assessment of a greater number of critical job skills than does the Logical Reasoning Test. A passing score has been established that will be applied uniformly to all applicants taking the test. There is one passing score that is based on the combination of all three tests rather than individual passing scores for each test. Thus, a very high score on one test can compensate for a lower score on another test.

Each applicant will be notified about his/her pass or fail status within 30 days of taking the tests. The actual test scores will not be disseminated. Those who pass the tests will be instructed regarding the next steps.

BIODATA INVENTORY

Directions for the Biodata Inventory are as follows:

This inventory contains 47 questions about yourself.

You are to read each question and select the answer that BEST describes you from the choices provided. Answer the questions honestly; doing otherwise will negatively affect your score.

Look at the example question below.

S1. In connection with your work, in which of the following have you taken the most pride?

A. Having been able to avoid any major controversies.
B. Having gotten where you are on your own.
C. Having been able to work smoothly with people.
D. Having provided a lot of new ideas, good or bad.
E. Having been able to do well whatever management has requested.

In this example, you would select the answer that BEST describes what YOU honestly take pride in with regard to your work. You would completely blacken the oval corresponding to your answer selection (A, B, C, D, or E).

You will have 45 minutes to complete this inventory.

You will record your answer to each question on the separate machine readable answer sheet in the section marked Biodata Inventory. Be sure to fill in the ovals you select completely with dark marks. As you are completing this inventory, please DO NOT write in the test booklet.

Two example biodata items are:

In connection with your work, in which of the following have you taken the most pride?

A. Having been able to avoid any major controversies.
B. Having gotten where you are on your own.
C. Having been able to work smoothly with people.
D. Having provided a lot of new ideas, good or bad.
E. Having been able to do well whatever management has requested.

When in a position at work or school which necessitated making decisions that affected others, how would others describe you?

A. As someone who appeared to weigh all logical alternatives before making a decision in a timely manner.
B. As someone who weighed all alternatives, but may have taken a long time to come to a decision.
C. As someone who makes decisions quickly without weighing the alternatives.
D. I have never been in this type of position

This test measures the following critical skills and abilities:

- Ability to Organize, Plan, and Prioritize
- Ability to Maintain a Positive Image
- Ability to Evaluate Information and Make Judgment Decisions
- Initiative and Motivation
- Ability to Adapt to Changing Situations
- Physical Requirements

LOGICAL REASONING TEST

General directions for the Logical Reasoning Test are as follows:

Each of the questions in the Logical Reasoning Test contains a reading passage followed by a lead-in phrase that introduces five response choices.

The Reading Passage

Questions in the Logical Reasoning Test are based on subject matter relevant to the Special Agent occupation but do not require job knowledge and do not always reflect true-to-fact job procedures. Therefore, in selecting your response, it is important that you accept every fact in the reading passage as true and that you use *only* the information given in the passage. Remember that you will not be judged on your knowledge of facts but rather on your ability to reason on the basis of given facts.

The Lead-In Phrase and the Response Choices

A lead-in phrase will follow every reading passage. This lead-in phrase will ask you to complete a sentence by selecting one among five response choices.

The lead-in phrase can be affirmative or negative:

- *From the information given above, it can be validly concluded that*
  OR
- *From the information given above, it CANNOT be validly concluded that*

It is important that you focus on the lead-in phrase in order to determine whether the question is affirmative or negative.

Affirmative lead-in phrases are followed by four invalid conclusions and one valid conclusion. Your task is to identify the valid conclusion. Negative lead-in phrases, on the contrary, are followed by four valid conclusions and one invalid conclusion, which will be your task to identify.

The lead-in phrase may also affect the response choices by circumscribing the inference to a certain set or situation. For example, the lead-in phrase F*rom the information given above it can be validly concluded that official court leave is granted to agents when* circumscribes the response choices to the context of circumstances in which official court leave is granted to agents.

LOGICAL REASONING TEST DIRECTIONS

To answer each question on the logic-based reasoning test, select the answer representing the only valid statement that can be made from the information contained in the paragraph. To identify the correct conclusion, it is essential that you use ONLY the information provided in the content paragraph.

Record your answer to each question on the machine-readable answer sheet. Make sure to completely fill in the circle that corresponds with your answer. You should provide only one answer for each question. Please do not write in the test booklet.

You have 90 minutes to read the questions and provide your responses. Do not start until I have instructed you to do so. I will give you a warning when you have one hour, 30 minutes, and 5 minutes remaining to complete the logical based reasoning test questions.

SAMPLE QUESTIONS

Question 1

Eventually, most citizens are summoned to serve on jury duty. If a government employee is asked to serve on a jury, official court leave is authorized with no charge to leave or loss of pay. Also, official court leave is always granted if the employee is summoned to appear as a witness in a judicial proceeding in which the government is a party. No fees rendered for service can be retained by the employee. Rather, they must be turned in to the agency in which he or she is employed. However, some payments designated as expenses by the courts, such as travel reimbursements, may be kept.

From the information given above, it can be validly concluded that official court leave

A) is not granted to individuals other than government employees who are summoned to serve as jurors or to appear as witnesses in judicial proceedings in which the government is a party
B) sometimes entails retention by government employees of fees received from the court for services rendered as jurors
C) is never accompanied by reimbursement for expenses incurred by government employees while serving as witnesses in judicial proceedings in which the government is a party
D) never entails loss of pay by government employees who are summoned to serve as jurors or to appear as witnesses in judicial proceedings in which the government is a party
E) is not always granted to government employees who are summoned to appear as witnesses in judicial proceedings in which the government is a party

The correct response is D. The information in the passage establishes two conditions under which court leave is authorized for government employees without charge to leave or loss of pay: (1) if the employee is asked to serve on a jury and (2) if the employee is summoned to appear as a witness in a judicial proceeding in which the government is a party. Response D reiterates this statement in negative form: *Official court leave never entails loss of pay by government employees who are summoned to serve as jurors or to appear as witnesses in judicial proceedings in which the government is a party.*

Response A is incorrect because the passage gives no information about court leave policies for non-government employees.

Response B is incorrect because it contradicts the information in the passage, which states that no fees rendered for service as a juror can be retained by a government employee.

Response C is incorrect because it contradicts the information in the passage, which states that some payments designated as expenses by the courts, such as travel reimbursements, may be kept by a government employee.

Response E is incorrect because it is contrary to the information in the passage, which establishes that official court leave is always granted to government employees if they are asked to serve on a jury or if they are summoned as a witness in a judicial proceeding in which the government is a party.

Question # 1 is an example of an easy question in which three of the incorrect response choices contradict the information in the passage, while one incorrect response (response A) is based on unwarranted assumptions about a set of individuals that is not discussed in the passage. More difficult errors of reasoning are illustrated in the next two sample questions.

Question 2
Whenever an investigator is involved in an intelligence operation, he or she is required to examine multiple hypotheses, thus avoiding the quick pursuit of only one path, which could turn out to be incorrect. In a recent terrorism case, which thus far has proved to be exceptionally complex and remains unresolved, several hypotheses were initially generated about the suspects, conspirators, motives, and implementation of the terrorist act. Most of these hypotheses have been disproved.

From the information given above, it can be validly concluded that

A) in any intelligence operation, an investigator who generates more than one hypothesis is more likely than not to succeed
B) at least one of the hypotheses generated for the terrorism case mentioned above is not likely to be disproved
C) if an investigator is not required to examine multiple hypotheses about a case, then he or she is not involved in an intelligence operation
D) whenever an investigator fails to solve a case, it can be assumed that, most probably, he/she failed to generate more than one hypothesis about the case
E) there are at least some investigative operations, other than those concerned with intelligence, that do not require the investigator to form more than one hypothesis

This question presents two aspects. One is the mandate to generate multiple hypotheses whenever an investigator conducts an intelligence operation. The second aspect is the interplay of possibilities and probabilities relative to the forming of hypotheses. The correct response, C, deals with the first aspect, while three of the four incorrect response choices deal with the second aspect. In the correct response, C, the inference (formally called a contra positive inference) represents a negative equivalent of the mandate found in the first sentence of the passage. The first sentence states an antecedent condition ("whenever an investigator is involved in an intelligence operation") from which follows a consequent condition ("he or she is required to examine multiple hypotheses"). If we transpose and negate these two conditions, as is done in C, we obtain an equivalent statement, in which the truth value of the original statement is retained.

Responses A, B, and D are based on unwarranted probabilistic inferences about (1) the likelihood that an investigator who generates more than one hypothesis will succeed (response A), the likelihood that at least one hypothesis will not be disproved in the terrorism case (response B), and the likelihood that an investigator who fails to solve a case will have failed to generate more than one hypothesis about it (response D). The passage provides no quantifying information from which such probabilistic inferences can be made. It only alludes to the *possibility* that a single hypothesis may be incorrect, which cannot be extrapolated into probabilities. In the context of probabilities, you should note that this test will not contain quantitative problems. You need to be alert only to verbal quantifying expressions such as "more likely than not," "unlikely," "most probably," etc.

Finally, in the case of response E, it is incorrect because the passage provides no information at all about investigative operations that may fall outside the set of intelligence operations.

Question 3
All forensic soil examiners compare the color, texture, and composition of two or more soils to determine if they share a common origin. Suppose, for example, that the suspect in a murder claims that soil recovered from her shovel-which actually came from a grave that she dug-was from her garden. The garden will be eliminated as the source of the soil on the shovel if and only if this soil is found to be dissimilar to soil samples taken from the garden.

From the information given above, it CANNOT be validly concluded that

A) upon analysis and comparison, the soil samples taken from the shovel and the garden of the above-mentioned suspect will be dissimilar if the grave was not dug in the garden
B) analysts who are not involved in the comparison of soil samples are not forensic soil examiners
C) if, as a result of analysis and comparison, the suspect's garden is confirmed as the source of the soil on the shovel, then the soil samples taken from the garden and the shovel were found to be similar
D) if an analyst is involved in the comparison of soil samples, then he or she will be classified as a forensic soil examiner
E) if the soil samples taken from the shovel and the garden of the above-mentioned suspect are similar, then it can be assumed that the grave was dug in the garden

This question is an example of a difficult question. In the first place, it asks you to identify the only response choice that *does not* follow from the given information, which in and of itself makes the question slightly more difficult to analyze. Nonetheless, the difficulty of the question stems primarily from the logical complexity of its response choices. (If you are asking yourself why such complex reasoning must be included in the test, please bear in mind that the reason is, exclusively, relevance to the job. The information you will have to analyze on the job, including that found in legal manuals, will be generally as complex as this question, and frequently more so.)

The correct response is D. It represents the only fallacy found among the response choices. The fallacy is formally called a converse fallacy. The passage states that *all forensic soil examiners compare the color, texture, and composition of two or more soils*. From this information nothing can be concluded about whether or not there are analysts other than forensic soil examiners who carry out such comparisons. The information in the passage tells us only that the set of *forensic soil examiners* is entirely included in the set of *analysts who carry out soil comparisons* but tells us nothing about the composition or extension of the second set.

Response A is not a fallacy. The passage states (1) that the suspect's garden will be eliminated as the source of soil on the shovel if and only if this soil is found to be dissimilar to soil samples taken from the garden and (2) that the soil on the shovel came from a grave that the suspect dug. It follows that the soil samples will be dissimilar if the grave was not dug in the garden.

In the context of this question and this response, it is pertinent to note the use of the biconditional *if and only if*. A biconditional statement is defined as one in which the conditions included in the statement are interchangeable without affecting the truth value of the statement. Thus, to say that *the suspect's garden will be eliminated as the source of soil on the shovel if and only if this soil is found to be dissimilar to soil samples taken from the garden* is the same as saying that *the soil on the shovel will be found to be dissimilar to soil samples taken from the garden if and only if the garden is eliminated as the source of soil on the shovel.* This interchangeability of conditions permits the inference in response C: The statement in the passage establishes that *the suspect's garden will be eliminated as the source of soil on the shovel if and only if this soil is found to be dissimilar to soil samples taken from the garden.* It follows that *if the garden is confirmed as the source of the soil on the shovel, then this soil must be similar to soil samples taken from the garden.* In symbols, when we say *p if and only if q*, we are saying both that *if p then q and if q then p*. Hence, if we negate *p*, the negation of *q* must follow.

Both response B and response E illustrate the same type of inference that was illustrated before in question # 2 (Response C) except that, in question # 3, response B illustrates the inference (formally called a contra positive) in the context of sets, while response E illustrates it in the context of a conditional statement. These are discussed immediately below.

Relative to response B, the passage states that all forensic soil examiners analyze and compare soil samples. The transposed negative equivalent of this statement follows necessarily: analysts who are not involved in the comparison of soil samples are not forensic soil examiners.

Relative to response E, it represents the transposed negative equivalent of the statement in response A and hence retains the same truth value. Response A states that *if the grave was not dug in the garden then the soil samples taken from the shovel and the garden will be dissimilar.* Response E transposes and negates these conditions: *if the soil samples taken from the shovel and the garden are similar, then it can be assumed that the grave was dug in the garden.*

SITUATIONAL JUDGMENT TEST

General directions for the Situational Judgment Test are as follows:

This booklet contains 33 descriptions of problem situations. Each problem situation has between three and five alternative actions that might be taken to deal with the problem. You are to make two judgments for each problem.

First, decide which alternative you would MOST LIKELY choose in response to the problem. It might not be exactly what you would do in that situation, but it should be the alternative that comes closest to what you would actually do. Record your answers on the answer sheet by blackening the appropriate letter in the column labeled MOST LIKELY.

Second, decide which alternative you would be LEAST LIKELY to choose in that situation. Blacken the letter of that alternative in the column labeled LEAST LIKELY.

As you are taking the test, please DO NOT write in the test booklet. All of your responses will be recorded on the separate answer sheet in the section marked Situational Judgment Test. Be sure to fill in the ovals you select completely with dark black marks. You will have 1 hour and 30 minutes to complete this test.

Here is an example item:

You are shopping when you notice a man robbing the store. What would you do?

A. Leave the store as quickly as possible and call the police.
B. Try to apprehend the robber yourself.
C. Follow the man and call the police as soon as he appears settled somewhere.
D. Nothing, as you do not wish to get involved in the matter.

As shown in the example below, the respondent thought alternative B was the action that she would most likely take in the situation and thus, blackened the B for item 1 in the MOST LIKELY column. The respondent thought alternative D was the least likely thing she would do. Thus, the D was filled in for item 1 in the LEAST LIKELY column.

This test measures the following critical skills and abilities:

- Ability to Organize, Plan, and Prioritize
- Ability to Relate Effectively with Others
- Ability to Maintain a Positive Image
- Ability to Evaluate Information and Make Judgment Decisions Initiative and Motivation
- Ability to Adapt to Changing Situations

SECTION IV: PHASE 2 TESTS

Introduction to the Phase 2 Tests

Only applicants who pass the Phase 1 tests and are informed that they are still being considered in the selection process will take the Phase 2 tests. When applicants arrive for the testing process, they will be checked in and asked to provide their driver's license. This license will be held by the Test Administrator until the testing is complete. A trained FBI employee will run the testing session. Two tests comprise the Phase 2 testing process. These are:

- Structured Interview
- Written Exercise

On the following pages, more information is provided about each test, including the critical skills and abilities being measured by the tests.

Tips for Taking the Phase 2 Tests

- Be yourself.
- The evaluators will be taking notes during the interview to assist them in documenting the exercises. Do not let this distract you.
- Do not make assumptions about what the evaluators are looking for. The interview instructions are straight forward. There are no trick questions.
- Read the written exercise instructions carefully. Make sure you understand what the exercise requires. Do not go beyond the material which is provided; that is, do not make up facts.
- You may write on the written exercise materials.
- You should ask the administrator any questions you have regarding instructions for the tests.

Scoring

Scores on the Structured Interview and written exercise will be combined to arrive at a final score. The Interview will be weighted three times as much as the written exercise, which is a relatively narrow test measuring only a few critical skills and abilities required for the job. A passing score has been established that will be applied uniformly to all applicants taking the test. There is one passing score that is based on combined interview and written simulation performance rather than individual passing scores for each test.

STRUCTURED INTERVIEW
TIME LIMIT: 1 HOUR

The structured interview consists of 16 standard questions that will be asked of applicants. The interview will be administered by a panel of three evaluators. The interview will take one hour to administer and an additional 20 minutes to score. The evaluators will be FBI Special Agents who have been trained thoroughly how to rate the applicant's performance on the interview using standardized scoring criteria. After the Structured Interview is complete, the three evaluators will provide independent ratings of each applicant's performance. After the independent ratings have been made, the three evaluators will compare their ratings and resolve any discrepancies. The final consensus ratings will serve as the applicant's score.

When the applicant enters the room with the three member panel, the following directions will be read:

> "We'd like to spend the next hour getting to know more about you. During the interview, we will ask you to tell us how you've dealt with various different kinds of situations in the past. In answering our questions, you can describe family, work, school, or social situations and how you handled them. We'd like you to tell us what you did in the situation, even if it was a team effort. We will be asking you 16 questions. Feel free to take a few moments to think about the answer you would like to give for each question. You'll be doing most of the talking during the interview.
>
> One final instruction before we start. In response to each question, please be as specific and detailed as possible in describing the situation, your actions, and the outcome of your actions."

The interview will then commence. The panel members will rotate in asking questions of the interviewee, in turn. If an applicant cannot think of an answer to a question, the interviewer will suggest that they move onto the next question and return to the question that could not be answered at the end of the interview. As long as the interviewee provides an answer at some point, she/he will not be penalized. If, however, the interviewee fails to answer one or more questions prior to the end of the interview, this will adversely affect his or her scores.

The interview measures the following critical skills and abilities:

- Ability to Communicate Orally
- Ability to Organize, Plan, and Prioritize
- Ability to Relate Effectively with Others
- Ability to Maintain a Positive Image
- Ability to Evaluate Information and Make Judgment Decisions
- Initiative and Motivation
- Ability to Adapt to Changing Situations
- Physical Requirements

WRITTEN EXERCISE
TIME LIMIT: 90 MINUTES

At the start of this exercise, the following materials will be distributed to each applicant:

- Written exercise instructions
- Summaries of interviews
- List of Approved Reimbursements
- List of Approved Charges
- Summary of Expenses Submitted

A checklist will accompany these materials describing the contents. Applicants will record their Social Security Number on the checklist and then compare this listing against the actual materials. If any materials are missing, you should raise your hand for assistance. Applicants will be asked to initial the checklist to verify that all of the materials were provided.

In this exercise, the applicant is to assume that she/he is an investigative reporter working for a large metropolitan newspaper. Recently, a tip was received from a person who believed that a company was being overcharged for services. The materials provided to applicants are reports of several interviews and records relevant to this case. Convinced that there is clear evidence of over-charging, the applicant's job is to write a memorandum to convince the editor of the newspaper to allow him/her to write an article on the case.

In preparing the response, be sure to write legibly. Responses cannot be evaluated if they cannot be read.

This exercise measures the following skills and abilities:

- Ability to Communicate in Writing
- Ability to Attend to Detail
- Ability to Evaluate and Make Judgment Decisions

QUESTIONS & ANSWERS ON THE FBI

1. When was the FBI founded?

In 1908, Attorney General Charles Bonaparte directed that Department of Justice investigations be handled by a small group of special investigators. This group was formed as the Bureau of Investigation and, in 1935, the present name of Federal Bureau of Investigation was designed by Congress.

2. Who is the head of the FBI?

The head of the FBI is the Director.

3. How is the Director of the FBI appointed to his office?

Legislation enacted in June 1968 provides that the Director of the FBI shall be appointed by the President with the advice and consent of the Senate.

4. What guidelines were used in setting up the FBI as a career service?

FBI positions are filled on the basis of ability and character without political interference, and performance and achievement are the requirements for promotion within the organization.

5. What safeguards are there against abuses of authority by the FBI and its Director?

The FBI's activities and operations are under constant scrutiny and review by the Attorney General, committees of Congress, the Office of Management and Budget, the courts, and the Nation's press.

ADMINISTRATIVE MATTERS

6. What kind of training do FBI Agents receive?

All FBI Agents initially must graduate from a 15-week course at the FBI Academy located on the U.S. Marine Corps Base at Quantico, Virginia. It is a tough and demanding course in which the new Agent receives intensified training in such diverse subjects as Constitutional law, Federal criminal procedure, collection and preservation of evidence, investigative techniques, scientific crime detection, firearms, and defensive tactics. Periodically throughout an Agent's career he or she will receive refresher training designed to keep him or her up to date on the latest procedures and techniques of their profession.

7. Why is law a desirable educational qualification for the Special Agent position?

In addition to having a knowledge of a suspect's rights and the applicability of Federal law to a given situation, FBI Agents must, during the course of a criminal investigation, collect evidence which is legally admissible to prove the guilt of the criminal. A legal education provides training in analyzing a set of facts and applying laws and regulations to them.

8. Why is accounting an alternate educational qualification for the Special Agent position?

Accounting is an alternative educational requirement because investigations of many matters under the jurisdiction of the FBI, such as bank embezzlements, frauds against the government, tort claims, Renegotiation Act cases, and other white-collar crimes require expert knowledge of accounting practices and procedures.

9. Does the FBI investigate domestic terrorism that originates in foreign countries?

Yes.

10. How often are Special Agents rotated in their assignments?

There are no specific tours of duty. Special Agent assignments are based upon the needs of the Bureau, and Agents must be available at any time for general or special assignment anywhere in the United States or its territories.

FBI JURISDICTION

11. What are the primary functions of the FBI and its Agents?

The FBI investigates violations of certain Federal statutes, collects evidence in cases in which the United States is or may be an interested party, and performs other duties specifically imposed by law or Presidential directive.

12. Then the FBI does not investigate all violations of Federal and Constitutional law?

True. The FBI can investigate a matter only when it has authority to do so under a law passed by Congress or on instructions of the President or the Attorney General.

13. What is the FBI's jurisdiction in the field of organized crime?

Most of the Federal statutes enacted to combat organized crime are aimed at eradicating interstate gambling, large-scale intrastate gambling, hoodlum loan-sharking, gangland infiltration of legitimate business, and interstate travel in aid of racketeering. Other statutes often utilized are those dealing with interstate transportation of stolen property, fraudulent bankruptcies and bank loans, extortion, thefts from interstate shipments, and labor racketeering.

14. What does the FBI do with facts and evidence gathered during an investigation?

If a possible violation of Federal law under the jurisdiction of the FBI has occurred, the FBI will conduct an investigation and thereafter present the facts of the case to the appropriate United States Attorney or Department of Justice official who will determine whether or not prosecution or further action is warranted. The FBI does not give an opinion or decide whether an individual will be prosecuted.

15. Are the CIA and the Secret Service part of the FBI?

No. The FBI is the investigative arm of the Department of Justice. The Secret Service is an agency of the Treasury Department, while the Central Intelligence Agency is an independent member of the Executive branch of the government.

16. Does an FBI Agent have powers of arrest or any authority outside the United States and its territories?

No.

17. Does the FBI investigate matters involving narcotics or income tax violations?

No. Narcotics are under the jurisdiction of the Drug Enforcement Administration in the Justice Department, while the Treasury Department handles tax matters. As a matter of cooperation, however, information developed by the FBI during the course of its investigations that relates to matters handled by other Federal, state, or local agencies is promptly disseminated to the agency having primary investigative responsibility.

18. Isn't the FBI a type of national police force?

Definitely not. The FBI is a fact-finding organization investigating violations of Federal laws and its authority is strictly limited to matters within its jurisdiction.

19. Wouldn't a national police agency be the most effective force against crime?

No. The same objective can be accomplished through cooperation of the various law enforcement agencies without surrendering to the democratically repugnant concept of a centralized, powerful police force.

20. What authority do FBI Agents have to make arrests?

FBI Agents may make arrests without a warrant for any Federal offense committed in their presence, or when they have reasonable grounds to believe that the person to be arrested has committed or is attempting to commit a felony violation of United States laws. Agents may also make arrests by warrant.

21. What is the general policy of the FBI regarding arrests by Agents?

Agents do not make arrests for *investigation* or *on suspicion.* Before arrests are made, if at all possible, the facts of each case are presented to the United States Attorney who decides whether or not a Federal violation has occurred and, if so, he may authorize Agents to file a complaint which serves as the basis of the arrest warrant.

22. How can I get a FBI security clearance?

The FBI does not issue security clearances. It does conduct applicant-type investigations in certain cases at the request of other government agencies concerning individuals requiring security clearances. The results of these investigations are furnished to the requesting agency which then decides whether or not to grant the individual a security clearance.

23. Does the FBI propose passage of new laws it feels are necessary to fight crime?

No. Proposing new legislation such as this is the responsibility of the Department of Justice; however, on the basis of investigative experience, the FBI may furnish comments or observations on legislative matters to the Department of Justice for its consideration.

24. Can the FBI be *called in* to investigate a serious crime, such as murder, when the local police are unable to solve the case?

No. The FBI has no authority to investigate local crimes that are not within FBI jurisdiction. The FBI will, however, render all possible assistance to the local police through the FBI Laboratory and Identification Division.

25. Briefly, what is the function of the FBI in the field of civil rights?

It is to objectively investigate alleged violations of the civil rights statutes within FBI jurisdiction and furnish the results of these investigations to the Department of Justice for a determination of whether further action or prosecution is desired.

26. If a crime is committed that is a violation of both local and federal laws, does the FBI *take over* the investigation?

No. State and local law enforcement agencies are not subordinate to the FBI and the FBI has no authority over them. Through cooperation, the investigative resources of the FBI and the local agency are pooled in a common effort to solve the case.

27. Are not FBI informants employees of the Bureau, much the same as Special Agents, except that they conduct only undercover investigations?

No. Informants are not hired or trained employees of the FBI, although they may receive compensation in some instances for their expenses and information. Informants are simply individuals who furnish information to the FBI on a confidential basis.

CRIMINAL INVESTIGATIONS

28. If a crime is committed on a military reservation, what is the jurisdiction of the FBI?

Generally, if only military personnel are involved, the matter will be handled by military authorities, unless the crime concerns government property or funds, in which case the FBI has jurisdiction. The FBI also has responsibility when only civilians not subject to military law are involved.

29. Does the FBI investigate ALL bank robberies?

The FBI has jurisdiction over robberies of financial institutions which are (1) members of the Federal Reserve System; (2) insured by the Federal Deposit Insurance Corporation or Federal Savings and Loan Insurance Corporation; **(3)** organized under the laws of the United States; or **(4)** federally insured credit unions.

30. If a child is missing under circumstances indicating that a kidnapping has occurred, but no interstate transportation is known, will the FBI begin an investigation?

Yes. The law provides that unless the victim is located or released within 24 hours, it is presumed that he has been transported interstate.

31. Isn't it true that the criminal work of the FBI is concerned with only serious Federal crimes such as bank robbery, kidnapping, and extortion?

No. The FBI's jurisdiction includes a wide range of responsibilities in both the criminal and security fields.

32. Does the FBI advocate payment of money that may be demanded by a criminal in an extortion or kidnapping case?

This is a decision that must be made by the family or person from whom the ransom is being demanded.

33. Does the FBI have any authority to investigate crimes involving thefts of large sums of money, jewelry or property?

Under the Interstate Transportation of Stolen Property Statute, the FBI investigates cases wherein stolen property valued at more than $5,000 is transported across state lines.

34. What is the basis for the FBI's jurisdiction in bombing cases?

Bombing investigations conducted by the FBI are handled primarily under the provisions of the Organized Crime Control Act of 1970. This Act, among other provisions, prohibits the use of explosives or incendiary devices against property used by the Federal government, federally funded activities, or activities which affect interstate commerce.

35. On what basis does the FBI select its *ten most wanted fugitives*?

This selection is based on several items, including the fugitive's past criminal record, the threat posed to the community, the seriousness of the crime for which the fugitive is sought, and whether nationwide publicity is likely to assist in apprehension.

36. Why does the FBI conduct investigations to locate some criminals under the Unlawful Flight Statute and not others?

The fugitive must be wanted by local authorities for prosecution, or confinement after conviction, for a crime which is a felony. Local authorities must have information that the individual has fled interstate, request FBI assistance to locate him, and agree to extradite and prosecute upon apprehension.

37. Does the FBI investigate graft and corruption in local government and in state and local police departments?

In certain instances, the FBI does investigate graft and corruption in local government and in state and local police departments under the Hobbs Act of the Anti-Racketeering Statute, the Interstate Transportation in Aid of Racketeering Statute, and the Organized Crime Control Act of 1970.

38. Are civil rights investigations a significant part of FBI caseload?

Yes.

39. How many people are convicted of crimes each year in cases investigated by the FBI?

Each year approximately 50,000 individuals are convicted of crimes in FBI cases.

40. When the FBI recovers stolen property, why is it not returned immediately in all instances to the owner?

Such property is often used as evidence in the trial of the thief. The disposition of recovered property is controlled by the United States Attorney or the federal court.

41. Will the FBI investigate the murder or suspected murder of a Federal employee who is killed while performing his official duties?

Yes, but only if the employee is in one of the categories covered by the statute governing assaults and killings of Federal officers or if there is evidence of a violation of the statute governing conspiracies to impede or injure Federal officers.

42. If a citizen furnishes facts to the FBI and there is a question as to whether the facts constitute a Federal violation, who decides the question?

The FBI will present the facts to the United States Attorney who then determines whether a Federal violation has occurred and whether the facts warrant prosecutive action.

43. What is the policy of the FBI concerning the use of firearms?

An FBI Agent is trained to use firearms only in self-defense or to safeguard the lives of other persons.

44. If FBI Agents have authority only in the United States and its possessions and FBI jurisdiction is generally based on interstate transactions, how can the FBI investigate crimes on the high seas?

The United States Constitution specifically grants Congress authority to pass laws governing crimes on the high seas. The FBI has jurisdiction over many of these crimes pursuant to Congressional enactment.

SECURITY MATTERS

45. To whom should I report information about espionage, sabotage and subversive activities?

Information of this type should be reported immediately to the FBI.

46. Does the FBI compile a list of organizations it has designated as subversive?

No. The FBI is strictly a fact-finding agency and does not designate or label organizations.

47. What internal security matters does the FBI investigate?

The FBI has investigative jurisdiction of matters relating to sabotage, espionage, counterespionage, treason, insurrection and rebellion, seditious conspiracy advocating overthrow of the government, and other matters affecting the national security.

48. What are the primary sources of FBI authority to investigate subversive groups?

The FBI's authority in this area is based on Congressional enactments and orders of the Attorney General.

49. Does the FBI investigate white hate groups as well as revolutionary groups?

Yes. The FBI is charged with internal security responsibilities and any group which follows a policy of violation, and in any way violates laws over which the FBI has jurisdiction, will be thoroughly and impartially investigated.

50. Does the FBI investigate crimes against foreign diplomatic officials in this country?
Under the Act for the Protection of Foreign Officials and Official Guests of the United States, the FBI investigates murders, kidnappings and assaults against such individuals as well as damage to property of foreign governments in the United States. Jurisdiction under this Act is held concurrently with local authorities and the FBI investigates when the crimes committed would adversely affect the conduct of United States foreign affairs.

51. Does the FBI investigate foreign-inspired terrorist acts?
Yes. The FBI investigates such acts when and if directed against targets in the United States. These investigations cover terrorist hijackings, kidnappings, bombings and assaults when against foreign officials.

52. Does the FBI have representatives abroad? If so, what is their function?
Yes. The FBI has representatives in a few of the large foreign capitals for the purpose of effecting liaison with foreign police agencies in matters of mutual interest.

FBI COOPERATIVE SERVICES

53. Who has their fingerprints in FBI files?
The prints of criminals, aliens, government applicants and military personnel form the large part of FBI fingerprint records. In addition, many citizens voluntarily submit their fingerprints for personal identification reasons.

54. Does the FBI conduct fingerprint examinations for private individuals?
No. The FBI's Latent Fingerprint Section conducts latent fingerprint examinations only for law enforcement agencies and officials or for other Federal agencies.

55. If a person is arrested, fingerprinted, and the charge is later dismissed, how can the fingerprint record in the FBI be changed to reflect dismissal of the charge?
The FBI strongly urges all police agencies submitting arrest fingerprint cards to follow the case and submit a final disposition for the completion of the records maintained by the FBI. The information submitted, including dismissal of the charge if appropriate, will be placed on the fingerprint record.

56. Will the FBI furnish fingerprint records to private citizens?
Yes. Pursuant to Department of Justice Order 556-73, an individual may obtain a copy of his or her arrest record by submitting a written request directly to the FBI Identification Division, together with a set of rolled inked fingerprint impressions taken on a fingerprint card which indicates the individual's name and birth data. There is a required fee for this service.

57. Does the FBI exchange fingerprint information with foreign police agencies?
Yes. The FBI exchanges fingerprint information with 84 countries on a cooperative basis.

58. Will the FBI look for a missing person?

No. However, the FBI will post a stop notice in the files of the Identification Division at the request of relatives or law enforcement agencies and will notify the inquirer of any information received regarding the missing person's whereabouts.

59. What is the function of the FBI Disaster Squad?

The function of the FBI Disaster Squad is to identify, through fingerprints, the victims of disasters. The services of this specially trained group are available upon request of local law enforcement and governmental agencies or transportation companies following a catastrophe where identification of victims is a problem.

60. Does the FBI's Disaster Squad go automatically to a scene of ANY disaster to assist in identifying the victims?

No. The services of the FBI Disaster Squad are made available only at the request of a ranking law enforcement official or transportation agency involved. It can assist in identifying Americans in disasters abroad only at the specific invitation of the country involved.

61. What, if any, is the difference in training received by Special Agents at the FBI Academy and local police officers attending the FBI National Academy?

Special Agents of the FBI receive training specifically designed to enable them to handle investigative responsibilities of Federal offenses. The FBI National Academy curriculum is designed to enhance the administrative potential of local, county and state police. The emphasis is on local problems rather than Federal.

62. What other training assistance is afforded local law enforcement officers?

Approximately 25,000 local, county and state law enforcement officers receive specialized training at the FBI Academy located on the Marine Corps Base at Quantico, Virginia, each year. This training is determined by the needs of local law enforcement agencies. In addition, the FBI has more than 5,000 Special Agents qualified to instruct local law enforcement officers in various phases of their work. They are available on request to assist in training programs being conducted by these agencies in the United States.

63. Is the FBI National Academy available only to United States police officers?

No. Although the whole concept of the FBI National Academy is based upon the needs of law enforcement within our own nation, as a cooperation measure a limited number of officers from foreign countries are accepted in each session.

64. What is the National Crime Information Center?

The National Crime Information Center, popularly known as NCIC, is a computerized information system established by the FBI as a service to all criminal justice agencies – local, state and Federal. NCIC stores documented information on serialized stolen property, wanted persons for whom an arrest warrant is outstanding, and criminal histories on individuals arrested and fingerprinted for serious or significant offenses. This information can be instantly retrieved over a vast communications network through the use of telecommunications equipment located in criminal justice agencies in various locations in the United States, Canada, and Puerto Rico.

65. If an individual is being sought by local police for committing a crime, what assistance can be rendered by the FBI to locate the fugitive?

A stop will be placed against the fugitive's fingerprints in the FBI Identification Division and the local police will be immediately notified of the receipt of any additional fingerprints of the fugitive. The fugitive's name and identifying data will also be entered into the National Crime Information Center. Any criminal justice agency which subsequently inquires about this individual will be advised of his or her fugitive status. In addition, the FBI may conduct active investigation to locate the wanted person under Federal unlawful flight statutes.

66. Does the FBI furnish local police and other law enforcement agencies the identities of persons suspected of committing crimes?

Yes. Information coming to the attention of the FBI regarding local crimes is promptly furnished to the appropriate local law enforcement agency. Each year, approximately a million items of criminal intelligence-type information were disseminated to Federal, state and local agencies.

67. If an FBI informant furnishes information regarding a crime not within the jurisdiction of the FBI, does the FBI conduct investigations to verify the information or to prove the violation?

No. This information is expeditiously furnished to the agency having jurisdiction over the alleged violation, and the agency is advised that the information has not been verified by FBI investigation.

68. Does the FBI Laboratory conduct examinations of evidence for anyone other than the FBI?

Yes. The facilities and scientific expertise of the FBI Laboratory are available to all duly constituted law enforcement agencies in the United States in their investigation of criminal matters. Over 30 percent of the examinations conducted by the FBI Laboratory during the year are for outside agencies.

69. Does the FBI Laboratory charge other agencies for conducting scientific examinations of evidence?

As a cooperative measure, no charge is made for these examinations. In addition, FBI Laboratory experts will appear in court as required to testify to the results of their examinations at no cost to the local agency.

70. Does the FBI keep statistics on criminal offenses committed in the United States?

Yes. The FBI collects criminal data from police departments across the nation and compiles it into four quarterly reports as well as a comprehensive annual report. This statistical data is published by the Government Printing Office as the Uniform Crime Reports.

71. Are statistics maintained by the FBI on the number of persons confined to penal institutions and on divorces, liquor consumption, cigarette consumption, deaths and marriages?

No. These statistics are compiled by the Bureau of the Census and can be found in its annual publication entitled STATISTICAL ABSTRACT OF THE UNITED STATES.

72. Can FBI Agents or FBI Headquarters furnish legal advice?

No.

73. Will the FBI recommend schools or courses to be taken by students?

No. As a matter of policy, the FBI does not recommend specific schools to be attended or courses of study to be pursued.

74. Can the FBI send wanted posters and flyers on fugitives to individuals on request?

No. Wanted posters and flyers relating to fugitives currently being sought by the FBI are sent primarily to law enforcement agencies and selected individuals and organizations which are likely to produce information regarding the fugitive's location.

75. How can I contact the FBI if I have information to report?

The front page of most telephone directories lists the telephone number of the nearest FBI field office, all of which are open 24 hours a day, including Saturday, Sunday and holidays. Additional information concerning matters in this booklet can be obtained from any field office or by writing to: Federal Bureau of Investigation, United States Department of Justice, Washington, D.C. 20535.

76. Is the FBI an independent agency?

No. It is a bureau of, and in, the United States Department of Justice, which is a cabinet department.

HOW TO TAKE A TEST

I. YOU MUST PASS AN EXAMINATION

A. WHAT EVERY CANDIDATE SHOULD KNOW

Examination applicants often ask us for help in preparing for the written test. What can I study in advance? What kinds of questions will be asked? How will the test be given? How will the papers be graded?

As an applicant for a civil service examination, you may be wondering about some of these things. Our purpose here is to suggest effective methods of advance study and to describe civil service examinations.

Your chances for success on this examination can be increased if you know how to prepare. Those "pre-examination jitters" can be reduced if you know what to expect. You can even experience an adventure in good citizenship if you know why civil service exams are given.

B. WHY ARE CIVIL SERVICE EXAMINATIONS GIVEN?

Civil service examinations are important to you in two ways. As a citizen, you want public jobs filled by employees who know how to do their work. As a job seeker, you want a fair chance to compete for that job on an equal footing with other candidates. The best-known means of accomplishing this two-fold goal is the competitive examination.

Exams are widely publicized throughout the nation. They may be administered for jobs in federal, state, city, municipal, town or village governments or agencies.

Any citizen may apply, with some limitations, such as the age or residence of applicants. Your experience and education may be reviewed to see whether you meet the requirements for the particular examination. When these requirements exist, they are reasonable and applied consistently to all applicants. Thus, a competitive examination may cause you some uneasiness now, but it is your privilege and safeguard.

C. HOW ARE CIVIL SERVICE EXAMS DEVELOPED?

Examinations are carefully written by trained technicians who are specialists in the field known as "psychological measurement," in consultation with recognized authorities in the field of work that the test will cover. These experts recommend the subject matter areas or skills to be tested; only those knowledges or skills important to your success on the job are included. The most reliable books and source materials available are used as references. Together, the experts and technicians judge the difficulty level of the questions.

Test technicians know how to phrase questions so that the problem is clearly stated. Their ethics do not permit "trick" or "catch" questions. Questions may have been tried out on sample groups, or subjected to statistical analysis, to determine their usefulness.

Written tests are often used in combination with performance tests, ratings of training and experience, and oral interviews. All of these measures combine to form the best-known means of finding the right person for the right job.

II. HOW TO PASS THE WRITTEN TEST

A. NATURE OF THE EXAMINATION

To prepare intelligently for civil service examinations, you should know how they differ from school examinations you have taken. In school you were assigned certain definite pages to read or subjects to cover. The examination questions were quite detailed and usually emphasized memory. Civil service exams, on the other hand, try to discover your present ability to perform the duties of a position, plus your potentiality to learn these duties. In other words, a civil service exam attempts to predict how successful you will be. Questions cover such a broad area that they cannot be as minute and detailed as school exam questions.

In the public service similar kinds of work, or positions, are grouped together in one "class." This process is known as *position-classification*. All the positions in a class are paid according to the salary range for that class. One class title covers all of these positions, and they are all tested by the same examination.

B. FOUR BASIC STEPS

1) Study the announcement

How, then, can you know what subjects to study? Our best answer is: "Learn as much as possible about the class of positions for which you've applied." The exam will test the knowledge, skills and abilities needed to do the work.

Your most valuable source of information about the position you want is the official exam announcement. This announcement lists the training and experience qualifications. Check these standards and apply only if you come reasonably close to meeting them.

The brief description of the position in the examination announcement offers some clues to the subjects which will be tested. Think about the job itself. Review the duties in your mind. Can you perform them, or are there some in which you are rusty? Fill in the blank spots in your preparation.

Many jurisdictions preview the written test in the exam announcement by including a section called "Knowledge and Abilities Required," "Scope of the Examination," or some similar heading. Here you will find out specifically what fields will be tested.

2) Review your own background

Once you learn in general what the position is all about, and what you need to know to do the work, ask yourself which subjects you already know fairly well and which need improvement. You may wonder whether to concentrate on improving your strong areas or on building some background in your fields of weakness. When the announcement has specified "some knowledge" or "considerable knowledge," or has used adjectives like "beginning principles of..." or "advanced ... methods," you can get a clue as to the number and difficulty of questions to be asked in any given field. More questions, and hence broader coverage, would be included for those subjects which are more important in the work. Now weigh your strengths and weaknesses against the job requirements and prepare accordingly.

3) Determine the level of the position

Another way to tell how intensively you should prepare is to understand the level of the job for which you are applying. Is it the entering level? In other words, is this the position in which beginners in a field of work are hired? Or is it an intermediate or advanced level? Sometimes this is indicated by such words as "Junior" or "Senior" in the class title. Other jurisdictions use Roman numerals to designate the level – Clerk I, Clerk II, for example. The word "Supervisor" sometimes appears in the title. If the level is not indicated by the title, check the description of duties. Will you be working under very close supervision, or will you have responsibility for independent decisions in this work?

4) Choose appropriate study materials

Now that you know the subjects to be examined and the relative amount of each subject to be covered, you can choose suitable study materials. For beginning level jobs, or even advanced ones, if you have a pronounced weakness in some aspect of your training, read a modern, standard textbook in that field. Be sure it is up to date and has general coverage. Such books are normally available at your library, and the librarian will be glad to help you locate one. For entry-level positions, questions of appropriate difficulty are chosen – neither highly advanced questions, nor those too simple. Such questions require careful thought but not advanced training.

If the position for which you are applying is technical or advanced, you will read more advanced, specialized material. If you are already familiar with the basic principles of your field, elementary textbooks would waste your time. Concentrate on advanced textbooks and technical periodicals. Think through the concepts and review difficult problems in your field.

These are all general sources. You can get more ideas on your own initiative, following these leads. For example, training manuals and publications of the government agency which employs workers in your field can be useful, particularly for technical and professional positions. A letter or visit to the government department involved may result in more specific study suggestions, and certainly will provide you with a more definite idea of the exact nature of the position you are seeking.

III. KINDS OF TESTS

Tests are used for purposes other than measuring knowledge and ability to perform specified duties. For some positions, it is equally important to test ability to make adjustments to new situations or to profit from training. In others, basic mental abilities not dependent on information are essential. Questions which test these things may not appear as pertinent to the duties of the position as those which test for knowledge and information. Yet they are often highly important parts of a fair examination. For very general questions, it is almost impossible to help you direct your study efforts. What we can do is to point out some of the more common of these general abilities needed in public service positions and describe some typical questions.

1) General information

Broad, general information has been found useful for predicting job success in some kinds of work. This is tested in a variety of ways, from vocabulary lists to questions about current events. Basic background in some field of work, such as sociology or economics, may be sampled in a group of questions. Often these are principles which have become familiar to most persons through exposure rather than through formal training. It is difficult to advise you how to study for these questions; being alert to the world around you is our best suggestion.

2) Verbal ability

An example of an ability needed in many positions is verbal or language ability. Verbal ability is, in brief, the ability to use and understand words. Vocabulary and grammar tests are typical measures of this ability. Reading comprehension or paragraph interpretation questions are common in many kinds of civil service tests. You are given a paragraph of written material and asked to find its central meaning.

3) Numerical ability

Number skills can be tested by the familiar arithmetic problem, by checking paired lists of numbers to see which are alike and which are different, or by interpreting charts and graphs. In the latter test, a graph may be printed in the test booklet which you are asked to use as the basis for answering questions.

4) Observation

A popular test for law-enforcement positions is the observation test. A picture is shown to you for several minutes, then taken away. Questions about the picture test your ability to observe both details and larger elements.

5) Following directions

In many positions in the public service, the employee must be able to carry out written instructions dependably and accurately. You may be given a chart with several columns, each column listing a variety of information. The questions require you to carry out directions involving the information given in the chart.

6) Skills and aptitudes

Performance tests effectively measure some manual skills and aptitudes. When the skill is one in which you are trained, such as typing or shorthand, you can practice. These tests are often very much like those given in business school or high school courses. For many of the other skills and aptitudes, however, no short-time preparation can be made. Skills and abilities natural to you or that you have developed throughout your lifetime are being tested.

Many of the general questions just described provide all the data needed to answer the questions and ask you to use your reasoning ability to find the answers. Your best preparation for these tests, as well as for tests of facts and ideas, is to be at your physical and mental best. You, no doubt, have your own methods of getting into an exam-taking mood and keeping "in shape." The next section lists some ideas on this subject.

IV. KINDS OF QUESTIONS

Only rarely is the "essay" question, which you answer in narrative form, used in civil service tests. Civil service tests are usually of the short-answer type. Full instructions for answering these questions will be given to you at the examination. But in case this is your first experience with short-answer questions and separate answer sheets, here is what you need to know:

1) Multiple-choice Questions

Most popular of the short-answer questions is the "multiple choice" or "best answer" question. It can be used, for example, to test for factual knowledge, ability to solve problems or judgment in meeting situations found at work.

A multiple-choice question is normally one of three types—

- It can begin with an incomplete statement followed by several possible endings. You are to find the one ending which *best* completes the statement, although some of the others may not be entirely wrong.
- It can also be a complete statement in the form of a question which is answered by choosing one of the statements listed.
- It can be in the form of a problem – again you select the best answer.

Here is an example of a multiple-choice question with a discussion which should give you some clues as to the method for choosing the right answer:

When an employee has a complaint about his assignment, the action which will *best* help him overcome his difficulty is to

A. discuss his difficulty with his coworkers
B. take the problem to the head of the organization
C. take the problem to the person who gave him the assignment
D. say nothing to anyone about his complaint

In answering this question, you should study each of the choices to find which is best. Consider choice "A" – Certainly an employee may discuss his complaint with fellow employees, but no change or improvement can result, and the complaint remains unresolved. Choice "B" is a poor choice since the head of the organization probably does not know what assignment you have been given, and taking your problem to him is known as "going over the head" of the supervisor. The supervisor, or person who made the assignment, is the person who can clarify it or correct any injustice. Choice "C" is, therefore, correct. To say nothing, as in choice "D," is unwise. Supervisors have and interest in knowing the problems employees are facing, and the employee is seeking a solution to his problem.

2) True/False Questions

The "true/false" or "right/wrong" form of question is sometimes used. Here a complete statement is given. Your job is to decide whether the statement is right or wrong.

SAMPLE: A person-to-person long-distance telephone call costs less than a station-to-station call to the same city.

This statement is wrong, or false, since person-to-person calls are more expensive.

This is not a complete list of all possible question forms, although most of the others are variations of these common types. You will always get complete directions for answering questions. Be sure you understand *how* to mark your answers – ask questions until you do.

V. RECORDING YOUR ANSWERS

For an examination with very few applicants, you may be told to record your answers in the test booklet itself. Separate answer sheets are much more common. If this separate answer sheet is to be scored by machine – and this is often the case – it is highly important that you mark your answers correctly in order to get credit.

An electric scoring machine is often used in civil service offices because of the speed with which papers can be scored. Machine-scored answer sheets must be marked with a pencil, which will be given to you. This pencil has a high graphite content which responds to the electric scoring machine. As a matter of fact, stray dots may register as answers, so do not let your pencil rest on the answer sheet while you are pondering the correct answer. Also, if your pencil lead breaks or is otherwise defective, ask for another.

Since the answer sheet will be dropped in a slot in the scoring machine, be careful not to bend the corners or get the paper crumpled.

The answer sheet normally has five vertical columns of numbers, with 30 numbers to a column. These numbers correspond to the question numbers in your test booklet. After each number, going across the page are four or five pairs of dotted lines. These short dotted lines have small letters or numbers above them. The first two pairs may also have a "T" or "F" above the letters. This indicates that the first two pairs only are to be used if the questions are of the true-false type. If the questions are multiple choice, disregard the "T" and "F" and pay attention only to the small letters or numbers.

Answer your questions in the manner of the sample that follows:

32. The largest city in the United States is
    - A. Washington, D.C.
    - B. New York City
    - C. Chicago
    - D. Detroit
    - E. San Francisco

1) Choose the answer you think is best. (New York City is the largest, so "B" is correct.)
2) Find the row of dotted lines numbered the same as the question you are answering. (Find row number 32)
3) Find the pair of dotted lines corresponding to the answer. (Find the pair of lines under the mark "B.")
4) Make a solid black mark between the dotted lines.

VI. BEFORE THE TEST

Common sense will help you find procedures to follow to get ready for an examination. Too many of us, however, overlook these sensible measures. Indeed, nervousness and fatigue have been found to be the most serious reasons why applicants fail to do their best on civil service tests. Here is a list of reminders:

- Begin your preparation early – Don't wait until the last minute to go scurrying around for books and materials or to find out what the position is all about.
- Prepare continuously – An hour a night for a week is better than an all-night cram session. This has been definitely established. What is more, a night a

week for a month will return better dividends than crowding your study into a shorter period of time.

- Locate the place of the exam – You have been sent a notice telling you when and where to report for the examination. If the location is in a different town or otherwise unfamiliar to you, it would be well to inquire the best route and learn something about the building.
- Relax the night before the test – Allow your mind to rest. Do not study at all that night. Plan some mild recreation or diversion; then go to bed early and get a good night's sleep.
- Get up early enough to make a leisurely trip to the place for the test – This way unforeseen events, traffic snarls, unfamiliar buildings, etc. will not upset you.
- Dress comfortably – A written test is not a fashion show. You will be known by number and not by name, so wear something comfortable.
- Leave excess paraphernalia at home – Shopping bags and odd bundles will get in your way. You need bring only the items mentioned in the official notice you received; usually everything you need is provided. Do not bring reference books to the exam. They will only confuse those last minutes and be taken away from you when in the test room.
- Arrive somewhat ahead of time – If because of transportation schedules you must get there very early, bring a newspaper or magazine to take your mind off yourself while waiting.
- Locate the examination room – When you have found the proper room, you will be directed to the seat or part of the room where you will sit. Sometimes you are given a sheet of instructions to read while you are waiting. Do not fill out any forms until you are told to do so; just read them and be prepared.
- Relax and prepare to listen to the instructions
- If you have any physical problem that may keep you from doing your best, be sure to tell the test administrator. If you are sick or in poor health, you really cannot do your best on the exam. You can come back and take the test some other time.

VII. AT THE TEST

The day of the test is here and you have the test booklet in your hand. The temptation to get going is very strong. Caution! There is more to success than knowing the right answers. You must know how to identify your papers and understand variations in the type of short-answer question used in this particular examination. Follow these suggestions for maximum results from your efforts:

1) Cooperate with the monitor

The test administrator has a duty to create a situation in which you can be as much at ease as possible. He will give instructions, tell you when to begin, check to see that you are marking your answer sheet correctly, and so on. He is not there to guard you, although he will see that your competitors do not take unfair advantage. He wants to help you do your best.

2) Listen to all instructions

Don't jump the gun! Wait until you understand all directions. In most civil service tests you get more time than you need to answer the questions. So don't be in a hurry.

Read each word of instructions until you clearly understand the meaning. Study the examples, listen to all announcements and follow directions. Ask questions if you do not understand what to do.

3) Identify your papers

Civil service exams are usually identified by number only. You will be assigned a number; you must not put your name on your test papers. Be sure to copy your number correctly. Since more than one exam may be given, copy your exact examination title.

4) Plan your time

Unless you are told that a test is a "speed" or "rate of work" test, speed itself is usually not important. Time enough to answer all the questions will be provided, but this does not mean that you have all day. An overall time limit has been set. Divide the total time (in minutes) by the number of questions to determine the approximate time you have for each question.

5) Do not linger over difficult questions

If you come across a difficult question, mark it with a paper clip (useful to have along) and come back to it when you have been through the booklet. One caution if you do this – be sure to skip a number on your answer sheet as well. Check often to be sure that you have not lost your place and that you are marking in the row numbered the same as the question you are answering.

6) Read the questions

Be sure you know what the question asks! Many capable people are unsuccessful because they failed to *read* the questions correctly.

7) Answer all questions

Unless you have been instructed that a penalty will be deducted for incorrect answers, it is better to guess than to omit a question.

8) Speed tests

It is often better NOT to guess on speed tests. It has been found that on timed tests people are tempted to spend the last few seconds before time is called in marking answers at random – without even reading them – in the hope of picking up a few extra points. To discourage this practice, the instructions may warn you that your score will be "corrected" for guessing. That is, a penalty will be applied. The incorrect answers will be deducted from the correct ones, or some other penalty formula will be used.

9) Review your answers

If you finish before time is called, go back to the questions you guessed or omitted to give them further thought. Review other answers if you have time.

10) Return your test materials

If you are ready to leave before others have finished or time is called, take ALL your materials to the monitor and leave quietly. Never take any test material with you. The monitor can discover whose papers are not complete, and taking a test booklet may be grounds for disqualification.

VIII. EXAMINATION TECHNIQUES

1) Read the general instructions carefully. These are usually printed on the first page of the exam booklet. As a rule, these instructions refer to the timing of the examination; the fact that you should not start work until the signal and must stop work at a signal, etc. If there are any *special* instructions, such as a choice of questions to be answered, make sure that you note this instruction carefully.

2) When you are ready to start work on the examination, that is as soon as the signal has been given, read the instructions to each question booklet, underline any key words or phrases, such as *least, best, outline, describe* and the like. In this way you will tend to answer as requested rather than discover on reviewing your paper that you *listed without describing*, that you selected the *worst* choice rather than the *best* choice, etc.

3) If the examination is of the objective or multiple-choice type – that is, each question will also give a series of possible answers: A, B, C or D, and you are called upon to select the best answer and write the letter next to that answer on your answer paper – it is advisable to start answering each question in turn. There may be anywhere from 50 to 100 such questions in the three or four hours allotted and you can see how much time would be taken if you read through all the questions before beginning to answer any. Furthermore, if you come across a question or group of questions which you know would be difficult to answer, it would undoubtedly affect your handling of all the other questions.

4) If the examination is of the essay type and contains but a few questions, it is a moot point as to whether you should read all the questions before starting to answer any one. Of course, if you are given a choice – say five out of seven and the like – then it is essential to read all the questions so you can eliminate the two that are most difficult. If, however, you are asked to answer all the questions, there may be danger in trying to answer the easiest one first because you may find that you will spend too much time on it. The best technique is to answer the first question, then proceed to the second, etc.

5) Time your answers. Before the exam begins, write down the time it started, then add the time allowed for the examination and write down the time it must be completed, then divide the time available somewhat as follows:
   - If 3-1/2 hours are allowed, that would be 210 minutes. If you have 80 objective-type questions, that would be an average of 2-1/2 minutes per question. Allow yourself no more than 2 minutes per question, or a total of 160 minutes, which will permit about 50 minutes to review.
   - If for the time allotment of 210 minutes there are 7 essay questions to answer, that would average about 30 minutes a question. Give yourself only 25 minutes per question so that you have about 35 minutes to review.

6) The most important instruction is to *read each question* and make sure you know what is wanted. The second most important instruction is to *time yourself properly* so that you answer every question. The third most

important instruction is to *answer every question.* Guess if you have to but include something for each question. Remember that you will receive no credit for a blank and will probably receive some credit if you write something in answer to an essay question. If you guess a letter – say "B" for a multiple-choice question – you may have guessed right. If you leave a blank as an answer to a multiple-choice question, the examiners may respect your feelings but it will not add a point to your score. Some exams may penalize you for wrong answers, so in such cases *only*, you may not want to guess unless you have some basis for your answer.

7) Suggestions

a. Objective-type questions

1. Examine the question booklet for proper sequence of pages and questions
2. Read all instructions carefully
3. Skip any question which seems too difficult; return to it after all other questions have been answered
4. Apportion your time properly; do not spend too much time on any single question or group of questions
5. Note and underline key words – *all, most, fewest, least, best, worst, same, opposite,* etc.
6. Pay particular attention to negatives
7. Note unusual option, e.g., unduly long, short, complex, different or similar in content to the body of the question
8. Observe the use of "hedging" words – *probably, may, most likely,* etc.
9. Make sure that your answer is put next to the same number as the question
10. Do not second-guess unless you have good reason to believe the second answer is definitely more correct
11. Cross out original answer if you decide another answer is more accurate; do not erase until you are ready to hand your paper in
12. Answer all questions; guess unless instructed otherwise
13. Leave time for review

b. Essay questions

1. Read each question carefully
2. Determine exactly what is wanted. Underline key words or phrases.
3. Decide on outline or paragraph answer
4. Include many different points and elements unless asked to develop any one or two points or elements
5. Show impartiality by giving pros and cons unless directed to select one side only
6. Make and write down any assumptions you find necessary to answer the questions
7. Watch your English, grammar, punctuation and choice of words
8. Time your answers; don't crowd material

8) Answering the essay question

Most essay questions can be answered by framing the specific response around several key words or ideas. Here are a few such key words or ideas:

M's: manpower, materials, methods, money, management
P's: purpose, program, policy, plan, procedure, practice, problems, pitfalls, personnel, public relations

a. Six basic steps in handling problems:
   1. Preliminary plan and background development
   2. Collect information, data and facts
   3. Analyze and interpret information, data and facts
   4. Analyze and develop solutions as well as make recommendations
   5. Prepare report and sell recommendations
   6. Install recommendations and follow up effectiveness

b. Pitfalls to avoid
   1. *Taking things for granted* – A statement of the situation does not necessarily imply that each of the elements is necessarily true; for example, a complaint may be invalid and biased so that all that can be taken for granted is that a complaint has been registered
   2. *Considering only one side of a situation* – Wherever possible, indicate several alternatives and then point out the reasons you selected the best one
   3. *Failing to indicate follow up* – Whenever your answer indicates action on your part, make certain that you will take proper follow-up action to see how successful your recommendations, procedures or actions turn out to be
   4. *Taking too long in answering any single question* – Remember to time your answers properly

IX. AFTER THE TEST

Scoring procedures differ in detail among civil service jurisdictions although the general principles are the same. Whether the papers are hand-scored or graded by machine we have described, they are nearly always graded by number. That is, the person who marks the paper knows only the number – never the name – of the applicant. Not until all the papers have been graded will they be matched with names. If other tests, such as training and experience or oral interview ratings have been given, scores will be combined. Different parts of the examination usually have different weights. For example, the written test might count 60 percent of the final grade, and a rating of training and experience 40 percent. In many jurisdictions, veterans will have a certain number of points added to their grades.

After the final grade has been determined, the names are placed in grade order and an eligible list is established. There are various methods for resolving ties between those who get the same final grade – probably the most common is to place first the name of the person whose application was received first. Job offers are made from the eligible list in the order the names appear on it. You will be notified of your grade and your rank as soon as all these computations have been made. This will be done as rapidly as possible.

People who are found to meet the requirements in the announcement are called "eligibles." Their names are put on a list of eligible candidates. An eligible's chances of getting a job depend on how high he stands on this list and how fast agencies are filling jobs from the list.

When a job is to be filled from a list of eligibles, the agency asks for the names of people on the list of eligibles for that job. When the civil service commission receives this request, it sends to the agency the names of the three people highest on this list. Or, if the job to be filled has specialized requirements, the office sends the agency the names of the top three persons who meet these requirements from the general list.

The appointing officer makes a choice from among the three people whose names were sent to him. If the selected person accepts the appointment, the names of the others are put back on the list to be considered for future openings.

That is the rule in hiring from all kinds of eligible lists, whether they are for typist, carpenter, chemist, or something else. For every vacancy, the appointing officer has his choice of any one of the top three eligibles on the list. This explains why the person whose name is on top of the list sometimes does not get an appointment when some of the persons lower on the list do. If the appointing officer chooses the second or third eligible, the No. 1 eligible does not get a job at once, but stays on the list until he is appointed or the list is terminated.

X. HOW TO PASS THE INTERVIEW TEST

The examination for which you applied requires an oral interview test. You have already taken the written test and you are now being called for the interview test – the final part of the formal examination.

You may think that it is not possible to prepare for an interview test and that there are no procedures to follow during an interview. Our purpose is to point out some things you can do in advance that will help you and some good rules to follow and pitfalls to avoid while you are being interviewed.

What is an interview supposed to test?

The written examination is designed to test the technical knowledge and competence of the candidate; the oral is designed to evaluate intangible qualities, not readily measured otherwise, and to establish a list showing the relative fitness of each candidate – as measured against his competitors – for the position sought. Scoring is not on the basis of "right" and "wrong," but on a sliding scale of values ranging from "not passable" to "outstanding." As a matter of fact, it is possible to achieve a relatively low score without a single "incorrect" answer because of evident weakness in the qualities being measured.

Occasionally, an examination may consist entirely of an oral test – either an individual or a group oral. In such cases, information is sought concerning the technical knowledges and abilities of the candidate, since there has been no written examination for this purpose. More commonly, however, an oral test is used to supplement a written examination.

Who conducts interviews?

The composition of oral boards varies among different jurisdictions. In nearly all, a representative of the personnel department serves as chairman. One of the members of the board may be a representative of the department in which the candidate would work. In some cases, "outside experts" are used, and, frequently, a businessman or some other representative of the general public is asked to serve. Labor and management or other special groups may be represented. The aim is to secure the services of experts in the appropriate field.

However the board is composed, it is a good idea (and not at all improper or unethical) to ascertain in advance of the interview who the members are and what groups they represent. When you are introduced to them, you will have some idea of their backgrounds and interests, and at least you will not stutter and stammer over their names.

What should be done before the interview?

While knowledge about the board members is useful and takes some of the surprise element out of the interview, there is other preparation which is more substantive. It *is* possible to prepare for an oral interview – in several ways:

1) Keep a copy of your application and review it carefully before the interview

This may be the only document before the oral board, and the starting point of the interview. Know what education and experience you have listed there, and the sequence and dates of all of it. Sometimes the board will ask you to review the highlights of your experience for them; you should not have to hem and haw doing it.

2) Study the class specification and the examination announcement

Usually, the oral board has one or both of these to guide them. The qualities, characteristics or knowledges required by the position sought are stated in these documents. They offer valuable clues as to the nature of the oral interview. For example, if the job involves supervisory responsibilities, the announcement will usually indicate that knowledge of modern supervisory methods and the qualifications of the candidate as a supervisor will be tested. If so, you can expect such questions, frequently in the form of a hypothetical situation which you are expected to solve. NEVER go into an oral without knowledge of the duties and responsibilities of the job you seek.

3) Think through each qualification required

Try to visualize the kind of questions you would ask if you were a board member. How well could you answer them? Try especially to appraise your own knowledge and background in each area, *measured against the job sought*, and identify any areas in which you are weak. Be critical and realistic – do not flatter yourself.

4) Do some general reading in areas in which you feel you may be weak

For example, if the job involves supervision and your past experience has NOT, some general reading in supervisory methods and practices, particularly in the field of human relations, might be useful. Do NOT study agency procedures or detailed manuals. The oral board will be testing your understanding and capacity, not your memory.

5) Get a good night's sleep and watch your general health and mental attitude

You will want a clear head at the interview. Take care of a cold or any other minor ailment, and of course, no hangovers.

What should be done on the day of the interview?

Now comes the day of the interview itself. Give yourself plenty of time to get there. Plan to arrive somewhat ahead of the scheduled time, particularly if your appointment is in the fore part of the day. If a previous candidate fails to appear, the board might be ready for you a bit early. By early afternoon an oral board is almost invariably behind schedule if there are many candidates, and you may have to wait.

Take along a book or magazine to read, or your application to review, but leave any extraneous material in the waiting room when you go in for your interview. In any event, relax and compose yourself.

The matter of dress is important. The board is forming impressions about you – from your experience, your manners, your attitude, and your appearance. Give your personal appearance careful attention. Dress your best, but not your flashiest. Choose conservative, appropriate clothing, and be sure it is immaculate. This is a business interview, and your appearance should indicate that you regard it as such. Besides, being well groomed and properly dressed will help boost your confidence.

Sooner or later, someone will call your name and escort you into the interview room. *This is it.* From here on you are on your own. It is too late for any more preparation. But remember, you asked for this opportunity to prove your fitness, and you are here because your request was granted.

What happens when you go in?

The usual sequence of events will be as follows: The clerk (who is often the board stenographer) will introduce you to the chairman of the oral board, who will introduce you to the other members of the board. Acknowledge the introductions before you sit down. Do not be surprised if you find a microphone facing you or a stenotypist sitting by. Oral interviews are usually recorded in the event of an appeal or other review.

Usually the chairman of the board will open the interview by reviewing the highlights of your education and work experience from your application – primarily for the benefit of the other members of the board, as well as to get the material into the record. Do not interrupt or comment unless there is an error or significant misinterpretation; if that is the case, do not hesitate. But do not quibble about insignificant matters. Also, he will usually ask you some question about your education, experience or your present job – partly to get you to start talking and to establish the interviewing "rapport." He may start the actual questioning, or turn it over to one of the other members. Frequently, each member undertakes the questioning on a particular area, one in which he is perhaps most competent, so you can expect each member to participate in the examination. Because time is limited, you may also expect some rather abrupt switches in the direction the questioning takes, so do not be upset by it. Normally, a board member will not pursue a single line of questioning unless he discovers a particular strength or weakness.

After each member has participated, the chairman will usually ask whether any member has any further questions, then will ask you if you have anything you wish to add. Unless you are expecting this question, it may floor you. Worse, it may start you off on an extended, extemporaneous speech. The board is not usually seeking more information. The question is principally to offer you a last opportunity to present further qualifications or to indicate that you have nothing to add. So, if you feel that a significant qualification or characteristic has been overlooked, it is proper to point it out in a sentence or so. Do not compliment the board on the thoroughness of their examination – they have been sketchy, and you know it. If you wish, merely say, "No thank you, I have nothing further to add." This is a point where you can "talk yourself out" of a good impression or fail to present an important bit of information. Remember, *you close the interview yourself.*

The chairman will then say, "That is all, Mr. ______, thank you." Do not be startled; the interview is over, and quicker than you think. Thank him, gather your belongings and take your leave. Save your sigh of relief for the other side of the door.

How to put your best foot forward

Throughout this entire process, you may feel that the board individually and collectively is trying to pierce your defenses, seek out your hidden weaknesses and embarrass and confuse you. Actually, this is not true. They are obliged to make an appraisal of your qualifications for the job you are seeking, and they want to see you in your best light. Remember, they must interview all candidates and a non-cooperative candidate may become a failure in spite of their best efforts to bring out his qualifications. Here are 15 suggestions that will help you:

1) Be natural – Keep your attitude confident, not cocky

If you are not confident that you can do the job, do not expect the board to be. Do not apologize for your weaknesses, try to bring out your strong points. The board is interested in a positive, not negative, presentation. Cockiness will antagonize any board member and make him wonder if you are covering up a weakness by a false show of strength.

2) Get comfortable, but don't lounge or sprawl

Sit erectly but not stiffly. A careless posture may lead the board to conclude that you are careless in other things, or at least that you are not impressed by the importance of the occasion. Either conclusion is natural, even if incorrect. Do not fuss with your clothing, a pencil or an ashtray. Your hands may occasionally be useful to emphasize a point; do not let them become a point of distraction.

3) Do not wisecrack or make small talk

This is a serious situation, and your attitude should show that you consider it as such. Further, the time of the board is limited – they do not want to waste it, and neither should you.

4) Do not exaggerate your experience or abilities

In the first place, from information in the application or other interviews and sources, the board may know more about you than you think. Secondly, you probably will not get away with it. An experienced board is rather adept at spotting such a situation, so do not take the chance.

5) If you know a board member, do not make a point of it, yet do not hide it

Certainly you are not fooling him, and probably not the other members of the board. Do not try to take advantage of your acquaintanceship – it will probably do you little good.

6) Do not dominate the interview

Let the board do that. They will give you the clues – do not assume that you have to do all the talking. Realize that the board has a number of questions to ask you, and do not try to take up all the interview time by showing off your extensive knowledge of the answer to the first one.

7) Be attentive

You only have 20 minutes or so, and you should keep your attention at its sharpest throughout. When a member is addressing a problem or question to you, give him your undivided attention. Address your reply principally to him, but do not exclude the other board members.

8) Do not interrupt

A board member may be stating a problem for you to analyze. He will ask you a question when the time comes. Let him state the problem, and wait for the question.

9) Make sure you understand the question

Do not try to answer until you are sure what the question is. If it is not clear, restate it in your own words or ask the board member to clarify it for you. However, do not haggle about minor elements.

10) Reply promptly but not hastily

A common entry on oral board rating sheets is "candidate responded readily," or "candidate hesitated in replies." Respond as promptly and quickly as you can, but do not jump to a hasty, ill-considered answer.

11) Do not be peremptory in your answers

A brief answer is proper – but do not fire your answer back. That is a losing game from your point of view. The board member can probably ask questions much faster than you can answer them.

12) Do not try to create the answer you think the board member wants

He is interested in what kind of mind you have and how it works – not in playing games. Furthermore, he can usually spot this practice and will actually grade you down on it.

13) Do not switch sides in your reply merely to agree with a board member

Frequently, a member will take a contrary position merely to draw you out and to see if you are willing and able to defend your point of view. Do not start a debate, yet do not surrender a good position. If a position is worth taking, it is worth defending.

14) Do not be afraid to admit an error in judgment if you are shown to be wrong

The board knows that you are forced to reply without any opportunity for careful consideration. Your answer may be demonstrably wrong. If so, admit it and get on with the interview.

15) Do not dwell at length on your present job

The opening question may relate to your present assignment. Answer the question but do not go into an extended discussion. You are being examined for a *new* job, not your present one. As a matter of fact, try to phrase ALL your answers in terms of the job for which you are being examined.

Basis of Rating

Probably you will forget most of these "do's" and "don'ts" when you walk into the oral interview room. Even remembering them all will not ensure you a passing grade. Perhaps you did not have the qualifications in the first place. But remembering them will help you to put your best foot forward, without treading on the toes of the board members.

Rumor and popular opinion to the contrary notwithstanding, an oral board wants you to make the best appearance possible. They know you are under pressure – but they also want to see how you respond to it as a guide to what your reaction would be under the pressures of the job you seek. They will be influenced by the degree of poise you display, the personal traits you show and the manner in which you respond.

EXAMINATION SECTION

EXAMINATION SECTION
TEST 1

Directions: This inventory contains 50 questions about yourself. You are to read each question and select the answer that best describes you from the choices provided. *PRINT THE LETTER OF YOUR ANSWER IN THE SPACE AT THE RIGHT.*

1) What has given you the most difficulty in any job that you have had? 1. _____

A. A supervisor who watched over my work too closely
B. A supervisor who gave inconsistent direction
C. Disagreements or gossip among co-workers
D. Having to deal with too many insignificant details

2) I _______________ put off doing a chore that I could have taken care of right away. 2. _____

A. often
B. sometimes
C. seldom
D. never

3) During high school, the number of clubs or organizations I belonged/ belong to is: 3. _____

A. 0
B. 1 or 2
C. 2 to 3
D. more than 3

4) In the past, when I have given a speech or presentation, I was likely to have prepared ahead of time: 4. _____

A. much less than others did
B. less than others
C. more than others
D. about the same as others

5) When working as a member of a team, I prefer to: 5. _____

A. take on challenging tasks but not take the lead
B. do less complex tasks
C. take the lead
D. keep a low profile

6) Generally, in my work assignments, I would prefer to work: 6. ______

A. on one thing at a time.
B. on a couple of things at a time.
C. on many things at the same time.
D. on something I have never done before.

7) In the course of a week, the thing that gives me the greatest satisfaction is 7. ______

A. coming up with a new or unique way to handle a situation.
B. helping other people to solve problems.
C. having free time to devote to personal interests.
D. being told I have done a good job.

8) My health or fitness has ________________ limited my ability to perform certain tasks. 8. ______

A. often
B. sometimes
C. seldom
D. never

9) In the past, when faced with an ethical dilemma, my first step has usually been to 9. ______

A. identify the issues that are in conflict
B. reflect on the punishment or rewards likely to result from either course of action
C. try to find someone else who is more appropriate for making such a decision
D. identify the people and organizations likely to be affected by the decision

10) My leadership style could be best described as 10. ______

A. autocratic
B. democratic/participative
C. permissive/laissez faire
D. motivational

11) In the past, when I have been part of a team, I most often felt 11. _____

A. as if I were a cut above, and ready to lead
B. a sense of equality and belonging
C. uncertain about the next step
D. isolated and marginalized

12) I usually enjoy thinking about the plusses and minuses of alternative approaches to solving a problem: 12. _____

A. very true for me—describes me perfectly
B. somewhat true of me
C. somewhat false for me
D. absolutely false for me—doesn't describe me at all

13) When I have participated in team activities in the past and found that other group members performed better than I have, I most often 13. _____

A. examined the skills and strategies that made them so successful
B. made a last-gasp attempt to measure up
C. tried to reconfigure the team members so that I wouldn't end up looking bad
D. resented the easier set of circumstances that made such success possible

14) In the past, when I failed to adequately learn a skill, concept or body of knowledge, the failure was most often the result of 14. _____

A. other peoples' interference with my approach to learning or solving the problem
B. poor instruction
C. having too little time to adequately study and practice
D. a study plan that aimed too high, without learning the basics first

15) My energy is usually highest when 15. _____

A. I work as part of a collaborative team
B. I work completely on my own
C. I work mostly on my own, with input from others when I ask for it
D. I work with ongoing evaluations from superiors

16) My own work standards are 16. _____

A. usually completely different from those of others
B. usually in tune with those of others
C. always frustratingly more demanding than those of others
D. sometimes different from others, but easily adapted to fit the group

17) In the past, when I have worked with a group on a task for which I had little experience, I have most often 17. _____

A. asked questions and contributed as much as I was able
B. tried to alter the parameters of the task in order to suit my own abilities
C. asked for direction and hoped for clear guidance
D. I don't recall being in this situation.

18) How much do you agree with the following statement: "Unless I am assigned to a team that is made up of people just like myself, the team is not likely to succeed." 18. _____

A. Strongly agree
B. Agree somewhat
C. Disagree somewhat
D. Strongly disagree

19) I am ________________ giving other people feedback on their work because ____________________. 19. _____

A. very comfortable; I usually know more about what it takes to succeed than they do
B. comfortable; it is a normal and useful part of teamwork
C. uncomfortable; I don't usually have anything to add
D. very uncomfortable; I'm afraid I will be resented or rejected

20) In my career, I have changed jobs 20. _____

A. only through promotion
B. once or twice
C. on the average, every few years
D. never

21) In the past, whenever I've been unable to achieve all that I set out to do in a given time period, I have 21. _____

A. tried to figure out where I came up short, and devised new strategies
B. looked for ways to redefine "success"
C. felt angry or hopeless
D. I have never failed to achieve what I've set out to do.

22) Other people have _______________ referred to me as an over-achiever. 22. _____

A. always
B. often
C. occasionally
D. never

23) When it comes to competitiveness, I am 23. _____

A. much more competitive than others
B. slightly more competitive than others
C. about as competitive as others
D. generally less competitive than others

24) In the past, when I have achieved an important goal, I have 24. _____

A. not made a big deal of it, as it is only one small step toward an ultimate goal
B. often gone back and tried to imagine how it could have been achieved more successfully
C. enjoyed the feeling of satisfaction for a while, before moving on to another goal
D. tried to make the feeling of accomplishment last for as long as I could

25) My first impressions of people 25. _____

A. are almost always dead-on
B. usually give an incomplete perception that evolves over time
C. are often wrong, to my delight
D. are often wrong, to my disappointment

26) When assigned a task, I believe 26. _____

A. success is imperative, and I'll do anything to achieve it
B. success is important, and I focus on doing my best
C. my investment in the success of the task correlates to my opinion of the task's importance
D. my investment in the success of the task correlates to my opinion of the task's achievability

27) When trying to evaluate whether I have succeeded on a certain task, I rely mostly on 27. _____

A. my own gut feeling
B. the opinions of peers
C. a list of objective criteria
D. people who fill leadership positions and are in a position to judge

28) If I fail to do something well, 28. _____

A. it usually isn't my fault
B. it's probably time to give someone else a chance
C. I'll look for feedback, reflect on it, and approach it differently another time
D. I'll redouble my efforts, and won't give up until I succeed

29) At work or in school, when somebody has stood up to me or disagreed with me, I have tended to 29. _____

A. make a mental note that the person is an enemy who can't be trusted
B. react angrily and heatedly, and then tried to make amends afterward
C. listen carefully and assume that the person's opinion deserves respect
D. apologize and try to soothe the person

30) In the past, when an assigned task has been altered during the course of my work, my reaction has usually been to 30. _____

A. adapt my strategy to fit the new circumstances
B. wish that the people who first assigned it could make up their minds
C. wonder what I've been doing wrong
D. This has never happened to me

31) When times get tough, I usually 31. _____

A. become emotionally fragile or volatile
B. feel more stressed, but make the effort to meet demands
C. become depressed and find it more difficult to work
D. tend to engage in unhealthy behaviors such as overeating or getting less sleep

32) I second-guess my decisions 32. _____

A. almost never
B. when there is evidence to suggest that another way might be better
C. when I feel poorly about myself or my performance
D. constantly, always mindful of the different available courses of action

33) When I engage in an activity that requires moderate physical exertion, I usually 33. _____

A. push myself to ratchet up the physical demands of the activity
B. feel challenged and energized
C. come up with ways to make it less strenuous
D. feel winded and depleted

34) If it were up to me, my success on a certain task would be defined by 34. _____

A. myself alone
B. a set of fair and objective criteria
C. my friends
D. the strictest standards available

35) When I have been assigned to work in a group in the past, I have usually 35. _____

A. insisted on a leadership position
B. been asked to assume a leadership position
C. participated as an equal, and deferred to others when their opinions merited it
D. been frozen out of decision-making by the more aggressive group members

36) When my regular work schedule changes, I most often 36. _____

A. try to stick with my proven formula for success
B. feel angry and resentful at the whimsy of outside forces
C. laugh it off as the result of a bureaucracy that often works against logic
D. try to go with the flow and produce results

37) If somebody tries to talk me out of a decision, I am most likely to 37. _____

A. tell them they are wasting their time
B. say I agree with them to minimize conflict, and then stick to my original plan
C. try to figure out where they are coming from
D. ask what I can do to make them happy

38) When I find a task to be unpleasant, but necessary, 38. _____

A. it is usually difficult to motivate myself to work on the task
B. I try to pass it on to someone who will enjoy it more
C. I am able to motivate myself to complete the task satisfactorily
D. I place the task low on my priorities list

39) It seems as if it is ________________ the case that some people find what I say to be rude or offensive. 39. _____

A. always
B. often
C. sometimes
D. never

40) When I have finished a particular task, I usually find that the time it took to complete was 40. _____

A. about what I had expected and planned for
B. more than I had expected and planned for
C. less than I had expected and planned for
D. other more or less than I had planned for, with no consistent means of predicting either

41) When I undertake a task with several different parts, I usually 41. _____

A. tackle the easiest work first
B. start organizing the different parts into categories that I can prioritize
C. start working on them in no particular order—it all has to get done anyway
D. have a difficult time deciding which part to do first

42) When I am assigned a new project, I'm usually 42. _____

A. a little apprehensive about adding to my workload
B. hopeful that it will be more interesting than the drudgery that takes up most of my time
C. excited to take on something new and different
D. nervous about whether I'm up to the task

43) On the occasions when I have been in a position to lead others, I have most often tried to lead by 43. _____

A. isolating and marginalizing the weak links
B. offering appropriate rewards and punishments
C. trying to inspire confidence and innovation
D. allowing decisions to be made by other group members

44) My own academic career has been one characterized by 44. _____

A. achievement beyond even my own expectations
B. hard work
C. success without having to try very hard
D. bitter disappointment in those charged with the task of educating me

45) I believe that when a group composed of talented people fails to achieve an assigned task, it is usually the case that 45. _____

A. the group failed to appoint a leader who could have directed their talents toward a result
B. the group probably didn't do as good a job at communicating as they could have
C. some group members were working harder than others
D. the people who assigned the task had unrealistic expectations

46) I feel that whatever success I have achieved in life has been attributable largely to 46. _____

A. myself alone
B. hard work and the support of others
C. the fact that tasks were clearly defined and not too difficult
D. pure luck

47) In my academic career, I have tended to focus the most energy on course work that 47. _____

A. allowed me to express my creativity
B. I knew would later help to advance my career
C. challenged me to think in new and different ways
D. involved memorization and repetition

48) I usually get a physical workout __________ times a week. 48. _____

A. 0-1
B. 2-3
C. 3-5
D. 5-7

49) Of the following, my favorite academic subjects could be most accurately described as 49. _____

A. the empirical subjects, such as math and science
B. expressive and creative subjects such as art
C. subjects that involved a lot of reading, such as history and English literature
D. entirely dependent on how the subjects were taught, and in what kind of environment

50) Of the following, the information sources I tend to trust the most are 50. _____

A. network television news programs
B. Internet blogs
C. professional and scholarly journals, such as *Scientific American*
D. other print media such as newspapers and magazines

Biodata Inventory
Key to Exercises

Note: In a biographical inventory, which asks for factual data, there are no right or wrong answers. It may also be true that for a particular question, more than one answer reflects a trait or viewpoint that might qualify one as a special agent: there is no single type of person or personality type that is acceptable. At the same time, there are some qualities or experiences that would probably suggest that a person is less than an ideal candidate. Generally, you are likely to be considered "qualified" if your answers tend to reveal the skills and abilities that the Biodata Inventory is designed to look for:

- *Ability to Organize, Plan, and Prioritize*
- *Ability to Maintain a Positive Image*
- *Ability to Evaluate Information and Make Judgment Decisions*
- *Initiative and Motivation*
- *Ability to Adapt to Changing Situations*
- *Physical Requirements*

The following responses are the ones most indicative of these skills and abilities:

1. No choice here is better than the others; all describe a problem.
2. D
3. D
4. C
5. A or C

6. No answer is inherently better than the others; candidate suitability will probably depend on the task at hand.
7. A or B
8. D
9. A
10. B or D

11. B
12. A or B
13. A
14. D
15. A

16. D
17. A
18. C or D
19. B
20. None is "right," but choice C is the least desirable, labeling you as one who can't stick with a job.

21. A
22. None is "right," but choice D is the least desirable—it's better to have over-achieved at least once or twice.
23. None is "right," but choice D is the least desirable.
24. C
25. B

Biodata Inventory
Key to Exercises (continued)

26. B
27. C
28. C
29. C
30. A

31. B
32. B
33. B
34. B
35. B or C

36. D
37. C
38. C
39. D
40. A

41. B
42. C
43. C
44. B
45. B

46. B
47. C
48. D
49. None is the "right" answer, but A or C are the best choices.
50. C

PERSONALITY/AUTOBIOGRAPHICAL INVENTORY
EXAMINATION SECTION
TEST 1

DIRECTIONS: Each question or incomplete statement is followed by several suggested answers or completions. Select the one that BEST answers the question or completes the statement. *PRINT THE LETTER OF THE CORRECT ANSWER IN THE SPACE AT THE RIGHT.*

1. While a senior in high school, I was absent 1.____

   A. never
   B. seldom
   C. frequently
   D. more than 10 days
   E. only when I felt bored

2. While in high school, I failed classes 2.____

   A. never
   B. once
   C. twice
   D. more than twice
   E. at least four times

3. During class discussions in my high school classes, I usually 3.____

   A. listened without participating
   B. participated as much as possible
   C. listened until I had something to add to the discussion
   D. disagreed with others simply for the sake of argument
   E. laughed at stupid ideas

4. My high school grade point average (on a 4.0 scale) was 4.____

   A. 2.0 or lower
   B. 2.1 to 2.5
   C. 2.6 to 3.0
   D. 3.1 to 3.5
   E. 3.6 to 4.0

5. As a high school student, I completed my assignments 5.____

   A. as close to the due date as I could manage
   B. whenever the teacher gave me an extension
   C. frequently
   D. on time
   E. when they were interesting

6. While in high school, I participated in 6.____

   A. athletic and nonathletic extracurricular activities
   B. athletic extracurricular activities
   C. nonathletic extracurricular activities
   D. no extracurricular activities
   E. mandatory after-school programs

7. In high school, I made the honor roll 7.____

   A. several times
   B. once
   C. more than once
   D. twice
   E. I can't remember if I made the honor roll

8. Upon graduation from high school, I received 8.___

A. academic and nonacademic honors
B. academic honors
C. nonacademic honors
D. no honors
E. I can't remember if I received honors

9. While attending high school, I worked at a paid job or as a volunteer 9.___

A. never
B. every so often
C. 5 to 10 hours a month
D. more than 10 hours a month
E. more than 15 hours a month

10. During my senior year of high school, I skipped school 10.___

A. whenever I could
B. once a week
C. several times a week
D. not at all
E. when I got bored

11. I was suspended from high school 11.___

A. not at all
B. once or twice
C. once or twice, for fighting
D. several times
E. more times than I can remember

12. During high school, my fellow students and teachers considered me 12.___

A. above average
B. below average
C. average
D. underachieving
E. underachieving and prone to fighting

13. The ability to ______ is most important to a Police Officer. 13.___

A. draw his/her gun quickly
B. see over great distances and difficult terrain
C. verbally and physically intimidate criminals
D. communicate effectively in circumstances which can be dangerous
E. hear over great distances

14. I began planning for college 14.___

A. when my parents told me to
B. when I entered high school
C. during my junior year
D. during my senior year
E. when I signed up for my SAT (or other standardized) exam

15. An effective leader is someone who 15.____

A. inspires confidence in his/her followers
B. inspires fear in his/her followers
C. tells subordinates exactly what they should do
D. creates an environment in which subordinates feel insecure about their job security and performance
E. makes as few decisions as possible

16. I prepared myself for college by 16.____

A. learning how to get extensions on major assignments
B. working as many hours as possible at my after-school job
C. spending as much time with my friends as possible
D. getting good grades and participating in extracurricular activities
E. watching television shows about college kids

17. I paid for college by 17.____

A. supplementing my parents contributions with my own earnings
B. relying on scholarships, loans, and my own earnings
C. relying on my parents and student loans
D. relying on my parents to pay my tuition, room and board
E. relying on sources not listed here

18. While a college student, I spent my summers and holiday breaks 18.____

A. in summer or remedial classes
B. traveling
C. working
D. relaxing
E. spending time with my friends

19. My final college grade point average (on a 4.0 scale) was 19.____

A. 3.8 to 4.0 B. 3.5 to 3.8 C. 3.0 to 3.5
D. 2.5 to 3.0 E. 2.0 to 2.5

20. As a college student, I cut classes 20.____

A. frequently B. when I didn't like them
C. sometimes D. rarely
E. when I needed the sleep

21. In college, I received academic honors 21.____

A. not at all B. once
C. twice D. several times
E. I can't remember if I received academic honors

22. While in college, I declared a major 22.____

A. during my first year B. during my sophomore year
C. during my junior year D. during my senior year
E. several times

23. While on patrol as a Police Officer, you spot someone attempting to flee the scene of a crime. Your first reaction is to 23.__

A. draw your weapon
B. observe the person until he or she completes the fleeing
C. identify yourself as a Police Officer
D. fire your weapon over the person's head in order to scare him or her
E. call immediately for backup

24. As a college student, I failed ______ classes. 24.__

A. no
B. two
C. three
D. four
E. more than four

25. Friends describe me as 25.__

A. introverted
B. hot-tempered
C. unpredictable
D. quiet
E. easygoing

KEY (CORRECT ANSWERS)

PLEASE NOTE: The answers listed are the best answers. However, you are to answer the exam honestly. Your personal answer may differ from the *best* answers.

1. A
2. A
3. C
4. E
5. D
6. A
7. A
8. A
9. E
10. D
11. A
12. A
13. D
14. B
15. A
16. D
17. B
18. C
19. A
20. D
21. D
22. A
23. C
24. A
25. E

TEST 2

DIRECTIONS: Each question or incomplete statement is followed by several suggested answers or completions. Select the one that BEST answers the question or completes the statement. *PRINT THE LETTER OF THE CORRECT ANSWER IN THE SPACE AT THE RIGHT.*

1. As a Police Officer, you apprehend three men whom you believe are in the country illegally. However, none of the men speaks English, and you don't speak their language. Your reaction should be to 1.____

   A. draw your weapon so that they understand the seriousness of the situation
   B. take them into custody, where they will have access to a translator
   C. attempt to communicate through hand gestures and shouting
   D. call for a translator to come and meet you at your location
   E. pretend you understand their language and apprehend them

2. During my college classes, I preferred to 2.____

   A. remain silent during class discussions
   B. do other homework during class discussions
   C. participate frequently in class discussions
   D. argue with others as much as possible
   E. laugh at the stupid opinions of others

3. As a Police Officer, you are chasing a small group of people who are running away from the scene of a crime. During your pursuit, one member of the group is left behind. You see that she is injured and in need of medical attention. Your reaction is to 3.____

   A. fire your weapon at the group members to get them to stop
   B. cease pursuit of the group members and take the woman into custody
   C. continue pursuit of the group members, leaving the woman behind since acting ill is a common trick
   D. radio for backup to stay with the woman while medical help arrives while you continue pursuit of the group members
   E. radio for backup to continue pursuit of the group members while you stay with the woman and wait for medical help to arrive

4. As a college student, I was placed on academic probation 4.____

   A. not at all
   B. once
   C. twice
   D. three times
   E. more than three times

5. At work, being a team player means to 5.____

   A. compromise your ideals and beliefs
   B. compensate for the incompetence of others
   C. count on others to compensate for my inexperience
   D. cooperate with others to get a project finished
   E. rely on others to get the job done

6. As a Police Officer, you confront someone you believe has just committed a crime. After identifying yourself, you notice the suspect holding something that looks like a knife. Your FIRST reaction should be to 6._____

   A. draw your weapon and fire
   B. call immediately for backup
   C. keep your weapon drawn until you get the suspect into a position that is controllable
   D. ask the suspect if he is armed
   E. talk to the suspect without drawing your weapon

7. My friends from college remember me primarily as a(n) 7._____

   A. person who loved to party
   B. ambitious student
   C. athlete
   D. joker
   E. fighter

8. My college experience is memorable primarily because of 8._____

   A. the friends I made
   B. the sorority/fraternity I was able to join
   C. the social activities I participated in
   D. my academic achievements
   E. the money I spent

9. A friend who is applying for a job asks you to help him pass the mandatory drug test by substituting a sample of your urine for his. You should 9._____

   A. help him by supplying the sample
   B. help him by supplying the sample and insisting he seek drug counseling
   C. supply the sample, but tell him that this is the only time you'll help in this way
   D. call the police
   E. refuse

10. As a college student, I handed in my assignments 10._____

    A. when they were due
    B. whenever I could get an extension
    C. when they were interesting
    D. when my friends reminded me to
    E. when I was able to

11. At work you are accused of a minor infraction which you didn't commit. Your first reaction is to 11._____

    A. call a lawyer
    B. speak to your supervisor about the mistake
    C. call the police
    D. yell at the person who did commit the infraction
    E. accept the consequences regardless of your guilt or innocence

12. While on patrol, you are surprised by a large group of disorderly teenage gang members. You are greatly outnumbered. 12.___
As a Police Officer, your first reaction is to

A. draw your weapon and identify yourself
B. get back into your vehicle and wait for help to arrive
C. call for backup
D. pretend you are part of a large group of police in the area
E. identify yourself and get the group members into a controllable position

13. As a college student, I began to prepare for final exams 13.___

A. the night before taking them
B. when the professor handed out the review sheets
C. several weeks before taking them
D. when my friends began to prepare for their exams
E. the morning of the exam

14. As a Police Officer in the field, you confront a small group of people you believe to be wanted criminals. Your most important consideration during this exchange should be 14.___

A. apprehension of criminals
B. safety of county citizens in nearby towns
C. safety of the criminals
D. number of criminals you must apprehend in order to receive a commendation
E. the amount of respect the criminals show to you and your position

15. At work, I am known as 15.___

A. popular B. quiet C. intense
D. easygoing E. dedicated

16. The most important quality in a coworker is 16.___

A. friendliness B. cleanliness
C. a good sense of humor D. dependability
E. good listening skills

17. In the past year, I have stayed home from work 17.___

A. frequently
B. only when I felt depressed
C. rarely
D. only when I felt overwhelmed
E. only to run important errands

18. As a Police Officer, the best way to collect information from a suspect during an interview is to 18.___

A. physically intimidate the suspect
B. verbally intimidate the suspect
C. threaten the suspect's family and/or friends with criminal prosecution
D. encourage a conversation with the suspect
E. sit in silence until the suspect begins speaking

19. For me, the best thing about college was the 19.____

A. chance to strengthen my friendships and develop new ones
B. chance to test my abilities and develop new ones
C. number of extracurricular activities and clubs
D. chance to socialize
E. chance to try several different majors

20. As an employee, my weakest skill is 20.____

A. controlling my temper
B. my organizational ability
C. my ability to effectively understand directions
D. my ability to effectively manage others
E. my ability to communicate my thoughts in writing

21. As a Police Officer, my greatest strength would be 21.____

A. my sense of loyalty
B. my organizational ability
C. punctuality
D. dedication
E. my ability to intimidate others

22. As a Police Officer, you find a group of suspicious youths gathered around a truck which is on fire. Your first reaction is to 22.____

A. call the fire department
B. arrest them all for destruction of property
C. draw your weapon and begin questioning them
D. return to your vehicle and wait for the fire department
E. instruct the group to remain while you return to your vehicle and request backup

23. If asked by my company to learn a new job-related skill, my reaction would be to 23.____

A. ask for a raise
B. ask for overtime pay
C. question the necessity of the skill
D. cooperate with some reluctance
E. cooperate with enthusiasm

24. When I disagree with others, I tend to 24.____

A. listen quietly despite my disagreement
B. laugh openly at the person I disagree with
C. ask the person to explain their views before I respond
D. leave the conversation before my anger gets the best of me
E. point out exactly why the person is wrong

25. When I find myself in a situation which is confusing or unclear, my reaction is to 25.____

A. pretend I am not confused
B. remain calm and, if necessary, ask someone else for clarification
C. grow frustrated and angry
D. walk away from the situation
E. immediately insist that someone explain things to me

KEY (CORRECT ANSWERS)

PLEASE NOTE: The answers listed are the best answers. However, you are to answer the exam honestly. Your personal answer may differ from the *best* answers.

1. B
2. C
3. E
4. A
5. D
6. C
7. B
8. D
9. E
10. A
11. B
12. E
13. C
14. A
15. E
16. D
17. C
18. D
19. B
20. E
21. D
22. A
23. E
24. C
25. B

TEST 3

DIRECTIONS: Each question or incomplete statement is followed by several suggested answers or completions. Select the one that BEST answers the question or completes the statement. *PRINT THE LETTER OF THE CORRECT ANSWER IN THE SPACE AT THE RIGHT.*

1. While on patrol as a Police Officer, you find a dead body lying in the open. Hiding a few feet away, behind some rocks, you find a suspicious person who is holding items which seem to have been taken from the dead body, including a pair of shoes and some jewelry. 1.____
You should

   A. apprehend the suspect and bring him to the station for further questioning
   B. arrest the suspect for murder and robbery
   C. arrest the suspect for murder
   D. subdue the suspect with force and check the area for his accomplices
   E. subdue the suspect with force and call for backup to check the area for his accomplices

2. If you were placed in a supervisory position, which of the following abilities would you consider to be most important to your job performance? 2.____

   A. Stubbornness
   B. The ability to hear all sides of a story before making a decision
   C. Kindness
   D. The ability to make and stick to a decision
   E. Patience

3. What is your highest level of education? 3.____

   A. Less than a high school diploma
   B. A high school diploma or equivalency
   C. A graduate of community college
   D. A graduate of a four-year accredited college
   E. A degree from graduate school

4. When asked to supervise other workers, your approach should be to 4.____

   A. ask for management wages since you're doing management work
   B. give the workers direction and supervise every aspect of the process
   C. give the workers direction and then allow them to do the job
   D. hand the workers their job specifications
   E. do the work yourself, since you're uncomfortable supervising others

5. Which of the following best describes you? 5.____

   A. Need little or no supervision
   B. Resent too much supervision
   C. Require as much supervision as my peers
   D. Require slightly more supervision than my peers
   E. Require close supervision

6. You accept a job which requires an ability to perform several tasks at once. What is the best way to handle such a position? 6.___

A. With strong organizational skills and a close attention to detail
B. By delegating the work to someone with strong organizational skills
C. Staying focused on one task at a time, no matter what happens
D. Working on one task at a time until each task is successfully completed
E. Asking my supervisor to help me

7. As a Police Officer, you take a suspected perpetrator into custody. After returning to the field, you notice that your gun is missing. You should 7.___

A. retrace your steps to see if you dropped it somewhere
B. report the loss immediately
C. ask your partner to borrow his or her gun
D. pretend that nothing's happened
E. rely on your hands for defense and protection

8. Which of the following best describes your behavior when you disagree with someone? You 8.___

A. state your own point of view as quickly and loudly as you can
B. listen quietly and keep your opinions to yourself
C. listen to the other person's perspective and then carefully point out all the flaws in their logic
D. list all of the ignorant people who agree with the opposing point of view
E. listen to the other person's perspective and then explain your own perspective

9. As a new Police Officer, you make several mistakes during your first week of work. You react by 9.___

A. learning from your mistakes and moving on
B. resigning
C. blaming it on your supervisor
D. refusing to talk about it
E. blaming yourself

10. My ability to communicate effectively with others is ________ average. 10.___

A. below B. about C. above D. far above E. far below

11. In which of the following areas are you most highly skilled? 11.___

A. Written communication
B. Oral communication
C. Ability to think quickly in difficult situations
D. Ability to work with a broad diversity of people and personalities
E. Organizational skills

12. As a Police Officer, you are assigned to work with a partner whom you dislike. You should 12.___

A. immediately report the problem to your supervisor
B. ask your partner not to speak to you during working hours
C. tell your colleagues about your differences
D. tell your partner why you dislike him/her
E. work with your partner regardless of your personal feelings

13. During high school, what was your most common after-school activity? 13.____

A. Remaining after school to participate in various clubs and organizations (such as band, sports, etc.)
B. Remaining after school to make up for missed classes
C. Remaining after school as punishment (detention, etc.)
D. Going straight to an after-school job
E. Spending the afternoon at home or with friends

14. During high school, in which of the following subjects did you receive the highest grades? 14.____

A. English, History, Social Studies
B. Math, Science
C. Vocational classes
D. My grades were consistent in all subjects
E. Classes I liked

15. When faced with an overwhelming number of duties at work, your reaction is to 15.____

A. do all of the work yourself, no matter what the cost
B. delegate some responsibilities to capable colleagues
C. immediately ask your supervisor for help
D. put off as much work as possible until you can get to it
E. take some time off to relax and clear your mind

16. As a Police Officer, your supervisor informs you that a prisoner whom you arrested has accused you of beating him. You know you are innocent. You react by 16.____

A. quitting your job
B. hiring a lawyer
C. challenging your supervisor to prove the charges against you
D. calmly telling your supervisor what really happened and presenting evidence to support your position
E. insisting that you be allowed to speak alone to the prisoner

17. Which of the following best describes your desk at your current or most recent job? 17.____

A. Messy and disorganized
B. Neat and organized
C. Messy but organized
D. Neat but disorganized
E. Messy

18. The ______ BEST describes your reasons for wanting tobecome a Police Officer* 18.____

A. ability to carry and use a weapon
B. excitement and challenges of the career
C. excellent salary and benefits package
D. chance to tell other people what to do
E. chance to help people find a better life

19. As a Police Officer in the field, you are approached by a man who is frantic but unable to speak English. After several minutes of trying to communicate, you realize that the man is asking you to come with him in order to help someone who has been hurt. You should 19.____

A. ignore him, since it might be a trap
B. call for backup
C. immediately offer to help the man
D. return to your vehicle and wait for the man to leave
E. radio your position and situation to another officer, then go with the man to offer help

20. When asked to take on extra responsibility at work, in order to help out a coworker who is overwhelmed, your response is to 20.___

A. ask for overtime pay
B. complain to your supervisor that you are being taken advantage of
C. help the coworker to the best of your ability
D. ask the coworker to come back some other time
E. give the coworker some advice on how to get his/her job done

21. At my last job, I was promoted 21.___

A. not at all
B. once
C. twice
D. three times
E. more than three times

22. As a Police Officer, you discover the body of a person whom you suspect to be a gang member. You also suspect that there are several other gang members hiding in the nearby vicinity. 22.___
Your first reaction should be to

A. begin a search of the nearby area for the other gang members
B. return to your vehicle and call for backup
C. return to your vehicle with the body of the person you found
D. check whether the person you found is dead or alive
E. draw your weapon and identify yourself

23. You are faced with an overwhelming deadline at work. Your reaction is to 23.___

A. procrastinate until the last minute
B. procrastinate until someone notices you need some help
C. notify your supervisor that you can't complete the work on your own
D. work in silence without asking any questions
E. arrange your schedule so that you can get the work done before the deadline

24. When you feel yourself under deadline pressures at work, your response is to 24.___

A. make sure you keep to a schedule which allows you to complete the work on time
B. wait until just before the deadline to complete the work
C. ask someone else to do the work
D. grow so obsessive about the work that your coworkers feel compelled to help you
E. ask your supervisor immediately for help

25. Which of the following best describes your appearance at your current or most recent position? 25.___

A. Well-groomed, neat, and clean
B. Unkempt, but dressed neatly
C. Messy and dirty clothing
D. Unshaven and untidy
E. Clean-shaven, but sloppily dressed

KEY (CORRECT ANSWERS)

PLEASE NOTE: The answers listed are the best answers. However, you are to answer the exam honestly. Your personal answers may differ from the *best* answers.

1. A
2. D
3. E
4. C
5. A
6. A
7. B
8. E
9. A
10. C
11. C
12. E
13. A
14. D
15. B
16. D
17. B
18. B
19. E
20. C
21. C
22. D
23. E
24. A
25. A

TEST 4

DIRECTIONS: Each question or incomplete statement is followed by several suggested answers or completions. Select the one that BEST answers the question or completes the statement. *PRINT THE LETTER OF THE CORRECT ANSWER IN THE SPACE AT THE RIGHT.*

1. Which of the following best describes the way you react to making a difficult decision? 1.___

   A. Consult with the people you're closest to before making the decision
   B. Make the decision entirely on your own
   C. Consult only with those people whom your decision will affect
   D. Consult with everyone you know, in an effort to make a decision that will please everyone
   E. Forget about the decision until you have to make it

2. If placed in a supervisory role, which of the following characteristics would you rely on most heavily when dealing with the employees you supervise? 2.___

   A. Kindness B. Cheeriness C. Honesty
   D. Hostility E. Aloofness

3. As a Police Officer, you are pursuing a suspect when he turns and pulls something out of his jacket that looks like a gun. You should 3.___

   A. run away and call for backup
   B. assure the man that you mean him no harm
   C. draw your gun and order the man to stop and drop his weapon
   D. draw your gun and fire a warning shot
   E. draw your gun and fire immediately

4. In addition to English, in which of the following languages are you also fluent? 4.___

   A. Spanish B. French C. Italian
   D. German E. Other

5. When confronted with gossip at work, your typical reaction is to 5.___

   A. participate
   B. listen without participating
   C. notify your supervisor
   D. excuse yourself from the discussion
   E. confront your coworkers about their problem

6. In the past two years, how many jobs have you held? 6.___

   A. None B. One C. Two
   D. Three E. More than three

7. In your current or most recent job, your favorite part of the job is the part which involves 7.___

   A. telling other people what they're doing wrong
   B. supervising others
   C. working without supervision to finish a project
   D. written communication
   E. oral communication

8. Your supervisor asks you about a colleague who is applying for a position which you also want. You react by 8._____

A. commenting honestly on the person's work performance
B. enhancing the person's negative traits
C. informing your supervisor about your colleague's personal problems
D. telling your supervisor that you would be better in the position
E. refusing to comment

9. As a Police Officer, you confiscate some contraband which was being imported by an illegal alien who is now in your custody. Your partner asks you not to turn the contraband in to your supervisor. 9._____
Your response is to

A. inform your supervisor of your partner's request immediately
B. tell your partner you feel uncomfortable with his request
C. pretend you didn't hear your partner's request
D. tell your supervisor and all your colleagues about your partner's request
E. give the contraband to your partner and let him handle it

10. Which of the following best describes your responsibilities in your last job? 10._____

A. Entirely supervisory
B. Much supervisory responsibility
C. Equal amounts of supervisory and nonsupervisory responsibility
D. Some supervisory responsibilities
E. No supervisory responsibilities

11. How much written communication did your previous or most recent job require of you? 11._____

A. A great deal of written communication
B. Some written communication
C. I don't remember
D. A small amount of written communication
E. No written communication

12. In the past two years, how many times have you been fired from a job? 12._____

A. None B. Once C. Twice D. Three times
E. More than three times

13. How much time have you spent working for volunteer organizations in the past year? 13._____

A. 10 to 20 hours per week B. 5 to 10 hours per week
C. 3 to 5 hours per week D. 1 to 3 hours per week
E. I have spent no time volunteering in the past year

14. Your efforts at volunteer work usually revolve around which of the following types of organizations? 14._____

A. Religious
B. Community-based organizations working to improve the community
C. Charity organizations working on behalf of the poor
D. Charity organizations working on behalf of the infirm or handicapped
E. Other

15. Which of the following best describes your professional history? 15.___
Promoted at

A. a much faster rate than coworkers
B. a slightly faster rate than coworkers
C. the same rate as coworkers
D. a slightly slower rate than coworkers
E. a much slower rate than coworkers

16. Which of the following qualities do you most appreciate in a coworker? 16.___

A. Friendliness
B. Dependability
C. Good looks
D. Silence
E. Forgiveness

17. When you disagree with a supervisor's instructions or opinion about how to complete a project, your reaction is to 17.___

A. inform your supervisor that you refuse to complete the project according to his or her instructions
B. inform your colleagues of your supervisor's incompetence
C. accept your supervisor's instructions in silence
D. voice your concerns and then complete the project according to your own instincts
E. voice your concerns and then complete the project according to your supervisor's instructions

18. Which of the following best describes your reaction to close supervision and specific direction from your supervisors? 18.___
You

A. listen carefully to the directions, and then figure out a way to do the job more effectively
B. complete the job according to the given specifications
C. show some initiative by doing the job your way
D. ask someone else to do the job for you
E. listen carefully to the directions, and then figure out a better way to do the job which will save more money

19. How should a Police Officer handle a situation in which he or she is offered a bribe not to issue a traffic ticket? 19.___

A. Pretend the bribe was never offered
B. Accept the money as evidence and release the person
C. Draw your weapon and call for backup
D. Refuse the bribe and then arrest the person
E. Accept the bribe and then arrest the person

20. At work, you are faced with a difficult decision. You react by 20.___

A. seeking advice from your colleagues
B. following your own path regardless of the consequences
C. asking your supervisor what you should do
D. keeping the difficulties to yourself
E. working for a solution which will please everyone

21. If asked to work with a person whom you dislike, your response would be 21.____

A. to ask your supervisor to allow you to work with someone else
B. to ask your coworker to transfer to another department or project
C. talk to your coworker about the proper way to behave at work
D. pretend the coworker is your best friend for the sake of your job
E. to set aside your personal differences in order to complete the job

22. As a supervisor, which of the following incentives would you use to motivate your employees? 22.____

A. Fear of losing their jobs
B. Fear of their supervisors
C. Allowing employees to provide their input on a number of policies
D. Encouraging employees to file secret reports regarding colleagues' transgressions
E. All of the above

23. A fellow Police Officer, with whom you enjoy a close friendship, has a substance-abuse problem which has gone undetected. You suspect the problem may be affecting his job. You would 23.____

A. ask the Police Officer if the problem is affecting his job performance
B. warn the Police Officer that he must seek counseling or you will report him
C. wait a few weeks to see whether the officer's problem really is affecting his job
D. discuss it with your supervisor
E. wait for the supervisor to discover the problem

24. In the past two months, you have missed work 24.____

A. zero times
B. once
C. twice
D. three times
E. more than three times

25. As a Police Officer, you are pursuing a group of robbers when you discover two small children who have been abandoned near a railroad crossing. You should 25.____

A. tell the children to stay put while you continue your pursuit
B. lock the children in your vehicle and continue your pursuit
C. stay with the children and radio for help in the pursuit of the robbers
D. use the children to set a trap for the robbers
E. ignore the children and continue your pursuit

KEY (CORRECT ANSWERS)

PLEASE NOTE: The answers listed are the best answers. However, you are to answer the exam honestly. Your personal answer may differ from the *best* answers.

1. A
2. C
3. C
4. A
5. D

6. B
7. C
8. A
9. A
10. D

11. B
12. A
13. C
14. B
15. A

16. B
17. E
18. B
19. D
20. A

21. E
22. C
23. D
24. A
25. C

EXAMINATION SECTION
TEST 1

For each of the following items, circle the answer that best reflects the accuracy of the given statement, according to your own values, opinions, and experience.

1) In most situations, I value cooperation over competition.

A. Very Accurate B. Moderately Accurate C. Neither Accurate nor Inaccurate D. Moderately Inaccurate E. Very Inaccurate

2) In work or in school, I've tried to do more than what's expected of me.

A. Very Accurate B. Moderately Accurate C. Neither Accurate nor Inaccurate D. Moderately Inaccurate E. Very Inaccurate

3) Most of my problems are caused by other people.

A. Very Accurate B. Moderately Accurate C. Neither Accurate nor Inaccurate D. Moderately Inaccurate E. Very Inaccurate

4) It's reasonable to say that a person's race is in some way related to the likelihood that he or she will commit a crime.

A. Very Accurate B. Moderately Accurate C. Neither Accurate nor Inaccurate D. Moderately Inaccurate E. Very Inaccurate

5) My respect for a person's authority relies entirely on my respect for them as an individual, and has nothing to do with his or her official position.

A. Very Accurate B. Moderately Accurate C. Neither Accurate nor Inaccurate D. Moderately Inaccurate E. Very Inaccurate

6) When I was in school, I never cheated on a test or assignment.

A. Very Accurate B. Moderately Accurate C. Neither Accurate nor Inaccurate D. Moderately Inaccurate E. Very Inaccurate

7) I feel comfortable around most people, even if they're strangers.

A. Very Accurate B. Moderately Accurate C. Neither Accurate nor Inaccurate D. Moderately Inaccurate E. Very Inaccurate

8) It's acceptable for an employee to borrow property from the workplace if the person who takes it intends to return it when he or she is finished with it.

A. Very Accurate B. Moderately Accurate C. Neither Accurate nor Inaccurate D. Moderately Inaccurate E. Very Inaccurate

9) If it's clear that a person is not likely to receive adequate punishment for a crime or infraction, it's only fair to inflict some form of discipline on that person to make up for any likely lapses in justice.

A. Very Accurate B. Moderately Accurate C. Neither Accurate nor Inaccurate D. Moderately Inaccurate E. Very Inaccurate

10) In previous work experience, I have been reluctant or unable to take on extra work or overtime on short notice.

A. Very Accurate | B. Moderately Accurate | C. Neither Accurate nor Inaccurate | D. Moderately Inaccurate | E. Very Inaccurate

11) The casual use of illegal substances, if it's done only recreationally and on weekends, has no effect on a person's performance on the job during the work week.

A. Very Accurate | B. Moderately Accurate | C. Neither Accurate nor Inaccurate | D. Moderately Inaccurate | E. Very Inaccurate

12) I am sometimes overwhelmed by events.

A. Very Accurate | B. Moderately Accurate | C. Neither Accurate nor Inaccurate | D. Moderately Inaccurate | E. Very Inaccurate

13) If I don't agree with a certain rule, I see nothing wrong with breaking it, as long as it doesn't hurt anyone else.

A. Very Accurate | B. Moderately Accurate | C. Neither Accurate nor Inaccurate | D. Moderately Inaccurate | E. Very Inaccurate

14) I get angry easily.

A. Very Accurate | B. Moderately Accurate | C. Neither Accurate nor Inaccurate | D. Moderately Inaccurate | E. Very Inaccurate

15) As long as an employee finishes all his work on time at the end of the day, there's nothing wrong with coming back from lunch late.

A. Very Accurate | B. Moderately Accurate | C. Neither Accurate nor Inaccurate | D. Moderately Inaccurate | E. Very Inaccurate

16) I enjoy beginning new things.

A. Very Accurate | B. Moderately Accurate | C. Neither Accurate nor Inaccurate | D. Moderately Inaccurate | E. Very Inaccurate

17) When I have a number of tasks to be done, I prioritize them and tackle them immediately in order of importance.

A. Very Accurate | B. Moderately Accurate | C. Neither Accurate nor Inaccurate | D. Moderately Inaccurate | E. Very Inaccurate

18) I would have no reservations about working for a supervisor who is of a different race or gender than I am.

A. Very Accurate | B. Moderately Accurate | C. Neither Accurate nor Inaccurate | D. Moderately Inaccurate | E. Very Inaccurate

19) I'd rather help other people to do better than punish them for doing wrong.

A. Very Accurate **B.** Moderately Accurate **C.** Neither Accurate nor Inaccurate **D.** Moderately Inaccurate **E.** Very Inaccurate

20) In the past, I've had personality clashes with fellow students or co-workers whom I disliked or with whom I disagreed.

A. Very Accurate **B.** Moderately Accurate **C.** Neither Accurate nor Inaccurate **D.** Moderately Inaccurate **E.** Very Inaccurate

21) Confrontations are usually unpleasant, but sometimes necessary.

A. Very Accurate **B.** Moderately Accurate **C.** Neither Accurate nor Inaccurate **D.** Moderately Inaccurate **E.** Very Inaccurate

22) I generally believe that other people have good intentions.

A. Very Accurate **B.** Moderately Accurate **C.** Neither Accurate nor Inaccurate **D.** Moderately Inaccurate **E.** Very Inaccurate

23) When I have a lot of information to sort through, I have difficulty making up my mind.

A. Very Accurate **B.** Moderately Accurate **C.** Neither Accurate nor Inaccurate **D.** Moderately Inaccurate **E.** Very Inaccurate

24) In tense situations, I choose my words with care.

A. Very Accurate **B.** Moderately Accurate **C.** Neither Accurate nor Inaccurate **D.** Moderately Inaccurate **E.** Very Inaccurate

25) A person who works through his or her lunch break should automatically be able to go home early.

A. Very Accurate **B.** Moderately Accurate **C.** Neither Accurate nor Inaccurate **D.** Moderately Inaccurate **E.** Very Inaccurate

: Experiences and Traits

For each of the 25 items, score your response according to the list below. Then add the scores of all 25 items to arrive at a single number.

1. A=4; B=3; C=2; D=1; E=0
2. A=4; B=3; C=2; D=1; E=0
3. A=0; B=1; C=2; D=3; E=4
4. A=0; B=1; C=2; D=3; E=4
5. A=0; B=1; C=2; D=3; E=4

6. A=4; B=3; C=2; D=1; E=0
7. A=4; B=3; C=2; D=1; E=0
8. A=0; B=1; C=2; D=3; E=4
9. A=0; B=1; C=2; D=3; E=4
10. A=0; B=1; C=2; D=3; E=4

11. A=0; B=1; C=2; D=3; E=4
12. A=0; B=1; C=2; D=3; E=4
13. A=0; B=1; C=2; D=3; E=4
14. A=0; B=1; C=2; D=3; E=4
15. A=0; B=1; C=2; D=3; E=4

16. A=4; B=3; C=2; D=1; E=0
17. A=4; B=3; C=2; D=1; E=0
18. A=4; B=3; C=2; D=1; E=0
19. A=4; B=3; C=2; D=1; E=0
20. A=0; B=1; C=2; D=3; E=4

21. A=4; B=3; C=2; D=1; E=0
22. A=4; B=3; C=2; D=1; E=0
23. A=0; B=1; C=2; D=3; E=4
24. A=4; B=3; C=2; D=1; E=0
25. A=0; B=1; C=2; D=3; E=4

The following scores serve as an approximate guide to your compatibility with a career in law enforcement—but should not be taken as the final word.

85-100 points	Most compatible
70-84 points	Compatible
50-69 points	Somewhat compatible
0-49 points	Incompatible

TEST 2

For each of the following items, circle the answer that best reflects the accuracy of the given statement, according to your own values, opinions, and experience.

1) I find it difficult to approach people I don't know well.

A. Very Accurate | B. Moderately Accurate | C. Neither Accurate nor Inaccurate | D. Moderately Inaccurate | E. Very Inaccurate

2) I'm not really interested in hearing about other people's problems.

A. Very Accurate | B. Moderately Accurate | C. Neither Accurate nor Inaccurate | D. Moderately Inaccurate | E. Very Inaccurate

3) Sometimes I don't know why I do the things I do.

A. Very Accurate | B. Moderately Accurate | C. Neither Accurate nor Inaccurate | D. Moderately Inaccurate | E. Very Inaccurate

4) I am hesitant to take charge of a group that has no clear leadership.

A. Very Accurate | B. Moderately Accurate | C. Neither Accurate nor Inaccurate | D. Moderately Inaccurate | E. Very Inaccurate

5) I enjoy examining myself and the direction my life is taking.

A. Very Accurate | B. Moderately Accurate | C. Neither Accurate nor Inaccurate | D. Moderately Inaccurate | E. Very Inaccurate

6) I believe there is no absolute right or wrong.

A. Very Accurate | B. Moderately Accurate | C. Neither Accurate nor Inaccurate | D. Moderately Inaccurate | E. Very Inaccurate

7) I always pay my bills on time.

A. Very Accurate | B. Moderately Accurate | C. Neither Accurate nor Inaccurate | D. Moderately Inaccurate | E. Very Inaccurate

8) In this world it's difficult to be both honest and successful.

A. Very Accurate | B. Moderately Accurate | C. Neither Accurate nor Inaccurate | D. Moderately Inaccurate | E. Very Inaccurate

9) I am intimidated by strong personalities.

A. Very Accurate | B. Moderately Accurate | C. Neither Accurate nor Inaccurate | D. Moderately Inaccurate | E. Very Inaccurate

10) In past work experience, I was unable to find value in work that wasn't personally rewarding to me.

A. Very Accurate B. Moderately Accurate C. Neither Accurate nor Inaccurate D. Moderately Inaccurate E. Very Inaccurate

11) I often do things I later regret.

A. Very Accurate B. Moderately Accurate C. Neither Accurate nor Inaccurate D. Moderately Inaccurate E. Very Inaccurate

12) I feel sympathy for those who are worse off than I am.

A. Very Accurate B. Moderately Accurate C. Neither Accurate nor Inaccurate D. Moderately Inaccurate E. Very Inaccurate

13) If a rule gets in the way of my doing my job well, I'll look for ways around it.

A. Very Accurate B. Moderately Accurate C. Neither Accurate nor Inaccurate D. Moderately Inaccurate E. Very Inaccurate

14) I think a person's dress and appearance are important in the work environment.

A. Very Accurate B. Moderately Accurate C. Neither Accurate nor Inaccurate D. Moderately Inaccurate E. Very Inaccurate

15) There have been times when my own personal use of drugs or alcohol has adversely affected my job performance.

A. Very Accurate B. Moderately Accurate C. Neither Accurate nor Inaccurate D. Moderately Inaccurate E. Very Inaccurate

16) In past work or school experience, I have never been in a position to supervise the work of others.

A. Very Accurate B. Moderately Accurate C. Neither Accurate nor Inaccurate D. Moderately Inaccurate E. Very Inaccurate

17) If I need to, I can talk other people into doing what I think is necessary.

A. Very Accurate B. Moderately Accurate C. Neither Accurate nor Inaccurate D. Moderately Inaccurate E. Very Inaccurate

18) I usually prefer order to chaos.

A. Very Accurate B. Moderately Accurate C. Neither Accurate nor Inaccurate D. Moderately Inaccurate E. Very Inaccurate

19) When I'm faced with an ethical dilemma, I listen to my conscience.

A. Very Accurate B. Moderately Accurate C. Neither Accurate nor Inaccurate D. Moderately Inaccurate E. Very Inaccurate

20) When I communicate with other people, I can easily sense their emotional state.

A. Very Accurate **B.** Moderately Accurate C. Neither Accurate nor Inaccurate **D.** Moderately Inaccurate **E.** Very Inaccurate

21) I set high standards for myself and others.

A. Very Accurate **B.** Moderately Accurate C. Neither Accurate nor Inaccurate **D.** Moderately Inaccurate **E.** Very Inaccurate

22) In school or at work, I am never late.

A. Very Accurate **B.** Moderately Accurate C. Neither Accurate nor Inaccurate **D.** Moderately Inaccurate **E.** Very Inaccurate

23) I sometimes make assumptions about people based on their racial or ethnic backgrounds.

A. Very Accurate **B.** Moderately Accurate C. Neither Accurate nor Inaccurate **D.** Moderately Inaccurate **E.** Very Inaccurate

24) I tend to focus on the positive aspects of a complex situation, rather than the negatives.

A. Very Accurate **B.** Moderately Accurate C. Neither Accurate nor Inaccurate **D.** Moderately Inaccurate **E.** Very Inaccurate

25) I can manage several tasks at the same time.

A. Very Accurate **B.** Moderately Accurate C. Neither Accurate nor Inaccurate **D.** Moderately Inaccurate **E.** Very Inaccurate

Experiences and Traits

For each of the 25 items, score your response according to the list below. Then add the scores of all 25 items to arrive at a single number.

1.	A=0; B=1; C=2; D=3; E=4
2.	A=0; B=1; C=2; D=3; E=4
3.	A=0; B=1; C=2; D=3; E=4
4.	A=0; B=1; C=2; D=3; E=4
5.	A=4; B=3; C=2; D=1; E=0
6.	A=0; B=1; C=2; D=3; E=4
7.	A=4; B=3; C=2; D=1; E=0
8.	A=0; B=1; C=2; D=3; E=4
9.	A=0; B=1; C=2; D=3; E=4
10.	A=0; B=1; C=2; D=3; E=4
11.	A=0; B=1; C=2; D=3; E=4
12.	A=4; B=3; C=2; D=1; E=0
13.	A=0; B=1; C=2; D=3; E=4
14.	A=4; B=3; C=2; D=1; E=0
15.	A=0; B=1; C=2; D=3; E=4
16.	A=0; B=1; C=2; D=3; E=4
17.	A=4; B=3; C=2; D=1; E=0
18.	A=4; B=3; C=2; D=1; E=0
19.	A=4; B=3; C=2; D=1; E=0
20.	A=4; B=3; C=2; D=1; E=0
21.	A=4; B=3; C=2; D=1; E=0
22.	A=4; B=3; C=2; D=1; E=0
23.	A=0; B=1; C=2; D=3; E=4
24.	A=4; B=3; C=2; D=1; E=0
25.	A=4; B=3; C=2; D=1; E=0

The following scores serve as an approximate guide to your compatibility with a career in law enforcement—but should not be taken as the final word.

85-100 points	Most compatible
70-84 points	Compatible
50-69 points	Somewhat compatible
0-49 points	Incompatible

EXAMINATION SECTION
TEST 1

DIRECTIONS: This section contains descriptions of problem situations. Each problem situation has four alternative actions that might be taken to deal with the problem. You are to make two judgments for each problem.

First, decide which alternative you would MOST LIKELY choose in response to the problem. It might not be exactly what you would do in that situation, but it should be the alternative that comes closest to what you would actually do. Record your answers on the answer sheet by writing the appropriate letter next to the prompt for MOST LIKELY.

Second, decide which alternative you would be LEAST LIKELY to choose in that situation. Write the letter of that alternative next to the prompt for LEAST LIKELY.

1. You realize that an error has been made in the documentation of evidence for a case. The amount of the cash reported seized at the scene is now significantly less than when it was originally recorded. You would 1.____

   A. go back and talk to everyone who was involved in the chain of custody
   B. immediately tell a supervisor about the problem
   C. consider it a clerical error and try to conceal the discrepancy while you try to figure out how it happenedbut tell a supervisor if you cannot figure out what happened
   D. consider that the mistake was made when the evidence was seized, and alter the log to reflect the existing amount

   Most likely: __________ Least likely: __________

2. You arc assigned to lead a search for evidence that may have been deposited somewhere within a large tract of woods. The recovery of this evidence is critical to the prosecution of the suspect in the crime. For this task, you are most likely to lead by 2.____

   A. blazing a trail for others to follow
   B. helping people choose the best course of action.
   C. punishing mistakes
   D. appealing to shared goals and values

   Most likely: __________ Least likely: __________

3. Your partner, who has become your oldest and dearest friend, recently admitted to you that he removed something from the evidence room that might suggest the innocence of a suspect whom he knew without a doubt to be guilty. Your supervisor has discovered that the evidence is missing, and your partner asks you to say that you forgot to log the evidence in. You know that this would easily resolve the situation. You would 3.____

   A. not go along with the idea to say the mistake was yours, and tell the supervisor what happened
   B. not go along with the idea, but would say nothing about your partner's ad Mission
   C. not go along with the idea, and encourage your partner to own up to what he did
   D. go along with your partner, he broke the rules but his intentions were good.

   Most likely: __________ Least likely: __________

4. You are having a telephone conversation with a supervisor who is leaving a confidential message to another agent in your office about facts petaining to an important case. You are on your cell phone, in a public area, suirounded by many unfamiliar people. In order to verify that you have correctly taken the message, you 4.___

   A. read the message back to the supervisor
   B. ask the supervisor to call you back later
   C. explain that you will call back when you can find a more private location
   D. ask the supervisor to repeat the message

   Most likely: ___________ Least likely: ___________

5. You're in a conversation with someone who has difficulty finding the proper words to say. You 5.___

   A. wait for the person to finish, and then offer a restatement of what you think she was trying to say
   B. gladly interrupt and supply the words for her
   C. wait for her to finish, and then ask a series of clarifying questions
   D. interrupt and ask that she take some time to think about it before speaking

   Most likely: ___________ Least likely: ___________

6. You are meeting with several other law enforcement officials and community members to determine a course of action for reducing drug trafficking in the area. In order to build a constructive relationship with officials and cohimunity members, you 6.___

   A. assure the group that you are an expert who has a long record of experience in these matters, and tell them how the problem can be solved
   B. advise them that the solution to the problem will be a primarily local concern
   C. ask for input from representatives from each group before making suggestions
   D. adopt a completely neutral tone of voice when addressing group members

   Most likely: ___________ Least likely: ___________

7. When working in a group, someone raises a question that you've already given a lot of thought. You're not sure, however, about how the question should best be answered. You decide to 7.___

   A. speak up, briefly explaining the different alternatives that occurred to you
   B. wait for somebody to mention something that has already occurred to you, and then voice your agreement
   C. advise the group that this is a thorny problem that probably can't be solved
   D. keep quiet and listen to the group's discussion, offering feedback when you think it's appropriate

   Most likely: ___________ Least likely: ___________

8. Completely by accident, you notice a significant error in a colleague's report. The report is about to be released to key decision-makers, and you have absolutely no responsibility for the report. You would most likely 8.____

A. spread the word about the error to the colleague's co-workers, in the hope that the information makes its way to the report's author
B. take a mental note of the error and mention it if anyone asks
C. keep quietit's not your responsibility and you don't want to create friction
D. find the person who wrote the report and point out the mistake

Most likely: __________ Least likely: __________

9. A detective who is often nasty to you and your colleagues has com-piled an impressive record of success in her investigationsnearly all have led to arrests, and every one of those arrests has ended in conviction. In going over one of the detective's reports, you notice that she has neglected to properly document the chain of custody for a piece of evidence. You aren't that familiar with the case, and don't know how important it is to the case. You have a feeling that the detective will be angry if you point out her mistake. You 9.____

A. do nothing and let her deal with the consequences
B. pull her aside and tell her about the mistake
C. tell her you noticed a mistake in her report, and ask her if she is interesed in knowing what it is
D. inform her supervisor and her partner about the mistake

Most likely: __________ Least likely: __________

10. A crime was recently committed. You believe that among the following, the most useful interview subject would probably be a(n) 10.____

A. informant
B. victim
C. suspect
D. witness

Most likely: __________ Least likely:__________

11. In order to complete a certain task, you need to ask a favor of a colleague whom you don't know very well. The best way to do this would be to 11.____

A. ask the colleague briefly for assistance, stating your reasons for asking
B. ask the colleague and offer to do something for him in return
C. tell the colleague there will be many intangible rewards associated wifh his cooperation
D. explain that one of the ways the colleague can gain favor with his superiors is to cooperate with you

Most likely: __________ Least likely: __________

12. With a team composed of you and your colleagues, you encounter a problem similar to one you have encountered when working within another team in the past. Together, you and your team come up with a solution that has the potential for success, even though it is significantly different from the one that worked for you in the past. Your reaction to this new solution is to 12.___

A. feel good about the team's originality and go along for the ride on this new plan
B. be concerned about the possibility of failure with the new solution, but accept that there may be more than one way to solve the problem
C. tell them there is a proven way to succeed in solving this problem, and insist that they adopt your solution
D. tell colleagues you're uneasy with the unknowns and variables involved in this new solution, and then urge them to go with your proven success

Most likely: ___________ Least likely: ___________

13. You have become so proficient at the documentation/paperwork part of your job that you actually now have some time to spare during work hours. With this extra time, you decide to 13.___

A. take initiative and propose a new project to the supervisor
B. see your supervisor and tell him or her you are ready for more work
C. take care of some personal errands that you have been unable to do because of work
D. take some of the pressure off existing work and take more time to complete existing tasks

Most likely: ___________ Least likely: ___________

14. Your investigative team is having a disagreement about strategy that has become a heated debate, with members divided nearly equally between two strategic choices. You think both choices have some merit, and don't feel strongly one way or the other about which is selected. You 14.___

A. take the side of the group that contains more of your friends and associates
B. calmly wait for them to work out their differences
C. try to figure out which side is more likely to win the argument before taking sides
D. calmly point out the benefits of both plans and suggest a compromise

Most likely: ___________ Least likely: ___________

15. You turn the corner at the office one day and spot a agent altering the evidence log, which has been left unattended. Later, you look and see that the entry was for an amount of an illicit substance, and the new entry appears to match the amount that exists in the evidence room. You are not sure how muen of the substance was initially collected. You would 15.___

A. ask the agent to return the missing evidence and tell him/her that if you see it happen again you will tell your supervisor
B. tell the agent you saw him making the change, and ask him why it was necessary
C. let the matter drop, you don't know that anything untoward occurred, and bringing it up will only result in bad feelings

D. tell other colleagues and try to confront the agent as a group to try to deal with the problem on your own

Most likely: __________ Least likely: __________

16. In developing an plan for investigating a crime spree that has taken place on both sides of the state line, a team encounters problems in how to coordinate the input of federal and state resources. The first step in solving this problem would be to 16.____

A. gather information
B. define the problem as completely as possible
C. envision contingencies
D. develop a plan for solving the problem

Most likely: __________ Least likely: __________

17. Because your work unit has recently become severely understaffed, you are asked to do perform a task that you believe is far beneath the skills and capabilities associated with your position. You respond to this request by 17.____

A. performing the task slowly or inadequately before resuming your more important work, in order to insure that you won't be asked again
B. doing what is asked, but asking a supervisor to make sure these tasks are evenly distributed among co-workers until the unit can be fully staffed
C. refusing it on the grounds of professional integrity
D. complying cheerfully and accepting the task as part of a new expanded job description

Most likely: __________ Least likely: __________

18. Your supervisor has decided to transfer you to an unfamiliar department as part of an agency restructuring of your organization. The department is in the same building and there will be no changes in compensation or benefits. Your reaction is to be 18.____

A. thrilled at the opportunity to push yourself and learn new skills
B. not to mind the transfer, because it is likely to teach you something new
C. entirely neutral, since you won't have to relocate or take a pay cut
D. disappointed that you will have to change your regular routine

Most likely: __________ Least likely: __________

19. Your investigative team has developed a plan for investigating a series of violent crimes that have occurred in the tri-state area. In developing the plan, your team must balance the need to conduct the investigation "by the book" meticulously gathering and documenting a body of evidence and testimony, with the need to catch the criminal before another person becomes a victim. The plan, in attempting to balance these concerns, includes a few procedures that involve certain risks. The team should attempt to minimize the consequences of risk-taking by 19.____

A. keeping the focus on capturing the suspect as soon as possible, and dealing with the consequences as they come
B. reworking the plan to avoid risk whenever possible
C. setting aside emotional concerns about victims and assembling an airtight case

D. planning ahead and preparing for each outcome

Most likely: __________ Least likely: __________

20. An informant has come forward to offer information about a crime. You believe it is important to understand the informant's motivation for coming forward, so you ask him about this 20.___

A. when he least expects it
B. after he has given an account, but before you have asked any questions
C. at the conclusion of the interview
D. at the beginning of the interview

Most likely: __________ Least likely: __________

21. You are faced with a problem that, try as you might, you're unable to solve. You 21.___

A. ask your most trusted associate
B. ask for input from several people who you know will have different viewpoints
C. drop it, hope that it won't become a significant concern, and move on to another task
D. shift your focus to another problem for a while before giving this prob-leih a fresh look

Most likely: __________ Least likely: __________

22. You are interviewing several witnesses to a particularly violent crime that was committed recently. One of the witnesses, an older woman, is so upset that she can barely speak coherently. Her testimony does not seem to make much sense, especially when compared to that of others. In continuing to interview her, you make a mental note to document her emotional state when you write up the interview, because strong emotional responses are likely to affect a person's 22.___

A. prior knowledge
B. intelligence
C. perceptions of current reality
D. reflexes

Most likely: __________ Least likely: __________

23. An informant in an ongoing investigation tells you that he resents having to work with you because you have adopted a superior attitude with him and made work unpleasant. The informant is working on the investigation as a condition of a prior court plea. Your best response would be to 23.___

A. tell the informant that you are not interested in his opinion of youhe is required to cooperate on the case
B. try to find out why the offender cannot work with you and tell him that his work is important to the case
C. consider the informant as rebellious, and inform the court that the terms of his sentencing have been violated
D. apologize to the offender and tell him you have been under a lot of strain

Most likely: __________ Least likely: __________

24. Within a few days, you will meet with supervisors for a scheduled work evaluation. For the review, you will 24.____

    A. take the evaluation as it comes and improvise your responses
    B. prepare a list of your accomplishments, skills, and ideas for how to contribute more to the organization
    C. assume that your performance will be criticized, and prepare for the attack
    D. undertake a little reflection on your failures and successes, but nothing elaborate

    Most likely: __________ Least likely: __________

25. You and your partner are in the middle of a very heated argument about the conduct of an investigation. You normally like your partner and get along very well with her, but you are so furious that you are about to say something very nasty that you know will hurt her feelings. Your most likely reaction would be to 25.____

    A. walk away immediately without saying a word.
    B. say what is on your mind and sort it out later
    C. say that you are too angry to talk right now and give yourself time to calm down
    D. leave the room while mumbling the comment in a low voice

    Most likely: __________ Least likely: __________

26. In casual conversation, a person asks you for information about your work as an FBI agent. You should 26.____

    A. explain that you are not supposed to talk about your responsibilities to outsiders
    B. refer the person to the public relations department
    C. speak vaguely and give out as few facts as possible
    D. be frank and tell the person as much factual information as you can about your general responsibilities

    Most likely: __________ Least likely: __________

27. In the field, you are in an isolated rural area and find yourself in a situ-ation with circam-stances you have never encountered before. You would be most likely to use your own judgement? 27.____

    A. When existing policy and rules appear to be unfair in their application
    B. When immediate action is necessary and the rules do not cover the situation
    C. Only if a superior is present
    D. Whenever a situation is not covered by established rules

    Most likely: __________ Least likely: __________

28. One of your colleagues has gone on vacation and his mother, an elderly woman who lives in another state, has filed a complaint with your officeshe thinks she may have been defrauded via an e-mail scam. The case has been assigned to Agent Broom, who works in your office. Your colleague phones you from his vacation and asks if you can find out more about her case. Your reaction is to 28.____

A. simply refuse to answer your colleague's questions
B. find the case file and tell the colleague what he wants to know
C. speak to your supervisor, explain the situation and ask for the information that your colleague wants.
D. ask the mother if she gives permission for you to find out more from Agent Broom

Most likely: __________ Least likely: __________

29. When working with team members, you offer what you think is a well-reasoned solution to a problem. Your team members reject it out of hand, saying that it could never work. In a later meeting with mid-level administrators, your supervisor makes the same suggestion. You 29.__

A. say nothing to the supervisor, but later make sure your team members understand that they should be more deferential to your judgement
B. make sure the supervisor knows you suggested the same solution, but were ignored
C. feel vindicated by the supervisor's concurrence, but don't feel the need to say anything
D. demand an apology from your team members for being so closed-minded

Most likely: __________ Least likely: __________

30. After your partner conducts an interview with an informant, the in-fohnant emerges from the interrogation room with some swelling around his right eye. You are pretty sure the swelling was not present when the informant entered the room. You 30.__

A. do nothingyou can't be certain your partner did anything wrong
B. immediately report the partner's abuse to a supervisor
C. ask other agents in the office if anything like this has ever happened before
D. confront your partner and ask what happened

Most likely: __________ Least likely: __________

31. You and another agent in your unit do not get along, to put it mildly. The problem is, you and she have been assigned to direct an investigation together, and in order to have a good outcome, the two of you need to get along. You 31.__

A. realize the destructive potential for run-ins with her, and quietly get yourself assigned to another case
B. make an effort to be civil, but if she isn't returning the favor, try to keep a low profile and get the work done
C. take this as a personal challenge and make it your mission to win her over
D. try to get your supervisors to understand the seriousness of the friction between you, and ask that they reassign her to another case

Most likely: __________ Least likely: __________

32. At the end of a busy day at work, you accidentally send an e-mail containing an attachment with some confidential case file information to the wrong person. Which of the following would be the best thing to do? 32.____

A. Forget what happened and send the e-mail to the correct person
B. Leave the office for the day and deal with it tomorrow
C. Explain to your supervisor what has happened and let her handle the issue
D. Immediately send another e-mail to the 'wrong' person explaining your mistake

Most likely: __________ Least likely: __________

33. A crime has just been committed at a bank, and you arrive at the scene first, before any local law enforcement personnel. Before the police arrive, a handful of bank officials arrive and ask to enter the crime scene. You would 33.____

A. requesl their cooperation in remaining outside the scene until the area can be properly secured
B. keep them out by any means necessary
C. tell them to take it up with the police when they arrive
D. defer to their wishes

Most likely: __________ Least likely: __________

34. You are interviewing the victim of a crime that was committed only about an hour ago. During the course of the interview you try to 34.____

A. maintain a calm and steady demeanor
B. make sure at least one other agent is present before beginning
C. get the facts by any means necessary
D. keep the victim away from others who are familiar to him/her

Most likely: __________ Least likely: __________

35. You inherit a large sum of money, and your financial advisor suggests two types of investments. In the first, you invest a moderate, set amount each year, and receive a modest guaranteed payoff at the end of the investment period. The second choice includes a much larger investment (most of your inheritance), but also has a larger potential payoff, with the possibility of losing all your money in an economic downturn. You choose Which type of investment would you choose? 35.____

A. a combination of the two
B. the first type of investment
C. the second type of investment
D. neither. You wouldn't risk your savings on investments.

Most likely: __________ Least likely: __________

36. You and your partner are working on a complex project that demands a great deal of effort from both of you. Your partner is frequently absent as a result of burnout and stress from his personal problems. You do not know much about the circumstances, nor have you known him for long. Your partner contributes very little to the project, and, as a result, you are putting in an excessive amount of overtime in order to keep the project moving ahead. You feel that your health may begin to suffer if you continue to work this many hours. You handle this situation by 36.___

A. raising the issue with your supervisor and request additional help to ensure that the project is completed on schedule
B. offering to help your partner deal with his personal problems
C. continuing to put in overtime to keep the project moving ahead
D. meeting with your partner to request that he does his share of the work

Most likely: ___________ Least likely: ___________

37. For the first time, you are assigned the lead on a case. You oversee a team of about five people. Your supervisor has assigned you a fairly clear-cut case, and in the end, despite a few logistical and technical problems, you and your team wrap things up fairly quickly. After a speedy conviction, you meet with a group of three supervisors, who congratulate you on your success. They then launch a critique of your leadership of the case that, while pointing out your strengths as a leader, can only be interpreted as somewhat unfavorable, given the team's logistical and technical problems. Most likely, your reaction is to feel that 37.___

A. it probably would not a good idea for you to assume leadership of a more difficult case in the future
B. you should keep this critique in mind the next time you take charge of a team
C. the bottom line is that the case resulted in a conviction, and this is the only measure that really matters
D. the members of your team really let you down with their mistakes

Most likely: ___________ Least likely: ___________

38. You and another agent are conducting an investigation together. You have noticed that the other agent is taking some shortcuts as he collects evidence and obtains statements from the victims and witnesses. These shortcuts are reducing the quality of the investigation. You would most likely 38.___

A. point out to the trooper the impact his shortcuts will have on the traffic investigation
B. notify your supervisor of the shortcuts being taken by the other agent
C. go back and redo those aspects of the investigation on which the agent has taken shortcuts
D. ignore the agent's work performance, since it is not your responsibility to monitor his performance

Most likely: ___________ Least likely: ___________

39. During a meeting, your and a group of supervisors are discussing your performance on a recently completed project. Using a list of objective cri-teria, the supervisors explain where you performed most successfully. They then shift their focus to areas in which your performance fell short of the stan-daps. Your reaction is to 39.____

A. launch a vigorous defense of your performance and explain why you think the standards are not appropriate in your case
B. listen carefully, ask for clarification when necessary, and then discuss with them why these shortcomings occurred
C. tell them you are very sorry and promise to do better in the future
D. explain that you did your best and are skeptical that any of them could have done better, given the circumstances

Most likely: __________ Least likely: __________

40. While you are conducting an investigation at a crime scene, a citizen walks past you and makes a demeaning and derogatory comment about your law enforcement responsibilities. You would most likely 40.____

A. ask the person to come back and explain why he made such a comment
B. ask the person to show you some identification, so that you can take his name down in case of further trouble
C. ignore the comment and continue with your work
D. confront the individual and demand an apology for the comment

Most likely: __________ Least likely: __________

41. You are working on a case under the direct supervision of a regional supervisor. In your opinion, she has her mind set on a plan that is mediocre, uninspired, and likely to meet only a minimal set of objectives. She is happy with having finally made a decision, wants to finalize, and makes a point of telling you not to try to talk her out of her plan. You think the plan is a waste of resources and perhaps even a mistake, even though most of your colleagues have already told you to let it go. How would you deal with the situation? 41.____

A. Quietly work to get transferred to another project.
B. Tell the supervisor that she is making a mistake, and try to convince her to change her mind.
C. Resist the temptation to try changing her mind.
D. Ask if she is certain she doesn't want to think it over one last time.

Most likely: __________ Least likely: __________

42. When interviewing a potential witness, you notice that she has a tendency to wander off the subject and talk about herself and her family for expended intervals. When you ask her where she was at about noon the day before yesterday, she launches into a long description of her normal daily rou-tine. You respond by 42.____

A. telling her sternly that your time is limited and you would like her to stick to answering your questions
B. waiting for a pause in her speech during which you can politely steer the conversation back toward her whereabouts yesterday at noon
C. cutting her off and repeating the question, as if she hadn't been speaking at all

D. letting her "talk herself out" and then repeating the question, this time in a more closed-ended format

Most likely: __________ Least likely: __________

43. You are the leader of an investigative team, and wonder about the role of praise in the team's success. As the leader, your philosophy about praise is that it 43.__

A. can improve performance if it is given when it is most appropriate
B. should almost always be withheld in order to make team members understand there is always room for improvement
C. should be given sparely, and reserved for truly exceptional achievements
D. should be given to team members evenand perhaps especially when they perform poorly, in order to boost their self-esteem

Most likely: __________ Least likely: __________

44. You are assigned to an investigation with Agent Stark, who is known to be somewhat inattentive to detail. His mistakes or omissions have resulted in at least one case dismissal that you know of. Throughout the course of the investigation, you 44.__

A. make it a point to be involved in every aspect of the investigation, accompanying Agent Stark on every interview, and insisting on collaboration in written work
B. leave Agent Stark mostly alone, and then go back and make correc-tiqns to his work and documentation when they are necessary
C. work to block Agent Stark's access to important witnesses, evidence, and case files, thereby minimizing the harm he is likely to do
D. document every one of Agent Stark's missteps and report them to your superiors as they occur, in order to avoid jeopardizing the case

Most likely: __________ Least likely: __________

45. An interview has strayed far beyond what you had intended. To redirect the subject's response, you say 45.__

A. "I'm interested in what you were saying a few minutes ago. Can you tell me more about it?"
B. "Why are we talking about this?"
C. "Let me ask the rest of the questions I need answered, then we can talk."
D. "This is interesting, but it isn't related to the business of this interview."

Most likely: __________ Least likely: __________

46. You have been asked to recruit a new detective to come work for your regional office. She is an up-and-coming star with a lot of potential, and you and your supervisor both feel she would be a good fit for your office. Unfortunately, despite your best efforts, she ends up seeking and receiving an assignment elsewhere. You later find out through your supervisor that you came off as seeming a little too aggressive and desperate. Your supervisor offers you some suggestions for how to handle this situation if it ever comes up again. Your reaction is to think that 46.__

A. putting you in charge of the detective's recruitment was a terrible idea to begin with

B. the detective's choice was her own loss; you made it clear that your office had the most to offer
C. you wish there was some way you could make it up to your supervisor
D. maybe you did come on too strong and should re-examine your methods

Most likely: __________ Least likely: __________

47. You have become aware that a colleague, who is nearing retirement and now working only part-time for the bureau, has been using office phone and fax facilities to run his own private investigation business. You think that he may have been warned about this once before and that he promised to stop. You have just found a fax for his business placed in your mailbox by mistake. You would most likely 47.____

A. Put the fax in your colleague's mailbox without saying anything to anyone.
B. Politely inform your colleague that you will tell your supervisor the next time you catch him using agency resources for his own private business.
C. Put the fax in your supervisor's mailbox without saying anything to anyone.
D. Give the fax to your co-worker and remind her that office equipment is not supposed to be used for personal use.

Most likely: __________ Least likely: __________

48. You arc working on a case with a detective in another regional office who has, once again, rescheduled your meeting appointment at the last minute. Apparently, he left a last-minute message for you this time, but you didn't get it because you were already on your way. This is not the first time you have canceled prior engagements to accommodate his schedule. Each time you have been inconvenienced and very irritated, but this is a very important case and he is a good detective when he is at work. How do you react to this person? 48.____

A. Tell the detective it is disrespectful and inconvenient when he makes last-minute changes to your schedule.
B. Don't let on that you are irritated, but ask the detective to give you longer notice the next time he has to cancel.
C. Maintain a cold professionalism when rescheduling the appointment.
D. Don't let on that you are irritated, but make a point to subject the detective to a few last-minute cancellations of his own, so he'll know how it feels.

Most likely: __________ Least likely: __________

49. A pharmacist has complained to the police department that several drug addicts in his neighborhood have been attempting to obtain drugs illegally, often by passing fake prescriptions. Based only on this information, during a Stakeout of the prescription counter, you would be most likely to find suspicious 49.____

A. a young African-American male in a hooded sweatshirton a hot day
B. a woman in her thirties who glances around furtively and brings a large amount of nonprescription items to the counter for purchase
C. a middle-aged man who appears homeless and is poorly groomed
D. None of the above should be regarded as suspicious on the basis of their appearance alone

Most likely: __________ Least likely: __________

50. At a work meeting, your supervisor mentions an interesting new assignment that has not been assigned yet. It sounds like something you could handle, though it would be demanding. You 50.__

A. grow increasingly nervous about the possibility that you would be assigned the job
B. immediately volunteer to handle the project yourself
C. tell the supervisor that you would be willing to take it on, but ask it might be possible to delegate some of your current workload
D. tell the supervisor that you would be willing to take it on, but only if yob receive a raise in pay

Most likely: __________ Least likely: __________

Situational Judgement
Key to Exercises

Note: While a few situations in the examination have one choice that is clearly better or worse than the others, some have two or even three choices that would be equally as goodor badas the rest. The key that follows should be taken as a rough guideline and not a definitive formula for success on the test. The answers below reflect the fact that the situational judgement test is designed to measure your:

•Ability to Organize, Plan, and Prioritize
•Ability to Relate Effectively with Others
•Ability to Maintain a Positive Image
•Ability to Evaluate Information and Make Judgment Decisions
•Ability to Adapt to Changing Situations Integrity

1. Most Likely: B; Least Likely: D
2. Most Likely: D; Least Likely: C
3. Most Likely: A or C; Least Likely: D
4. Most Likely: D; Least Likely: A
5. Most Likely: A or C; Least Likely: D

6. Most Likely: C; Least Likely: A or B
7. Most Likely: A; Least Likely: C
8. Most Likely: D; Least Likely: C
9. Most Likely: B; Least Likely: A
10. Most Likely: D; Least Likely: C

11. Most Likely: A; Least Likely: D
12. Most Likely: B; Least Likely: C
13. Most Likely: B; Least Likely: C or D
14. Most Likely: D; Least Likely: A, B or C
15. Most Likely: B; Least Likely: A

16. Most Likely: B; Least Likely : A, C or D
17. Most Likely: B; Least Likely: C
18. Most Likely: B; Least Likely: D
19. Most Likely: D; Least Likely: A, B or C
20. Most Likely: C; Least Likely: A, B or D

21. Most Likely: B; Least Likely: C
22. Most Likely: C; Least Likely: A, B or D
23. Most Likely: B; Least Likely: C
24. Most Likely: B; Least Likely: C
25. Most Likely: C; Least Likely: B

26. Most Likely: D; Least Likely: A
27. Most Likely: B; Least Likely: D
28. Most Likely: C; Least Likely: A
29. Most Likely: C; Least Likely: D

Situational Judgement
Key to Exercises

30. Most Likely: D; Least Likely: A
31. Most Likely: C; Least Likely: A or D
32. Most Likely: C; Least Likely: A
33. Most Likely: A; Least Likely: B, C or D
34. Most Likely: A; Least Likely: C or D
35. Most Likely: A; Least Likely: D

36. Most Likely: A; Least Likely: C
37. Most Likely: B; Least Likely: A, C or D
38. Most Likely: A; Least Likely: D
39. Most Likely: B; Least Likely: C or D
40. Most Likely: C; Least Likely: A, B or D

41. Most Likely: D; Least Likely: A
42. Most Likely: B; Least Likely: A
43. Most Likely: A; Least Likely: B or D
44. Most Likely: A; Least Likely: C
45. Most Likely: A; Least Likely: B

46. Most Likely: D; Least Likely: A or B
47. Most Likely: D; Least Likely: A
48. Most Likely: B; Least Likely: D
49. Most Likely: D; Least Likely: A, B or C
50. Most Likely: C; Least Likely: A or D

EXAMINATION SECTION
TEST 1

DIRECTIONS: Each question or incomplete statement is followed by several suggested answers or completions. Select the one that BEST answers the question or completes the statement. *PRINT THE LETTER OF THE CORRECT ANSWER IN THE SPACE AT THE RIGHT.*

Questions 1-3.

DIRECTIONS: Answer Questions 1 to 3 based on the following situation.

You are a school counselor in an academic and commercial high school. A senior boy by the name of Peter informs you that for years he has wished to prepare for the practice of medicine. His parents urged him to make this choice when an uncle, who was a doctor, promised to pay part of his college expenses, provided he enrolled in the medical course.

You have listened with interest to Peter's problem as he related it. You have talked to all of his teachers, studied his school records, checked his grades, and given him a battery of tests. All of his grades were below average. Tests revealed that he had slightly less than an average mental ability. Personality and adjustment tests revealed nothing wrong except a slight tendency to be dissatisfied with his family relationship. His clerical aptitude test score was low. Three mechanical aptitude tests, however, revealed high promise. Further questioning revealed that for years Peter had tinkered in his own shop with tools.

It appears that unwise family pressures had caused Peter to choose a life work beyond his ability to achieve.

1. Your FIRST step in handling this problem should be to 1._____

   A. tell the parents that they must agree to a search for another life goal
   B. inform the boy's parents that their son does not have the ability to succeed in a profession
   C. confer with the boy's parents and get them to, have the boy keep trying to gain entrance to a medical school
   D. see the boy's parents and suggest that they forget about his choice of a vocation for the present

2. You later arranged a meeting with Peter and during your interview with him, he stated that he wanted to learn more about various types of work before he chose. Under these conditions, you should 2._____

   A. advise him to take a variety of subjects as tryouts so that he will be able to make a wiser choice
   B. suggest that he learn something about the requirements of other jobs
   C. take him to the library and show him books to read on various types of work and try to given him insight into his abilities and interests
   D. tell him you feel that he is old enough to decide now

3. After thinking about it, Peter finally decided to prepare for work as a garage mechanic. You should then 3.____

   A. advise him to change to a trade school and take auto mechanics or machine shop and do that kind of work during the summer
   B. advise him to drop chemistry and biology but not give up completely the idea of becoming a doctor
   C. advise him to remain in school and take several more science subjects
   D. try to interest him in getting a job in a garage and attending night school

4. You are a judge in a juvenile court in a large city. A young girl fifteen years of age is brought before you. She is charged with the theft of a dress, perfume, and handbag from a large department store. The total value of the articles is $437. This is the first time the girl has been caught. She is from a middle class family. Her mother works in a factory in the daytime, and her father is employed in a local bank as an assistant cashier. Their combined income is about $40,000 a year. She is an only child. Her school record is good, and one test showed that she had better than average mental ability. 4.____
After having had a talk with the girl, it is your duty to make a decision. You FIRST would

   A. give her a severe scolding and release her, but make her pay the bill
   B. counsel with the girl and her parents and then give her another chance
   C. talk with the mother to find out whether the girl had ever been neglected
   D. inform the girl that you are thinking of sending her to a girls' training school

5. Wally is a bright five-year-old boy in a kindergarten group. Every day he wastes the time of the group by being slow in putting away materials at the end of the activity period. You, his teacher, know that at home his toys are picked up and put away by his mother or father when he tires of them. He is an only child. 5.____
You should

   A. tell his parents to force him to pick up things at home so that he will put away his materials when he is at school
   B. tell him to hurry because the group is waiting for him
   C. help him to put away his materials so the group will not be forced to wait
   D. send the group to the gymnasium to play a game which Wally likes, and have Wally lose out on the fun while he puts away his materials

6. Jimmy, a first-grade pupil, is active on the playground. In the schoolroom, however, he refuses to take part and frequently cries when told to do so. 6.____
In trying to remedy this situation, you, as his teacher, should

   A. advise him to take part at once because you think that he is afraid
   B. ask his parents to keep him at home for a year in the belief that he is not yet mature enough to begin school
   C. keep harmony in the class by permitting him to take part when he chooses to do so
   D. encourage him to take part gradually

7. Ralph, who is in the sixth grade, likes to make things with tools and seems to enjoy helping you keep the library books in order and the room decorated nicely. He finds arithmetic very difficult and often avoids it. He plays truant quite often. 7.____
In handling this truancy problem, you should

A. discuss why his offense is serious and try to get him to see the error of his ways
B. attempt to discover the causes of his difficulty and tell him you will excuse him from arithmetic if he does not skip school
C. compliment him on his mechanical ability and at the proper time assign him mechanical work in which arithmetic would be useful
D. tell him that staying out of school is an offense not to be tolerated

8. Harry sprinkled a foul-smelling drug around the classroom. The odor was so bad that it made some of the pupils ill and thus almost broke up school for the day. When the teacher discovered who did it, she forced Harry to apologize to the school and to stand before the class each morning for a week taking a smell of the drug from a vial which she kept in her possession. 8._____
In your judgment, this form of punishment

A. will cure him
B. is not quite severe enough for the offense
C. was carried on too long even though it produced the desired results
D. is apt to fail

9. For more than a month, various articles had been disappearing from the lockers in the school hallway. Finally, the instructor caught Jerry going through the coats in the lockers. He admitted the thefts. The instructor knew that Jerry's parents were very poor. He had no spending money, and his meals did not meet his needs. 9._____
His instructor should

A. give him a weekly amount which he can pay back sometime and also give him an apple, a sandwich, or candy when possible
B. help him find work so that he can take care of his own needs
C. show him that a thief always gets caught and then promise him a still worse penalty if he does it again
D. make an example of him by telling the students that he stole the articles

10. Jack, in the eighth grade, is always doing something to attract the attention of his classmates. He makes *bright* remarks during class, insists on talking more than his share of the time, acts up as he walks around the room to obtain a laugh, and even dresses, walks, and combs his hair in an unusual manner to attract attention. 10._____
His teachers think that

A. he should be separated from the group or otherwise punished until he learns not to disturb
B. the best way to handle him is to join with his classmates in smiling at his remarks and tricks because this cannot do a great deal of harm
C. the teacher should give him the attention he desires whenever he earns it by doing something worthwhile
D. the teacher should refuse to notice his behavior so it will return to normal again

11. The teacher has noticed lately that Mildred, age eight, answers out of turn, speaks when others are speaking, and wants to be the center of attention in every activity. She pouts or cries if another child is selected to do something for the teacher which she wishes to do. She has no sister but has a new baby brother. 11._____
The MOST probable explanation of her behavior is that

A. her behavior changed because she now has new duties at home
B. she is no longer the center of attention at home and is seeking more attention at school
C. she is being disobedient because she has been spoiled from babyhood
D. Mildred is probably suffering from some illness

12. You are an employment officer. It is your duty to talk with and refer individuals who are trying to secure work. There have been many inquiries regarding a particularly fine automotive mechanic's job in a well-known shop in the city. It offers a good chance to anyone who obtains it. It is up to you to fill this opening from a large group of men applying for this work. 12.____
You should select the man who

A. showed that he knew his trade and showed you the best set of written references and recommendations from his former employers
B. appeared to be most highly recommended by such previous employers as you were able to contact and answered the trade questions most satisfactorily
C. told you he had the best training and had the longest experience in the automotive field
D. appeared the most intelligent and answered the oral trade questions correctly

13. As head nurse in a leading hospital, you are faced with a serious problem. Two of your very efficient nurses are unable to cooperate and to avoid trouble. You have attempted to improve the situation by talking to both of them but their attitudes and relations have not improved. 13.____
It would be BEST to

A. dismiss the less efficient nurse and secure a more satisfactory employee to take her position
B. overlook their attitude toward each other as much as possible
C. assign each to unpleasant duties and thereby attempt to teach both that they should try to cooperate better with each other
D. place them on duty in different wards of the hospital so that they will not need to work together

14. You are a nurse in a city hospital assigned to a patient who demands too much of your time, thus causing you to neglect other duties. 14.____
The situation would BEST be handled agreeably by

A. referring her case to the hospital authorities
B. doing things requested by her to avoid offending her
C. explaining pleasantly but firmly why you are unable to grant all of her requests
D. paying no attention to her occasionally so she will not ask so often

15. You are a social case worker from a public welfare agency. You are charged with advising and assisting poor families which supposedly are in need of financial or medical aid. You are asked to investigate a family of six small children whose father is a ne'er-do-well and who is in a drunken condition most of the time. The mother has been frail and sickly for years. 15.____
Under these conditions, you should

A. give them a monthly allowance despite the father's drinking
B. refuse them all help so that the father might feel forced to work

C. take the children from the family and advise the mother to secure a divorce
D. give them a monthly allowance and have the father sent to a sanitarium or other institution for medical help

16. Virginia is an attractive girl in the ninth grade with ability somewhat above the average. She is nervous and worries a great deal about her schoolwork and about life in general. Her mother is very anxious for her to excel in school. She criticizes Virginia if her marks are not high and urges her to work harder. 16.____
If you were Virginia's teacher, the method you would use in helping Virginia is to

A. show the other pupils what fine work Virginia is doing, using her case as a model to inspire the others
B. talk to the mother, explaining that it may be dangerous to urge Virginia to earn high marks
C. encourage Virginia and her mother to continue as at present since it is likely to lead to high scholarship
D. tell Virginia that she should not study hard

17. The attitudes of three teachers in discussing the behavior of their pupils is shown in the four paragraphs that follow. 17.____
Which do you regard as BEST from the standpoint of development of the child?

A. When a child does what is wrong, he should be withdrawn from the group so that he may think over his poor behavior.
B. Teachers should watch children, stopping them promptly the instant they get into mischief. Privileges should be temporarily withdrawn because of offenses.
C. When a child misbehaves, he should be punished.
D. When a child misbehaves, the adult should explain what the right mode of behavior is and why it is right.

18. Teacher X will never admit that she is wrong. Every question in the classroom is taken as a challenge to her authority. Every comment on her work is regarded as unfair criticism. She makes sarcastic comments to her fellow workers but never apologizes. She can usually prove to her own satisfaction that she is right. She interrupts friends or students so often that no one is able to finish a discussion in her presence. 18.____
If you were the principal, you would

A. put up with the behavior since in a few more years she will be obliged to retire
B. tell her that she may lose her position if she does not change
C. have a serious talk with her and force her to see her behavior is educationally unsound
D. arrange for a psychiatrist to help her to understand her behavior and alter it

19. Dale shows shyness on the playground. He seems afraid to enter into the games and is so awkward when he plays that the boys do not like to choose him on their side. You are the director. 19.____
How can you assist him in overcoming this fear? You should

A. give him some easy task connected with the games, such as keeping score
B. allow him to watch or to do something with another pupil
C. advise him to learn to play
D. insist that he get into the games and play

20. A ten-year-old boy in the fourth grade suddenly begins to stutter. He is ashamed, and the children in his class are amused. 20.___
The teacher should

A. advise the parents to keep him out of school for a while because of his nervousness
B. compel him to recite in front of the class so that he will cure his stuttering
C. tell him he can stop if he wants to and then attempt to overlook the condition if it occurs again
D. refer him to a clinic for help

KEY (CORRECT ANSWERS)

1.	D	11.	B
2.	C	12.	B
3.	A	13.	D
4.	B	14.	C
5.	D	15.	D
6.	D	16.	B
7.	C	17.	D
8.	D	18.	D
9.	B	19.	A
10.	C	20.	D

TEST 2

DIRECTIONS: Each question or incomplete statement is followed by several suggested answers or completions. Select the one that BEST answers the question or completes the statement. *PRINT THE LETTER OF THE CORRECT ANSWER IN THE SPACE AT THE RIGHT.*

Questions 1-8.

DIRECTIONS: If you were judging social workers, which of the following personality traits would you consider the MOST important for a successful person in this type of work? Select ONE in each group, and mark its letter in the space at the right.

1. A. Aggressive and persuasive 1.____
   B. Determined and hard working
   C. Prudent and careful
   D. Helpful and kindly

2. A. Ambitious and spirited 2.____
   B. Tactful and diplomatic
   C. Persuasive and overbearing
   D. Cautious and prudent

3. A. *Slippery* and critical 3.____
   B. Pleasant appearing and apologetic
   C. Selfish and self-reliant
   D. Well-balanced and interested in people

4. A. Persevering and determined 4.____
   B. Considerate and understanding
   C. Outstanding and superior
   D. Friendly and spirited

5. A. Sympathetic and condescending 5.____
   B. Determined and superior
   C. Practical and experienced
   D. Self-confident and changeable

6. A. Sociable and sincere 6.____
   B. Self-reliant and theoretical
   C. Overbearing and forward
   D. Agreeable and congenial

7. A. Self-confident and assured 7.____
   B. Energetic and tactless
   C. Intelligent and ambitious
   D. Industrious and tolerant

8. A. Enthusiastic and eager 8.____
   B. Cheerful and apologetic
   C. Cordial and tolerant
   D. Analytical and intelligent

9. Geraldine, a junior in high school, is boasting constantly about something that she has done, or about the members of her family. Her companions think that she is conceited. A close study of her case shows the following possibilities.
The MOST likely cause of her boastful conduct is that 9.___

A. her father is a prominent man in town, highly respected by his fellow citizens
B. she has ability above the average and generally earns good marks
C. she lacks self-confidence and occasionally hints to her teacher that she is not quite as capable as her classmates
D. she has been spoiled by having had too much attention

10. Skippy, a high school senior, is a poor athlete. No matter how hard he tries, he seems unable to do well in sports. This worries him. He has expressed the opinion that he does not amount to much. He has had a physical examination and his poor athletic ability is not due to physical causes. Skippy can *probably* be helped if 10.___

A. his teachers urge him to put forth every effort to become good in athletics
B. teachers let him alone to fight the battle that everyone must fight sooner or later when he learns that someone else is better than he
C. his teachers study his case and help him to discover other things that he can do well
D. the coach places him in a special class known as the awkward squad and teaches him to improve his athletic ability

11. In order to help a child to avoid developing the feeling that others are ALWAYS better than he is, you should 11.___

A. assist him in becoming as successful as possible in the things he attempts
B. try to get him to see that he is as competent as anyone else
C. tell him never to admit that he is beaten
D. help him to be as successful as possible in the things he attempts and help him to do some one thing especially well

12. With pupils of extremely low mental ability, it is MOST justifiable to 12.___

A. give them the same work as the others get but realize that it will take them longer to do it
B. give them the same type of work as the others get but less of it
C. assign more extra curricular work and less from the regular curriculum; for example, use more handwork
D. place all of them in manual arts courses

13. You are a personnel manager in a large industrial plant engaged in the manufacture of vital instruments. It is your job to maintain good employee-employer relationships, increase the amount of work done, and keep the men happy and satisfied in their work. In other words, you are active in keeping up high standards of work by keeping everyone happy. 13.___
One of your experienced employees, Mr. Ryan, is engaged in the final inspection of shuttle o-rings. He apparently has fallen down in his work rating without any known reason. He holds an important job and must maintain a high degree of skill. The plant physician, after a thorough physical examination, says there is nothing wrong with him physically.
Under these conditions, you should

A. suggest that he might lose his job if he does not increase the quality and amount of work he does
B. talk with him and attempt to determine what is causing his trouble or what is worrying him
C. drop a word of praise occasionally so he might be helped to do better
D. suggest that it might help if he changed to a different type of work

14. Suppose that you found that Mr. Ryan was upset at work because of difficulties with his wife and his envy of a man who was promoted over him. 14.____
You should

A. try to explain to him why this man was promoted over him
B. to satisfy him, tell him that your plant promotes those first who were employed first, and casually suggest that his wife drop in to see you
C. give him some marital advice and suggest that he may be better off if he separated from his wife for a while
D. tell him you are interested only in his output and that he will have to work out his personal affairs by himself

15. You are a Red Cross director with an army unit in the field. A soldier, Jones, approaches you and tells you there is serious illness in his family, and he would like to go home. You agree, but upon looking into the matter the next day, you find that no one is actually sick in the soldier's family. 15.____
Under these conditions, you should

A. take no further action at present but later get the man a furlough because you can see that he is under serious strain and may become very ill
B. treat it as a humorous incident but be on the lookout so that it does not occur again
C. notify the commanding officer and get his opinion
D. deny the request and try to find out the real cause for the man's behavior

16. If Jones then saw you again, you should 16.____

A. tell him to pour out his troubles to you
B. scold him for his actions and explain the seriousness of such dishonesty
C. explain that taking vacations whenever he feels like it is impossible; offer assistance and try to find something to interest him
D. explain to him in a nice manner that you have shortened his furlough a few days

17. Jones then told you that he was sick and tired of the army and wanted to get away from it for a while. 17.____
You should

A. warn him of what would happen if he deserted and obtain a furlough for him
B. notify his commanding officer that the man should be watched
C. suggest an appointment be made for him with the psychiatrist
D. refuse to interest yourself in his problem because it is not your concern

18. If Jones also told you that his first sergeant was picking on him, you should 18.____

A. look into the matter to determine the truth by talking to a few people who know him
B. call the soldier's commanding officer and tell him about the situation

C. tell him to forget the incident since it really was not very serious
D. try to arrange to get the soldier transferred to another company

19. You are a dean in a secondary school. An intelligent child, Bob, sixteen years of age who is about to fail, has been referred to you. Prior to this time, the boy has been a good student and a very likable boy. Suddenly, he began to neglect his work.
Under these conditions, you should 19.___

A. go to the principal and suggest that the boy be deprived of a few privileges around school until his behavior improves
B. have a casual talk with the boy
C. learn about the boy's home life and outside activities
D. have a talk with the boy and tell him he must apply himself

20. If you should have a talk with Bob, your FIRST step will be to try to 20.___

A. make him feel that by improving his behavior it will please you
B. gain his confidence so he will feel free to tell his problem
C. impress him with the importance of your position
D. show him that he is developing some bad habits

21. You discover that one reason for Bob's poor attitude is the fact that he feels he is being left out of things.
Knowing this, you should 21.___

A. ask his friends to aid him in his studies
B. force him to engage in sports
C. tell him not to worry as things are bound to turn out all right
D. seek the help of his friends

22. If, in two months, you heard nothing more concerning Bob, you should 22.___

A. have one of his teachers send him to you
B. look into his current activities and then drop in and talk to him about how well he is progressing in his classes and social relations
C. inquire about him and then drop in casually and observe him
D. look at his school record to determine whether he had improved

23. Near the close of the school year, you notice a great improvement in Bob's behavior, and his grades have improved.
You then should 23.___

A. call the boy in and tell him you were disappointed in the amount of improvement shown because you knew he could do better
B. say nothing to him but inform his parents that he has improved
C. go to him and comment on his splendid improvement
D. give him a two-day holiday as a reward for the splendid improvement shown

24. Which of these teacher's opinions is CORRECT? 24.___

A. Mr. W. - "*I think some children are naturally quite mischievous and must be dealt with sternly.*"
B. Mr. X. - "*I have a pupil who causes a great deal of trouble. After I scold him, he quiets down and behaves himself.*"

C. Mr. Y. - "*Since every bit of misconduct has a cause, we should not be angry with a child who misbehaves any more than we should get angry at one who is ill.* "
D. Mr. Z. - "*Most misconduct can be traced right back to the home. It is the parents' fault.*"

25. You are a social case worker from a public welfare agency. One of your cases is Mr. Backus, an aged man whose failing health makes nursing care necessary. 25.____
Mr. Backus is dependent upon relief. An agency reports that he suffers from *senility and paralysis*. His only son is confined in the Veterans Hospital. There are no other relatives. Mr. Backus is receiving $320 per month, but he feels he should be receiving at least $600 per month on which to live since the high cost of living makes it very hard to get along on less. He has no savings. His landlady says that she does not wish to have him remain there because she cannot care for an invalid.
After a complete investigation of this case, you then should

A. arrange to increase Mr. Backus' pension to $600 a month and then try to get the landlady to keep him
B. place him in a home for old people at public expense
C. increase his pension to $600 a month and make arrangements with the owner of a nursing home to care for Mr. Backus
D. try to have the son support him

KEY (CORRECT ANSWERS)

1. D
2. B
3. D
4. B
5. C
6. A
7. D
8. C
9. C
10. C
11. D
12. C
13. B
14. A
15. D
16. C
17. C
18. A
19. C
20. B
21. D
22. B
23. C
24. C
25. C

LOGICAL REASONING

The reasoning test assesses how well applicants can read, understand, and apply critical thinking skills to factual situations. Before entering your job, you will receive training that requires reading, understanding, and applying a wealth of detailed, written materials. Although some information must be memorized, much of the information you will use must be learned through independent reasoning. The test is, therefore, designed to select trainees who will be able to handle the academic workload and who will subsequently be able to handle complex reasoning and decision-making situations on the job.

The Logical Reasoning Questions

These sample questions are similar to the questions you will find in actual tests in terms of difficulty and format. Some of the questions in the test will be harder and some will be easier than those shown here.

Some of the questions in this manual deal with topics related to general government business. However, all of the questions in the actual test will deal with topics related to the work performed in entry-level positions. *You should remember, however, that knowledge of job-specific subject matter is **NOT** required to answer correctly the questions in this manual or the questions in the actual test.*

The kind of reading these questions require you to do is different from ordinary reading in which you just follow the general meaning of a series of sentences or paragraphs to see what the writer is saying about the topic. Instead, it is the kind of reading you must do with complex material when you intend to take some action or draw some conclusion based on that material.

This test asks you to make logical conclusions based on facts given in various paragraphs, and answering requires careful reading and focused thought about exactly what is given and what **is not** given. Therefore, you should read each question and the answer choices for each question very carefully before choosing your answer. The information below will give you some suggestions about how to approach this part of the test and some information about how you can improve your reasoning skills.

About the Questions

Reading the Paragraph (The Beginning of the Question)

There may be facts in the paragraph that may not always be true everywhere. However, it is important for testing purposes that you **accept** every fact in the paragraph as given or true. Also remember that, in this part of the test, you are not being judged on your knowledge of facts, but rather on your ability to read and reason on the basis of the facts presented to you.

Example of a Paragraph:

Law enforcement agencies use scientific techniques to identify suspects or to establish guilt. One obvious application of such techniques is the examination of a crime scene. Some substances found at a crime scene yield valuable clues under microscopic examination. Clothing fibers, dirt particles, and even pollen grains may reveal important information to the careful investigator. Nothing can be overlooked because all substances found at a crime scene are potential sources of evidence.

Reading the Question Lead-in

Each paragraph is followed by a lead-in statement that asks you to complete a sentence by choosing one of several phrases (possible answers) labeled (A) to (E). The lead-in sentence may be either positive or negative, as shown in the examples below:

From the information given above, it can be validly concluded that,

or

From the information given above, it CANNOT be validly concluded that,

It is important to focus on the lead-in statement because if you skim over it, you may miss a "**NOT**" and answer that question incorrectly. Positive lead-in statements are followed by four false conclusions (set of possible answers) and one correct conclusion (the correct answer). Your task is to find the correct one. Negative lead-in statements, by contrast, give you four correct conclusions and only one false conclusion; the task in these types of questions is to determine the one conclusion that **cannot** be supported by the facts in the paragraph (the false conclusion). If you do not pay close attention to negative lead-in questions, you could jump to the conclusion that the first correct option you read must be the right answer. The lead-in statement may also limit the possible answers in some way. For example, a lead-in statement such as

"from the information given above, it can be validly concluded that, during a crime scene investigation"

means that there might be different answers based on other times and places, but for the purpose of the test question, only conditions during a crime scene investigation (as described in the lead-in) should be considered.

The lead-in statement is followed by the set of conclusions or possible alternatives from which you will choose the correct answer. There are always five alternatives, which appear as follows:

A) all substances that yield valuable clues under microscopic examination are substances found at a crime scene
B) some potential sources of evidence are substances that yield valuable clues under microscopic examination
C) some substances found at a crime scene are not potential sources of evidence
D) no potential sources of evidence are substances found at a crime scene
E) some substances that yield valuable clues under microscopic examination are not substances found at a crime scene

Reasoning About Categories

Sometimes the information that you work with is based on your knowledge of how things can be categorized or grouped and combined with your knowledge of facts about those categories. You may have information about several categories that can be combined in various ways. You can also draw conclusions from facts that are <u>not</u> true and from facts about different events or indicators that are linked together. To understand these statements better, consider the following situation:

Think of a situation in which you are in charge of searching a vacant building for a missing child. The building has six floors. You have assigned one group to begin searching on the first floor of the building and then to move up to the next higher floor as they complete their search. A second group is sent to the top floor to begin searching there and then to move down as they complete searching. The first two floors of the building once contained a retail store and, therefore, broken glass shelves and metal hooks litter those floors. The next three floors once contained offices and, although they do not have any metal or broken glass on the floors, these floors do have plenty of leftover paper trash everywhere. The top floor used to be a penthouse apartment, and it is the only floor in the building that is still carpeted.

This situation gives you six floors that have in the past been used for three different purposes. There are two groups of searchers with two different search patterns. Within this situation, there are various categories into which information can be sorted. As the searchers report back to you on their progress, your level of certainty will depend on the completeness of the information you receive from them.

For example, if one group leader reports back "We've just finished searching a floor that is carpeted, and the child is not here," you **can** conclude that the child is not on the penthouse apartment level of the building. However, if the other group leader calls to say "We've just finished searching a floor with a lot of glass debris all over the place," you **cannot** conclude that the retail part of the building has been completely searched because the leader only told you about one floor while there were two floors in that category (two floors with glass all over the floor). However, if the leader told you "We've just finished searching two floors full of glass and metal hooks, and we're moving on to search the next floor up, where there seems to be a lot of paper all over," then you **could** conclude that the entire retail section had been searched because you have information that is complete about that category.

As you study the logical reasoning test questions, you must use the type of approach described above to reason about categories of information and draw conclusions through the process of elimination.

Statements Using the Quantifier "All"

One of the biggest mistakes people make when they jump to conclusions without basing them on all the facts is to misinterpret statements beginning with "all." A sentence that begins with the words "all" or "every" gives you information about how two different groups are linked. If a librarian told you "All the books on this set of shelves are about law enforcement," you might be tempted to conclude that all of the library's books on law enforcement were on that set of shelves, but you would be wrong. That sentence simply tells you that the books on those shelves are a subcategory of the category of books on law enforcement. That sentence does **not** tell you anything about where other law enforcement books are located in the library. Therefore, you do not have any information on the rest of that category.

It is easier to recognize the error in this kind of thinking if you consider two linked groups of things that are of very different sizes. Suppose a neighbor describes a children's birthday party at his house, saying "all the children at the party spoke Spanish fluently." It would not be correct to conclude that "all people who could speak Spanish fluently attended this birthday party." In this case, it is easy to recognize that "all the children at the party who spoke Spanish fluently" is really a subgroup of the category of "all people who could speak Spanish."

Reasoning From Disproved Facts ("NONE" and "NOT" Statements)

A lot of useful information can be gained when you learn that something is **NOT** true or when you know that one group of things is **NOT** part of a particular category. This is the same as saying that there is no overlap at all between two groups of things. Here, you can draw conclusions about either group as it relates to the other since you can count on the fact that the two groups have no members in common. If you can say "no reptiles are warm-blooded," you can also say "no warm-blooded creatures are reptiles" because you know that the first statement means that there is no overlap between the two categories. Many investigations hinge on negative facts. In the logical reasoning test part, you will see phrases such as "It is not the case that" or "Not all of the" or many words that begin with the prefix "non-." All of these are ways to say that a negative fact has been established.

Sometimes our ordinary speech habits get in the way. Most people would not make a statement such as "Some of the pizza has no pepperoni" unless they are trying to suggest at the same time that some of the pizza does have pepperoni. By contrast, a detective might make a statement such as "some of the bloodstains were not human blood" simply because only part of the samples had come back from the laboratory. The rest of the bloodstains might or might not be human.

As you work through the sample questions and practice test in this manual, think about each negative phrase or term you find. Take care to assume only as much as is definitely indicated by the facts as given, **AND NO MORE.**

READING COMPREHENSION
UNDERSTANDING AND INTERPRETING WRITTEN MATERIAL
EXAMINATION SECTION
TEST 1

DIRECTIONS: Each question or incomplete statement is followed by several suggested answers or completions. Select the one that BEST answers the question or completes the statement. *PRINT THE LETTER OF THE CORRECT ANSWER IN THE SPACE AT THE RIGHT.*

Questions 1-2.

DIRECTIONS: Questions 1 and 2 are to be answered SOLELY on the basis of the information given in the following paragraph .

It is argued by some that the locale of the trial should be given little or no consideration. Facts are facts, they say, and if presented properly to a jury panel they will be productive of the same results regardless of where the trial is held. However, experience shows great differences in the methods of handling claims by juries. In some counties, large demands in personal injury suits are viewed with suspicion by the jury. In others, the jurors are liberal in dealing with someone else's funds.

1. According to the above paragraph, it would be ADVISABLE for an examiner on a personal injury case to 1.____

   A. get information as to the kind of verdicts that are usually awarded by juries in the county of trial
   B. give little or no consideration to the locale of the trial
   C. look for incomplete and improper presentation of facts to the jury if the verdict was not justified by the facts
   D. offer a high but realistic initial settlement figure so that no temptation is left to the claimant to gamble on the jury's verdict

2. According to the above statement, the argument that the location of a trial in a personal injury suit CANNOT counteract the weight of the evidence is 2.____

   A. basically sound
   B. disproven by the differences in awards for similar claims
   C. substantiated in those cases where the facts are properly and carefully presented to the injury
   D. supported by experience which shows great differences in the methods of handling claims by juries

Questions 3-6.

DIRECTIONS: Questions 3 through 6 are to be answered SOLELY on the basis of the following excerpt from a recorded annual report of the police department. This material should be read first and then referred to in answering these questions.

LEGAL BUREAU

One of the more important functions of this bureau is to analyze and furnish the department with pertinent information concerning Federal and State statutes and local laws which affect the department, law enforcement or crime prevention. In addition, all measure introduced in the State Legislature and the City Council which may affect this department are carefully reviewed by members of the Legal Bureau and, where necessary, opinions and recommendations thereon are prepared.

Another important function of this office is the prosecution of cases in the Criminal Courts. This is accomplished by assignment of attorneys who are members of the Legal Bureau to appear in those cases which are deemed to raise issues of importance to the department or questions of law which require technical presentation to facilitate proper determination; and also in those cases where request is made for such appearances by a judge or magistrate, some other official of the city, or a member of the force.

Proposed legislation was prepared and sponsored for introduction in the State Legislature and, at this writing, one of these proposals has already been enacted into law and five others are presently on the Governor's desk awaiting executive action. The new law prohibits the sale or possession of a hypodermic syringe or needle by an unauthorized person. The bureau's proposals awaiting executive action pertain to an amendment to the Criminal Procedure Law prohibiting desk officers from taking bail in gambling cases or in cases mentioned in the Criminal Procedure Law, including confidence men and swindlers as jostlers in the Penal Law; prohibiting the sale of switchblade knives of any size to children under 16 and bills extending the licensing period of gunsmiths.

The Legal Bureau has regularly cooperated with the Corporation Counsel and the District Attorneys in respect to matters affecting this department, and has continued to advise and represent the Police Athletic League, the Police Sports Association, the Police Relief Fund, and the Police Pension Fund.

3. Members of the Legal Bureau frequently appear in Criminal Court for the purpose of 3.___

   A. defending members of the Police Force
   B. raising issues of important to the Police Department
   C. prosecuting all offenders arrested by members of the Force
   D. facilitating proper determination of questions of law requiring technical presentation

4. The Legal Bureau sponsored a bill that would 4.___

   A. extend the licenses of gunsmiths
   B. prohibit the sale of switchblade knives to children of any size
   C. place confidence men and swindlers in the same category as jostlers in the Penal Law
   D. prohibit desk officers from admitting gamblers, confidence men, and swindlers to bail

5. One of the functions of the Legal Bureau is to 5.____

   A. review and make recommendations on proposed Federal laws affecting law enforcement
   B. prepare opinions on all measures introduced in the State Legislature and the City Council
   C. furnish the Police Department with pertinent information concerning all new Federal and State laws
   D. analyze all laws affecting the work of the Police Department

6. The one of the following that is NOT a function of the Legal Bureau is 6.____

   A. law enforcement and crime prevention
   B. prosecution of all cases in Women's Court
   C. advise and represent the Police Sports Association
   D. lecturing at the Police Academy

7. It is usual in public service for recruits to serve a probationary period before they receive tenured positions. The objective of this is to observe them in actual service, to teach them the duties of their position, and to provide a means for eliminating those who prove they are not suited for this kind of work. During this period, firings may be made at the discretion of the chief. 7.____
   Which one of the following is BEST supported by the above selection?

   A. Demonstrated fitness for the job is the basis for retention of probationary employees.
   B. Trial appointments protect the appointee from unfair dismissal practices.
   C. Public service employees need experience and instruction before permanent appointment.
   D. Exams must be given to determine the ability of probationary employees.

8. As the fundamental changes sought to be brought about in the inmates of a correctional institution can be accomplished only under good leadership, it follows that the quality of the staff whose duty it is to influence and guide the inmates in the right direction is more important than the physical facilities of the institution. 8.____
   Of the following, the MOST accurate conclusion based on the preceding statement is that

   A. the development of leadership is the fundamental change brought about in inmates by good quality staff
   B. the physical facilities of an institution are not very important in bringing about fundamental changes in the inmates
   C. with proper training the entire staff of a correctional institution can be developed into good leaders
   D. without good leadership the basic changes desired in the inmates of a correctional institution cannot be brought about

Questions 9-11.

DIRECTIONS: Questions 9 through 11 are to be answered SOLELY on the basis of the following paragraph.

The law enforcement agency is one of the most important agencies in the field of juvenile delinquency prevention. This is so not because of the social work connected with this problem, however, for this is not a police matter, but because the officers are usually the first to come in contact with the delinquent. The manner of arrest and detention makes a deep impression upon him and affects his life-long attitude toward society and the law. The juvenile court is perhaps the most important agency in this work. Contrary to the general opinion, however, it is not primarily concerned with putting children into correctional schools. The main purpose of the juvenile court is to save the child and to develop his emotional make-up in order that he can grow up to be a decent and well-balanced citizen. The system of probation is the means whereby the court seeks to accomplish these goals.

9. According to this paragraph, police work is an important part of a program to prevent juvenile delinquency because 9.___

A. social work is no longer considered important in juvenile delinquency prevention
B. police officers are the first to have contact with the delinquent
C. police officers jail the offender in order to be able to change his attitude toward society and the law
D. it is the first step in placing the delinquent in jail

10. According to this paragraph, the CHIEF purpose of the juvenile court is to 10.___

A. punish the child for his offense
B. select a suitable correctional school for the delinquent
C. use available means to help the delinquent become a better person
D. provide psychiatric care for the delinquent

11. According to this paragraph, the juvenile court directs the development of delinquents under its care CHIEFLY by 11.___

A. placing the child under probation
B. sending the child to a correctional school
C. keeping the delinquent in prison
D. returning the child to his home

Questions 12-14.

DIRECTIONS: Questions 12 through 14 are to be answered on the basis of the following paragraph.

An assassination is an act that consists of a plotted, attempted or actual murder of a prominent political figure by an individual who performs this act in other than a governmental role. This definition draws a distinction between political execution and assassination. An execution may be regarded as a political killing, but it is initiated by the organs of the state, while an assassination can always be characterized as an illegal act. A prominent figure must be the target of the killing, since the killing of lesser members of the political community is included within a wider category of internal political turmoil, namely, terrorism. Assassination is also to be distinguished from homicide. The target of the aggressive act must be a political figure rather than a private person. The killing of a prime minister by a member of an insurrectionist or underground group clearly qualifies as an assassination. So does an act by a deranged individual who tries to kill not just any individual, but the individual in his political role - as President, for example.

12. Assume that a nationally prominent political figure is charged with treason by the state, tried in a court of law, found guilty, and hanged by the state. According to the above passage, it would be MOST appropriate to regard his death as a(n) 12.____

    A. assassination
    B. execution
    C. aggressive act
    D. homicide

13. According to the above passage, which of the following statements is CORRECT? 13.____

    A. The assassination of a political figure is an illegal act.
    B. A private person may be the target of an assassination attempt.
    C. The killing of an obscure member of a political community is considered an assassination event.
    D. An execution may not be regarded as a political killing.

14. Of the following, the MOST appropriate title for this passage would be 14.____

    A. ASSASSINATION - LEGAL ASPECTS
    B. POLITICAL CAUSES OF ASSASSINATION
    C. ASSASSINATION - A DEFINITION
    D. CATEGORIES OF ASSASSINATION

Questions 15-17.

DIRECTIONS: Questions 15 through 17 are to be answered SOLELY on the basis of the following paragraph.

All applicants for an original license to operate a catering establishment shall be fingerprinted. This shall include the officers, employees, and stockholders of the company and the members of a partnership. In case of a change, by addition or substitution, occurring during the existence of a license, the person added or substituted shall be fingerprinted. However, in the case of a hotel containing more than 200 rooms, only the officer or manager filing the application is required to be fingerprinted. The police commissioner may also, at his discretion, exempt the employees and stockholders of any company. The fingerprints shall be taken on one copy of Form C.E. 20 and on two copies of C.E. 21. One copy of Form C.E. 21 shall accompany the application. Fingerprints are not required with a renewal application.

15. According to the above paragraph, an employee added to the payroll of a licensed catering establishment which is not in a hotel must be fingerprinted 15.____

    A. always
    B. unless he has been previously fingerprinted for another license
    C. unless exempted by the police commissioner
    D. only if he is the manager or an officer of the company

16. According to the above paragraph, it would be MOST accurate to state that 16.____

    A. Form C.E. 20 must accompany a renewal application
    B. Form C.E. 21 must accompany all applications
    C. Form C.E. 21 must accompany an original application
    D. both Forms C.E. 20 and C.E. 21 must accompany all applications

17. A hotel of 270 rooms has applied for a license to operate a catering establishment on the premises. 17.___
According to the instructions for fingerprinting given in the above paragraph, the _______ shall be fingerprinted.

A. officers, employees, and stockholders
B. officers and the manager
C. employees
D. officer filing the application

Questions 18-24.

DIRECTIONS: Read the following two paragraphs. Then answer the questions by selecting the answer
A - if the paragraphs indicate it is TRUE
B - if the paragraphs indicate it is PROBABLY true
C - if the paragraphs indicate it is PROBABLY false
D - if the paragraphs indicate it is FALSE

The fallacy underlying what some might call the eighteenth and nineteenth century misconceptions of the nature of scientific investigations seems to lie in a mistaken analogy. Those who said they were investigating the structure of the universe imagined themselves as the equivalent of the early explorers and map makers. The explorers of the fifteenth and sixteenth centuries had opened up new worlds with the aid of imperfect maps; in their accounts of distant lands, there had been some false and many ambiguous statements. But by the time everyone came to believe the world was round, the maps of distant continents were beginning to assume a fairly consistent pattern. By the seventeenth century, methods of measuring space and time had laid the foundations for an accurate geography.

On this basic issue there is far from complete agreement among philosophers *of* science today. You can, each of you, choose your side and find highly distinguished advocates for the point of view you have selected. However, in view of the revolution in physics, anyone who now asserts that science is an exploration of the universe must be prepared to shoulder a heavy burden of proof. To my mind, the analogy between the map maker and the scientist is false. A scientific theory is not even the first approximation to a map; it is not a need; it is a policy -- an economical and fruitful guide to action, by scientific investigators.

18. The author thinks that 18th and 19th century science followed the same technique as the 15th century geographers. 18.___

19. The author disagrees with the philosophers who are labelled realists. 19.___

20. The author believes there is a permanent structure to the universe. 20.___

21. A scientific theory is an economical guide to exploring what cannot be known absolutely. 21.___

22. Philosophers of science accept the relativity implications of recent research in physics. 22.___

23. It is a matter of time and effort before modern scientists will be as successful as the geographers. 23.___

24. The author believes in an indeterminate universe. 24.___

25. Borough X reports that its police force makes fewer arrests per thousand persons than any of the other boroughs. 25.____
From this statement, it is MOST probable that

A. sufficient information has not been given to warrant any conclusion
B. the police force of Borough X is less efficient
C. fewer crimes are being committed in Borough X
D. fewer crimes are being reported in Borough X

KEY (CORRECT ANSWERS)

1.	A	11.	A
2.	B	12.	B
3.	D	13.	A
4.	C	14.	C
5.	D	15.	C
6.	A	16.	C
7.	A	17.	D
8.	D	18.	D
9.	B	19.	B
10.	C	20.	D

21.	A
22.	D
23.	D
24.	B
25.	A

TEST 2

DIRECTIONS: Each question or incomplete statement is followed by several suggested answers or completions. Select the one that BEST answers the question or completes the statement. *PRINT THE LETTER OF THE CORRECT ANSWER IN THE SPACE AT THE RIGHT.*

Questions 1-2.

DIRECTIONS: Questions 1 and 2 are to be answered on the basis of the information given in the following passage.

Assume that a certain agency is having a problem at one of its work locations because a sizable portion of the staff at that location is regularly tardy in reporting to work. The management of the agency is primarily concerned about eliminating the problem and is not yet too concerned about taking any disciplinary action. An investigator is assigned to investigate to determine, if possible, what might be causing this problem.

After several interviews, the investigator sees that low morale created by poor supervision at this location is at least part of the problem. In addition, there is a problem of tardiness and lack of interest.

1. Given the goals of the investigation and assuming that the investigator was using a non-directive approach in this interview, of the following, the investigator's MOST effective response should be: 1.___

   A. You know, you are building a bad record of tardiness
   B. Can you tell me more about this situation?
   C. What kind of person is your superior?
   D. Do you think you are acting fairly towards the agency by being late so often?

2. Given the goals of the investigation and assuming the investigator was using a directed approach in this interview, of the following, the investigator's response should be: 2.___

   A. That doesn't seem like much of an excuse to me
   B. What do you mean by saying that you've lost interest?
   C. What problems are there with the supervision you are getting?
   D. How do you think your tardiness looks in your personnel record?

Questions 3-5.

DIRECTIONS: Questions 3 through 5 are to be answered SOLELY on the basis of the following passage.

As investigators, we are more concerned with the utilitarian than the philosophical aspects of ethics and ethical standards, procedures, and conduct. As a working consideration, we might view ethics as the science of doing the right thing at the right time in the right manner in conformity with the normal, everyday standards imposed by society; and in conformity with the judgment society would be expected to make concerning the rightness or wrongness of what we have done.

An ethical code might be considered a basic set of rules and regulations to which we must conform in the performance of investigative duties. Ethical standards, procedures, and conduct might be considered the logical workings of our ethical code in its everyday application to our work. Ethics also necessarily involves morals and morality. We must eventually answer the self-imposed question of whether or not we have acted in the right way in conducting our investigative activities in their individual and total aspects.

3. Of the following, the MOST suitable title for the above passage is 3.____

   A. THE IMPORTANCE OF RULES FOR INVESTIGATORS
   B. THE BASIC PHILOSOPHY OF A LAWFUL SOCIETY
   C. SCIENTIFIC ASPECTS OF INVESTIGATIONS
   D. ETHICAL GUIDELINES FOR THE CONDUCT OF INVESTIGATIONS

4. According to the above passage, ethical considerations for investigators involve 4.____

   A. special standards that are different from those which apply to the rest of society
   B. practices and procedures which cannot be evaluated by others
   C. individual judgments by investigators of the appropriateness of their own actions
   D. regulations which are based primarily upon a philosophical approach

5. Of the following, the author's PRINCIPAL purpose in writing the above passage seems to have been to 5.____

   A. emphasize the importance of self-criticism in investigative activities
   B. explain the relationship that exists between ethics and investigative conduct
   C. reduce the amount of unethical conduct in the area of investigations
   D. seek recognition by his fellow investigators for his academic treatment of the subject matter

Questions 6-8.

DIRECTIONS: Questions 6 through 8 are to be answered SOLELY on the basis of the following passage.

The investigator must remember that acts of omission can be as effective as acts of commission in affecting the determination of disputed issues. Acts of omission, such as failure to obtain available information or failure to verify dubious information, manifest themselves in miscarriages of justice and erroneous adjudications. An incomplete investigation is an erroneous investigation because a conclusion predicated upon inadequate facts is based on quicksand.

When an investigator throws up his hands and admits defeat, the reason for this action does not necessarily lie in his possible laziness and ineptitude. It is more likely that the investigator has made his conclusions after exhausting only those avenues of investigation of which he is aware. He has exercised good faith in his belief that nothing else can be done.

This tendency must be overcome by all investigators if they are to operate at top efficiency. If no suggestion for new or additional action can be found in any authority, an investigator should use his own initiative to cope with a given situation. No investigator should ever hesitate to set precedents. It is far better in the final analysis to attempt difficult solutions, even if the chances of error are obviously present, than it is to take refuge in the spineless adage: If you don't do anything, you don't do it wrong.

6. Of the following, the MOST suitable title for the above passage is 6.___

   A. THE NEED FOR RESOURCEFULNESS IN INVESTIGATIONS
   B. PROCEDURES FOR COMPLETING AN INVESTIGATION
   C. THE DEVELOPMENT OF STANDARDS FOR INVESTIGATORS
   D. THE CAUSES OF INCOMPLETE INVESTIGATIONS

7. Of the following, the author of this passage considers that the LEAST important consideration in developing new investigative methods is 7.___

   A. efficiency
   B. caution
   C. imagination
   D. thoroughness

8. According to this passage, which of the following statements is INCORRECT? 8.___

   A. Lack of creativity may lead to erroneous investigations .
   B. Acts of omission are sometimes as harmful as acts of commission.
   C. Some investigators who give up on a case are lazy or inept.
   D. An investigator who gives up on a case is usually not acting in good faith.

Questions 9-12.

DIRECTIONS: Questions 9 through 12 are to be answered on the basis of the following paragraph.

A report of investigation should not be weighed down by a mass of information which is hardly material or only remotely relevant, or which fails to prove a point, clarify an issue, or aid the inquiry even by indirection. Some investigative agencies, however, value the report for its own sake, considering it primarily as a justification of the investigative activity contained therein. Every step is listed to show that no logical measure has been overlooked and to demonstrate that the reporting agent is beyond criticism. This system serves to provide reviewing authorities with a ready means of checking subordinates and provides order, method, and routine to investigative activity. In addition, it may offer supervisors and investigators a sense of security; the investigator would know within fairly exact limits what is expected of him and the supervisor may be comforted by the knowledge that his organization may not be reasonably criticized in a particular case on the grounds of obvious omissions or inertia. To the state's attorney and others, however, who must take administrative action on the basis of the report, the irrelevant and immaterial information thwarts the purpose of the investigation by dimming the issues and obscuring the facts that are truly contributory to the proof.

9. From the point of view of the supervising investigator, a drawback of having the investigator prepare the type of report which the state's attorney would like is that it 9.___

   A. gives a biased and one-sided view of what should have been an impartial investigation
   B. has only limited usefulness as an indication that all proper investigative methods were used by the investigator
   C. overlooks logical measures, removing the responsibility for taking those measures which the investigator should otherwise have been expected to take
   D. sets fairly exact limits to what the supervisor can expect of the investigator

10. District attorneys do not like reports of investigations in which every step is listed because 10.____

A. their administrative action is then based on irrelevant and immaterial information
B. it places the investigator beyond criticism, making the responsibility of the district attorney that much greater
C. of the difficulty of finding among the mass of information the portion which is meaningful and useful
D. the inclusion of indirect or hardly material information is not in accord with the order in which the steps were taken

11. As expressed in the above paragraph, the type of report which MOST investigators prefer to prepare is 11.____

A. a step-by-step account of their activities, including both fruitful and unfruitful steps, since to do so provides order and method and gives them a sense of security
B. not made clear, even though current practice in some agencies is to include every step taken in the investigation
C. one from which useless and confusing information has been excluded because it is not helpful and is poor practice
D. one not weighed down by a mass of irrelevant information but one which shows within fairly exact limits what was expected of them

12. With regard to the type of information which an investigator should include in his report, the above paragraph expresses the opinion that 12.____

A. it is best to include in the report only that information which supports the conclusions of the investigator
B. reports should include all relevant and clarifying information and exclude information on inquiries which had no productive result
C. reports should include sufficient information to demonstrate that the investigator has been properly attending to his duties and all the information which contributes toward proof of what occurred in the case
D. the most logical thing to do is to list every step in the investigation and its result

Questions 13-17.

DIRECTIONS: Questions 13 through 17 are to be answered SOLELY on the basis of the following paragraph.

Those statutes of limitations which are of interest to a claim examiner are the ones affecting third party actions brought against an insured covered by a liability policy of insurance. Such statutes of limitations are legislative enactments limiting the time within which such actions at law may be brought. Research shows that such periods differ from state to state and vary within the states with the type of action brought. The laws of the jurisdiction in which the action is brought govern and determine the period within which the action may be instituted, regardless of the place of the cause of action or the residence of the parties at the time of cause of action. The period of time set by a statute of limitations for a tort action starts from the moment the alleged tort is committed. The period usually extends continuously until its expiration, upon which legal action may no longer be brought. However, there is a suspension of the running of the period when a defendant has concealed himself in order to avoid service of legal process. The suspension continues until the defendant discontinues his concealment and then the period starts running again. A defendant may, by his agreement or conduct, be legally barred from asserting the statute of limitations as a defense to an action. The insurance carrier for the defendant may, by the misrepresentation of the claims man, cause such a bar against use of the statute of limitations by the defendant. If the claim examiner of the insurance carrier has by his conduct or assertion lulled the plaintiff into a false sense of security by false representations, the defendant may be barred from setting up the statute of limitations as a defense.

13. Of the following, the MOST suitable title for the above paragraph is 13.__

   A. FRAUDULENT USE OF THE STATUTE OF LIMITATIONS
   B. PARTIES AT INTEREST IN A LAWSUIT
   C. THE CLAIM EXAMINER AND THE LAW
   D. THE STATUTE OF LIMITATIONS IN CLAIMS WORK

14. The period of time during which a third party action may be brought against an insured covered by a liability policy depends on 14.__

   A. the laws of the jurisdiction in which the action is brought
   B. where the cause of action which is the subject of the suit took place
   C. where the claimant lived at the time of the cause of action
   D. where the insured lived at the time of the cause of action

15. Time limits in third party actions which are set by the statutes of limitations described above are 15.__

   A. determined by claimant's place of residence at start of action
   B. different in a state for different actions
   C. the same from state to state for the same type of action
   D. the same within a state regardless of type of action

16. According to the above paragraph, grounds which may be legally used to prevent a defendant from using the statute of limitations as a defense in the action described are 16.__

   A. defendant's agreement or concealment; a charge of liability for death and injury
   B. defendant's agreement or conduct; misrepresentation by the claims man
   C. fraudulent concealment by claim examiner; a charge of liability for death or injury; defendant's agreement
   D. misrepresentation by claim examiner of carrier; defendant's agreement; plaintiff's concealment

17. Suppose an alleged tort was commited on January 1, 2008 and that the period in which action may be taken is set at three years by the statute of limitations. Suppose further that the defendant, in order to avoid service of legal process, had concealed himself from July 1, 2010 through December 31, 2010. 17.__
   In this case, the defendant may not use the statute of limitations as a defense unless action is brought by the plaintiff after _______, 2011.

   A. January 1
   B. February 28
   C. June 30
   D. August 1

Questions 18-20.

DIRECTIONS: Questions 18 through 20 are to be answered SOLELY on the basis of information contained in the following passage.

No matter how well the interrogator adjusts himself to the witness and how precisely he induces the witness to describe his observations, mistakes still can be made. The mistakes made by an experienced interrogator may be comparatively few, but as far as the witness is concerned, his path is full of pitfalls. Modern *witness psychology* has shown that even the most honest and trustworthy witnesses are apt to make grave mistakes in good faith. It is, therefore, necessary that the interrogator get an idea of the weak links in the testimony in order to check up on them in the event that something appears to be strange or not quite satisfactory.

Unfortunately, modern witness psychology does not yet offer any means of directly testing the credibility of testimony. It lacks precision and method, in spite of worthwhile attempts on the part of learned men. At the same time, witness psychology, through the gathering of many experiences concerning the weaknesses of human testimony, has been of invaluable service. It shows clearly that only evidence of a technical nature has absolute value as proof.

Testimony may be separated into the following stages: (1) perception, (2) observation, (3) mind fixation of the observed occurrences, in which fantasy, association of ideas, and personal judgment participate, and (4) expression in oral or written form, where the testimony is transferred from one witness to another or to the interrogator.

Each of these stages offers innumerable possibilities for the distortion of testimony.

18. The above passage indicates that having witnesses talk to each other before testifying is a practice which is GENERALLY 18.____

    A. *desirable,* since the witnesses will be able to correct each other's errors in observation before testimony
    B. *undesirable,* since the witnesses will collaborate on one story to tell the investigator
    C. *undesirable,* since one witness may distort his testimony because of what another witness may erroneously say
    D. *desirable,* since witnesses will become aware of discrepancies in their own testimony and can point out the discrepancies to the investigator

19. According to the above passage, the one of the following which would be the MOST reliable for use as evidence would be the testimony of a 19.____

    A. handwriting expert about a signature on a forged check
    B. trained police officer about the identity of a criminal
    C. laboratory technician about an accident he has observed
    D. psychologist who has interviewed any witnesses who relate conflicting stories

20. Concerning the validity of evidence, it is CLEAR from the above passage that 20.____

    A. only evidence of a technical nature is at all valuable
    B. the testimony of witnesses is so flawed that it is usually valueless

C. an investigator, by knowing modern witness psychology, will usually be able to perceive mistaken testimony
D. an investigator ought to expect mistakes in even the most reliable witness testimony

Questions 21-22.

DIRECTIONS: Questions 21 and 22 are to be answered SOLELY on the basis of the information contained in the passage below. This passage represents a report prepared by a subordinate superior concerning a school demonstration.

On April 1, a group of students, each holding an anti-apartheid sign, was involved in a demonstration on the grounds of Columbia University. The students began by locking the main entrance doors to the Administration Building and preventing faculty and students from entering or leaving the building.

The C.O. of the police detail at the scene requested additional assistance of four female detectives, an Emergency Service van, and a police photographer equipped with a Polaroid instamatic camera.

When the additional assistance arrived, the Commanding Officer directed the students to disperse. His justification for the order was that the demonstrators were violating the rights of other students and certain faculty members by denying them access to the Administration Building. The students ignored the order to disperse and the Commanding Officer of the police detail ordered them to be removed.

Another group of students who had been standing in front of the library were sympathetic toward the demonstrators and charged the police. Several police officers were injured during the ensuing hostilities.

Eventually, order was restored. That evening, the television coverage presented a neutral and fairly accurate account of the incident.

21. Which of the following statements MOST clearly and accurately reflects the contents of the report? 21.____

A. A large group of students, all of whom were holding anti-apartheid signs, was involved in a demonstration on the grounds of Columbia University.
B. A large group of students, some of whom were holding anti-apartheid signs, was involved in a demonstration on the grounds of Columbia University.
C. Each of a group of Columbia students carrying anti-apartheid signs was involved in a demonstration on the grounds of Columbia University.
D. Each of the students involved in the demonstration on the grounds of Columbia University was holding an anti-apartheid sign.

22. Which of the following statements MOST clearly and accurately reflects the contents of the report? 22.____

A. The Commanding Officer of the police detail justified his order that the demonstrators disperse when the additional assistance arrived.
B. When the additional assistance arrived, the Commanding Officer of the police detail justified his order that the demonstrators disperse.
C. The Commanding Officer of the police detail directed the students to disperse when the additional assistance arrived.
D. The Commanding Officer of the police detail requested additional assistance because the student demonstrators were violating the rights of other students and certain faculty members.

23. Which of the following statements MOST clearly and accurately reflects the contents of the report? 23.____

A. Another group of students charged the police because they were sympathetic toward the police.
B. The evening television coverage of the demonstration was fair and accurate.
C. The group of students who had been standing in front of the library was sympathetic toward the demonstrators.
D. Several police officers were injured during the hostilities which took place in front of the library.

Questions 24-25.

DIRECTIONS: Questions 24 and 25 are to be answered SOLELY on the basis of the information given in the following paragraph.

Credibility of a witness is usually governed by his character and is evidenced by his reputation for truthfulness. Personal or financial reasons or a criminal record may cause a witness to give false information to avoid being implicated. Age, sex, physical and mental abnormalities, loyalty, revenge, social and economic status, indulgence in alcohol, and the influence of other persons are some of the many factors which may affect the accuracy, willingness, or ability with which witnesses observe, interpret, and describe occurrences.

24. According to the above paragraph, a witness may, for personal reasons, give wrong information about an occurrence because he 24.____

A. wants to protect his reputation for truthfulness
B. wants to embarrass the investigator
C. doesn't want to become involved
D. doesn't really remember what happened

25. According to the above paragraph, factors which influence the witness of an occurrence may affect 25.____

A. not only what he tells about it but what he was able and wanted to see of it
B. only what he describes and interprets later but not what he actually sees at the time of the event
C. what he sees but not what he describes
D. what he is willing to see but not what he is able to see

KEY (CORRECT ANSWERS)

1. B
2. C
3. D
4. C
5. B

6. A
7. B
8. D
9. B
10. C

11. B
12. B
13. D
14. A
15. B

16. B
17. C
18. C
19. A
20. D

21. D
22. C
23. C
24. C
25. A

READING COMPREHENSION
UNDERSTANDING AND INTERPRETING WRITTEN MATERIAL
EXAMINATION SECTION
TEST 1

DIRECTIONS: Each question or incomplete statement is followed by several suggested answers or completions. Select the one that *BEST* answers the question or completes the statement. *PRINT THE LETTER OF THE CORRECT ANSWER IN THE SPACE AT THE RIGHT.*

Questions 1-5.

DIRECTIONS: The following passage is to be used as the *SOLE* basis for answering Questions 1 to 5. Read the selection carefully and base your answers *ONLY* on the information contained therein.

PASSAGE

Politicians, preachers, and moralists frequently inveigh against the breakdown of family and community morality. According to one variant of this position, it is because of a "moral breakdown" that we find so much "crime in the streets." This line of reasoning has a persuasive message for many white Americans – it carries surface plausibility and underlying racial prejudice. Family "breakdown," "immoral" delinquent gangs and African-Americans are all disproportionately found in the urban slums. There is, however, an important flaw in the implied argument of this modern morality tale. It is apparent that lower-class families have difficulty in maintaining control over their children. According to the modern morality tale, if parents were more responsible and less perverse, and exercised control over their children, there would be less delinquency. The parents, and later their children, are the villains. But the lack of control stems not from parental perversity but from parental poverty, that is, from the deprivations of lower-class status. Of course, personalities do vary, even in their degree of "perversity"; and there are undoubtedly elements of "perversity" among some parents who do not maintain control over their children. But the magnitude of the problem stems from major social forces that have a pervasive influence over the lives of so many people.

By increasing the amount and awareness of legitimate opportunities, and reducing the attractiveness of delinquent gangs and illegitimate behavior, it may be possible to reduce delinquency. But overcoming these deprivations may also have an indirect effect upon delinquency by influencing family structure. The key problem in the lower class family is the weak occupational economic position of the man. Since, in the United States, the man is expected to be the breadwinner above all else, he performs inadequately at his major role within the family. As a result the lower class man is not esteemed, even within his own family. Under these circumstances, he may also leave his family. It can therefore be expected that improvements made in occupational and economic opportunities for lower class men will strengthen their position within the family and thereby strengthen the stability of the family as a whole. It will also heighten the attractiveness of the father and the family in the eyes of the children and make additional resources available within the family. Such changes will make it possible for the family to maintain stronger controls over its children.

Some argue that the provision of opportunities is not enough–that lower class people differ in their subculture, or values, or goals, or motivations so that they would not take advantage of these opportunities. Although value modifications generally take place within the lower class to make life's values more in accord with life's circumstances, it appears that middle class values and goals are still retained. Lower class people frequently find it necessary to stretch their values and aspirations downward to accord with realistic opportunities, but they do not abandon middle class values. They may lessen their commitment to values so that some of the sting will be taken out of life's deprivations, but they do not abandon all values. In short, providing additional opportunities seems to be the key area for change.

QUESTIONS

1. According to the passage, which of the following statements concerning street crime and moral breakdown is CORRECT? 1.___

   A. The irresponsibility of parents in slum-areas is the root cause of moral breakdown and street crime.
   B. Moral breakdown is basically a result of street crime.
   C. Moral breakdown and street crime are aspects of larger and widespread social problems.
   D. Street crime is basically a result of moral breakdown.
   E. Moral breakdown and street crime are a response to the prejudice of many white Americans.

2. According to the passage, the problem of juvenile delinquency is basically a result of 2.___

   A. the overrepresentation of minority groups in lower class neighborhoods
   B. the poor social and economic conditions that are an inherent part of lower class life
   C. the unwillingness of parents to accept their responsibilities and exercise discipline
   D. the breakdown in family morality that is most pervasive among the lower class
   E. personality variations among lower class parents which prevent them from maintaining control over their children

3. According to the passage, the *central* problem of the lower class family is the 3.___

   A. absence of goal motivated behavior
   B. failure to develop a distinct subculture within poor communities
   C. dissatisfaction with middle class values
   D. inability of the father to adequately support his family
   E. attractiveness of delinquency and illegitimate behavior

4. According to the passage, providing greater occupational opportunities for lower class men will result in all of the following *EXCEPT* 4.___

   A. allowing families to maintain greater control over their children
   B. improving the standing of lower class fathers within their families
   C. reducing the amount of juvenile delinquency so that lower class neighborhoods are as safe as others in the city
   D. increasing the stability of lower class families
   E. enhancing the image of the family itself for lower class children

5. According to the passage, lower class people often make adjustments in their values. As a result, their values *generally* 5.____

   A. reflect the opportunities that are actually available to the lower class
   B. coincide exactly with middle class values
   C. depend upon a family structure that lacks a strong father figure
   D. include goals and aspirations that exceed their economic situation
   E. deny responsibility for the delinquent behavior of their children

Questions 6-10.

DIRECTIONS: Questions 6 to 10 are to be answered *SOLELY* on the basis of the following passage.

PASSAGE

Of all the groups claiming interference by restrictions on the dissemination of news, the one with the most pressing claim is the law enforcement agency. Due to the combination of a morbid interest in crimes of violence and fear that a vicious criminal may be at large, there is a demand by the public for a showing by the police of capability in solving a crime. Perhaps unwilling to acknowledge the existence of, and accept responsibility for, a degenerate element in its midst, the public tends to cast the blame for a successful crime on police failure to prevent it. Thus there is constant pressure on the police to demonstrate that the case is nearing solution and that the perpetrator will soon be in custody. To avoid the accusation of suppressing information to cover up malfeasance, there is a legitimate tendency on the part of the police to cooperate with the press and thus escape being cast in an unfavorable light. The ideal solution – from the point of view of the police-would be to allow them free rein in releasing information to reassure the public. However, this would not be consonant with the right of the accused to a fair trial with the presumption of innocence.

A distinguished committee of lawyers and jurists has developed a comprehensive code for police and law enforcement agencies. The committee's recommendations include the following:

A. Concerning the Defendant

   1. The release of information concerning the defendant shall be limited to his name, age, occupation, marital status, and personal data not related to the crime or the character of the defendant. His criminal record, prior medical and psychiatric history, or military disciplinary record, if any, shall not be released. No other information that is clearly prejudicial to the defendant shall be released.
   2. No statement of any nature made by the defendant, or the substance thereof, shall be released. No reference shall be made to any test taken by the defendant or that he has refused to take.
   3. The announcement of the arrest of the defendant may include, in addition to the information authorized above, the time, place, and manner of apprehension as well as the text or summary of the charge, information, or indictment. No comments shall be made relating to his guilt or innocence.
   4. News media shall not be permitted to interview the defendant with or without his attorney's consent, while he is in police custody.
   5. News media shall not be permitted to photograph or televise the defendant while he is in police custody except in a public place. This prohibition extends to such instances as where he is being interrogated, where he is being processed ("booked") following arrest, where he is in a lockup or detention facility, or where he is at a hospital bedside for identification purposes.
   6. Where the defendant is still at large, and it appears that he is a fugitive from justice, additional information that may reasonably and directly aid in effecting his apprehension, including his photograph, may be released.

B. Concerning the Crime, the Investigation, and the Arrest
   1. A general description of the crime shall be made available to the news media. Gruesome or sordid aspects which tend unduly to inflame public emotions shall not be released. Witnesses shall not be identified by name or otherwise, nor shall any comment be made concerning their credibility, their testimony, or their identification of the defendant.
   2. No comment on the apparent motivation or character of the perpetrator shall be made.
   3. No information concerning scientific evidence such as laboratory or ballistics tests or fingerprints shall be released.

C. General
   1. A member of the police agency shall be designated as the Information Officer responsible for the dissemination of all information to the news media. It will be the responsibility of the Information Officer to supervise the enforcement of these regulations and to solicit and encourage full cooperation of news media. No member of a police agency may furnish any information to news media without prior approval by the Information Officer. No interviews shall be permitted with investigating or arresting officers.
   2. Wherever feasible, the Information Officer will encourage news media to enter into pool arrangements so as to reduce confusion and interference with the orderly processes of law enforcement. It shall be a prime responsibility of the Information Officer to insure a calm and orderly atmosphere during the dissemination of information to the news media.

QUESTIONS

6. According to the passage, the tendency of the police to cooperate with the press by releasing information is based on the 6.___

   A. public's desire for evidence that the police are able to bring criminals to justice
   B. deterrent effect on other criminals which results from reports of police efficiency
   C. requirement of the courts for full disclosure of pertinent information
   D. assistance which unrestricted publicity provides in apprehending perpetrators who are still at large
   E. belief that charges of corruption cannot be avoided in any other way

7. Of the following, the *BASIC* purpose of the recommendations contained in the passage is to 7.___

   A. satisfy the public's curiosity concerning crime
   B. expedite the dissemination of information to the news media
   C. protect the defendant's right to a fair trial
   D. enhance the reputation of the police
   E. reduce interference by the news media in essential police functions

8. According to the recommendations contained in the passage, it would *NOT* be proper for a law enforcement agency to 8.___

   A. release information pertaining to how the defendant was caught
   B. discuss the testimony given by eyewitnesses
   C. distribute a written copy or synopsis of the indictment
   D. provide a general description of the crime in question
   E. disclose the occupation and marital status of the defendant

9. According to the recommendations contained in the passage, law enforcement agencies, under certain circumstances, would be able to 9.____

   A. permit a defendant to make a statement to the news media
   B. release information concerning the defendant's medical history which is not pertinent to the case
   C. describe to the news media evidence against the defendant in terms of probable guilt or innocence
   D. allow a defendant to be televised while in their custody in a non-public place
   E. provide a photograph of the defendant to the news media

10. According to the passage, the Information Officer in a police department is responsible for all of the following EXCEPT 10.____

   A. coordinating interviews of arresting officers by members of the news media
   B. enforcing regulations concerning dissemination of information to the news media
   C. fostering the use of pool arrangements by the news media
   D. approving in advance all requests by the news media for information
   E. preventing hectic and unruly situations when information is provided to the news media.

KEY (CORRECT ANSWERS)

1.	C	6.	A
2.	B	7.	C
3.	D	8.	B
4.	C	9.	E
5.	A	10.	A

TEST 2

DIRECTIONS: Each question or incomplete statement is followed by several suggested answers or completions. Select the one that *BEST* answers the question or completes the statement. *PRINT THE LETTER OF THE CORRECT ANSWER IN THE SPACE AT THE RIGHT.*

Questions 1-5.

DIRECTIONS: Questions 1 to 5 are to be answered *SOLELY* on the basis of the following passage.

PASSAGE

There is a hazy boundary between grateful citizens paying their respects to a proud profession, and "good" citizens involved in corruption, wishing to buy future favors. Once begun, however, the acceptance of small bribes and favors or similar practices can become "norms" or informal standards of cliques of policemen. A recruit can be socialized into accepting these illegal practices by mild, informal negative sanctions such as the withholding of group acceptance. If these unlawful practices are embraced, the recruit's membership group – the police force – and his reference group – the clique involved in illegal behavior – are no longer one and the same. In such circumstances the norms of the reference group (the illegal-oriented clique) would clearly take precedence over either the formal requisites of the membership group (police department regulations) or the formalized norms (legal statutes) of the larger society. When such conflicts are apparent a person can

1. conform to one, take the consequences of non-conformity to the other;
2. seek a compromise position by which he attempts to conform in part, though not wholly, to one or more sets of role expectations, in the hope that sanctions applied will be minimal.

If these reference group norms involving illegal activity become routinized with use they become an identifiable informal "code." Such codes are not unique to the police profession. A fully documented case study of training at a military academy, in which an informal pattern of behavior was assimilated along with the formal standards, clearly outlined the function of the informal norms, their dominance when in conflict with formal regulations, and the secretive nature of their existence to facilitate their effectiveness and subsequent preservation. This same secrecy could be demanded of a police "code" to insure its preservation. Although within the clique the code must be well defined, the ignorance of the lay public to even its existence would be a requisite to its continuous and effective use. Through participation in activity regimented by the "code," an increased group identity and cohesion among "code" practitioners would emerge.

Group identity requires winning of acceptance as a member of the inner group and, thereby, gaining access to the secrets of the occupation which are acquired through informal contacts with colleagues. Lack of this acceptance not only bars the neophyte from the inner secrets of the profession, but may isolate him socially and professionally from his colleagues and even his superiors. There isthe added fear that, in some circumstances in which he would need their support, they would avoid becoming involved, forcing him to face personal danger or public ridicule alone.

QUESTIONS

1. According to the passage, the reference group of a recruit who accepts corrupt practices is 1.____

   A. the police force of which the recruit is a member
   B. a loosely-structured group from which the recruit learns both formal and informal norms
   C. the coterie of officers who are involved in illegal activities
   D. society as a whole, of which the police are a component
   E. a professional organization which instructs the recruit in his responsibilities

2. According to the passage, allegiance by policemen to informally codified standards of behavior is *most likely* to result in 2.____

   A. increased attempts by most citizens to bribe police officers
   B. a decrease of mutual support among policemen
   C. greater awareness on the part of the public of such behavior
   D. decreased secrecy about police department practices
   E. stronger group identification among such policemen

3. According to the passage, the police recuit who is *NOT* accepted by the group which is involved in illegal behavior will 3.____

   A. be prevented from learning many confidential aspects of police work
   B. face less risk of public ridicule or personal danger
   C. be held in high esteem by his superiors
   D. gain social and professional stature among his colleagues
   E. be more likely to expose the activities of the group to the public

4. According to the passage, informal codes of illegal behavior function effectively only when they 4.____

   A. are tacitly accepted by the entire society
   B. permit formal standards to predominate whenever there is a conflict
   C. exist without being known to outsiders
   D. minimize the use of informal negative sanctions
   E. complement pre-existing norms within the police profession

5. According to the passage, a recruit who must deal with conflicting norms of different groups may 5.____

   A. not be able to distinguish between ordinary citizens and those involved in graft
   B. try to accommodate himself to the different roles he is expected to play
   C. be unaware of the informal codes of behavior within the police department
   D. accept one set of standards and thereby avoid any unpleasant consequences
   E. find that he is able to solve the problem by bringing the competing norms into conformity

Questions 6-10.

DIRECTIONS: Questions 6 to 10 are to be answered *SOLELY* on the basis of the following passage.

PASSAGE

THE CONCEPT OF AN OFFENSIVELY DEPLOYED PATROL FORCE

Police forces, in general, are defensively deployed, both in their organization and operation. That is, they are principally designed to act efficiently during or after the commission of a crime. This concept becomes quite clear when the distribution of available manpower of a police force is examined.

The defensive enforcement attitude is prevalent in the philosophy of the individual policeman. Most law enforcement officers seem to view the making of an arrest as one of their major goals. The reason for this attitude is obvious. Police administrators do not have available a measuring technique for evaluating an officer's crime prevention efforts, while an arrest is a measure of his defensive effectiveness.

One of the most serious drawbacks for any police force that is committed to a defensive action during a period of rising crime, is that it becomes, of necessity, a retrograde operation; that is, as more crime is committed, more manpower is utilized for investigation, with a corresponding decrease in crime prevention activities, thus encouraging more crime, more manpower for investigation, etc., etc. The logical extension of this situation is a police force that is completely overloaded with investigations, while crime runs rampant.

It is now appropriate to inquire into the effectiveness of defensive police strategy in the present crime situation. Determining the effectiveness of a police system and its strategy requires the use of absolute measurements. In particular, the effectiveness should be measured in terms of how well it attains its goals. By these measures, the defensive strategy used by the police does not appear to be effective.

If the goal of police action is to eliminate or substantially reduce crime, it is not succeeding. The number of crimes as well as the crime rate is increasing.

It seems completely self-evident that if it were possible to station a policeman at or about every house and building in the city, the amount of crime would be significantly reduced. It would be reduced not because a criminal would be caught after he committed a crime, but because he would not commit the crime, because of the fear of being caught. Thus the crime rate would be reduced by preventing the crime from happening, not by punishing the criminal (if caught) after the crime has been committed.

The solution is, of course, not a practical one but, nevertheless, it should serve as an ideal for an offensively deployed police force. In practice, the force should create the appearance of being everywhere at once.

In contrast to the defensive force, whose operation is retrograde, such an offensive force would be progressive in nature; that is, by preventing a crime from occurring, the manpower required for investigation would be reduced. Hence, it could be diverted toward the prevention of more crime, which would further reduce the investigations and manpower needed, etc. The logical extension of this situation is a force that is completely deployed to prevent crime.

The offensive force depicted above is, of course, a patrol force, but not in the sense of the conventional police patrol, which is very inflexible with regard to the time and place it can be deployed, which is heavily committed to answering complaints, and which is managed by "seat of the pants" techniques.

The specifications for an offensively deployed patrol force are as follows:

1. A patrol unit must pass by every point in the city, on the average of once every ten minutes.

2. The patrol unit must not be sent on a complaint, unless the complaint can be disposed of in less than ten minutes, or there is a crime or equivalent emergency situation in progress. If a unit does become involved, its territory must be covered by adjacent patrol units.
3. The patrol force must be deployed with due regard to the expected type and location of crime, based on an analysis of previous criminal activity for the particular season of the year, day of the week, hour of the day, etc.

QUESTIONS

6. Assume that a certain city has changed the nature of its motor patrol force from a defensive force to offensive deployment. 6._____
Which one of the following results will *MOST* logically follow if the patrol force is functioning in line with the principles discussed in the passage? The

   A. arrest rate for burglary will decrease
   B. number of complaints received will increase
   C. number of aggravated assaults will increase
   D. number of miles that the patrol vehicles travel will increase
   E. number of complaints answered by the patrol force will increase

7. According to the passage, which one of the following *MOST* accurately states the underlying purpose of offensively deployed patrol? To 7._____

   A. leave the patrol unit free to perform offensive patrol
   B. increase the number of criminals that are caught and punished
   C. catch so many criminals that the criminals are afraid to commit offenses
   D. make offenders so fearful of being caught that they refrainfrom committing offenses
   E. have a patrol unit pass every point in the city on the average of once every ten minutes

8. A certain police department has accepted the concept of offensive deployment. In implementing this concept, it has adopted a policy defining the basic responsibility for making initial investigations or crimes. 8._____
Which one of the following is *MOST* likely the policy this department has adopted, if it followed the terms of the passage?

   A. Basic responsibility for initial investigation of crimes is assigned to the patrol force.
   B. Basic responsibility for initial criminal investigation is assigned somewhere other than to the patrol units.
   C. As crime increases above normal levels, the basic responsibility for initial investigation of crime retrogrades to the patrol force.
   D. As crime increases above normal levels, the basic responsibility for initial investigation of crime retrogrades to the Detective Division.
   E. When crime is normal, basic responsibility for initial investigation of crime is divided between the Detective Division and the patrol force, depending on the availability of manpower in each.

9. Assume the following facts: The police department of a certain city has implemented the concept of an offensively deployed police force based on the recommendations contained in the passage. 9.___
Which one of the following results would *MOST* logically indicate that the patrol force is functioning ineffectively? The

A. crime rate has decreased
B. number of crime investigations by the patrol units has increased
C. percentage of crimes cleared by arrest has increased
D. number of prosecutions for crimes cleared by arrest has increased
E. average amount of time spent by the average officer answering complaints has decreased

10. According to the passage, which one of the following is the *MOST* probable reason why many individual policemen have accepted the philosophy of defensive enforcement? Because 10.___

A. of the retrograde philosophy
B. no technique exists for evaluating an officer's offensive efforts
C. most policemen believe in the effectiveness of the crime-investigation cycle
D. the goal of police action is to eliminate or substantially reduce crime
E. the effectiveness of defensive police strategy has never been evaluated

---

KEY (CORRECT ANSWERS)

1. C	6. D
2. E	7. D
3. A	8. B
4. C	9. B
5. B	10. B

Evaluating Conclusions in Light of Known Facts

EXAMINATION SECTION
TEST 1

DIRECTIONS: Each question or incomplete statement is followed by several suggested answers or completions. Select the one that BEST answers the question or completes the statement. *PRINT THE LETTER OF THE CORRECT ANSWER IN THE SPACE AT THE RIGHT.*

Questions 1-9.

DIRECTIONS: In questions 1-9, you will read a set of facts and a conclusion drawn from them. The conclusion may be valid or invalid, based on the facts–it's your task to determine the validity of the conclusion.

For each question, select the letter before the statement that BEST expresses the relationship between the given facts and the conclusion that has been drawn from them. Your choices are:

A. The facts prove the conclusion
B. The facts disprove the conclusion; or
C. The facts neither prove nor disprove the conclusion.

1. FACTS: If the supervisor retires, James, the assistant supervisor, will not be transferred to another department. James will be promoted to supervisor if he is not transferred. The supervisor retired. 1.____

   CONCLUSION: James will be promoted to supervisor.

   A. The facts prove the conclusion.
   B. The facts disprove the conclusion.
   C. The facts neither prove nor disprove the conclusion.

2. FACTS: In the town of Luray, every player on the softball team works at Luray National Bank. In addition, every player on the Luray softball team wears glasses. 2.____

   CONCLUSION: At least some of the people who work at Luray National Bank wear glasses.

   A. The facts prove the conclusion.
   B. The facts disprove the conclusion.
   C. The facts neither prove nor disprove the conclusion.

3. FACTS: The only time Henry and June go out to dinner is on an evening when they have childbirth classes. Their childbirth classes meet on Tuesdays and Thursdays 3.____

   CONCLUSION: Henry and June never go out to dinner on Friday or Saturday.

   A. The facts prove the conclusion.
   B. The facts disprove the conclusion.
   C. The facts neither prove nor disprove the conclusion.

4. FACTS: Every player on the field hockey team has at least one bruise. Everyone on the field hockey team also has scarred knees. 4.___

CONCLUSION: Most people with both bruises and scarred knees are field hockey players.

A. The facts prove the conclusion.
B. The facts disprove the conclusion.
C. The facts neither prove nor disprove the conclusion.

5. FACTS: In the chess tournament, Lance will win his match against Jane if Jane wins her match against Mathias. If Lance wins his match against Jane, Christine will not win her match against Jane. 5.___

CONCLUSION: Christine will not win her match against Jane if Jane wins her match against Mathias.

A. The facts prove the conclusion.
B. The facts disprove the conclusion.
C. The facts neither prove nor disprove the conclusion.

6. FACTS: No green lights on the machine are indicators for the belt drive status. Not all of the lights on the machine's upper panel are green. Some lights on the machine's lower panel are green. 6.___

CONCLUSION: The green lights on the machine's lower panel may be indicators for the belt drive status.

A. The facts prove the conclusion.
B. The facts disprove the conclusion.
C. The facts neither prove nor disprove the conclusion.

7. FACTS: At a small, one-room country school, there are eight students: Amy, Ben, Carla, Dan, Elliot, Francine, Greg, and Hannah. Each student is in either the 6th, 7th, or 8th grade. Either two or three students are in each grade. Amy, Dan, and Francine are all in different grades. Ben and Elliot are both in the 7th grade. Hannah and Carl are in the same grade. 7.___

CONCLUSION: Exactly three students are in the 7th grade.

A. The facts prove the conclusion.
B. The facts disprove the conclusion.
C. The facts neither prove nor disprove the conclusion.

8. FACTS: Two married couples are having lunch together. Two of the four people are German and two are Russian, but in each couple the nationality of a spouse is not necessarily the same as the other's. One person in the group is a teacher, the other a lawyer, one an engineer, and the other a writer. The teacher is a Russian man. The writer is Russian, and her husband is an engineer. One of the people, Mr. Stern, is German. 8.___

CONCLUSION: Mr. Stern's wife is a writer.

A. The facts prove the conclusion.
B. The facts disprove the conclusion.
C. The facts neither prove nor disprove the conclusion.

9. FACTS: The flume ride at the county fair is open only to children who are at least 36 inches tall. Lisa is 30 inches tall. John is shorter than Henry, but more than 10 inches taller than Lisa. 9.____

CONCLUSION: Lisa is the only one who can't ride the flume ride.

A. The facts prove the conclusion.
B. The facts disprove the conclusion.
C. The facts neither prove nor disprove the conclusion.

Questions 10-17.

DIRECTIONS: Questions 10-17 are based on the following reading passage. It is not your knowledge of the particular topic that is being tested, but your ability to reason based on what you have read. The passage is likely to detail several proposed courses of action and factors affecting these proposals. The reading passage is followed by a conclusion or outcome based on the facts in the passage, or a description of a decision taken regarding the situation. The conclusion is followed by a number of statements that have a possible connection to the conclusion. For each statement, you are to determine whether:

A. The statement proves the conclusion.
B. The statement supports the conclusion but does not prove it.
C. The statement disproves the conclusion.
D. The statement weakens the conclusion but does not disprove it.
E. The statement has no relevance to the conclusion.

Remember that the conclusion after the passage is to be accepted as the outcome of what actually happened, and that you are being asked to evaluate the impact each statement would have had on the conclusion.

PASSAGE:

The Grand Army of Foreign Wars, a national veteran's organization, is struggling to maintain its National Home, where the widowed spouses and orphans of deceased members are housed together in a small village-like community. The Home is open to spouses and children who are bereaved for any reason, regardless of whether the member's death was related to military service, but a new global conflict has led to a dramatic surge in the number of members' deaths: many veterans who re-enlisted for the conflict have been killed in action.

The Grand Army of Foreign Wars is considering several options for handling the increased number of applications for housing at the National Home, which has been traditionally supported by membership dues. At its national convention, it will choose only one of the following:

The first idea is a one-time $50 tax on all members, above and beyond the dues they pay already. Since the organization has more than a million members, this tax should be sufficient for the construction and maintenance of new housing for applicants on the existing grounds of the National Home. The idea is opposed, however, by some older members who live on fixed incomes. These members object in principle to the taxation of Grand Army members. The Grand Army has never imposed a tax on its members.

The second idea is to launch a national fund-raising drive and public relations campaign that will attract donations for the National Home. Several national celebrities are members of the organization, and other celebrities could be attracted to the cause. Many Grand Army members are wary of this approach, however: in the past, the net receipts of some fund-raising efforts have been relatively insignificant, given the costs of staging them.

A third approach, suggested by many of the younger members, is to have new applicants share some of the costs of construction and maintenance. The spouses and children would pay an up-front "enrollment" fee, based on a sliding scale proportionate to their income and assets, and then a monthly fee adjusted similarly to contribute to maintenance costs. Many older members are strongly opposed to this idea, as it is in direct contradiction to the principles on which the organization was founded more than a century ago.

The fourth option is simply to maintain the status quo, focus the organization's efforts on supporting the families who already live at the National Home, and wait to accept new applicants based on attrition.

CONCLUSION: At its annual national convention, the Grand Army of Foreign Wars votes to impose a one-time tax of $10 on each member for the purpose of expanding and supporting the National Home to welcome a larger number of applicants. The tax is considered to be the solution most likely to produce the funds needed to accommodate the growing number of applicants.

10. Actuarial studies have shown that because the Grand Army's membership consists mostly of older veterans from earlier wars, the organization's membership will suffer a precipitous decline in numbers in about five years. 10.___

A.
B.
C.
D.
E.

11. After passage of the funding measure, a splinter group of older members appeals for the "sliding scale" provision to be applied to the tax, so that some members may be allowed to contribute less based on their income. 11.___

A.
B.
C.
D.
E.

12. The original charter of the Grand Army of Foreign Wars specifically states that the organization will not levy any taxes or duties on its members beyond its modest annual dues. It takes a super-majority of attending delegates at the national convention to make alterations to the charter. 12.____

A.
B.
C.
D.
E.

13. Six months before Grand Army of Foreign Wars'national convention, the Internal Revenue Service rules that because it is an organization that engages in political lobbying, the Grand Army must no longer enjoy its own federal tax-exempt status. 13.____

A.
B.
C.
D.
E.

14. Two months before the national convention, Dirk Rockwell, arguably the country's most famous film actor, announces in a nationally televised interview that he has been saddened to learn of the plight of the National Home, and that he is going to make it his own personal crusade to see that it is able to house and support a greater number of widowed spouses and orphans in the future. 14.____

A.
B.
C.
D.
E.

15. The Grand Army's final estimate is that the cost of expanding the National Home to accommodate the increased number of applicants will be about $61 million. 15.____

A.
B.
C.
D.
E.

16. Just before the national convention, the federal Department of Veterans Affairs announces steep cuts in the benefits package that is currently offered to the widowed spouses and orphans of veterans. 16.____

A.
B.
C.
D.

17. After the national convention, the Grand Army of Foreign Wars begins charging a modest "start-up" fee to all families who apply for residence at the national home. 17.___

A.
B.
C.
D.
E.

Questions 18-25.

DIRECTIONS: Questions 18-25 each provide four factual statements and a conclusion based on these statements. After reading the entire question, you will decide whether:
A. The conclusion is proved by statements 1-4;
B. The conclusion is disproved by statements 1-4; or
C. The facts are not sufficient to prove or disprove the conclusion.

18. FACTUAL STATEMENTS: 18.___

1. In the Field Day high jump competition, Martha jumped higher than Frank.
2. Carl jumped higher than Ignacio.
3. I gnacio jumped higher than Frank.
4. Dan jumped higher than Carl.

CONCLUSION: Frank finished last in the high jump competition.

A. The conclusion is proved by statements 1-4.
B. The conclusion is disproved by statements 1-4.
C. The facts are not sufficient to prove or disprove the conclusion.

19. FACTUAL STATEMENTS: 19.___

1. The door to the hammer mill chamber is locked if light 6 is red.
2. The door to the hammer mill chamber is locked only when the mill is operating.
3. If the mill is not operating, light 6 is blue.
4. Light 6 is blue.

CONCLUSION: The door to the hammer mill chamber is locked.

A. The conclusion is proved by statements 1-4.
B. The conclusion is disproved by statements 1-4.
C. The facts are not sufficient to prove or disprove the conclusion.

20. FACTUAL STATEMENTS: 20.____

1. Ziegfried, the lion tamer at the circus, has demanded ten additional minutes of performance time during each show.
2. If Ziegfried is allowed his ten additional minutes per show, he will attempt to teach Kimba the tiger to shoot a basketball.
3. If Kimba learns how to shoot a basketball, then Ziegfried was not given his ten additional minutes.
4. Ziegfried was given his ten additional minutes.

CONCLUSION: Despite Ziegfried's efforts, Kimba did not learn how to shoot a basketball.

A. The conclusion is proved by statements 1-4.
B. The conclusion is disproved by statements 1-4.
C. The facts are not sufficient to prove or disprove the conclusion.

21. FACTUAL STATEMENTS: 21.____

1. If Stan goes to counseling, Sara won't divorce him.
2. If Sara divorces Stan, she'll move back to Texas.
3. If Sara doesn't divorce Stan, Irene will be disappointed.
4. Stan goes to counseling.

CONCLUSION: Irene will be disappointed.

A. The conclusion is proved by statements 1-4.
B. The conclusion is disproved by statements 1-4.
C. The facts are not sufficient to prove or disprove the conclusion.

22. FACTUAL STATEMENTS: 22.____

1. If Delia is promoted to district manager, Claudia will have to be promoted to team leader.
2. Delia will be promoted to district manager unless she misses her fourth-quarter sales quota.
3. If Claudia is promoted to team leader, Thomas will be promoted to assistant team leader.
4. Delia meets her fourth-quarter sales quota.

CONCLUSION: Thomas is promoted to assistant team leader.

A. The conclusion is proved by statements 1-4.
B. The conclusion is disproved by statements 1-4.
C. The facts are not sufficient to prove or disprove the conclusion.

23. FACTUAL STATEMENTS: 23.___

1. Clone D is identical to Clone B.
2. Clone B is not identical to Clone A.
3. Clone D is not identical to Clone C.
4. Clone E is not identical to the clones that are identical to Clone B.

CONCLUSION: Clone E is identical to Clone D.

A. The conclusion is proved by statements 1-4.
B. The conclusion is disproved by statements 1-4.
C. The facts are not sufficient to prove or disprove the conclusion.

24. FACTUAL STATEMENTS: 24.___

1. In the Stafford Tower, each floor is occupied by a single business.
2. Big G Staffing is on a floor between CyberGraphics and MainEvent.
3. Gasco is on the floor directly below CyberGraphics and three floors above Treehorn Audio.
4. MainEvent is five floors below EZ Tax and four floors below Treehorn Audio.

CONCLUSION: EZ Tax is on a floor between Gasco and MainEvent.

A. The conclusion is proved by statements 1-4.
B. The conclusion is disproved by statements 1-4.
C. The facts are not sufficient to prove or disprove the conclusion.

25. FACTUAL STATEMENTS: 25.___

1. Only county roads lead to Nicodemus.
2. All the roads from Hill City to Graham County are federal highways.
3. Some of the roads from Plainville lead to Nicodemus.
4. Some of the roads running from Hill City lead to Strong City.

CONCLUSION: Some of the roads from Plainville are county roads.

A. The conclusion is proved by statements 1-4.
B. The conclusion is disproved by statements 1-4.
C. The facts are not sufficient to prove or disprove the conclusion.

KEY (CORRECT ANSWERS)

1. A
2. A
3. A
4. C
5. A

6. B
7. A
8. A
9. A
10. E

11. A
12. D
13. E
14. D
15. B

16. B
17. C
18. A
19. B
20. A

21. A
22. A
23. B
24. A
25. A

TEST 2

DIRECTIONS: Each question or incomplete statement is followed by several suggested answers or completions. Select the one that BEST answers the question or completes the statement. *PRINT THE LETTER OF THE CORRECT ANSWER IN THE SPACE AT THE RIGHT.*

Questions 1-9.

DIRECTIONS: In questions 1-9, you will read a set of facts and a conclusion drawn from them. The conclusion may be valid or invalid, based on the facts-it's your task to determine the validity of the conclusion.

For each question, select the letter before the statement that BEST expresses the relationship between the given facts and the conclusion that has been drawn from them. Your choices are:

A. The facts prove the conclusion
B. The facts disprove the conclusion; or
C. The facts neither prove nor disprove the conclusion.

1. FACTS: Some employees in the testing department are statisticians. Most of the statisticians who work in the testing department are projection specialists. Tom Wilks works in the testing department. 1.____

   CONCLUSION: Tom Wilks is a statistician.

   A. The facts prove the conclusion.
   B. The facts disprove the conclusion.
   C. The facts neither prove nor disprove the conclusion.

2. FACTS: Ten coins are split among Hank, Lawrence, and Gail. If Lawrence gives his coins to Hank, then Hank will have more coins than Gail. If Gail gives her coins to Lawrence, then Lawrence will have more coins than Hank. 2.____

   CONCLUSION: Hank has six coins.

   A. The facts prove the conclusion.
   B. The facts disprove the conclusion.
   C. The facts neither prove nor disprove the conclusion.

3. FACTS: Nobody loves everybody. Janet loves Ken. Ken loves everybody who loves Janet. 3.____

   CONCLUSION: Everybody loves Janet.

   A. The facts prove the conclusion.
   B. The facts disprove the conclusion.
   C. The facts neither prove nor disprove the conclusion.

4. FACTS: Most of the Torres family lives in East Los Angeles. Many people in East Los Angeles celebrate Cinco de Mayo. Joe is a member of the Torres family. 4._____

CONCLUSION: Joe lives in East Los Angeles.

A. The facts prove the conclusion.
B. The facts disprove the conclusion.
C. The facts neither prove nor disprove the conclusion.

5. FACTS: Five professionals each occupy one story of a five-story office building. Dr. Kane's office is above Dr. Assad's. Dr. Johnson's office is between Dr. Kane's and Dr. Conlon's. Dr. Steen's office is between Dr. Conlon's and Dr. Assad's. Dr. Johnson is on the fourth story. 5._____

CONCLUSION: Dr. Kane occupies the top story.

A. The facts prove the conclusion.
B. The facts disprove the conclusion.
C. The facts neither prove nor disprove the conclusion.

6. FACTS: To be eligible for membership in the Yukon Society, a person must be able to either tunnel through a snowbank while wearing only a T-shirt and shorts, or hold his breath for two minutes under water that is 50° F. Ray can only hold his breath for a minute and a half. 6._____

CONCLUSION: Ray can still become a member of the Yukon Society by tunneling through a snowbank while wearing a T-shirt and shorts.

A. The facts prove the conclusion.
B. The facts disprove the conclusion.
C. The facts neither prove nor disprove the conclusion.

7. FACTS: A mark is worth five plunks. You can exchange four sharps for a tinplot. It takes eight marks to buy a sharp. 7._____

CONCLUSION: A sharp is the most valuable.

A. The facts prove the conclusion.
B. The facts disprove the conclusion.
C. The facts neither prove nor disprove the conclusion.

8. FACTS: There are gibbons, as well as lemurs, who like to play in the trees at the monkey house. All those who like to play in the trees at the monkey house are fed lettuce and bananas. 8._____

CONCLUSION: Lemurs and gibbons are types of monkeys.

A. The facts prove the conclusion.
B. The facts disprove the conclusion.
C. The facts neither prove nor disprove the conclusion.

9. FACTS: None of the Blackfoot tribes is a Salishan Indian tribe. Sal-ishan Indians came from the northern Pacific Coast. All Salishan Indians live east of the Continental Divide. 9.___

CONCLUSION: No Blackfoot tribes live east of the Continental Divide.

A. The facts prove the conclusion.
B. The facts disprove the conclusion.
C. The facts neither prove nor disprove the conclusion.

Questions 10-17.

DIRECTIONS: Questions 10-17 are based on the following reading passage. It is not your knowledge of the particular topic that is being tested, but your ability to reason based on what you have read. The passage is likely to detail several proposed courses of action and factors affecting these proposals. The reading passage is followed by a conclusion or outcome based on the facts in the passage, or a description of a decision taken regarding the situation. The conclusion is followed by a number of statements that have a possible connection to the conclusion. For each statement, you are to determine whether:

A. The statement proves the conclusion.
B. The statement supports the conclusion but does not prove it.
C. The statement disproves the conclusion.
D. The statement weakens the conclusion but does not disprove it.
E. The statement has no relevance to the conclusion.

Remember that the conclusion after the passage is to be accepted as the outcome of what actually happened, and that you are being asked to evaluate the impact each statement would have had on the conclusion.

PASSAGE:

On August 12, Beverly Willey reported that she was in the elevator late on the previous evening after leaving her office on the 16th floor of a large office building. In her report, she states that a man got on the elevator at the 11th floor, pulled her off the elevator, assaulted her, and stole her purse. Ms. Willey reported that she had seen the man in the elevators and hallways of the building before. She believes that the man works in the building. Her description of him is as follows: he is tall, unshaven, with wavy brown hair and a scar on his left cheek. He walks with a pronounced limp, often dragging his left foot behind his right.

CONCLUSION: After Beverly Willey makes her report, the police arrest a 43-year-man, Barton Black, and charge him with her assault.

10. Barton Black is a former Marine who served in Vietnam, where he sustained shrapnel wounds to the left side of his face and suffered nerve damage in his left leg. 10.___

A.
B.
C.
D.
E.

11. When they arrived at his residence to question him, detectives were greeted at the door by Barton Black, who was tall and clean-shaven. 11.____

A.
B.
C.
D.
E.

12. Barton Black was booked into the county jail several days after Beverly Willey's assault. 12.____

A.
B.
C.
D.
E.

13. Upon further investigation, detectives discover that Beverly Willey does not work at the office building. 13.____

A.
B.
C.
D.
E.

14. Upon further investigation, detectives discover that Barton Black does not work at the office building. 14.____

A.
B.
C.
D.
E.

15. In the spring of the following year, Barton Black is convicted of assaulting Beverly Willey on August 11. 15.____

A.
B.
C.
D.
E.

16. During their investigation of the assault, detectives determine that Beverly Willey was assaulted on the 12th floor of the office building. 16.____

A.
B.
C.
D.
E.

17. The day after Beverly Willey's assault, Barton Black fled the area and was never seen again. 17.___

A.
B.
C.
D.
E.

Questions 18-25.

DIRECTIONS: Questions 18-25 each provide four factual statements and a conclusion based on these statements. After reading the entire question, you will decide whether:

A. The conclusion is proved by statements 1-4;
B. The conclusion is disproved by statements 1-4; or
C. The facts are not sufficient to prove or disprove the conclusion.

18. FACTUAL STATEMENTS: 18.___

1. Among five spice jars on the shelf, the sage is to the right of the parsley.
2. The pepper is to the left of the basil.
3. The nutmeg is between the sage and the pepper.
4. The pepper is the second spice from the left.

CONCLUSION: The sage is the farthest to the right.

A. The conclusion is proved by statements 1-4.
B. The conclusion is disproved by statements 1-4.
C. The facts are not sufficient to prove or disprove the conclusion.

19. FACTUAL STATEMENTS: 19.___

1. Gear X rotates in a clockwise direction if Switch C is in the OFF position
2. Gear X will rotate in a counter-clockwise direction if Switch C is ON.
3. If Gear X is rotating in a clockwise direction, then Gear Y will not be rotating at all.
4. Switch C is ON.

CONCLUSION: Gear X is rotating in a counter-clockwise direction.

A. The conclusion is proved by statements 1-4.
B. The conclusion is disproved by statements 1-4.
C. The facts are not sufficient to prove or disprove the conclusion.

20. FACTUAL STATEMENTS: 20.____
1. Lane will leave for the Toronto meeting today only if Terence, Rourke, and Jackson all file their marketing reports by the end of the work day.
2. Rourke will file her report on time only if Ganz submits last quarter's data.
3. If Terence attends the security meeting, he will attend it with Jackson, and they will not file their marketing reports by the end of the work day.
4. Ganz submits last quarter's data to Rourke.

CONCLUSION: Lane will leave for the Toronto meeting today.

A. The conclusion is proved by statements 1-4.
B. The conclusion is disproved by statements 1-4.
C. The facts are not sufficient to prove or disprove the conclusion.

21. FACTUAL STATEMENTS: 21.____

1. Bob is in second place in the Boston Marathon.
2. Gregory is winning the Boston Marathon.
3. There are four miles to go in the race, and Bob is gaining on Gregory at the rate of 100 yards every minute.
4. There are 1760 yards in a mile, and Gregory's usual pace during the Boston Marathon is one mile every six minutes.

CONCLUSION: Bob wins the Boston Marathon.

A. The conclusion is proved by statements 1-4.
B. The conclusion is disproved by statements 1-4.
C. The facts are not sufficient to prove or disprove the conclusion.

22. FACTUAL STATEMENTS: 22.____

1. Four brothers are named Earl, John, Gary, and Pete.
2. Earl and Pete are unmarried.
3. John is shorter than the youngest of the four.
4. The oldest brother is married, and is also the tallest.

CONCLUSION: Gary is the oldest brother.

A. The conclusion is proved by statements 1-4.
B. The conclusion is disproved by statements 1-4.
C. The facts are not sufficient to prove or disprove the conclusion.

23. FACTUAL STATEMENTS: 23.____

1. Brigade X is ten miles from the demilitarized zone.
2. If General Woundwort gives the order, Brigade X will advance to the demilitarized zone, but not quickly enough to reach the zone before the conflict begins.
3. Brigade Y, five miles behind Brigade X, will not advance unless General Woundwort gives the order.
4. Brigade Y advances.

CONCLUSION: Brigade X reaches the demilitarized zone before the conflict begins.

A. The conclusion is proved by statements 1-4.
B. The conclusion is disproved by statements 1-4.
C. The facts are not sufficient to prove or disprove the conclusion.

24. FACTUAL STATEMENTS: 24.___

1. Jerry has decided to take a cab from Fullerton to Elverton.
2. Chubby Cab charges $5 plus $3 a mile.
3. Orange Cab charges $7.50 but gives free mileage for the first 5 miles.
4. After the first 5 miles, Orange Cab charges $2.50 a mile.

CONCLUSION: Orange Cab is the cheaper fare from Fullerton to Elverton.

A. The conclusion is proved by statements 1-4.
B. The conclusion is disproved by statements 1-4.
C. The facts are not sufficient to prove or disprove the conclusion.

25. FACTUAL STATEMENTS: 25.___

1. Dan is never in class when his friend Lucy is absent.
2. Lucy is never absent unless her mother is sick.
3. If Lucy is in class, Sergio is in class also
4. Sergio is never in class when Dalton is absent.

CONCLUSION: If Lucy is absent, Dalton may be in class.

A. The conclusion is proved by statements 1-4.
B. The conclusion is disproved by statements 1-4.
C. The facts are not sufficient to prove or disprove the conclusion.

KEY (CORRECT ANSWERS)

1. C
2. B
3. B
4. C
5. C

6. A
7. B
8. C
9. C
10. B

11. E
12. B
13. D
14. E
15. A

16. E
17. C
18. C
19. A
20. C

21. C
22. A
23. B
24. C
25. B

LOGICAL REASONING
EVALUATING CONCLUSIONS IN LIGHT OF KNOWN FACTS

EXAMINATION SECTION
TEST 1

COMMENTARY

This section is designed to provide practice questions in evaluating conclusions when you are given specific data to work with.

We suggest you do the questions three at a time, consulting the answer key and then the solution section for any questions you may have missed. It's a good idea to try the questions again a week before the exam.

In the validity of conclusion type of question, you are first given a reading passage which describes a particular situation. The passage may be on any topic, as it is not your knowledge of the topic that is being tested, but your reasoning abilities. The passage is likely to detail several proposed courses of action and factors affecting these proposals. The reading passage is followed by a conclusion based on the facts in the passage, or a description of a decision taken regarding the situation. The conclusion is followed by a number of statements which have a possible connection to the conclusion. For each statement, you are to determine whether:

A. The statement proves the conclusion.
B. The statement supports the conclusion but does not prove it.
C. The statement disproves the conclusion.
D. The statement weakens the conclusion but does not disprove it.
E. The statement has no relevance to the conclusion.

Remember that the conclusion after the passage is to be accepted as the outcome of what actually happened, and that you are being asked to evaluate the impact each statement would have had on the conclusion.
Questions 1-8 are based on the following paragraph.

In May of 1993, Mr. Bryan inherited a clothing store on Main Street in a small New England town. The store has specialized in selling quality men's and women's clothing since 1885. Business has been stable throughout the years, neither increasing nor decreasing. He has an opportunity to buy two adjacent stores which would enable him to add a wider range and style of clothing. In order to do this, he would have to borrow a substantial amount of money. He also risks losing the goodwill of his present clientele.

CONCLUSION: On November 7, 1993, Mr. Bryan tells the owner of the two adjacent stores that he has decided not to purchase them. He feels that it would be best to simply maintain his present marketing position, as there would not be enough new business to support an expansion.

A. The statement proves the conclusion.
B. The statement supports the conclusion but does not prove it.
C. The statement disproves the conclusion.
D. The statement weakens the conclusion.
E. The statement is irrelevant to the conclusion.

1. A large new branch of the county's community college holds its first classes in September of 1993. 1.__

2. The town's largest factory shuts down with no indication that it will reopen. 2.__

3. The 1990 United States Census showed that the number of children per household dropped from 2.4 to 2.1 since the 1980 census. 3.__

4. Mr. Bryan's brother tells him of a new clothing boutique specializing in casual women's clothing which is opening soon. 4.__

5. Mr. Bryan's sister buys her baby several items for Christmas at Mr. Bryan's store. 5.__

6. Mrs. McIntyre, the President of the Town Council, brings Mr. Bryan a home-baked pumpkin pie in honor of his store's 100th anniversary. They discuss the changes that have taken place in the town, and she comments on how his store has maintained the same look and feel over the years. 6.__

7. In October of 1993, Mr. Bryan's aunt lends him $50,000. 7.__

8. The Town Council has just announced that the town is eligible for funding from a federal project designed to encourage the location of new businesses in the central districts of cities and towns. 8.__

Questions 9-18 are based on the following paragraph.

A proposal has been put before the legislative body of a small European country to require air bags in all automobiles manufactured for domestic use in that country after 1999. The air bag, made of nylon or plastic, is designed to inflate automatically within a car at the impact of a collision, thus protecting front-seat occupants from being thrown forward. There has been much support of the measure from consumer groups, the insurance industry, key legislators, and the general public. The country's automobile manufacturers, who contend the new crash equipment would add up to $1,000 to car prices and provide no more protection than existing seat belts, are against the proposed legislation.

CONCLUSION: On April 21, 1994, the legislature passed legislation requiring air bags in all automobiles manufactured for domestic use in that country after 1999.

A. The statement proves the conclusion.
B. The statement supports the conclusion but does not prove it.
C. The statement disproves the conclusion.
D. The statement weakens the conclusion.
E. The statement is irrelevant to the conclusion.

9. A study has shown that 59% of car occupants do not use seat belts. 9.__

10. The country's Department of Transportation has estimated that the crash protection equipment would save up to 5,900 lives each year. 10.__

11. On April 27, 1993, Augusta Raneoni was named head of an advisory committee to gather and analyze data on the costs, benefits, and feasibility of the proposed legislation on air bags in automobiles. 11.__

12. Consumer groups and the insurance industry accuse the legislature of rejecting passage of the regulation for political reasons. 12.____

13. A study by the Committee on Imports and Exports projected that the sales of imported cars would rise dramatically in 1999 because imported cars do not have to include air bags, and can be sold more cheaply. 13.____

14. Research has shown that air bags, if produced on a large scale, would cost about $200 apiece, and would provide more reliable protection than any other type of seat belt. 14.____

15. Auto sales in 1991 have increased 3% over the previous year. 15.____

16. A Department of Transportation report in July of 2000 credits a drop in automobile deaths of 4,100 to the use of air bags. 16.____

17. In June of 1994, the lobbyist of the largest insurance company receives a bonus for her work on the passage of the air bag legislation. 17.____

18. In 2000, the stock in crash protection equipment has risen three-fold over the previous year. 18.____

Questions 19-25 are based on the following paragraph.

On a national television talk show, Joan Rivera, a famous comedienne, has recently insulted the physical appearances of a famous actress and the dead wife of an ex-President. There has been a flurry of controversy over her comments, and much discussion of the incident has appeared in the press. Most of the comments have been negative. It appears that this time she might have gone too far. There have been cancellations of two of her five scheduled performances in the two weeks since the show was televised, and Joan's been receiving a lot of negative mail. Because of the controversy, she has an interview with a national news magazine at the end of the week, and her press agent is strongly urging her to apologize publicly. She feels strongly that her comments were no worse than any other she has ever made, and that the whole incident will *blow over* soon. She respects her press agent's judgment, however, as his assessment of public sentiment tends to be very accurate.

CONCLUSION: Joan does not apologize publicly, and during the interview she challenges the actress to a weight-losing contest. For every pound the actress loses, Joan says she will donate $1 to the Cellulite Prevention League.

A. The statement proves the conclusion.
B. The statement supports the conclusion but does not prove it.
C. The statement disproves the conclusion.
D. The statement weakens the conclusion.
E. The statement is irrelevant to the conclusion.

19. Joan's mother, who she is very fond of, is very upset about Joan's comments. 19.____

20. Six months after the interview, Joan's income has doubled. 20.____

21. Joan's agent is pleased with the way Joan handles the interview. 21._

22. Joan's sister has been appointed Treasurer of the Cellulite Prevention League. In her report, she states that Joan's $12 contribution is the only amount that has been donated to the League in its first six months. 22._

23. The magazine receives many letters commending Joan for the courage it took for her to apologize publicly in the interview. 23._

24. Immediately after the interview appears, another one of Joan's performances is cancelled. 24._

25. Due to a printers strike, the article was not published until the following week. 25._

Questions 26-30 are based on the following paragraph.

The law-making body of Country X must decide what to do about the issue of videotaping television shows for home use. There is currently no law against taping shows directly from the TV as long as the videotapes are not used for commercial purposes. The increasing popularity of pay TV and satellite systems, combined with the increasing number of homes that own video-cassette recorders, has caused a great deal of concern in some segments of the entertainment industry. Companies that own the rights to films, popular television shows, and sporting events feel that their copyright privileges are being violated, and they are seeking compensation or the banning of TV home videotaping. Legislation has been introduced to make it illegal to videotape television programs for home use. Separate proposed legislation is also pending that would continue to allow videotaping of TV shows for home use, but would place a tax of 10% on each videocassette that is purchased for home use. The income from that tax would then be proportionately distributed as royalties to those owning the rights to programs being aired. A weighted point system coupled with the averaging of several national viewing rating systems would be used to determine the royalties. There is a great deal of lobbying being done for both bills, as the manufacturers of videocassette recorders and videocassettes are against the passage of the bills.

CONCLUSION: The legislature of Country X rejects both bills by a wide margin.

A. The statement proves the conclusion.
B. The statement supports the conclusion but does not prove it.
C. The statement disproves the conclusion.
D. The statement weakens the conclusion.
E. The statement is irrelevant to the conclusion.

26. Country X's Department of Taxation hires 500 new employees to handle the increased paperwork created by the new tax on videocassettes. 26._

27. A study conducted by the country's most prestigious accounting firm shows that the cost of implementing the proposed new videocassette tax would be greater than the income expected from it. 27._

28. It is estimated that 80% of all those working in the entertainment industry, excluding performers, own video-cassette recorders. 28.____

29. The head of Country X's law enforcement agency states that legislation banning the home taping of TV shows would be unenforceable. 29.____

30. Financial experts predict that unless a tax is placed on videocassettes, several large companies in the entertainment industry will have to file for bankruptcy. 30.____

Questions 31-38.

DIRECTIONS: The following questions 31 through 38 are variations on the type of question you just had. It is important that you read the question very carefully to determine exactly what is required.

31. In this question, select the choice that is most relevant to the conclusion. 31.____

1. The Buffalo Bills football team is in second place in its division.
2. The New England Patriots are in first place in the same division.
3. There are two games left to play in the season, and the Bills will not play the Patriots again.
4. The New England Patriots won ten games and lost four games, and the Buffalo Bills have won eight games and lost six games.

CONCLUSION: The Buffalo Bills win their division.

A. The conclusion is proved by sentences 1-4.
B. The conclusion is disproved by sentences 1-4.
C. The facts are not sufficient to prove or disprove the conclusion.

32. In this question, select the choice that is most relevant to the conclusion. 32.____

1. On the planet of Zeinon there are only two different eye colors and only two different hair colors.
2. Half of those beings with purple hair have golden eyes.
3. There are more inhabitants with purple hair than there are inhabitants with silver hair.
4. One-third of those with silver hair have green eyes.

CONCLUSION: There are more golden-eyed beings on Zeinon than green-eyed ones.

A. The conclusion is proved by sentences 1-4.
B. The conclusion is disproved by sentences 1-4.
C. The facts are not sufficient to prove or disprove the conclusion.

33. In this question, select the choice that is most relevant to the conclusion. 33.____
John and Kevin are leaving Amaranth to go to school in Bethany. They've decided to rent a small truck to move their possessions. Joe's Truck Rental charges $100 plus 30¢ a mile. National Movers charges $50 more but gives free mileage for the first 100 miles. After the first 100 miles, they charge 25¢ a mile.

CONCLUSION: John and Kevin rent their truck from National Movers because it is cheaper.

A. The conclusion is proved by the facts in the above paragraph.
B. The conclusion is disproved by the facts in the above paragraph.
C. The facts are not sufficient to prove or disprove the conclusion.

34. For this question, select the choice that supports the information given in the passage. 34.___

Municipalities in Country X are divided into villages, towns, and cities. A village has a population of 5,000 or less. The population of a town ranges from 5,001 to 15,000. In order to be incorporated as a city, the municipality must have a population over 15,000. If, after a village becomes a town, or a town becomes a city, the population drops below the minimum required (for example, the population of a city goes below 15,000), and stays below the minimum for more than ten years, it loses its current status, and drops to the next category. As soon as a municipality rises in population to the next category (village to town, for example), however, it is immediately reclassified to the next category.

In the 1970 census, Plainfield had a population of 12,000. Between 1970 and 1980, Plainfield grew 10%, and between 1980 and 1990 Plainfield grew another 20%. The population of Springdale doubled from 1970 to 1980, and increased 25% from 1980 to 1990. The city of Smallville's population, 20,283, has not changed significantly in the last twenty years. Granton had a population of 25,000 people in 1960, and has decreased 25% in each ten year period since then. Ellenville had a population of 4,283 in 1960, and grew 5% in each ten year period since 1960.

In 1990,

A. Plainfield, Smallville, and Granton are cities
B. Smallville is a city, Granton is a town, and Ellenville is a village
C. Springdale, Granton, and Ellenville are towns
D. Plainfield and Smallville are cities, and Ellenville is a town

35. For this question, select the choice that is most relevant to the conclusion. 35.___

A study was done for a major food distributing firm to determine if there is any difference in the kind of caffeine containing products used by people of different ages. A sample of one thousand people between the ages of twenty and fifty were drawn from selected areas in the country. They were divided equally into three groups.

Those individuals who were 20-29 were designated Group A, those 30-39 were Group B, and those 40-50 were placed in Group C.

It was found that on the average, Group A drank 1.8 cups of coffee, Group B 3.1, and Group C 2.5 cups of coffee daily. Group A drank 2.1 cups of tea, Group B drank 1.2, and Group C drank 2.6 cups of tea daily. Group A drank 3.1 8-ounce glasses of cola, Group B drank 1.9, and Group C drank 1.5 glasses of cola daily.

CONCLUSION: According to the study, the average person in the 20-29 age group drinks less tea daily than the average person in the 40-50 age group, but drinks more coffee daily than the average person in the 30-39 age group drinks cola.

A. The conclusion is proved by the facts in the above paragraph.
B. The conclusion is disproved by the facts in the above paragraph.
C. The facts are not sufficient to prove or disprove the conclusion.

36. For this question, select the choice that is most relevant to the conclusion. 36.____

1. Mary is taller than Jane but shorter than Dale.
2. Fred is taller than Mary but shorter than Steven.
3. Dale is shorter than Steven but taller than Elizabeth.
4. Elizabeth is taller than Mary but not as tall as Fred.

CONCLUSION: Dale is taller than Fred.

A. The conclusion is proved by sentences 1-4.
B. The conclusion is disproved by sentences 1-4.
C. The facts are not sufficient to prove or disprove the conclusion.

37. For this question, select the choice that is most relevant to the conclusion. 37.____

1. Main Street is between Spring Street and Glenn Blvd.
2. Hawley Avenue is one block south of Spring Street and three blocks north of Main Street.
3. Glenn Street is five blocks south of Elm and four blocks south of Main.
4. All the streets mentioned are parallel to one another.

CONCLUSION: Elm Street is between Hawley Avenue and Glenn Blvd.

A. The conclusion is proved by the facts in sentences 1-4.
B. The conclusion is disproved by the facts in sentences 1-4.
C. The facts are not sufficient to prove or disprove the conclusion.

38. For this question, select the choice that is most relevant to the conclusion. 38.____

1. Train A leaves the town of Hampshire every day at 5:50 A.M. and arrives in New London at 6:42 A.M.
2. Train A leaves New London at 7:00 A.M. and arrives in Kellogsville at 8:42 A.M.
3. Train B leaves Kellogsville at 8:00 A.M. and arrives in Hampshire at 10:42 A.M.
4. Due to the need for repairs, there is just one railroad track between New London and Hampshire.

CONCLUSION: It is impossible for Train A and Train B to follow these schedules without colliding.

A. The conclusion is proved by the facts in the above paragraph.
B. The conclusion is disproved by the facts in the above passage.
C. The facts are not sufficient to prove or disprove the conclusion.

KEY (CORRECT ANSWERS)

1.	D	11.	C	21.	D	31.	C
2.	B	12.	C	22.	A	32.	A
3.	E	13.	D	23.	C	33.	C
4.	B	14.	B	24.	B	34.	B
5.	C	15.	E	25.	E	35.	B
6.	D	16.	B	26.	C	36.	C
7.	B	17.	A	27.	B	37.	A
8.	A	18.	B	28.	E	38.	B
9.	B	19.	D	29.	B		
10.	B	20.	E	30.	D		

SOLUTIONS TO QUESTIONS

1. The answer is D. This statement weakens the conclusion, but does not disprove it. If a new branch of the community college opened in September, it could possibly bring in new business for Mr. Bryant. Since it states in the conclusion that Mr. Bryant felt there would not be enough new business to support the additional stores, this would tend to disprove the conclusion. Choice C would not be correct because it's possible that he felt that the students would not have enough additional money to support his new venture, or would not be interested in his clothing styles. It's also possible that the majority of the students already live in the area, so that they wouldn't really be a new customer population. This type of question is tricky, and can initially be very confusing, so don't feel badly if you missed it. Most people need to practice with a few of these types of questions before they feel comfortable recognizing exactly what they're being asked to do.

2. The answer is B. It supports the conclusion because the closing of the factory would probably take money and customers out of the town, causing Mr. Bryant to lose some of his present business. It doesn't prove the conclusion, however, because we don't know how large the factory was. It's possible that only a small percentage of the population was employed there, or that they found other jobs.

3. The answer is E. The fact that the number of children per household dropped slightly nationwide from 1970 to 1980 is irrelevant. Statistics showing a drop nationwide doesn't mean that there was a drop in the number of children per household in Mr. Bryant's hometown. This is a tricky question, as choice B, supporting the conclusion but not proving it, may seem reasonable. If the number of children per household declined nationwide, then it may not seem unreasonable to feel that this would support Mr. Bryant's decision not to expand his business. However, we're preparing you for promotional exams, not "real life." One of the difficult things about taking exams is that sometimes you're forced to make a choice between two statements that both seem like they could be the possible answer. What you need to do in that case is choose the <u>best</u> choice. Becoming annoyed or frustrated with the question won't really help much. If there's a review of the exam, you can certainly appeal the question. There have been many cases where, after an appeal, two possible choices have been allowed as correct answers. We've included this question, however, to help you see what to do should you get a question like this. It's most important not to get rattled, and to select the <u>best</u> choice. In this case, the connection between the statistical information and Mr. Bryant's decision is pretty remote. If the question had said that the number of children in Mr. Bryant's <u>town</u> had decreased, then choice B would have been a more reasonable choice. It could also help in this situation to visualize the situation. Picture Mr. Bryant in his armchair reading that, nationwide, the average number of children per household has declined slightly. How likely would this be to influence his decision, especially since he sells men's and women's clothing? It would take a while for this decline in population to show up, and we're not even sure if it applies to Mr. Bryant's hometown. Don't feel badly if you missed this, it was tricky. The more of these you do, the more comfortable you'll feel.

4. The answer is B. If a new clothing boutique specializing in casual women's clothing were to open soon, this would lend support to Mr. Bryant's decision not to expand, but would not prove that he had actually made the decision not to expand. A new women's clothing boutique would most likely be in competition with his existing business, thus making any possible expansion a riskier venture. We can't be sure from this, however, that he didn't go ahead and expand his business despite the increased competition. Choice A, proves the conclusion, would only be the answer if we could be absolutely sure from the statement that Mr. Bryant had actually not expanded his business.

5. The answer is C. This statement disproves the conclusion. In order for his sister to buy several items for her baby at Mr. Bryant's store, he would have to have changed his business to include children's clothing.

6. The answer is A. It definitely proves the conclusion. The passage states that Mr. Bryant's store had been in business since 1885. A pie baked in honor of his store's 100th anniversary would have to be presented sometime in 1985. The conclusion states that he made his decision not to expand on November 7, 1983. If, more than a year later Mrs. MacIntyre comments that his store has maintained the same look and feel over the years, it could not have been expanded, or otherwise significantly changed.

7. The answer is D. If Mr. Bryant's aunt lent him $50,000 in October, this would tend to weaken the conclusion, which took place in November. Because it was stated that Mr. Bryant would need to borrow money in order to expand his business, it would be logical to assume that if he borrowed money he had decided to expand his business, weakening the conclusion. The reason C, disproves the conclusion, is not the correct answer is because we can't be sure Mr. Bryant didn't borrow the money for another reason.

8. The answer is B. If Mr. Bryant's town is eligible for federal funds to encourage the location of new businesses in the central district, this would tend to support his decision not to expand his business. Funds to encourage new business would increase the likelihood of there being additional competition for Mr. Bryant's store to contend with. Since we can't say for sure that there would be direct competition from a new business, however, choice A would be incorrect. Note that this is also a tricky question. You might have thought that the new funds weakened the conclusion because it would mean that Mr. Bryant could easily get the money he needed. Mr. Bryant is expanding his present business, not creating a new business. Therefore he is not eligible for the funding.

9. The answer is B. This is a very tricky question. It's stated that 59% of car occupants don't use seat belts. The legislature is considering the use of air bags because of safety issues. The advantage of air bags over seat belts is that they inflate upon impact, and don't require car occupants to do anything with them ahead of time. Since the population has strongly resisted using seat belts, the air bags could become even more important in saving lives. Since saving lives is the purpose of the proposed legislation, the information that a small percentage of people use seat belts could be helpful to the passage of the legislation. We can't be sure that this is reason enough for the legislature to vote for the legislation, however, so choice A is incorrect.

10. The answer is B, as the information that 5,900 lives could be saved would tend to support the conclusion. Saving that many lives through the use of air bags could be a very persuasive reason to vote for the legislation. Since we don't know for sure that it's enough of a compelling reason for the legislature to vote for the legislation, however, choice A could not be the answer.

11. The answer is C, disproves the conclusion. If the legislation had been passed as stated in the conclusion, there would be no reason to appoint someone head of an advisory committee six days later to analyze the "feasibility of the proposed legislation." The key word here is "proposed." If it has been proposed, it means it hasn't been passed. This contradicts the conclusion and therefore disproves it.

12. The answer is C, disproves the conclusion. If the legislation had passed, there would be no reason for supporters of the legislation to accuse the legislature of rejecting the legislation for political reasons. This question may have seemed so obvious that you might have thought there was a trick to it. Exams usually have a few obvious questions, which will trip you up if you begin reading too much into them.

13. The answer is D, as this would tend to disprove the conclusion. A projected dramatic rise in imported cars could be very harmful to the country's economy and could be a very good reason for some legislators to vote against the proposed legislation. It would be assuming too much to choose C, however, because we don't know if they actually did vote against it.

14. The answer is B. This information would tend to support the passage of the legislation. The estimate of the cost of the air bags is $800 less than the cost estimated by opponents, and it's stated that the protection would be more reliable than any other type of seat belt. Both of these would be good arguments in favor of passing the legislation. Since we don't know for sure, however, how persuasive they actually were, choice A would not be the correct choice.

15. The answer is E, as this is irrelevant information. It really doesn't matter whether auto sales in 1981 have increased slightly over the previous year. If the air bag legislation were to go into effect in 1984, that might make the information somehow more relevant. But the air bag legislation would not take effect until 1989, so the information is irrelevant, since it tells us nothing about the state of the auto industry then.

16. The answer is B, supports the conclusion. This is a tricky question. While at first it might seem to prove the conclusion, we can't be sure that the air bag legislation is responsible for the drop in automobile deaths. It's possible air bags came into popular use without the legislation, or with different legislation. There's no way we can be sure that it was the proposed legislation mandating the use of air bags that was responsible.

17. The answer is A. If, in June of 1984, the lobbyist received a bonus "for her work on the air bag legislation," we can be sure that the legislation passed. This proves the conclusion.

18. The answer is B. This is another tricky question. A three fold stock increase would strongly suggest that the legislation had been passed, but it's possible that factors other than the air bag legislation caused the increase. Note that the stock is in "crash protection equipment." Nowhere in the statement does it say air bags. Seat belts, motorcycle helmets, and collapsible bumpers are all crash protection equipment and could have contributed to the increase. This is just another reminder to read carefully because the questions are often designed to mislead you.

19. The answer is D. This would tend to weaken the conclusion because Marsha is very fond of her mother and she would not want to upset her unnecessarily. It does not prove it, however, because if Marsha strongly feels she is right, she probably wouldn't let her mother's opinion sway her. Choice E would also not be correct, because we cannot assume that Marsha's mother's opinion is of so little importance to her as to be considered irrelevant.

20. The answer is E. The statement is irrelevant. We are told that Marsha's income has doubled but we are not told why. The phrase "six months after the interview" can be misleading in that it leads us to assume that the increase and the interview are related. Her income could have doubled because she regained her popularity but it could also have come from stocks or some other business venture. Because we are not given any reason for her income doubling, it would be impossible to say whether or not this statement proves or disproves the conclusion. Choice E is the best choice of the five possible choices. One of the problems with promotional exams is that sometimes you need to select a choice you're not crazy about. In this case, "not having enough information to make a determination" would be the best choice. However, that's not an option, so you're forced to work with what you've got. On these exams it's sometimes like voting for President, you have to pick the "lesser of the two evils" or the least awful choice. In this case, the information is more irrelevant to the conclusion than it is anything else.

21. The answer is D, weakens the conclusion. We've been told that Marsha's agent feels that she should apologize. If he is pleased with her interview, then it would tend to weaken the conclusion but not disprove it. We can't be sure that he hasn't had a change of heart, or that there weren't other parts of the interview he liked so much that they outweighed her unwillingness to apologize.

22. The answer is A. The conclusion states that Marsha will donate $1 to the Cellulite Prevention League for every pound the actress loses. Marsha's sister's financial report on the League's activities directly supports and proves the conclusion.

23. The answer is C, disproves the conclusion. If the magazine receives many letters commending Marsha for her courage in apologizing, this directly contradicts the conclusion, which states that Marsha didn't apologize.

24. The answer is B. It was stated in the passage that two of Marsha's performances were cancelled after the controversy first occurred. The cancellation of another performance immediately after her interview was published would tend to support the conclusion that she refused to apologize. Because we can't be sure, however, that her performance wasn't cancelled for another reason, choice A would be incorrect.

25. The answer is E, as this information is irrelevant. Postponing the article an extra week does not affect Marsha's decision or the public's reaction to it.

26. The answer is C. If 500 new employees are hired to handle the "increased paperwork created by the new tax on videocassettes", this would directly contradict the conclusion, which states that the legislature defeated both bills. (They should all be this easy.)

27. The answer is B. The results of the study would support the conclusion. If implementing the legislation was going to be so costly, it is likely that the legislature would vote against it. Choice A is not the answer, however, because we can't be sure that the legislature didn't pass it anyway.

28. The answer is E. It's irrelevant to the conclusion that 80% of all those working in the entertainment industry own videocassette recorders. Sometimes if you're not sure about these, it can help a lot to try and visualize the situation. Why would someone voting on this legislation care about this fact? It doesn't seem to be the kind of information that would make any difference or impact upon the conclusion.

29. The answer is B. The head of the law enforcement agency's statement that the legislation would be unenforceable would support the conclusion. It's possible that many legislators would question why they should bother to pass legislation that would be impossible to enforce. Choice A would be incorrect however, because we can't be sure that the legislation wasn't passed in spite of his statement.

30. The answer is D. This would tend to weaken the conclusion because the prospect of several large companies going bankrupt would seem to be a good argument in favor of the legislation. The possible loss of jobs and businesses would be a good reason for some people to vote for the legislation. We can't be sure, however, that this would be a compelling enough reason to ensure passage of the legislation so choice C is incorrect.

This concludes our section on the "Validity of Conclusion" type of questions.

We hope these weren't too horrible for you. It's important to keep in mind exactly what you've been given and exactly what they want you to do with it. It's also necessary to remember that you may have to choose between two possible answers. In that case you must choose the one that seems the best. Sometimes you may think there is no good answer. You will probably be right but you can't let that upset you. Just choose the one you dislike the least.

We want to repeat that it is unlikely that this exact format will appear on the exam. The skills required to answer these questions, however, are the same as those you'll need for the exam so we suggest that you review this section before taking the actual exam.

31. The answer is C. This next set of questions requires you to "switch gears" slightly, and get used to different formats. In this type of question, you have to decide whether the conclusion is proved by the facts given, disproved by the facts given, or neither because not enough information has been provided. Fortunately, unlike the previous questions, you don't have to decide whether particular facts support or don't support the conclusion. This type of question is more straight forward, but the reasoning behind it is the same. We are told that the Bills have won two games less than the Patriots, and that the Patriots are in first place and the Bills are in second place. We are also told that there are two games left to play, and that they won't play each other again. The conclusion states that the Bills won the division. Is there anything in the four statements that would prove this? We have no idea what the outcome of the last two games of the season was. The

Bills and Patriots could have ended up tied at the end of the season, or the Bills could have lost both or one of their last games while the Patriots did the same. There might even be another team tied for first or second place with the Bills or Patriots. Since we don't know for sure, Choice A is incorrect. Choice B is trickier. It might seem at first glance that the best the Bills could do would be to tie the Patriots if the Patriots lost their last two games and the Bills won their last two games. But it would be too much to assume that there is no procedure for a tiebreaker that wouldn't give the Bills the division championship. Since we don't know what the rules are in the event of a tie (for example, what if a tie was decided on the results of what happened when the two teams had played each other, or on the best record in the division, or on most points scored?), we can't say for sure that it would be impossible for the Bills to win their division. For this reason, choice C is the answer, as we don't have enough information to prove or disprove the conclusion. This question looked more difficult than it actually was. It's important to disregard any factors outside of the actual question, and to focus only on what you've been given. In this case, as on all of these types of questions, what you know or don't know about a subject is actually irrelevant. It's best to concentrate only on the actual facts given.

32. The answer is A. The conclusion is proved by the facts given.

In this type of problem it is usually best to pull as many facts as possible from the sentences and then put them into a simpler form. The phrasing and the order of exam questions are designed to be confusing so you need to restate things as clearly as possible by eliminating the extras.

Sentence 1 tells us that there are only two possible colors for eyes and two for hair. Looking at the other sentences we learn that eyes are either green or gold and that hair is either silver or purple. If half the beings with purple hair have golden eyes then the other half must have green eyes since it is the only other eye color. Likewise, if one-third of those with silver hair have green eyes the other two-thirds must have golden eyes.

This information makes it clear that there are more golden-eyed beings on Zeinon than green-eyed ones. It doesn't matter that we don't know exactly how many are actually living on the planet. The number of those with gold eyes (1/2 plus 2/3) will always be greater than the number of those with green eyes (1/2 plus 1/3), no matter what the actual figures might be. Sentence 3 is totally irrelevant because even if there were more silver-haired inhabitants it would not affect the conclusion.

33. The answer is C. The conclusion is neither proved nor disproved by the facts because we don't know how many miles Bethany is from Amoranth.

With this type of question, if you're not sure how to approach it you can always substitute in a range of "real numbers" to see what the result would be. If they were 200 miles apart Joe's Truck Rental would be cheaper because they would charge a total of $160 while National Movers would charge $175.

Joe's - $100 plus .30 x 200 (or $60) = $160
National - $150 plus .25 x 100 (or $25) = $175

If the towns were 600 miles apart, however, National Movers would be cheaper. The cost of renting from National would be $275 compared to the $280 charged by Joe's Trucking.

Joe's - $100 plus .30 x 600 (or $180) = $280
National - $150 plus .25 x 500 (or $125) = $275

34. The answer is B. We've varied the format once more, but the reasoning is similar. This is a tedious question that is more like a math question, but we wanted to give you some practice with this type, just in case. You won't be able to do this question if you've forgotten how to do percents. Many exams require this knowledge, so if you feel you need a review we suggest you read Booklets 1, 2 or 3 in this series.

The only way to attack this problem is to go through each choice until you find the one that is correct. Choice A states that Plainfield, Smallville and Granton are cities. Let's begin with Plainfield. The passage states that in 1960 Plainfield had a population of 12,000, and that it grew 10% between 1960 and 1970, and another 20% between 1970 and 1980. Ten percent of 12,000 is 1200 (12,000 x .10 = 1200). Therefore, the population grew from 12,000 in 1960 to 12,000 + 1200 between 1960 and 1970. At the time of the 1970 Census, Plainfield's population was 13,200. It then grew another 20% between 1970 and 1980, so, 13,200 x .20 = 2640. 13,200 plus the additional increase of 2640 would make the population of Plainfield 15,840. This would qualify it as a city, since its population is over 15,000. Since a change upward in the population of a municipality is re-classified immediately, Plainfield would have become a city right away. So far, statement A is true. The passage states that Smallville's population has not changed significantly in the last twenty years. Since Smallville's population was 20,283, Smallville would still be a city. Granton had a population of 25,000 (what a coincidence that so many of these places have such nice, even numbers) in 1950. The population has decreased 25% in each ten year period since that time. So from 1950 to 1960 the population decreased 25%. 25,000 x .25 = 6,250. 25,000 minus 6,250 = 18,750. So the population of Granton in 1960 would have been 18,750. (Or you could have saved a step and multiplied 25,000 by .75 to get 18,750.) The population from 1960 to 1970 decreased an additional 25%. So: 18,750 x .25 = 4687.50. 18,750 minus 4687.50 = 14,062.50. Or: 18,750 x .75 = 14,062.50. (Don't let the fact that a half of a person is involved confuse you, these are exam questions, not real life.) From 1970 to 1980 the population decreased an additional 25%. This would mean that Granton's population was below 15,000 for more than ten years, so it's status as a city would have changed to that of a town, which would make choice A incorrect, since it states that Granton is a city.

Choice B states that Smallville is a city and Granton is a town which we know to be true from the information above. Choice B is correct so far. We next need to determine if Ellenville is a village. Ellenville had a population of 4,283 in 1950, and increased 5% in each ten year period since 1950. 4,283 x .05 = 214.15. 4,283 plus 214.15 = 4,497.15, so Ellenville's population from 1950 to 1960 increased to 4,497.15. (Or: 4,283 x 1.05 - 4,497.15.) From 1960 to 1970 Ellenville's population increased another 5%: 4,497.15 x .05 = 224.86. 4,497.15 plus 224.86 = 4,772.01 (or: 4,497.15 x 1.05 = 4,722.01.) From 1970 to 1980, Ellenville's population increased another 5%: 4,722.01 x .05 = 236.1. 4722.01 plus 236.10 = 4958.11. (Or: 4,722.01 x 1.05 = 4958.11.).

Ellenville's population is still under 5,000 in 1980 so it would continue to be classified as a village. Since all three statements in choice B are true, Choice B must be the answer. However, we'll go through the other choices. Choice C states that Springdale is a town. The passage tells us that the population of Springdale doubled from 1960 to 1970, and increased

25% from 1970 to 1980. It doesn't give us any actual population figures, however, so it's impossible to know what the population of Springdale is, making Choice C incorrect. Choice C also states that Granton is a town, which is true, and that Ellenville is a town, which is false (from Choice B we know it's a village). Choice D states that Plainfield and Smallville are cities, which is information we already know is true, and that Ellenville is a town. Since Ellenville is a village, Choice D is also incorrect.

This was a lot of work for just one question and we doubt you'll get one like this on this section of the exam, but we included it just in case. On an exam, you can always put a check mark next to a question like this and come back to it later, if you feel you're pressed for time and could spend your time more productively on other, less time consuming problems.

35. The answer is B. This question requires very careful reading. It's best to break the conclusion down into smaller parts in order to solve the problem. The first half of the conclusion states that the average person in the 20-29 age group (Group A) drinks less tea daily than the average person in the 40-50 age group (Group C). The average person in Group A drinks 2.1 cups of tea daily, while the average person in Group C drinks 2.6 cups of tea daily. Since 2.1 is less than 2.6, the conclusion is correct so far. The second half of the conclusion states that the average person in Group A drinks more coffee daily than the average person in the 30-39 age group (Group B) drinks cola. The average person in Group A drinks 1.8 cups of coffee daily while the average person in Group B drinks 1.9 glasses of cola. This disproves the conclusion, which states that the average person in Group A drinks more coffee daily than the average person in Group B drinks cola.

36. The answer is C. The easiest way to approach a problem that deals with the relationship between a number of different people or things is to set up a diagram. This type of problem is usually too confusing to do in your head. For this particular problem the "diagram" could be a line, one end of which would be labelled tall and the other end labelled short. Then, taking one sentence at a time, place the people on the line to see where they fall in relation to one another.

The diagram of the first sentence would look like this:

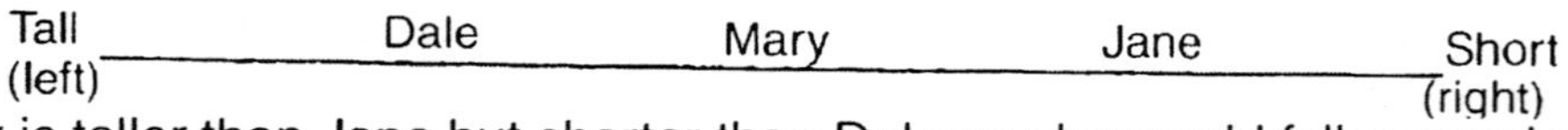

Mary is taller than Jane but shorter than Dale so she would fall somewhere between the two of them. We have placed tall on the left and labelled it left just to make the explanation easier. You could just as easily have reversed the position.

The second sentence places Fred somewhere to the left of Mary because he is taller than she is. Steven would be to the left of Fred for the same reason. At this point we don't know whether Steven and Fred are taller or shorter than Dale. The new diagram would look like this:

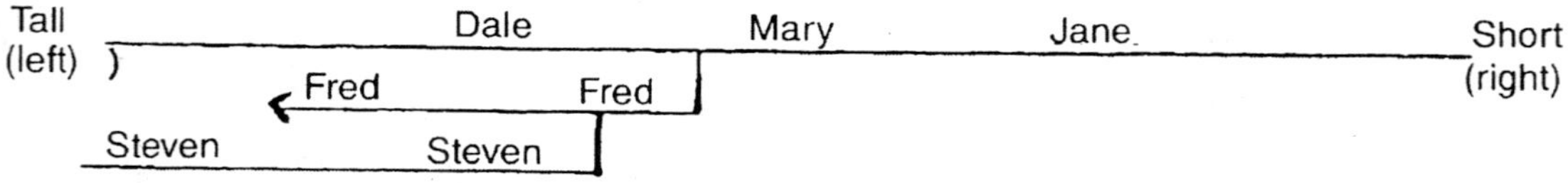

The third stentence introduces Elizabeth, presenting a new problem. Elizabeth can be anywhere to the right of Dale. Don't make the mistake of assuming she falls between Dale and Mary. At this point we don't know where she fits in relation to Mary, Jane, or even Fred.

We do get information about Steven, however. He is taller than Dale so he would be to the left of Dale. Since he is also taller than Fred (see sentence two) we know that Steven is the tallest person thus far. The diagram would now look like this:

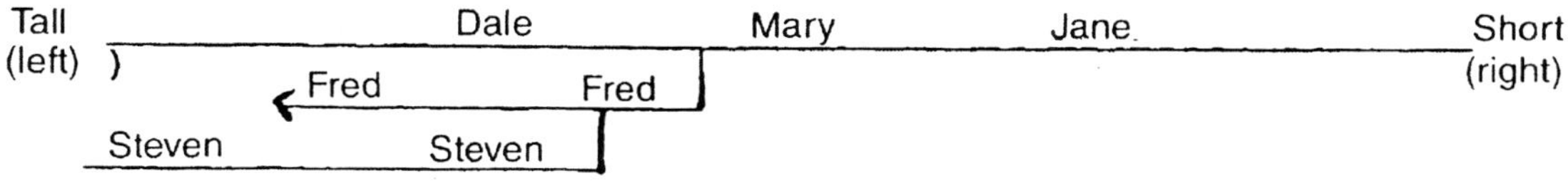

Fred's height is somewhere between Steven and Mary, Elizabeth's anywhere between Dale and the end of the line.

The fourth sentence tells us where Elizabeth stands, in relation to Fred and the others in the problem. The fact that she is taller than Mary means she is also taller than Jane. The final diagram would look like this:

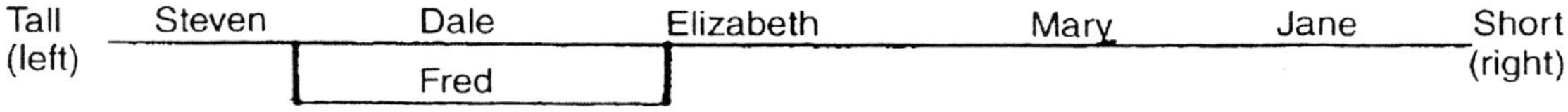

We still don't know whether Dale or Fred is taller, however. Therefore, the conclusion that Dale is taller than Fred can't be proved. It also can't be disproved because we don't know for sure that he isn't. The answer has to be Choice C, as the conclusion can't be proved or disproved.

37. The answer is A. This is another problem that is easiest for most people if they make a diagram. Sentence 1 states that Main Street is between Spring Street and Glenn Blvd. At this point we don't know if they are next to each other or if they are separated by a number of streets. Therefore, you should leave space between streets as you plot your first diagram.

The order of the streets could go either:

Spring St.	or	Glenn Blvd.
Main St.		Main St.
Glenn Blvd.		Spring St.

Sentence 2 states that Hawley Street is one block south of Spring Street and 3 blocks north of Main Street. Because most people think in terms of north as above and south as below and because it was stated that Hawley is one block south of Spring Street and three blocks north of Main Street, the next diagram could look like this:

Spring
Hawley
______
______
Main
Glenn

The third sentence states that Glenn Street is five blocks south of Elm and four blocks south of Main. It could look like this:

Spring
Hawley
_____
Elm
Main
_____
_____
_____
Glenn

The conclusion states that Elm Street is between Hawley Avenue and Glenn Blvd. From the above diagram we can see that this is the case.

38. The answer is B. For most people the best way to do this problem is to draw a diagram, plotting the course of both trains. Sentence 1 states that train A leaves Hampshire at 5:50 a.m. and reaches New London at 6:42. Your first diagram might look like this: 38.___

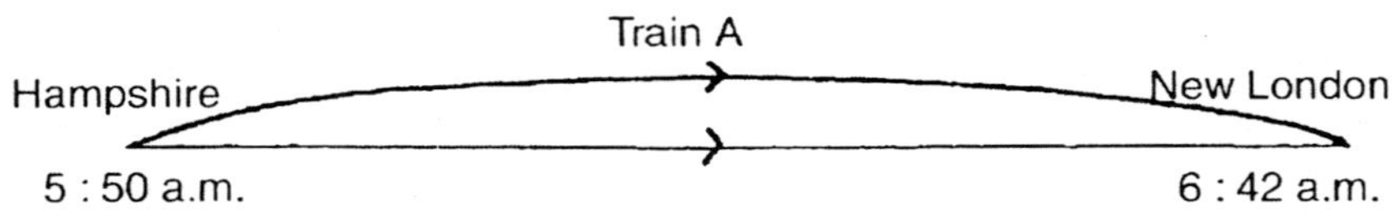

Sentence 2 states that the train leaves New London at 7:00 a.m. and arrives in Kellogsville at 8:42 a.m. The diagram might now look like this:

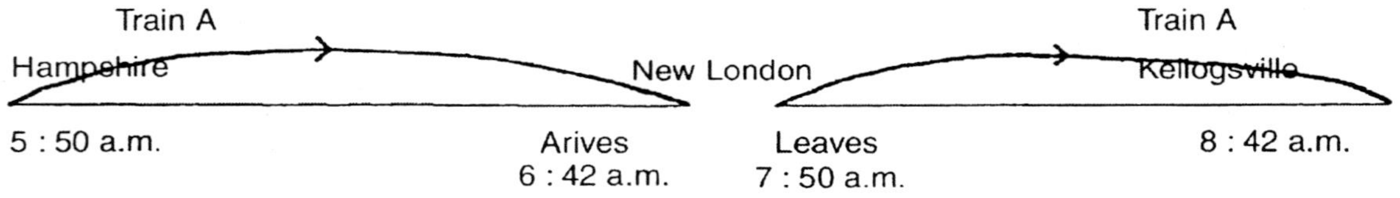

Sentence 3 gives us the rest of the information that must be included in the diagram. It introduces Train B, which moves in the opposite direction, leaving Kellogsville at 8:00 a.m. and arriving at Hampshire at 10:42 a.m. The final diagram might look like this:

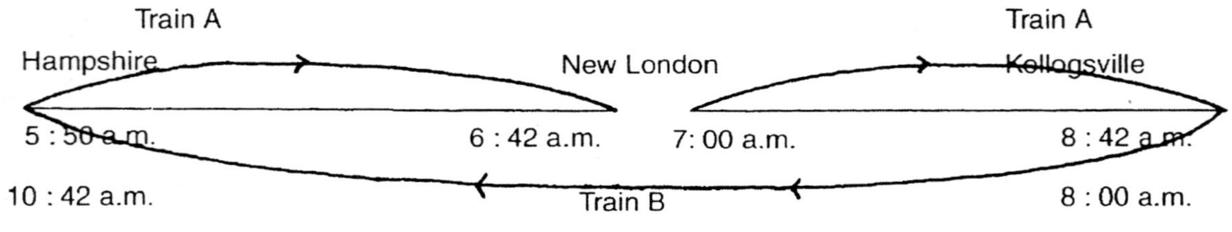

As you can see from the diagram, the routes of the two trains will overlap somewhere between Kellogsville and New London. If you read sentence 4 quickly and assumed that that was the section with only one track, you probably would have assumed that there would have had to be a collision. Sentence 4 states, however, that there is only one railroad track between New London and Hampshire. That is the only section, then, where the two trains could collide. By the time Train B gets to that section, however, Train A will have passed it. The two trains will pass each other somewhere between New London and Kellogsville, not New London and Hampshire.

EXAMINATION SECTION
TEST 1

DIRECTIONS: Each question or incomplete statement is followed by several suggested answers or completions. Select the one that BEST answers the question or completes the statement. *PRINT THE LETTER OF THE CORRECT ANSWER IN THE SPACE AT THE RIGHT.*

Questions 1 -9

Questions 1 through 9 measure your ability to (1) determine whether statements from witnesses say essentially the same thing and (2) determine the evidence needed to make it reasonably certain that a particular conclusion is true.

1. Which of the following pairs of statements say essentially the same thing in two different ways? 1.____

   I. If you get your feet wet, you will catch a cold.
   If you catch a cold, you must have gotten your feet wet.

   II. If I am nominated, I will run for office.
   I will run for office only if I am nominated.

   A. I only
   B. I and II
   C. II only
   D. Neither I nor II

2. Which of the following pairs of statements say essentially the same thing in two different ways? 2.____

   I. The enzyme Rhopsin cannot be present if the bacterium Trilox is absent.
   Rhopsin and Trilox always appear together.

   II. A member of PENSA has an IQ of at least 175.
   A person with an IQ of less than 175 is not a member of PENSA.

   A. I only
   B. I and II
   C. II only
   D. Neither I nor II

3. Which of the following pairs of statements say essentially the same thing in two different ways? 3.____

   I. None of Finer High School's sophomores will be going to the prom.
   No student at Finer High School who is going to the prom is a sophomore.

   II. If you have 20/20 vision, you may carry a firearm.
   You may not carry a firearm unless you have 20/20 vision.

   A. I only
   B. I and II
   C. II only
   D. Neither I nor II

4. Which of the following pairs of statements say essentially the same thing in two different ways? 4.___

    I. If the family doesn't pay the ransom, they will never see their son again.
    It is necessary for the family to pay the ransom in order for them to see their son again.

    II. If it is raining, I am carrying an umbrella.
    If I am carrying an umbrella, it is raining.

    A. I only
    B. I and II
    C. II only
    D. Neither I nor II

5. Summary of Evidence Collected to Date: 5.___
In the county's maternity wards, over the past year, only one baby was born who did not share a birthday with any other baby.
Prematurely Drawn Conclusion: At least one baby was born on the same day as another baby in the county's maternity wards.
Which of the following pieces of evidence, if any, would make it *reasonably certain* that the conclusion drawn is true?

    A. More than 365 babies were born in the county's maternity wards over the past year
    B. No pairs of twins were born over the past year in the county's maternity wards
    C. More than one baby was born in the county's maternity wards over the past year
    D. None of these

6. Summary of Evidence Collected to Date: 6.___
Every claims adjustor for MetroLife drives only a Ford sedan when on the job.
Prematurely Drawn Conclusion: A person who works for MetroLife and drives a Ford sedan is a claims adjustor.
Which of the following pieces of evidence, if any, would make it *reasonably certain* that the conclusion drawn is true?

    A. Most people who work for MetroLife are claims adjustors
    B. Some people who work for MetroLife are not claims adjustors
    C. Most people who work for MetroLife drive Ford sedans
    D. None of these

7. Summary of Evidence Collected to Date: 7.___
Mason will speak to Zisk if Zisk will speak to Ronaldson.
Prematurely Drawn Conclusion: Jones will not speak to Zisk if Zisk will speak to Ronaldson
Which of the following pieces of evidence, if any, would make it *reasonably certain* that the conclusion drawn is true?

    A. If Zisk will speak to Mason, then Ronaldson will not speak to Jones
    B. If Mason will speak to Zisk, then Jones will not speak to Zisk
    C. If Ronaldson will speak to Jones, then Jones will speak to Ronaldson
    D. None of these

8. Summary of Evidence Collected to Date: 8.____
No blue lights on the machine are indicators for the belt drive status.
Prematurely Drawn Conclusion: Some of the lights on the lower panel are not indicators for the belt drive status.
Which of the following pieces of evidence, if any, would make it *reasonably certain* that the conclusion drawn is true?

A. No lights on the machine's lower panel are blue
B. An indicator light for the machine's belt drive status is either green or red
C. Some lights on the machine's lower panel are blue
D. None of these

9. Summary of Evidence Collected to Date: 9.____
Of the four Sweeney sisters, two are married, three have brown eyes, and three are doctors.
Prematurely Drawn Conclusion: Two of the Sweeney sisters are brown-eyed, married doctors.
Which of the following pieces of evidence, if any, would make it *reasonably certain* that the conclusion drawn is true?

A. The sister who does not have brown eyes is married
B. The sister who does not have brown eyes is not a doctor, and one who is not married is not a doctor
C. Every Sweeney sister with brown eyes is a doctor
D. None of these

Questions 10-14

Questions 10 through 14 refer to Map #5 and measure your ability to orient yourself within a given section of town, neighborhood or particular area. Each of the questions describes a starting point and a destination. Assume that you are driving a car in the area shown on the map accompanying the questions. Use the map as a basis for the shortest way to get from one point to another without breaking the law.

On the map, a street marked by arrows, or by arrows and the words "One Way," indicates one-way travel, and should be assumed to be one-way for the entire length, even when there are breaks or jogs in the street. EXCEPTION: A street that does not have the same name over the full length.

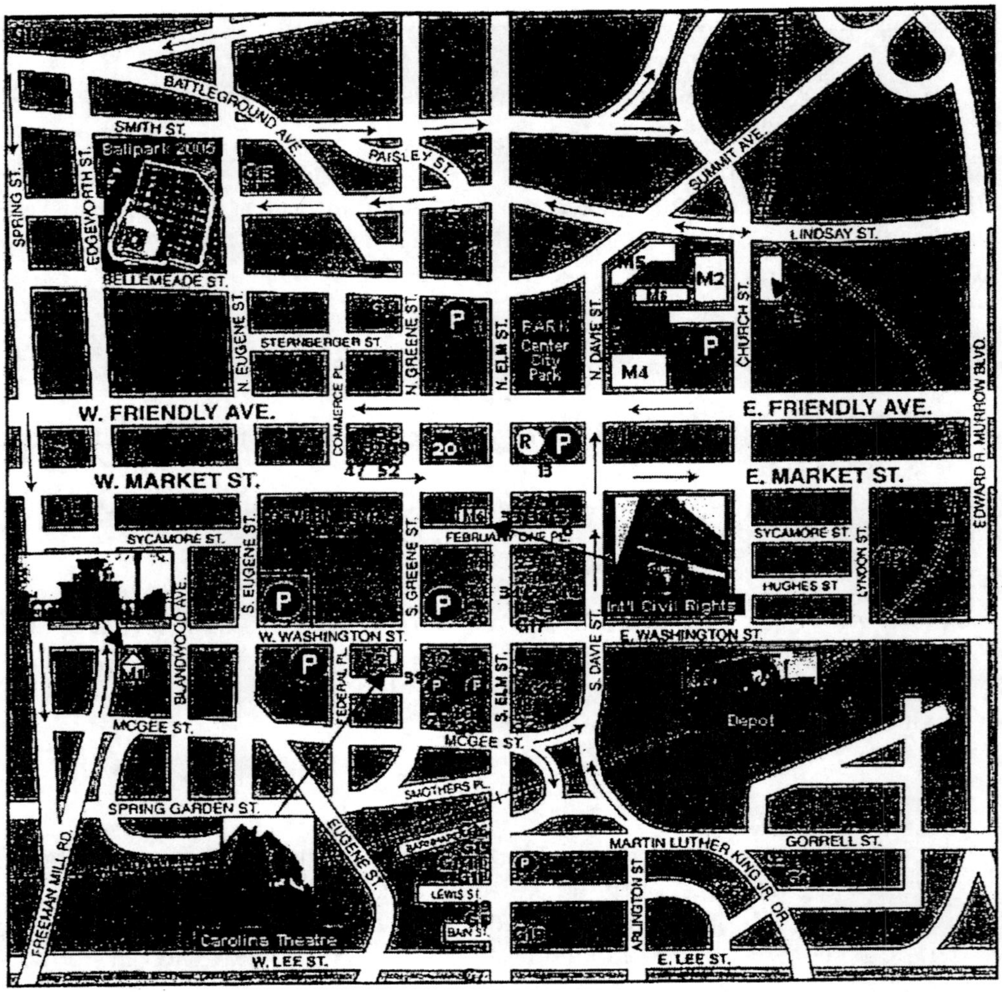

Map #5

10. The shortest legal way from the depot to Center City Park is 10.____

A. north on Church, west on Market, north on Elm
B. east on Washington, north on Edward R. Murrow Blvd., west on Friendly Ave.
C. west on Washington, north on Greene, east on Market, north on Davie
D. north on Church, west on Friendly Ave.

11. The shortest legal way from the Governmental Plaza to the ballpark is 11.____

A. west on Market, north on Edgeworth
B. west on Market, north on Eugene
C. north on Greene, west on Lindsay
D. north on Commerce Place, west on Bellemeade

12. The shortest legal way from the International Civil Rights Building to the building marked "M3" on the map is 12.____

A. east on February One Place, north on Davie, east on Friendly Ave., north on Church
B. south on Elm, west on Washington, north on Greene, east on Market, north on Church
C. north on Elm, east on Market, north on Church
D. north on Elm, east on Lindsay, south on Church

13. The shortest legal way from the ballpark to the Carolina Theatre is 13.____

A. east on Lindsay, south on Greene
B. south on Edgeworth, east on Friendly Ave., south on Greene
C. east on Bellemeade, south on Elm, west on Washington
D. south on Eugene, east on Washington

14. A car traveling north or south on Church Street may NOT go 14.____

A. west onto Friendly Ave.
B. west onto Lindsay
C. east onto Market
D. west onto Smith

Questions 15-19

Questions 15 through 19 refer to Figure #5, on the following page, and measure your ability to understand written descriptions of events. Each question presents a description of an accident or event and asks you which of the five drawings in Figure #5 BEST represents it.

In the drawings, the following symbols are used:

Moving vehicle:  Non-moving vehicle: 

Pedestrian or bicyclist: ●

The path and direction of travel of a vehicle or pedestrian is indicated by a solid line.

The path and direction of travel of each vehicle or pedestrian directly involved in a collision from the point of impact is indicated by a dotted line.

In the space at the right, print the letter of the drawing that best fits the descriptions written below:

15. A driver heading south on Ohio runs a red light and strikes the front of a car headed west on Grand. He glances off and leaves the roadway at the southwest corner of Grand and Ohio. 15.____

16. A driver heading east on Grand drifts into the oncoming lane as it travels through the intersection of Grand and Ohio, and strikes an oncoming car head-on. 16.____

17. A driver heading east on Grand veers into the oncoming lane, sideswipes a westbound car and overcorrects as he swerves back into his lane. He leaves the roadway near the southeast corner of Grand and Ohio. 17.___

18. A driver heading east on Grand strikes the front of a car that is traveling north on Ohio and has run a red light. After striking the front of the northbound car, the driver veers left and leaves the roadway at the northeast corner of Grand and Ohio. 18.___

19. A driver heading east on Grand is traveling above the speed limit and clips the rear end of another eastbound car. The driver then veers to the left and leaves the roadway at the northeast corner of Grand and Ohio. 19.___

FIGURE #5

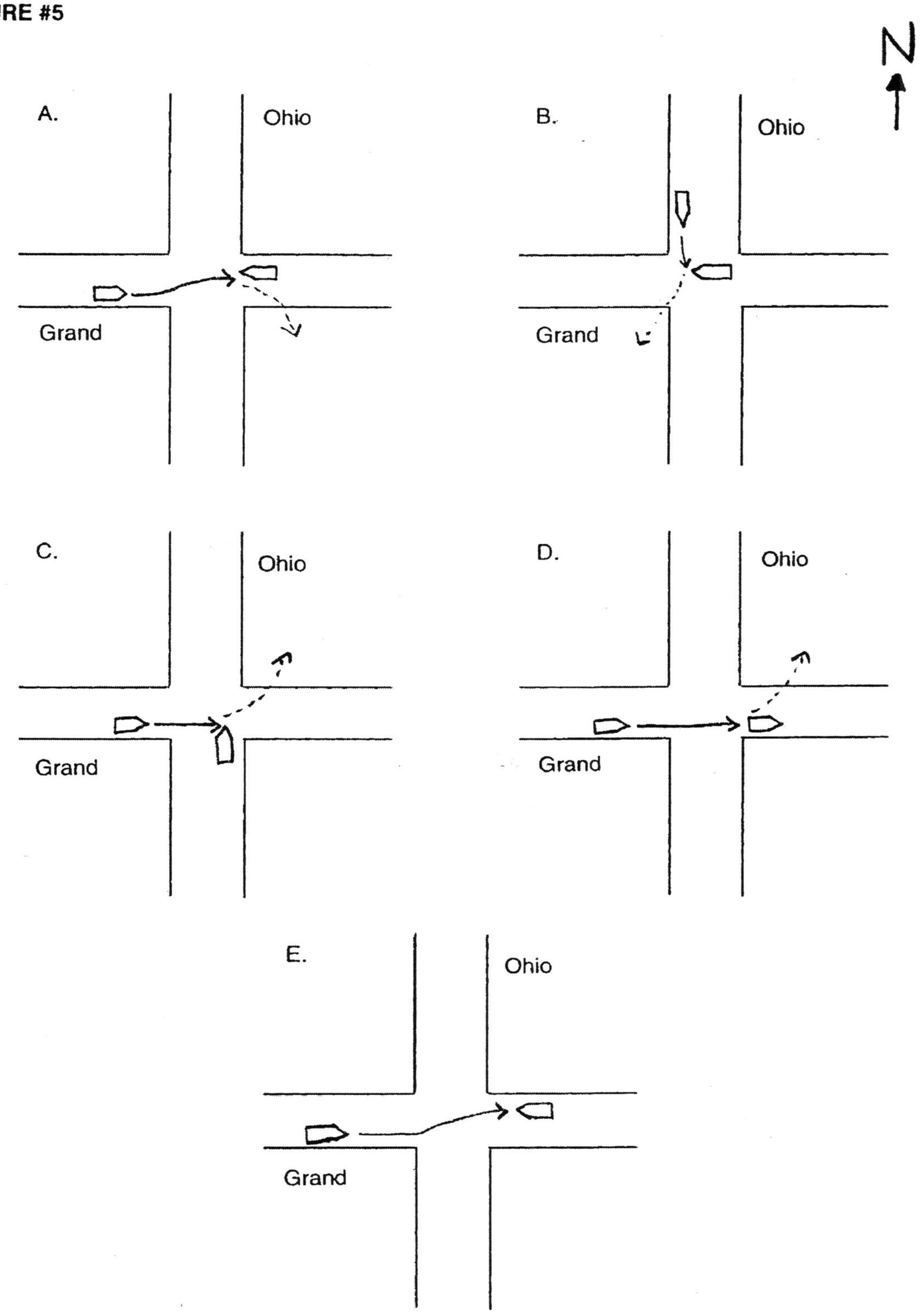
N
A.
Ohio
Grand
B.
Ohio
Grand
C.
Ohio
Grand
D.
Ohio
Grand
E.
Ohio
Grand

Questions 20-22

In questions 20 through 22, choose the word or phrase CLOSEST in meaning to the word or phrase printed in capital letters.

20. PETITION 20.___

A. appeal
B. law
C. oath
D. opposition

21. MALPRACTICE 21.___

A. commission
B. mayhem
C. error
D. misconduct

22. EXONERATE 22.___

A. incriminate
B. accuse
C. lengthen
D. acquit

Questions 23-25

Questions 23 through 25 measure your ability to do fieldwork-related arithmetic. Each question presents a separate arithmetic problem for you to solve.

23. Officers Lane and Bryant visited another city as part of an investigation. Because each is from a different precinct, they agree to split all expenses. With her credit card, Lane paid $70 for food and $150 for lodging. Bryant wrote checks for gas ($50) and entertainment ($40). 23.___
How much does Bryant owe Lane?

A. $65 B. $90 C. $155 D. $210

24. In a remote mountain pass, two search-and-rescue teams, one from Silverton and one from Durango, combine to look for a family that disappeared in a recent snowstorm. The combined team is composed of 20 members. Which of the following statements could NOT be true? 24.___

A. The Durango team has a dozen members
B. The Silverton team has only one member
C. The Durango team has two more members than the Silverton team
D. The Silverton team has one more member than the Durango team

25. Three people in the department share a vehicle for a period of one year. The average number of miles traveled per month by each person is 150. How many miles will be added to the car's odometer at the end of the year? 25.___

A. 1,800 B. 2,400 C. 3,600 D. 5,400

KEY (CORRECT ANSWERS)

1. D
2. C
3. A
4. A
5. A

6. D
7. B
8. C
9. B
10. D

11. D
12. C
13. D
14. D
15. B

16. E
17. A
18. C
19. D
20. A

21. D
22. D
23. A
24. D
25. D

TEST 2

DIRECTIONS: Each question or incomplete statement is followed by several suggested answers or completions. Select the one that BEST answers the question or completes the statement. *PRINT THE LETTER OF THE CORRECT ANSWER IN THE SPACE AT THE RIGHT.*

Questions 1-9

Questions 1 through 9 measure your ability to (1) determine whether statements from witnesses say essentially the same thing and (2) determine the evidence needed to make it reasonably certain that a particular conclusion is true.

To do well on this part of the test, you do NOT have to have a working knowledge of police procedures and techniques. Nor do you have to have any more familiarity with criminals and criminal behavior than that acquired from reading newspapers, listening to radio or watching TV. To do well in this part, you must read and reason carefully.

1. Which of the following pairs of statements say essentially the same thing in two different ways? 1.____
   I. If there is life on Mars, we should fund NASA.
      Either there is life on Mars, or we should not fund NASA.
   II. All Eagle Scouts are teenage boys.
      All teenage boys are Eagle Scouts.

   A. I only
   B. I and II
   C. II only
   D. Neither I nor II

2. Which of the following pairs of statements say essentially the same thing in two different ways? 2.____
   I. If that notebook is missing its front cover, it definitely belongs to Carter.
      Carter's notebook is the only one missing its front cover.
   II. If it's hot, the pool is open.
      The pool is open if it's hot.

   A. I only
   B. I and II
   C. II only
   D. Neither I nor II

3. Which of the following pairs of statements say essentially the same thing in two different ways? 3.____
   I. Nobody who works at the mill is without benefits.
      Everyone who works at the mill has benefits.
   II. We will fund the program only if at least 100 people sign the petition.
      Either we will fund the program or at least 100 people will sign the petition.

   A. I only
   B. I and II
   C. II only
   D. Neither I nor II

4. Which of the following pairs of statements say essentially the same thing in two different ways? 4.____

   I. If the new parts arrive, Mr. Luther's request has been answered.
   Mr. Luther requested new parts to arrive.

   II. The machine's test cycle will not run unless the operation cycle is not running.
   The machine's test cycle must be running in order for the operation cycle to run.

A. I only
B. I and II
C. II only
D. Neither I nor II

5. Summary of Evidence Collected to Date: 5.____

   I. To become a member of the East Side Crips, a kid must be either "jumped in" or steal a squad car without getting caught.
   II. Sid, a kid on the East Side, was caught stealing a squad car.

<u>Prematurely Drawn Conclusion:</u> Sid did not become a member of the East Side Crips.
Which of the following pieces of evidence, if any, would make it *reasonably certain* that the conclusion drawn is true?

A. "Jumping in" is not allowed in prison
B. Sid was not "jumped in"
C. Sid's stealing the squad car had nothing to do with wanting to join the East Side Crips
D. None of these

6. <u>Summary of Evidence Collected to Date:</u> 6.____

   I. Jones, a Precinct 8 officer, has more arrests than Smith.
   II. Smith and Watson have exactly the same number of arrests.

<u>Prematurely Drawn Conclusion:</u> Watson is not a Precinct 8 officer.
Which of the following pieces of evidence, if any, would make it *reasonably certain* that the conclusion drawn is true?

A. All the officers in Precinct 8 have more arrests than Watson
B. All the officers in Precinct 8 have fewer arrests than Watson
C. Watson has fewer arrests than Jones
D. None of these

7. <u>Summary of Evidence Collected to Date:</u> 7.____

   I. Twenty one-dollar bills are divided among Frances, Kerry and Brian.
   II. If Kerry gives her dollar bills to Frances, then Frances will have more money than Brian.

<u>Prematurely Drawn Conclusion:</u> Frances has twelve dollars.
Which of the following pieces of evidence, if any, would make it *reasonably certain* that the conclusion drawn is true?

A. If Brian gives his dollars to Kerry, then Kerry will have more money than Frances
B. Brian has two dollars
C. If Kerry gives her dollars to Brian, Brian will still have less money than Frances
D. None of these

8. <u>Summary of Evidence Collected to Date:</u> 8.___

I. The street sweepers will be here at noon today.

II. Residents on the west side of the street should move their cars before noon.

Prematurely Drawn Conclusion: Today is Wednesday.

Which of the following pieces of evidence, if any, would make it *reasonably certain* that the conclusion drawn is true?

A. The street sweepers never sweep the east side of the street on Wednesday
B. The street sweepers arrive at noon every other day
C. There is no parking allowed on the west side of the street on Wednesday
D. None of these

9. Summary of Evidence Collected to Date: 9.___

The only time the warning light comes on is when there is a power surge.

Prematurely Drawn Conclusion: The warning light does not come on if the air conditioner is not running.

Which of the following pieces of evidence, if any, would make it *reasonably certain* that the conclusion drawn is true?

A. The air conditioner does not turn on if the warning light is on
B. Sometimes a power surge is caused by the dishwasher
C. There is only a power surge when the air conditioner turns on
D. None of these

Questions 10-14

Questions 10 through 14 refer to Map #6 and measure your ability to orient yourself within a given section of town, neighborhood or particular area. Each of the questions describes a starting point and a destination. Assume that you are driving a car in the area shown on the map accompanying the questions. Use the map as a basis for the shortest way to get from one point to another without breaking the law.

On the map, a street marked by arrows, or by arrows and the words "One Way," indicates one-way travel, and should be assumed to be one-way for the entire length, even when there are breaks or jogs in the street. EXCEPTION: A street that does not have the same name over the full length.

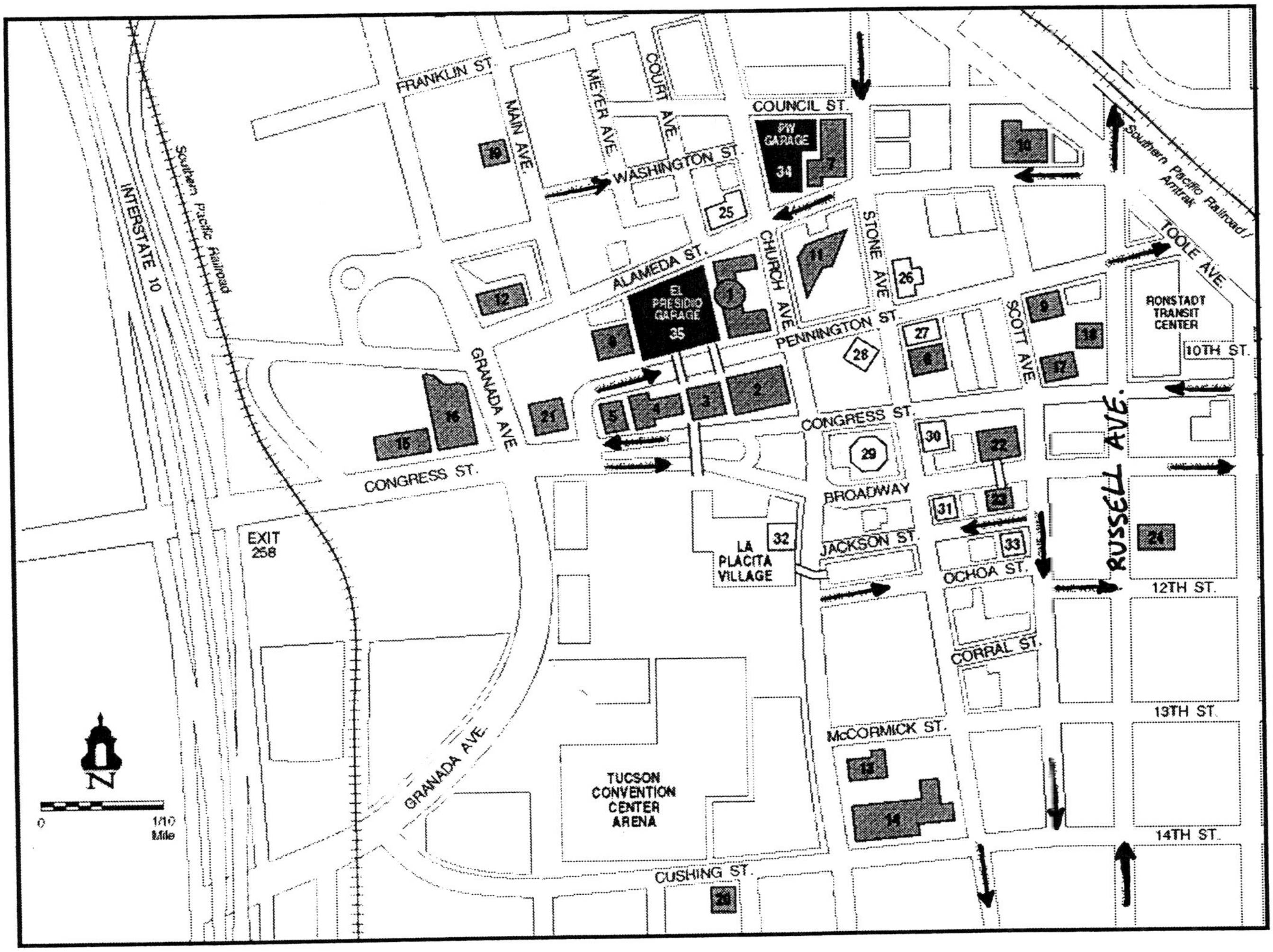

Map #6

PIMA COUNTY

1 Old Courthouse
2 Superior Court Building
3 Administration Building
4 Health and Welfare Building
5 Mechanical Building
6 Legal Services Building
7 County/City Public Works Center

CITY OF TUCSON

8 City Hall
9 City Hall Annex
10 Alameda Plaza City Court Building
11 Public Library - Main Branch
12 Tucson Water Building
13 Fire Department Headquarters
14 Police Department Building

10. The shortest legal way from the Public Library to the Alameda Plaza City Court Building is 10.___

A. north on Stone Ave., east on Alameda
B. south on Stone Ave., east on Congress, north on Russell Ave., west on Alameda
C. south on Stone Ave., east on Pennington, north on Russell Ave., west on Alameda
D. south on Church Ave., east on Pennington, north on Russell Ave., west on Alameda

11. The shortest legal way from City Hall to the Police Department is 11.___

A. east on Congress, south on Scott Ave., west on 14th
B. east on Pennington, south on Stone Ave.
C. east on Congress, south on Stone Ave.
D. east on Pennington, south on Church Ave.

12. The shortest legal way from the Tucson Water Building to the Legal Service Building is 12.___

A. south on Granada Ave., east on Congress, north to east on Pennington, south on Stone Ave.
B. east on Alameda, south on Church Ave., east on Pennington, south on Stone Ave.
C. north on Granada Ave., east on Washington, south on Church Ave., east on Pennington, south on Stone Ave.
D. south on Granada Ave., east on Cushing, north on Stone Ave.

13. The shortest legal way from the Tucson Convention Center Arena to the City Hall Annex is 13.___

A. west on Cushing, north on Granada Ave., east on Congress, east on Broadway, north on Scott Ave.
B. east on Cushing, north on Church Ave., east on Pennington
C. east on Cushing, north on Russell Ave., west on Pennington
D. east on Cushing, north on Stone Ave., east on Pennington

14. The shortest legal way from the Ronstadt Transit Center to the Fire Department is 14.___

A. west on Pennington , south on Stone Ave., west on McCormick
B. west on Congress, south on Russell Ave., west on 13th
C. west on Congress, south on Church Ave.
D. west on Pennington, south on Church Ave.

Questions 15-19

Questions 15 through 19 refer to Figure #6, on the following page, and measure your ability to understand written descriptions of events. Each question presents a description of an accident or event and asks you which of the five drawings in Figure #6 BEST represents it.

In the drawings, the following symbols are used:

Moving vehicle:  Non-moving vehicle: 

Pedestrian or bicyclist: 

The path and direction of travel of a vehicle or pedestrian is indicated by a solid line.

The path and direction of travel of each vehicle or pedestrian directly involved in a collision from the point of impact is indicated by a dotted line.

In the space at the right, print the letter of the drawing that best fits the descriptions written below:

15. A bicyclist heading southwest on Rose travels into the intersection, sideswipes a car that is heading east on Page, and veers right, leaving the roadway at the northwest corner of Page and Mill. 15._____

16. A driver traveling north on Mill swerves right to avoid a bicyclist that is traveling southwest on Rose. The driver strikes the rear end of a car parked on Rose. The bicyclist continues through the intersection and travels west on Page. 16._____

17. A bicyclist heading southwest on Rose travels into the intersection, sideswipes a car that is heading east on Page, and veers right, striking the rear end of a car parked in the westbound lane on Page. 17._____

18. A driver traveling east on Page swerves left to avoid a bicyclist that is traveling southwest on Rose. The driver strikes the rear end of a car parked on Mill. The bicyclist continues through the intersection and travels west on Page. 18._____

19. A bicyclist heading southwest on Rose enters the intersection and sideswipes a car that is swerving left to avoid her. The bicyclist veers left and collides with a car parked in the southbound lane on Mill. The driver of the car veers left and collides with a car parked in the northbound lane on Mill. 19._____

FIGURE #6

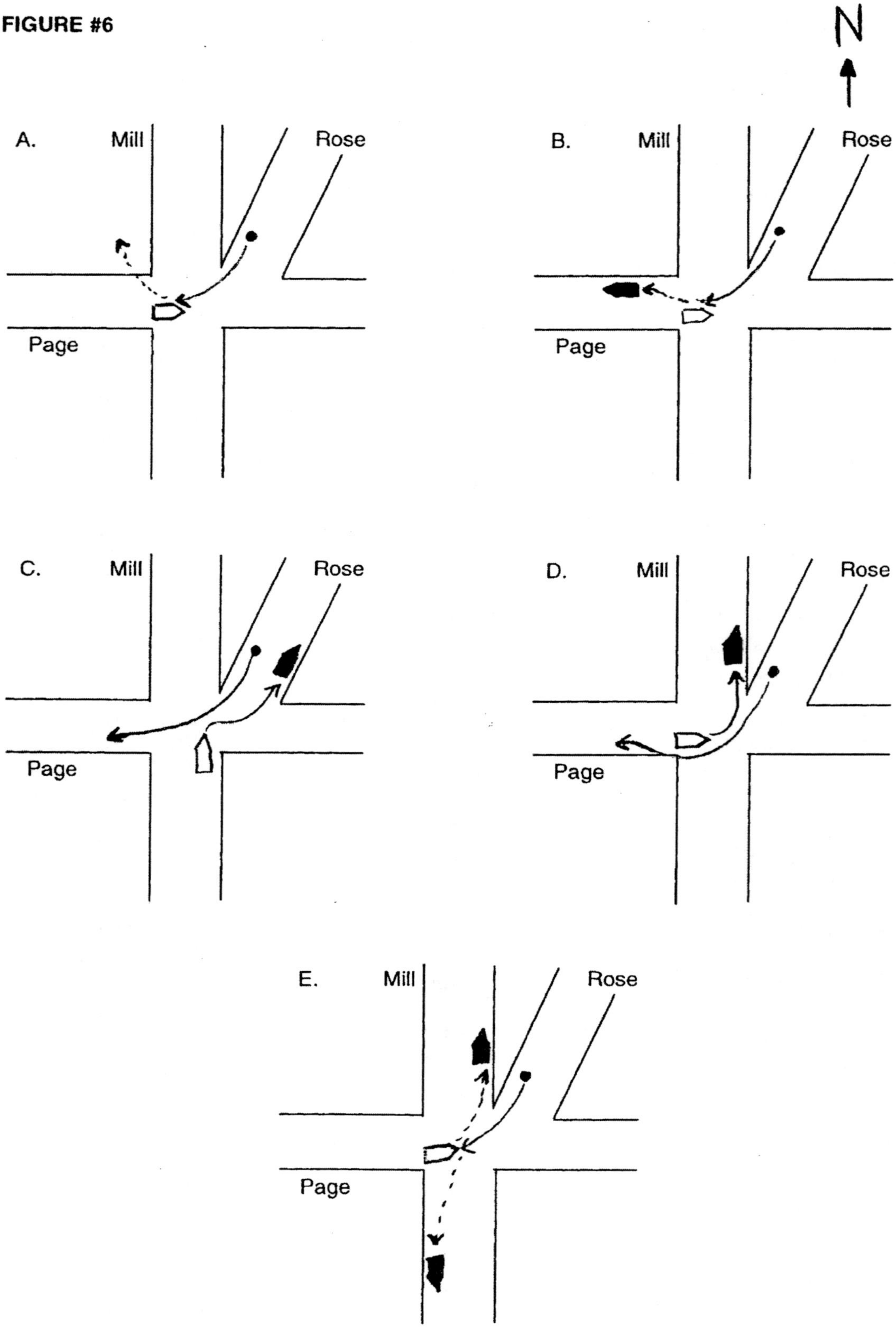
N
A.
Mill
Rose
Page
B.
Mill
Rose
Page
C.
Mill
Rose
Page
D.
Mill
Rose
Page
E.
Mill
Rose
Page

Questions 20-22

In questions 20 through 22, choose the word or phrase CLOSEST in meaning to the word or phrase printed in capital letters.

20. WAIVE 20._____

A. cease
B. surrender
C. prevent
D. die

21. DEPOSITION 21._____

A. settlement
B. deterioration
C. testimony
D. character

22. IMMUNITY 22._____

A. exposure
B. accusation
C. protection
D. exchange

Questions 23-25

Questions 23 through 25 measure your ability to do fieldwork-related arithmetic. Each question presents a separate arithmetic problem for you to solve.

23. Dean, a claims investigator, is reading a 445-page case record in his spare time at work. He has already read 157 pages. If Dean reads 24 pages a day, he should finish reading the rest of the record in ______ days. 23._____

A. 7 B. 12 C. 19 D. 24

24. The Fire Department owns four cars. The Department of Sanitation owns twice as many cars as the Fire Department. The Department of Parks and Recreation owns one fewer car than the Department of Sanitation. The Department of Parks and Recreation is buying new tires for each of its cars. Each tire costs $100. How much is the Department of Parks and Recreation going to spend on tires? 24._____

A. $400 B. $2,800 C. $3,200 D. $4,900

25. A dance hall is about 5,000 square feet. The local ordinance does not allow more than 50 people per every 100 square feet of commercial space. The maximum occupancy of the hall is 25._____

A. 500 B. 2,500 C. 5,000 D. 25,000

KEY (CORRECT ANSWERS)

1. D
2. B
3. A
4. A
5. B
6. D
7. D
8. D
9. C
10. C
11. D
12. A
13. B
14. C
15. A
16. C
17. B
18. D
19. E
20. B
21. C
22. C
23. B
24. B
25. B

EXAMINATION SECTION
TEST 1

DIRECTIONS: Each question or incomplete statement is followed by several suggested answers or completions. Select the one that BEST answers the question or completes the statement. *PRINT THE LETTER OF THE CORRECT ANSWER IN THE SPACE AT THE RIGHT.*

Questions 1 -9

Questions 1 through 9 measure your ability to (1) determine whether statements from witnesses say essentially the same thing and (2) determine the evidence needed to make it reasonably certain that a particular conclusion is true.

1. Which of the following pairs of statements say essentially the same thing in two different ways? 1.____

   I. The only time the machine's red light is on is when the door is locked.
   If the machine's door is locked, the red light is on.

   II. Some gray-jacketed cables are connected to the blower.
   If a cable is connected to the blower, it must be gray-jacketed.

   A. I only
   B. I and II
   C. II only
   D. Neither I nor II

2. Which of the following pairs of statements say essentially the same thing in two different ways? 2.____

   I. If you live on Maple Street, your child is in the Valley District.
   If your child is in the Valley District, you must live on Maple Street.

   II. All the Smith children are brown-eyed.
   If a child is brown-eyed, it is not one of the Smith children

   A. I only
   B. I and II
   C. II only
   D. Neither I nor II

3. Which of the following pairs of statements say essentially the same thing in two different ways? 3.____

   I. If it's Monday, Mrs. James will be here.
   Mrs. James is here every Monday.

   II. Most people in the Drama Club do not have stage fright, but everyone in the Drama Club wants to be noticed.
   Some people in the Drama Club have stage fright and want to be noticed.

   A. I only
   B. I and II
   C. II only
   D. Neither I nor II

4. Which of the following pairs of statements say essentially the same thing in two different ways? 4.___

   I. If you are older than 65, you will get a senior's discount.
   Either you will get a senior's discount, or you are not older than 65.

   II. Every cadet in Officer Johnson's class has passed the firearms safety course.
   No cadet that has failed the firearms safety course is in Officer Johnson's class.

   A. I only
   B. I and II
   C. II only
   D. Neither I nor II

5. Summary of Evidence Collected to Date: 5.___
Most people in the Greenlawn housing project do not have criminal records.
Prematurely Drawn Conclusion: Some people in Greenlawn who have been crime victims have criminal records themselves.
Which of the following pieces of evidence, if any, would make it *reasonably certain* that the conclusion drawn is true?

   A. Some of those who live in the Greenlawn project have been arrested or convicted of "victimless" crimes
   B. Most people in Greenlawn have been the victims of crime
   C. Everyone in Greenlawn has been the victim of crime
   D. None of these

6. Summary of Evidence Collected to Date: 6.___
Every drug dealer in the Oak Lawn neighborhood wears blue and carries a Glock.
Prematurely Drawn Conclusion: A person in the Oak Lawn neighborhood who carries a Glock is a drug dealer.
Which of the following pieces of evidence, if any, would make it *reasonably certain* that the conclusion drawn is true?

   A. In the Oak Lawn neighborhood, only drug dealers wear blue
   B. Drug dealers in Oak Lawn only carry Glocks when they're dealing drugs
   C. In the Oak Lawn neighborhood, only drug dealers carry Glocks
   D. None of these

7. Summary of Evidence Collected to Date: 7.___

   I. Dr. Jones is older than Dr. Gupta.
   II. Dr. Gupta and Dr. Unruh were born on the same day.

Prematurely Drawn Conclusion: Dr. Gupta does not work in the emergency room.
Which of the following pieces of evidence, if any, would make it *reasonably certain* that the conclusion drawn is true?

   A. Dr. Jones is older than Dr. Unruh
   B. Dr. Jones works in the emergency room
   C. Every doctor in the emergency room is older then Dr. Unruh
   D. None of these

8. Summary of Evidence Collected to Date: 8.____
   I. On the street, a "dose" of a certain drug contains four "drams."
   II. A person can trade three "rolls" of a drug for a "plunk."

   Prematurely Drawn Conclusion: A plunk is the most valuable amount of the drug on the street.
   Which of the following pieces of evidence, if any, would make it *reasonably certain* that the conclusion drawn is true?

   A. A person can trade five doses for two rolls
   B. A dram contains two rolls
   C. A roll is larger than a dram
   D. None of these

9. Summary of Evidence Collected to Date: 9.____
   Sam is a good writer and editor.
   Prematurely Drawn Conclusion: Sam is qualified for the job.
   Which of the following pieces of evidence, if any, would make it *reasonably certain* that the conclusion drawn is true?

   A. The job calls for good writing and editing skills
   B. A person who is not a good editor could still apply for the job on the strength of his/her writing skills
   C. If Sam applies for the job, he must be both a good writer and editor
   D. None of these

Questions 10-14

Questions 10 through 14 refer to Map #7 and measure your ability to orient yourself within a given section of town, neighborhood or particular area. Each of the questions describes a starting point and a destination. Assume that you are driving a car in the area shown on the map accompanying the questions. Use the map as a basis for the shortest way to get from one point to another without breaking the law.

On the map, a street marked by arrows, or by arrows and the words "One Way," indicates one-way travel, and should be assumed to be one-way for the entire length, even when there are breaks or jogs in the street. EXCEPTION: A street that does not have the same name over the full length.

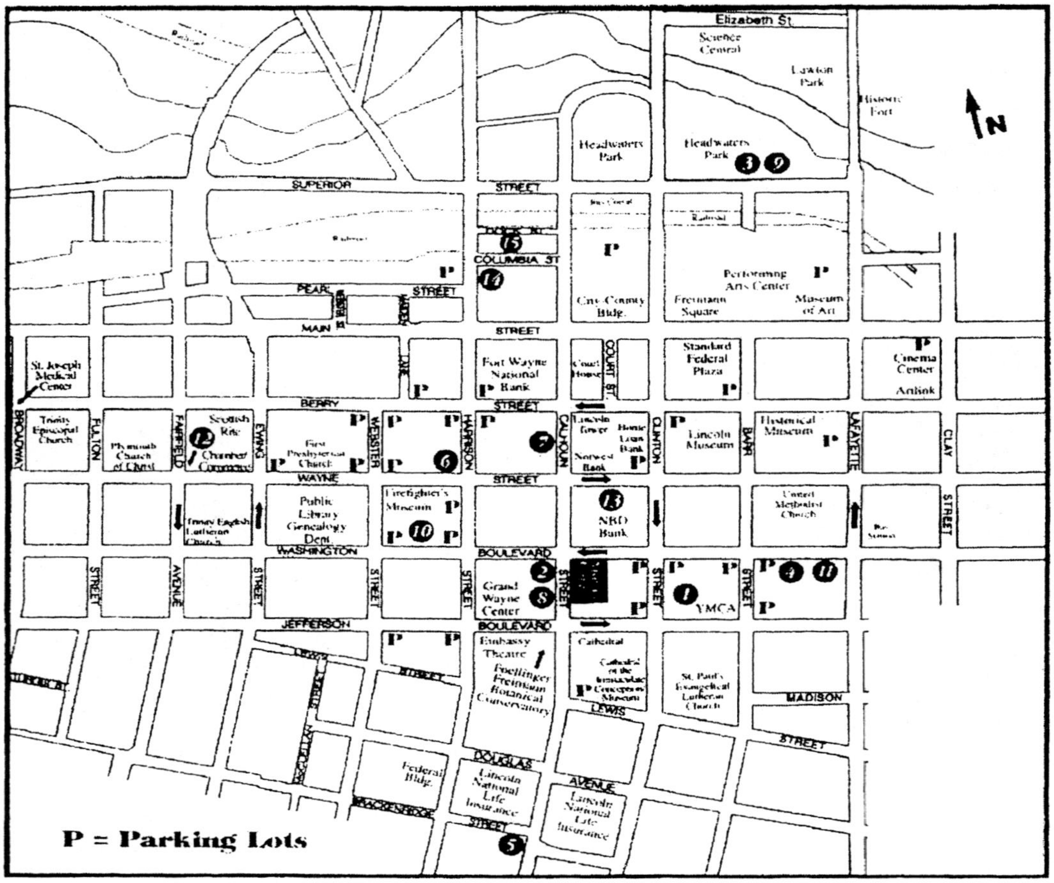

Map #7

10. The shortest legal way from Trinity Episcopal Church to Science Central is 10.____

 A. east on Berry, north on Clinton, east on Elizabeth
 B. east on Berry, north on Lafayette, west on Elizabeth
 C. north on Fulton, east on Main, north on Lafayette, west on Elizabeth
 D. north on Fulton, east on Main, north on Calhoun

11. The shortest legal way from the Grand Wayne Center to the Museum of Art is 11.____

 A. north on Harrison, east on Superior, south on Lafayette
 B. east on Washington Blvd., north on Lafayette
 C. east on Jefferson Blvd., north on Clinton, east on Main
 D. east on Jefferson Blvd., north on Lafayette

12. The shortest legal way from the Embassy Theatre to the City/County Building is 12.____

 A. west on Jefferson Blvd., north on Ewing, east on Main
 B. east on Jefferson Blvd., north on Lafayette, west on Main
 C. east on Jefferson Blvd., north on Clinton
 D. north on Harrison, east on Main

13. The shortest legal way from the YMCA to the Firefighter's Museum is 13._____

A. west on Jefferson Blvd., north on Webster
B. north on Barr, west on Washington Blvd., north on Webster
C. north on Barr, west on Wayne
D. north on Barr, west on Berry, south on Webster

14. The shortest legal way from the Historic Fort to Freimann Square is 14._____

A. north on Lafayette, west on Elizabeth, south on Clinton
B. north on Lafayette, west on Elizabeth, west/south on Calhoun, east on Main
C. south on Lafayette, west on Main
D. south on Lafayette, west on Superior, south on Clinton

Questions 15-19

Questions 15 through 19 refer to Figure #7, on the following page, and measure your ability to understand written descriptions of events. Each question presents a description of an accident or event and asks you which of the five drawings in Figure #7 BEST represents it.

In the drawings, the following symbols are used:

Moving vehicle:    Non-moving vehicle: 

Pedestrian or bicyclist: ●

The path and direction of travel of a vehicle or pedestrian is indicated by a solid line.

The path and direction of travel of each vehicle or pedestrian directly involved in a collision from the point of impact is indicated by a dotted line.

In the space at the right, print the letter of the drawing that best fits the descriptions written below:

15. A driver headed northeast on Cary strikes a car in the intersection and is diverted north, where he collides with the rear of a car that is traveling north on Park. The northbound car is knocked into the rear of another car that is traveling north ahead of it. 15._____

16. A driver headed northeast on Cary strikes a car in the intersection and is diverted north, where he collides head-on with a car stopped at a traffic light in the southbound lane on Park. 16._____

17. A driver headed northeast on Cary strikes a car in the intersection and is diverted east, where he collides head-on with a car stopped at a traffic light in the westbound lane on Roble. 17._____

18. A driver headed east on Roble collides with the left front of a car that is turning right from Knox onto Roble. The driver swerves right after the collision and collides head-on with another car headed north on Park. 18._____

19. A driver headed northeast on Cary strikes a car in the intersection and is diverted north, where he collides with the rear of a car parked in the northbound lane on Park. 19._____

FIGURE #7

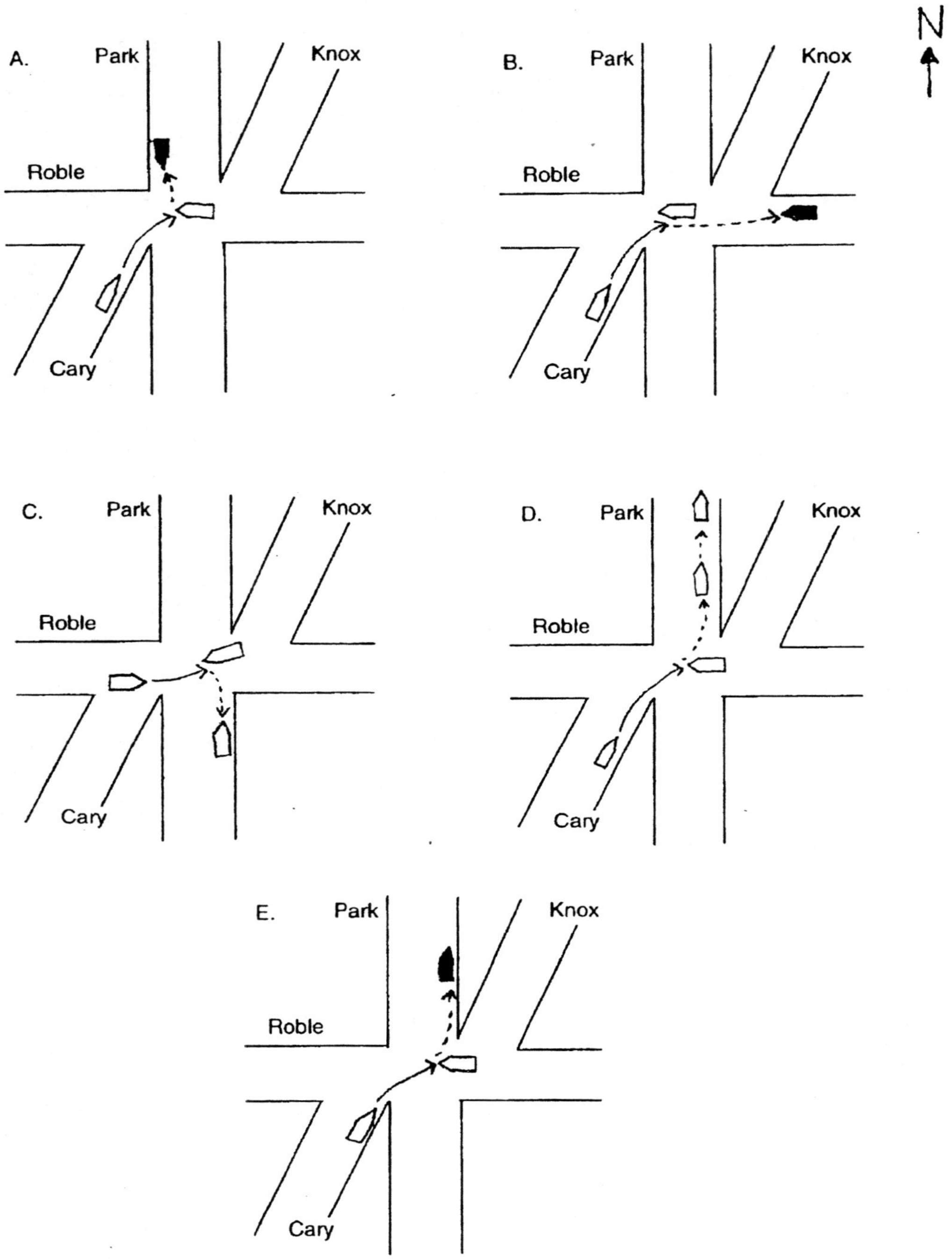
N
A.
Park
Knox
Roble
Cary
B.
Park
Knox
Roble
Cary
C.
Park
Knox
Roble
Cary
D.
Park
Knox
Roble
Cary
E.
Park
Knox
Roble
Cary

Questions 20-22

In questions 20 through 22, choose the word or phrase CLOSEST in meaning to the word or phrase printed in capital letters.

20. JURISDICTION 20.____

A. authority
B. decision
C. judgment
D. argument

21. PROXY 21.____

A. neighbor
B. agent
C. enforcer
D. impostor

22. LARCENY 22.____

A. theft
B. assault
C. deceit
D. gentleness

Questions 23-25

Questions 23 through 25 measure your ability to do fieldwork-related arithmetic. Each question presents a separate arithmetic problem for you to solve.

23. Mr. Long has 14 employees. He has four more male employees than female employees. How many female employees does he have? 23.____

A. 4 B. 5 C. 9 D. 10

24. A box of latex gloves costs $18. A crate has 12 boxes, each of which contains 48 gloves. How much does a crate of latex gloves cost? 24.____

A. $216 B. $328 C. $576 D. $864

25. In a single week, the Department of Parking collected 540 quarters, 623 dimes and 146 nickels from its parking meters. What was the total revenue collected from the meters during the week? 25.____

A. $135.00 B. $154.00 C. $204.60 D. $270.30

KEY (CORRECT ANSWERS)

1.	A	11.	D
2.	C	12.	D
3.	A	13.	B
4.	B	14.	A
5.	C	15.	D
6.	C	16.	A
7.	C	17.	B
8.	A	18.	C
9.	A	19.	E
10.	C	20.	A

21.	B
22.	A
23.	B
24.	A
25.	C

TEST 2

DIRECTIONS: Each question or incomplete statement is followed by several suggested answers or completions. Select the one that BEST answers the question or completes the statement. *PRINT THE LETTER OF THE CORRECT ANSWER IN THE SPACE AT THE RIGHT.*

Questions 1-9

Questions 1 through 9 measure your ability to (1) determine whether statements from witnesses say essentially the same thing and (2) determine the evidence needed to make it reasonably certain that a particular conclusion is true.

To do well on this part of the test, you do NOT have to have a working knowledge of police procedures and techniques. Nor do you have to have any more familiarity with criminals and criminal behavior than that acquired from reading newspapers, listening to radio or watching TV. To do well in this part, you must read and reason carefully.

1. Which of the following pairs of statements say essentially the same thing in two different ways? 1.____

   I. If the garbage is collected today, it is definitely Wednesday.
   The garbage is collected every Wednesday.

   II. Nobody has no answer to the question.
   Everybody has at least one answer to the question.

   A. I only
   B. I and II
   C. II only
   D. Neither I nor II

2. Which of the following pairs of statements say essentially the same thing in two different ways? 2.____

   I. If it rains, the streets will be wet.
   If the streets are wet, it has rained.

   II. All of the Duluth Five are immune from prosecution.
   No member of the Duluth Five can be prosecuted.

   A. I only
   B. I and II
   C. II only
   D. Neither I nor II

3. Which of the following pairs of statements say essentially the same thing in two different ways? 3.____

   I. Ms. Friar will accept her promotion if and only if she is offered a 10% raise.
   For Ms. Friar to accept her promotion, it is necessary that she be offered a 10% raise.

   II. If the hydraulic lines are flushed, it is definitely inspection day.
   The hydraulic lines are flushed only on inspection days.

   A. I only
   B. I and II
   C. II only
   D. Neither I nor II

4. Which of the following pairs of statements say essentially the same thing in two different ways? 4.___

   I. If you are tall you will get onto the basketball team.
   Unless you are tall you will not get onto the basketball team.

   II. That raven is black.
   If that bird is black, it's a raven.

   A. I only
   B. I and II
   C. II only
   D. Neither I nor II

5. Summary of Evidence Collected to Date: 5.___
Every member of the Rotary Club is retired.
Prematurely Drawn Conclusion: At least some people in the planning commission are retired.
Which of the following pieces of evidence, if any, would make it *reasonably certain* that the conclusion drawn is true?

   A. Retirement is a condition for membership in the Rotary Club
   B. Every member of the planning commission has been in the Rotary Club at one time
   C. Every member of the Rotary Club is also on the planning commission
   D. None of these

6. Summary of Evidence Collected to Date: 6.___
Some of the SWAT team snipers have poor aim.
Prematurely Drawn Conclusion: The snipers on the SWAT team with the worst aim also have 20/20 vision.
Which of the following pieces of evidence, if any, would make it *reasonably certain* that the conclusion drawn is true?

   A. Some of the SWAT team snipers have 20/20 vision
   B. Every sniper on the SWAT team has 20/20 vision
   C. Some snipers on the SWAT team wear corrective lenses
   D. None of these

7. Summary of Evidence Collected to Date: 7.___
The only time Garson hears voices is on a day when he doesn't take his medication.
Prematurely Drawn Conclusion: On Fridays, Garson never hears voices.
Which of the following pieces of evidence, if any, would make it *reasonably certain* that the conclusion drawn is true?

   A. Garson is supposed to take his medication every day
   B. Garson usually undergoes shock therapy on Fridays
   C. Garson usually takes his medication and undergoes shock therapy on Fridays
   D. None of these

8. <u>Summary of Evidence Collected to Date</u>: 8._____
Among the three maintenance workersFrank, Lily and JeanFrank is not the tallest.
<u>Prematurely Drawn Conclusion:</u> Lily is the tallest.
Which of the following pieces of evidence, if any, would make it *reasonably certain* that the conclusion drawn is true?

A. Jean is not the tallest
B. Frank is the shortest
C. Jean is the shortest
D. None of these

9. <u>Summary of Evidence Collected to Date</u>: 9._____
Doctor Lyons went to the cafeteria for lunch today and did not eat dessert.
<u>Prematurely Drawn Conclusion:</u> The cafeteria did not serve dessert.
Which of the following pieces of evidence, if any, would make it *reasonably certain* that the conclusion drawn is true?

A. Dr. Lyons never eats dessert
B. When the cafeteria serves dessert, Dr. Lyons always eats it
C. The cafeteria rarely serves dessert when Dr. Lyons eats there
D. None of these

Questions 10-14

Questions 10 through 14 refer to Map #8 and measure your ability to orient yourself within a given section of town, neighborhood or particular area. Each of the questions describes a starting point and a destination. Assume that you are driving a car in the area shown on the map accompanying the questions. Use the map as a basis for the shortest way to get from one point to another without breaking the law.

On the map, a street marked by arrows, or by arrows and the words "One Way," indicates one-way travel, and should be assumed to be one-way for the entire length, even when there are breaks or jogs in the street. EXCEPTION: A street that does not have the same name over the full length.

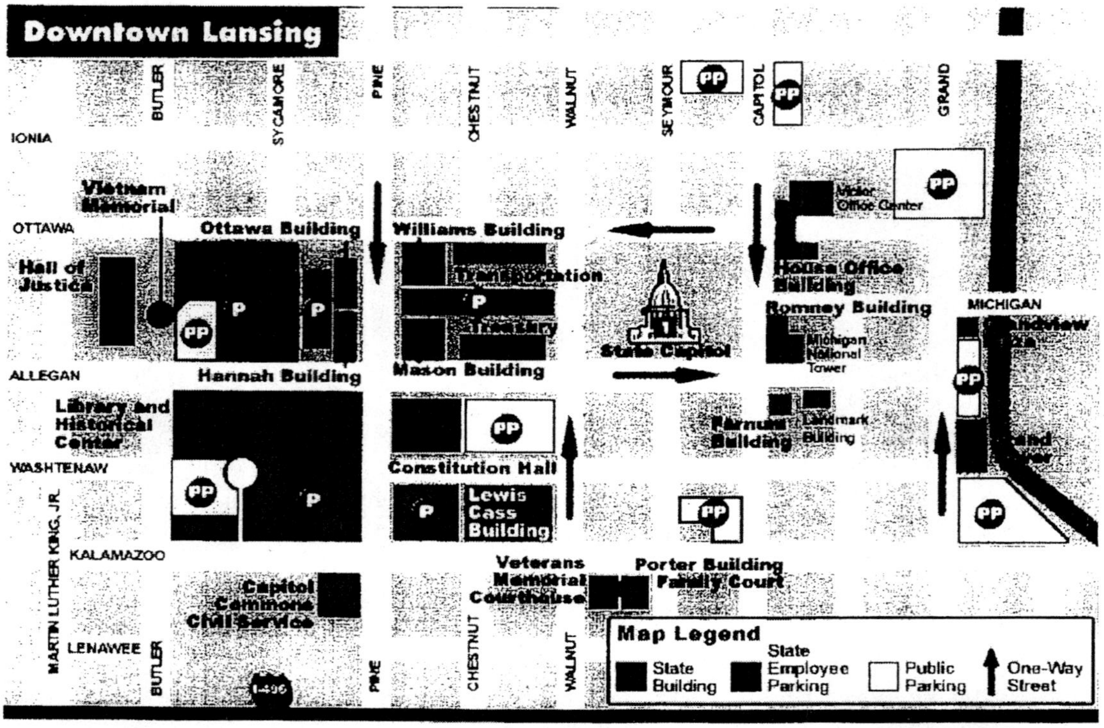

Map #8

10. The shortest legal way from the Library and Historical Center to Grandview Plaza is 10.____

A. south on Butler, east on Kalamazoo, north on Grand
B. east on Allegan, north on Grand
C. north on Butler, east on Ionia, south on Grand
D. north on Martin Luther King, Jr., east on Ottawa, south on Pine, east on Allegan, north on Grand

11. The shortest legal way from the Victor Office Center to the Mason Building is 11.____

A. west on Ottawa, south on Pine
B. south on Capitol, west on Allegan, north on Pine
C. south on Capitol, west on Washtenaw, north on Walnut, west on Allegan
D. west on Ottawa, north on Seymour, west on Ionia, south on Pine

12. The shortest legal way from the Treasury to the Hall of Justice is 12.____

A. north on Walnut, west on Ottawa, south on Martin Luther King, Jr.
B. west on Allegan
C. east on Allegan, north on Grand, west on Ottawa, south on Martin Luther King, Jr.
D. south on Walnut, west on Kalamazoo, north on Martin Luther King, Jr.

13. The shortest legal way from the Veterans Memorial Courthouse to the House Office Building is 13.____

A. north on Walnut, east on Ottawa
B. east on Kalamazoo, north on Capitol
C. east on Kalamazoo, north on Grand, west on Ottawa
D. north on Walnut, east on Allegan, north on Capitol

14. The shortest legal way from Grand Tower to Constitution Hall is 14.____

A. west on Washtenaw
B. north on Grand, west on Allegan, south on Pine
C. north on Grand, west on Ottawa, south on Pine
D. south on Grand, west on Kalamazoo, north on Pine

Questions 15-19

Questions 15 through 19 refer to Figure #8, on the following page, and measure your ability to understand written descriptions of events. Each question presents a description of an accident or event and asks you which of the five drawings in Figure #8 BEST represents it.

In the drawings, the following symbols are used:

Moving vehicle:  Non-moving vehicle: 

Pedestrian or bicyclist: 

The path and direction of travel of a vehicle or pedestrian is indicated by a solid line.
The path and direction of travel of each vehicle or pedestrian directly involved in a collision from the point of impact is indicated by a dotted line.
In the space at the right, print the letter of the drawing that best fits the descriptions written below:

15. A driver headed west on Holly runs a red light and turns left. He sideswipes a car headed south in the intersection, and then flees south on Bay. The southbound car is diverted into the rear end of a car parked in the southbound lane on Bay. 15.____

16. A driver headed east on Holly runs a red light. Another driver headed south through the intersection slams on her brakes just in time to avoid a serious collision. The eastbound driver glances off the front of the southbound car and continues east, where he collides with a car parked in the eastbound lane on Holly. 16.____

17. A driver headed east on Holly runs a red light. She strikes the left front of a westbound car that is turning left from Holly onto Bay, and then veers left and strikes the rear end of a car parked in the northbound lane on Bay. 17.____

18. A driver headed north on Bay strikes the right front of a car heading south in the intersection of Bay and Holly. After the collision, the driver veers left and collides with the rear end of a car parked in the westbound lane of Holly. The southbound car veers left and collides with the rear end of a car in the eastbound lane on Holly. 18.____

19. A driver headed north on Bay strikes the left front of a car heading south in the intersection of Bay and Holly. After the collision, the driver continues north and collides with the rear end of a car parked in the northbound lane. The southbound car continues south and collides with the rear end of a car in the southbound lane. 19.___

FIGURE #8

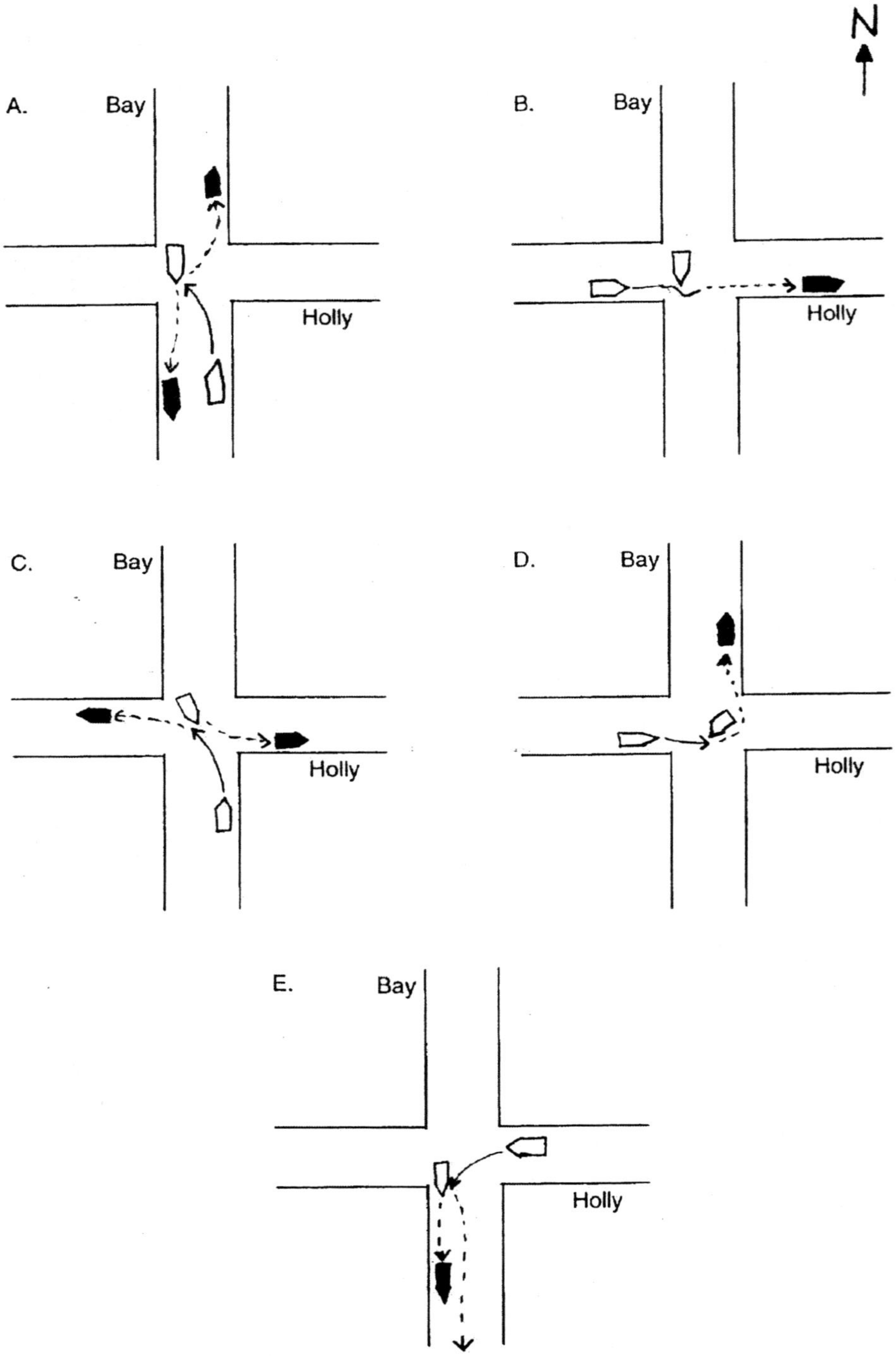

Questions 20-22

In questions 20 through 22, choose the word or phrase CLOSEST in meaning to the word or phrase printed in capital letters.

20. LIABLE 20.____

A. sensitive
B. dishonest
C. responsible
D. valid

21. CLAIM 21.____

A. debt
B. period
C. denial
D. banishment

22. ADMISSIBLE 22.____

A. false
B. conclusive
C. acceptable
D. indisputable

Questions 23-25

Questions 23 through 25 measure your ability to do fieldwork-related arithmetic. Each question presents a separate arithmetic problem for you to solve.

23. Three departments divide an $800 payment. Department 1 takes $270, and Department 2 takes $150 more than Department 3. How much does Department 2 take? 23.____

A. $150 B. $190 C. $340 D. $490

24. Detective Smalley cleared 100 murder cases in five years. Each year he cleared six more than he cleared in the previous year. How many cases did he clear during the first year? 24.____

A. 6 B. 8 C. 12 D. 18

25. The purchasing agent bought three binders for $2 each, four reams of copier paper for $3 each and five packs of black pens for $7 each. How much did the agent spend? 25.____

A. $12.00 B. $25.20 C. $53.00 D. $72.00

KEY (CORRECT ANSWERS)

1. C
2. C
3. B
4. D
5. C

6. B
7. D
8. C
9. B
10. B

11. A
12. A
13. C
14. A
15. E

16. B
17. D
18. C
19. A
20. C

21. A
22. C
23. C
24. B
25. C

EXAMINATION SECTION
TEST 1

DIRECTIONS: Each question or incomplete statement is followed by several suggested answers or completions. Select the one that BEST answers the question or completes the statement. *PRINT THE LETTER OF THE CORRECT ANSWER IN THE SPACE AT THE RIGHT.*

1. Agent Jenner's team took on 25 cases last year and solved 17. The ratio of unsolved cases to the number of solved cases is 1.____

   A. 17:25
   B. 8:25
   C. 17:8
   D. 8:17

2. If x is an odd number, then $x + 1$ is 2.____

   A. an even number.
   B. an odd number.
   C. divisible by x
   D. a prime number

3. Which of the following statements is logically equivalent to the one below? 3.____
   "If you work for Excorp, you are a millionaire."

   A. If you do not work for Excorp, you are not a millionaire.
   B. If you do not work for Excorp, you may be a millionaire.
   C. If you are not a millionaire, you do not work for Excorp.
   D. If you are a millionaire, you work for Excorp.

4. Of the following, which is the largest fraction? 4.____

   A. 7/8
   B. 4/5
   C. 3/4
   D. 7/9

5. A hexagon has ______ sides. 5.____

   A. 5
   B. 6
   C. 7
   D. 8

6. A rectangle is 5 inches wide and 2 inches tall. The perimeter of the rectangle is ______ inches. 6.____

   A. 7
   B. 10
   C. 14
   D. 20

7. Which of the following must contain only right angles? 7.___

   I. square
   II. rectangle
   III. parallelogram
   IV. right triangle

   A. I only
   B. I and II
   C. I, II and III
   D. I, II, III and IV

8. In the annual promotion examinations, 8.___

   1. Marcus scored higher than Franklin.
   2. Taggart scored higher than Rosewood.
   3. Rosewood scored higher than Franklin.
   4. Yarnell scored higher than Taggart.

   Which of the following pieces of information would allow all five agents to be ranked in the order of their performance on the examination?

   A. Rosewood scored higher than Marcus.
   B. Yarnell had the highest score.
   C. Marcus, scored higher than Taggart.
   D. Yarnell scored higher than Marcus.

9. Carter closed 4 cases last month. Bloom closed 3 times as many-cases as Carter. Which of these will show the total number of cases closed by Bloom? 9.___

   A. The product of 4 and 3.
   B. The quotient of 4 and 3.
   C. The difference between 12 and 4.
   D. The quotient of 12 and 3.

10. 45/9 =12 - y 10.___
    y =

    A. 6 B. 7 C. 8 D. 9

11. Agent Langley recently started work on her new job. She worked 20% more hours in her third week than she did in the second week. She worked 30% more hours during her second week than her first, and she worked 10% less during her first week than her regularly scheduled weekly hours. If Agent Langley worked 46 hours in her third week on the job, approximately what are her regularly scheduled weekly work hours? 11.___

    A. 33 B. 38 C. 40 D. 48

12. In the Niagara office, there are *x* men and *y* women. The ratio of the number of men to the total number of people in the Niagara office would be expressed 12.___

    A. $(x - y):x$ B. $x:y$ C. $x:(x+y)$ D. $(x+y):x$

13. How many, faces does a triangular prism have? 13.____

A. 3 B. 4 C. 5 D. 6

14. The Maloneys, whose house was assessed at $ 100,000, paid $3000 in property taxes last year. If the Joneses paid the same rate, how much property tax did they pay on their house, assessed at $155,000? 14.____

A. $3333 B. $4200 C. $4650 D. $5640

15. Warren invested $6,000 in AmNex stock a year ago. Today the value of Warren's investment has risen to $7,200. If Warren had invested $15,000 a year ago instead of $6000, what would his investment be worth today? 15.____

A. $16,400 B. $18,000 C. $22,500 D. $33,000

16. The best estimate of the capacity of an ordinary drinking glass is 16.____

A. 3 liters
B. 30 cups
C. 300 milliliters
D. 30 fluid ounces

17. The fraction 3/5, expressed as a percent, is 17.____

A. 30% B. 35% C. 60% D. 80%

18. What is the missing number in the following sequence? 28, 31,37,?, 58 18.____

A. 43 B. 46 C. 48 D. 49

19. Bob, Tom, Gary, and Claire all work in Alexandria. One is an administrative assistant, one a supervisor, one a detective, and one a special agent. 19.____

1. Bob and Gary have lunch with the special agent.
2. Claire and Tom carpool with the detective.
3. Gary works in the same building as the administrative assistant and the detective.

Given the information above, the detective

A. must be Bob
B. must be Claire
C. must be Gary
D. cannot be determined from the given information

20. 20 / 0.8 = 20.____

A. 16 B. 24 C. 25 D. 27

21. A pyramid has a square base. How many edges does the pyramid have? 21.____

A. 4 B. 6 C. 8 D. 10

22. The menu at Al 's Restaurant offers 5 entrees, 4 sides, and 3 desserts. If a meal consists of an entree, a side, and a dessert, how many possible meals can be chosen from Al's menu? 22._

A. 25 B. 30 C. 60 D. 90

23. Agent Turco is marking off a perimeter in the shape of a regular polygon and plans to enclose it with orange tape. Which of the following pieces of information can be used to determine the total length of tape Agent Turco will need? 23._

I. The length of one side of the perimeter to be cordoned off
II. The number of sides on the perimeter
III. The distance from the center of the cordoned-off area to one side of the perimeter
IV. The area enclosed by the perimeter

A. I only
B. I and II
C. II and III
D. I, II and IV

24. A victim's purse contains only nickels and dimes. The ratio of nickels to dimes is 3: 4. There are 28 coins in all. What is the value of the dimes? 24._

A. $0.80 B. $1.60 C. $2.10 D. $2.40

25. Agent Brooks is examining a crime scene. Given the marks on the road, she concludes that a tire, on the truck that left tracks at the scene, traveled 82 inches in one full rotation. The approximate diameter of the tire that left the track is _______ inches. 25._

A. 13 B. 26 C. 32 D. 41

26. 2/4 ? 2/3 26._

In order to denote the relationship between the two numbers above, which of the following mathematical symbols belongs between the two numbers above

A. $=$ B. $<$ C. $\geq$ D. $>$

27. Aaron is twice as old as Bob. Five years ago, Aaron was 3 times as old as Bob. How old is Bob now? 27._

A. 8 B. 10 C. 15 D. 20

28. Detective Sturgis is directing a search over a rectangular grid that has sides of lengths x and y. He wants to cover the rectangle by using the smallest number of identical square search zones possible. The zones are to be placed adjacent to each other and are not to be exceed the area of the rectangle. The side length of each zone would be represented by the 28._

A. largest number that can divide both x and y
B. smallest number that is divisible by both x and y
C. difference between x and y
D. remainder of $x \div y$

29. At 3:00, the hands of a round analog clock are at a ______^{o} angle to each other 29.____

A. 45
B. 90
C. 180
D. 240

30. The county planning commission must decide how to use a 240-acre parcel of land. The commission sets aside 24 acres for watershed protection and an additional 88 acres for recreation. How many acres of land are set aside for watershed protection and recreation? 30.____

A. 64
B. 88
C. 112
D. 128

31. Which of the following always has four sides that are each equal in measure? 31.____

I. square
II. rectangle
III. parallelogram
IV. rhombus

A. I only
B. I and II
C. I and IV
D. I, II and III

32. Mr. Alexis is younger than 50 years of age. His age is a multiple of 3, 5, and 6. Mr. Alexis's age 32.____

A. is 15
B. is 30
C. is 40
D. can't be determined from the given information

33. On Friday morning the temperature was 78°F. By noon it had gone up 5°F, and by sundown it had gone down another 2°F. What was the temperature at sundown? 33.____

A. 71°F
B. 75°F
C. 81°F
D. 83°F

34. Of the following, the best estimate of the weight of a commercial delivery truck is 34.____

A. 300 ounces
B. 3000 grams
C. 3000 pounds
D. 300 tons

35. Each day that Scranton is late, he earns 5 demerits. Scranton has been late on each of the last 8 days. How many demerits did Scranton earn during that period? 35._

A. 15
B. 20
C. 40
D. 85

36. Smith, Taylor and Long solved a total of 56 cases during the last year. Smith solved 4 more cases than Taylor, and Long solved twice as many cases as Taylor. Which of the following is a reasonable conclusion? 36._

A. Taylor solved exactly half the total cases.
B. Smith and long solved an equal number of cases.
C. Long solved the most cases.
D. Smith solved the least number of cases.

37. Rectangle Q is 6 inches wide and 4 inches tall. Rectangle R is 5 inches wide and 3 inches tall. The perimeter of rectangle Q is _______ inches longer than the perimeter of rectangle R. 37._

A. 1
B. 2
C. 3
D. 4

38. Agent Stuckey cordons off a crime scene, outlining a square whose area is about 125 square yards. Which of the following measures, in yards, would be closest to the length of one side of this square? 38._

A. 9.5
B. 10
C. 11
D. 13

39. A binar is worth four sepetas. You can trade 3 hirseths for a jelet. You can trade 5 binars for 2 hirseths. 39._
Which is most valuable?

A. Binar
B. Sepeta
C. Jelet
D. It cannot be determined from the information given

40. Harkin and Laws are in business together. They have agreed to split the profits in a ratio of 60% to 40%. The total profits are $80,000. The largest share of the profits equals. 40._

A. $36,000
B. $40,000
C. $48,000
D. $60,000

41. In the five-story Cl]aremont Building, each floor is occupied by the offices of a professional. 41.____

1. Ms. Garrity's story is above Mr. Ishmael's.
2. Ms. Johnson's story is between Ms. Garrity's and Dr. Hortense's.
3. Ms. Penelope's story is between Dr. Hortense's and Mr. Ishmael's.
4. Ms. Johnson is on the fourth story.

Who occupies the second story?

A. Ms. Penelope
B. Ms. Garrity
C. Mr. Ishmael
D. It cannot be determined from the given information.

42. Agent Grimley can complete an average of 18 pages of paperwork during his 30-minute lunch break. He has 380 pages of paperwork outstanding. How many hours will it take him to complete this amount? 42.____

A. 9
B. 11
C. 13
D. 15

43. Which of the following fractions is the smallest? 43.____

A. 7/32
B. 7/8
C. 9/16
D. 3/4

44. Which of the following figures has only one pair of parallel lines? 44.____

A. Trapezoid
B. Hexagon
C. Parallelogram
D. Rhombus

45. The only time Henry and June patrol together is on an evening when Henry is assigned to the 12th precinct. Henry is assigned to the 12th precinct on Tuesdays and Thursdays. Based only on the information above, which of the following must be true? 45.____

A. Henry and June usually patrol on Thursday.
B. Henry and June would not be patrolling together if Henry were not assigned to the 12th precinct.
C. Henry and June never patrol on Friday or Saturday.
D. Henry and June patrol at least eight times a month.

46. When 123,456 is divided by 12, the remainder is 46.____

A. 0
B. 18
C. 144
D. 10,288

47. Agent Speer uses his cell phone to interview a potential witness. The first minute of the call costs $1.23, and each additional minute costs 89 cents. The total cost of the call is $15.47. If x is used to represent the total of minutes talked, which of the following equations can be used to solve the problem? 47._

A. 1.23 + 0.89(x-1)= 15.47
B. (1.23 + 0.89)(x-1)= 15.47
C. (1.23 + 0.89)x= 15.47
D. 1.23 + 0.89=15.47

48. Ms. Stanislaus is paid on commission. She receives 6% of the total real estate sales that are conducted by her office. Last year, Ms. Stanislaus made $420,000. How much real estate did her office sell? 48._

A. $2.52 million
B. $6.6 million
C. $7 million
D. $8.3 million

49. An agent interviews 26 people in an apartment building. She discovers that 14 knew the victim; 10 knew the suspect; and 5 were at home when the crime was committed. Four knew both the victim and the suspect; three knew the victim and were at home when the crime was committed; and one knew the suspect and was at home when the crime was committed. None of the 26 people knows both the victim and the suspect, and was at home when the crime was committed.
How many of the people interviewed know neither the victim nor the suspect, and were not at home when the crime was committed? 49._

A. 3
B. 5
C. 8
D. The answer cannot be determined from the given information.

50. Mrs. Nesbit drove 150 miles in 2 hours and 30 minutes. Which of the following formulas will give Mrs. Nesbit's average speed in miles per hour? 50._

A. 150 multiplied by 2.5
B. 150 multiplied by 150
C. 150 divided by 2.5
D. 150 divided by 2.3

KEY (CORRECT ANSWERS)

1.	D	11.	A	21.	C	31.	C	41.	A
2.	A	12.	C	22.	C	32.	B	42.	B
3.	C	13.	C	23.	B	33.	C	43.	A
4.	A	14.	C	24.	B	34.	C	44.	A
5.	B	15.	B	25.	B	35.	C	45.	C
6.	C	16.	C	26.	B	36.	C	46.	A
7.	B	17.	C	27.	B	37.	D	47.	A
8.	A	18.	B	28.	A	38.	C	48.	C
9.	A	19.	A	29.	B	39.	C	49.	B
10.	B	20.	C	30.	C	40.	C	50.	C

TEST 2

DIRECTIONS: Each question or incomplete statement is followed by several suggested answers or completions. Select the one that BEST answers the question or completes the statement. *PRINT THE LETTER OF THE CORRECT ANSWER IN THE SPACE AT THE RIGHT.*

1. What is the missing number in the following series of numbers? 1, 4, 9,?, 25 1.___

   A. 12
   B. 15
   C. 16
   D. 18

2. During the course of her investigations, Agent Stearns drove these distances in one week: 102.4, 187.6,89.4, and 206.0 miles. 2.___
   To calculate how many gallons of gas Agent Stearns consumed during this week, it is necessary to know the

   A. cost per gallon of gasoline
   B. number of trips made by Agent Steams during the week
   C. average number of miles per gallon of gasoline for Agent Stearns' car
   D. average speed, in miles per hour, driven by Agent Stearns during these trips

3. Which of these is NOT equal to 2.87? 3.___

   A. 2.87 ÷ 0.1
   B. 7.2-4.33
   C. 287%
   D. 0.0287 x 100

4. The best estimate of 281 x 324 is 4.___

   A. 900
   B. 9,000
   C. 90,000
   D. 900,000

5. In the annual promotion examinations, 5.___
   1. Marcus scored higher than Franklin.
   2. Taggart scored higher than Rosewood.
   3. Rosewood scored higher than Franklin.
   4. Yarnell scored higher than Taggart.

   Based only on the information above, which of the following must be true?

   A. Franklin had the lowest score.
   B. Rosewood scored higher than Yarnell.
   C. Taggart scored higher than Marcus.
   D. Taggart had the highest score.

6. Gerald patrols from 2:45 pm to 5:15 pm each day. How long does he patrol each day? 6.___

   A. 1 hour and 45 minutes
   B. 2 hours and 30 minutes
   C. 3 hours and 15 minutes
   D. 3 hours and 30 minutes

7. On the first day of the year, the Granada Division opened 4 cases. After 9 days, they had opened 36 cases. After 15 days, they had opened 60 cases. At this rate, how many cases will the Granada Division have opened after 21 days? 7.____

A. 66
B. 84
C. 111
D. 120

8. Of the 400 people who work at Galatea Inc., 90 work in administrative or supervisory positions and 230 work in production. Exactly 20 people occupy positions that are classified as both production and administrative/ supervisory in nature. What is the probability that an employee of Galatea is in a position that is classified as *neither* administrative/ supervisory or production? 8.____

A. 1/4
B. 1/14
C. 3/20
D. 3/4

9. An officer is trying to arrange four men in a lineup. Each man is wearing a different colored shirt. The man in the blue shirtthe main suspectcannot be placed on either end of the row because he begins to shout disruptively. He insists on being placed immediately next to the man in the white shirt. How many different ways can the officer arrange the men in the lineup? 9.____

A. 1
B. 2
C. 4
D. 6

10. 8/16 ? 16/32 10.____
In order to denote the relationship between the two numbers above, which of the following mathematical symbols belongs between the two numbers above?

A. =
B. <
C. ≥
D. #

11. 30 Alkan employees walk to work; 90 take public transportation; 30 ride their bicycles; and 150 drive or carpool. What percentage of these employees ride their bicycles to work? 11.____

A. 5
B. 10
C. 25
D. 30

12. The comptroller of the Hudson office plans to buy 3 dozen forms for each person in the office. 28 people work in the office. If the forms cost $4.80 per package, what other information is needed to calculate the amount the comptroller will need to spend on forms? 12.___

A. The number of tasks that will require forms.
B. The number of forms per package.
C. The number of forms in a dozen.
D. The number of people who will use the forms.

13. How many edges does a cube have? 13.___

A. 6
B. 8
C. 10
D. 12

14. To be eligible for membership in the Black Berets, a person must be able to either swim underwater for at least a minute, or complete the Iron Man triathlon in less than eleven hours. Jennifer has run the Iron Man several times and her best time was 12:45:42. Which of the following statements must be true? 14.___

A. No member of the Black Berets is capable of running the Iron Man triathlon in less than eleven hours.
B. Jenniter can become a member of the Black Berets by swimming underwater for at least one minute.
C. Some members of the Black Berets have never swum underwater for more than a minute.
D. Jennifer cannot become a member of the Black Berets.

15. Hearns has a roll of crime scene tape 12 yards long. He needs 40 feet of tape to close off the crime scene. To find out if he has enough tape, Hearns should first 15.___

A. multiply 40 by 3
B. multiply 40 by 12
C. multiply 12 by 12
D. multiply 12 by 3

16. On Sunday, Frank builds a deck for his family in the back yard. He plans to use 30 redwood boards, and will need 12 screws for each board. To be safe, Frank buys 30 more screws than he needs. How many screws did he buy? 16.___

A. 300
B. 360
C. 390
D. 400

17. Of the following fractions, which is smallest? 17.___

A. 8/15
B. 5/6
C. 11/20
D. 7/12

18. 4% of 650 is 18.____

A. 24
B. 26
C. 72
D. 260

19. There are two sets of numbers, A and B. Each number in set A is related in the same way to the number below it in B: 19.____
A: 1, 3, 5
B: 6, 18,30
If the number in A is 9, one way to find out its corresponding number in set B is to

A. add 9 and 2
B. subtract 2 from 9
C. add 9 and 6
D. multiply 9 by 6

20. A random canvass on Boxelder Street shows that 42 out of 80 people have parked illegally in the past month. If 2,000 people live in the Boxelder neighborhood, what is the best prediction of the total number who will park illegally in a month? 20.____

A. 120
B. 280
C. 420
D. 1000

21. An employer administers random drug screenings to 40 out of every 100 employees. Of those employees screened, one out of every 20 tests positive for some kind of controlled substance. Based on the testing process described above, which of the following is true? 21.____

A. Every batch of 100 employees will have about two employees who have a controlled substance in their systems.
B. To achieve a representative sample, the employer should test a larger number of employees.
C. About 2 percent of the employees screened test positive for a controlled substance
D. About 5 percent of the employees screened test positive for a controlled substance

22. 4 tickets to the Murphy Follies cost $9.00. How much will a dozen tickets cost? 22.____

A. $16.00
B. $27.00
C. $36.00
D. $42.50

23. Officials estimate that of 320,000 people who attended the parade left behind 40 tons of garbage. A ton equals 2000 pounds. How many pounds of garbage did each person leave behind at the parade? 23.____

A. 1/4
B. 1/2
C. 1 1/4
D. 2 1/3

24. Agents Harris and Nieman discover a cardboard box filled with an illicit substance The box is 60 inches long, 18 inches wide, and 24 inches high. What is the approximate volume of the substance, in cubic feet? 24.___

A. 7.5 B. 15 C. 19 D. 24

25. Agent Lopez does not work if Agent Hingis is not working. 25.___
Given the above conclusion, which of the following would also be true?

I. Agent Hingis may work when Agent Lopez is not working.
II. Agent Lopez and Agent Hingis may work at the same time.
III. Agent Lopez may work when Agent Hingis does not.

A. I only B. II only C. II and III D. I and II
E. I and III

26. Of the following, which is the largest? 26.___

A. 1/4 B. 3/5 C. 9/20 D. 1/2

27. Larry, Moe and Curly each have some coins in a pants pocket. 27.___

1. Larry has three quarters and two dimes.
2. Moe has two dimes and a nickel.
3. Curly has three nickels and a penny.

To be guaranteed of receiving at least one coin of each denomination, and without looking at any of the coins before accepting them, you must

A. take four coins each from Larry and Curly
B. take all five of Larry's coins, all four of Moe's, and three of Curly's
C. take three coins from Larry, two from Moe, and three from Curly
D. take four coins from Larry, two from Moe, and two from Curly

28. Greeley drove 1500 miles in 25 hours, and Earnhart drove 900 miles in 15 hours. Greeley's average speed was 28.___

A. equal to Earnhart's average speed.
B. 3 mph faster than Earnhart's.
C. 5 mph faster than Earnhart's.
D. 2 mph slower than Earnhart's.

29. *Agent Horner runs an eight-minute mile. At this average rate, how long will it take him to run a 26-mile marathon?* 29.___
Which of the following problems can be solved using the same mathematical operations that would be used to solve the problem above?

A. A clerk has to place a shipment of 480 cans on 22 shelves. If each shelf will contain the same number of cans, how many cans will the clerk place on each shelf?
B. The average laptop computer weighs 3.4 pounds. What would be the weight of a shipment of 1500 laptop computers?
C. Agent Dickey ran 26 miles in 320 minutes. On average, how long did it take her to run a mile?
D. A bag of sand weighs 80 pounds. How many sandbags can be made from 5 tons of sand?

30. Together, two items of evidence, *x* and *y*, weigh one pound. If item * weighs 11 ounces, item *y* weighs 30._____

A. 5 ounces
B. 9 ounces
C. 13 ounces
D. 1.2 pounds

31. Agent Farkus interviews 30 people at the airport. 16 speak French; 16 speak Spanish, and 11 speak English. 5 speak both French and English, and of these, only 3 speak Spanish as well. 5 speak only English, and 8 speak only Spanish. How many of the 30 speak only French? 31._____

A. 3
B. 7
C. 9
D. The answer cannot be determined from the given information.

32. A crime was committed in a classroom that contained 2 teachers, 3 aides, 4 girls and 5 boys. Assuming that one of these committed the crime, what is the probability that the crime was committed by either an aide or a girl? 32._____

A. 1/14
B. 3/14
C. 7/14
D. 9/14

33. Which of the following has two pairs of opposite sides that are parallel? 33._____

I. square
II. rectangle
III. rhombus
IV. parallelogram

A. I only
B. I and II
C. I, II and IV
D. I, II, III and IV

34. Throughout the day, a preset traffic light functions as follows: it is red for 30 seconds, yellow for 15 seconds, and green for 45 seconds. What is the chance that the light is green at any given moment? 34._____

A. 30%
B. 45%
C. 50%
D. 65%

35. After an employee embezzled 20% of its Sunday donations, St Leo's Church had $2000 left. The original amount of the donations was 35._____

A. $500
B. $1500
C. $2500
D. $3000

36. Michaels estimates that he spends a third of his travel budget on gasoline and a quarter of it on meals. If his travel budget is $300 for the month, how much is left over for other expenses? 36.___

A. $114.29
B. $125.00
C. $144.00
D. $175.50

37. 56/7 = x - 5 37.___
x =

A. 13
B. 14
C. 15
D. 16

38. What is the missing number in the following sequence? 79,67,55,43, ? 38.___

A. 34
B. 32
C. 31
D. 30

39. Officer Hardy confiscated 8 cases of beer from the party. There are 24 cans in a case. How many cans of beer did Officer Hardy confiscate? 39.___

A. 160
B. 172
C. 184
D. 192

40. Which of the following numbers is a multiple of 12 and a factor of 2400? 40.___

A. 48
B. 36
C. 8
D. 3

41. According to the state bureau of crime statistics, the number of burglary victims was 184% larger this year than it was in the previous year. In other words, the number of burglary victims 41.___

A. almost tripled
B. almost doubled
C. almost quadrupled
D. more than tripled

42. 7 is _______ % of 140. 42.____

A. .5
B. 1.5
C. 5
D. 12

43. 4 + x/6 = 6 43.____
x=

A. 2
B. 12
C. 16
D. 10

44. A store is advertising a sale in which all merchandise is priced at 30% off the original price. If an item from the store originally cost *x* dollars, who much will it cost during the sale? 44.____

A. 3*x*
B. x - .3
C. 1.3 *x*
D. .7*x*

45. What is the rule for the following sequence of numbers? 18 , 25 ,32 , 39 ,46 45.____

A. Each number in the sequence is 7 more than the previous number.
B. Each number in the sequence is 8 more than the previous number.
C. Each number in the sequence is 11 more than the previous number.
D. Each number in the sequence is 13 more than the previous number.

46. Two numbers relate to each other in the ratio 3:5. Added together, the numbers equal 80. The smallest of the two numbers is 46.____

A. 15
B. 25
C. 30
D. 50

47. Which of the following statements is logically equivalent to the one below? 47.____
"The *Agassiz* will launch if it does not rain."

A. If it does not rain, the Agassiz will not launch.
B. If the Agassiz did not launch, it did not rain.
C. If it rains, the Agassiz may launch.
D. If it rains, the Agassiz will not launch.

48. Which two consecutive, positive whole numbers have a product equal to 1122? 48.____

A. 36 and 37
B. 33 and 34
C. 22 and 51
D. 11 and 102

49. Increasing a number by 4 1/2% is equivalent to multiplying it by 49.___

A. .045
B. .45
C. 1.045
D. 1.45

50. Gerald's wage of $ 10 per hour is increased by 5%. If Gerald now works 8 hours, what will he be paid? 50.___

A. $82.50
B. $84.00
C. $85.00
D. $88.50

KEY (CORRECT ANSWERS)

1. C	11. B	21. D	31. B	41. A
2. C	12. B	22. B	32. C	42. C
3. A	13. D	23. A	33. D	43. B
4. C	14. B	24. B	34. C	44. D
5. A	15. D	25. D	35. C	45. A
6. B	16. C	26. B	36. B	46. C
7. B	17. A	27. A	37. A	47. D
8. A	18. B	28. A	38. C	48. B
9. C	19. D	29. B	39. D	49. C
10. A	20. D	30. A	40. A	50. B

INTERPRETING STATISTICAL DATA GRAPHS, CHARTS AND TABLES

EXAMINATION SECTION
TEST 1

DIRECTIONS: Each question or incomplete statement is followed by several suggested answers or completions. Select the one that BEST answers the question or completes the statement. *PRINT THE LETTER OF THE CORRECT ANSWER IN THE SPACE AT THE RIGHT.*

Questions 1-5.

DIRECTIONS: Questions 1 through 5 are to be answered SOLELY on the basis of the contents of the following graph.

3-YEAR STUDY OF ACTIONS
DIRECTLY LEADING TO ASSAULTS ON
DETECTIVES/INVESTIGATORS
NUMBER OF INJURIES

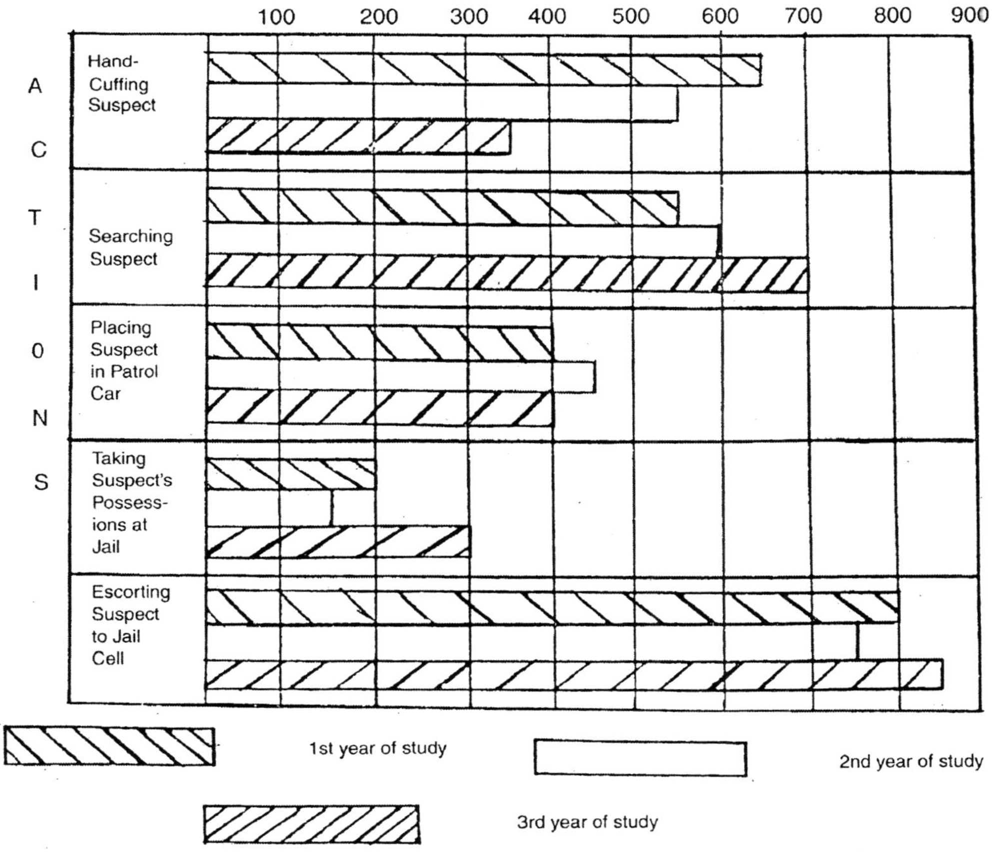

1. Which one of the following MOST closely approximates the number of assaults on Detectives/Investigators for all five actions during the second year of the study? 1.___

   A. 1850 B. 2450 C. 2500 D. 5050

2. Which one of the following conditions led to the GREATEST increase in number of assaults on Detectives/Investigators between the 2nd and 3rd years of the study? 2.___

   A. Handcuffing the suspect
   B. Searching the suspect
   C. Taking the suspect's possessions at the jail
   D. Escorting the suspect to the jail cell

3. Which one of the following MOST closely approximates the TOTAL number of Detective/Investigator injuries attributed to placing the suspect in patrol car for the three years of the study? 3.___

   A. 750 B. 1050 C. 1250 D. 1550

4. Which one of the following actions resulted in the GREATEST number of assaults on Detectives/Investigators throughout the three years of the study? 4.___

   A. Taking the suspect's possessions at the jail
   B. Handcuffing the suspect
   C. Placing the suspect in the patrol car
   D. Escorting the suspect to the jail cell

5. Compared to the first year, the number of assaults in the third year of the study attributable to all five situations was 5.___

   A. 300 more B. 300 fewer
   C. 600 more D. the same

KEY (CORRECT ANSWERS)

1. C
2. C
3. C
4. D
5. D

TEST 2

Questions 1-5.

DIRECTIONS: Questions 1 through 5 are to be answered SOLELY on the basis of the information given in the table below. The numbers which have been omitted from the table can be calculated from the other numbers which are given.

NUMBER OF DWELLING UNITS CONSTRUCTED

Year	Private one-family houses	In private apt. houses	In public housing	Total dwelling units
1996	4,500	500	600	5,600
1997	9,200	5,300	2,800	17,300
1998	8,900	12,800	6,800	28,500
1999	12,100	15,500	7,100	34,700
2000	?	12,200	14,100	39,200
2001	10,200	26,000	8,600	44,800
2002	10,300	17,900	7,400	35,600
2003	11,800	18,900	7,700	38,400
2004	12,700	22,100	8,400	43,200
2005	13,300	24,300	8,100	45,700
TOTALS	105,900	?	?	?

1. According to this table, the AVERAGE number of public housing units constructed yearly during the period 1996 through 2005 was 1.____

   A. 7,160 B. 6,180 C. 7,610 D. 6,810

2. Of the following, the two years in which the number of private one-family homes constructed was GREATEST for the two years together is 2.____

   A. 1998 and 1999
   B. 1997 and 2003
   C. 1998 and 2004
   D. 2001 and 2002

3. For the entire period of 1996 through 2005, the TOTAL of all private one-family houses constructed exceeded the total of all public housing units constructed by 3.____

   A. 34,300 B. 45,700 C. 50,000 D. 83,900

4. Of the total number of private apartment house dwelling units constructed in the ten years given in the table, the percentage which was constructed in 2002 was MOST NEARLY 4.____

   A. 5% B. 11% C. 16% D. 21%

5. Considering dwelling units of all types, the average number constructed annually in the period from 2001 through 2005 was greater than the average number constructed annually in the period from 1996 through 2000 by 5.____

   A. 16,480 B. 33,320 C. 79,300 D. 82,400

KEY (CORRECT ANSWERS)

1. A
2. C
3. A
4. B
5. A

TEST 3

Questions 1-5.

DIRECTIONS: Questions 1 through 5 are to be answered SOLELY on the basis of the information contained in the two tables shown below.

TABLE 1 Yearly Incidence of Traffic Violations in Community Y

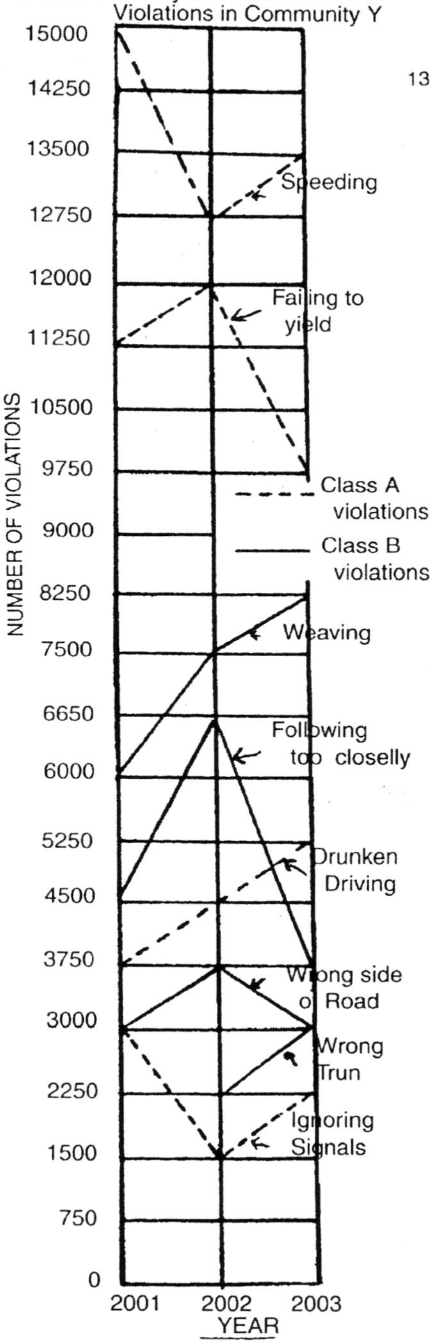

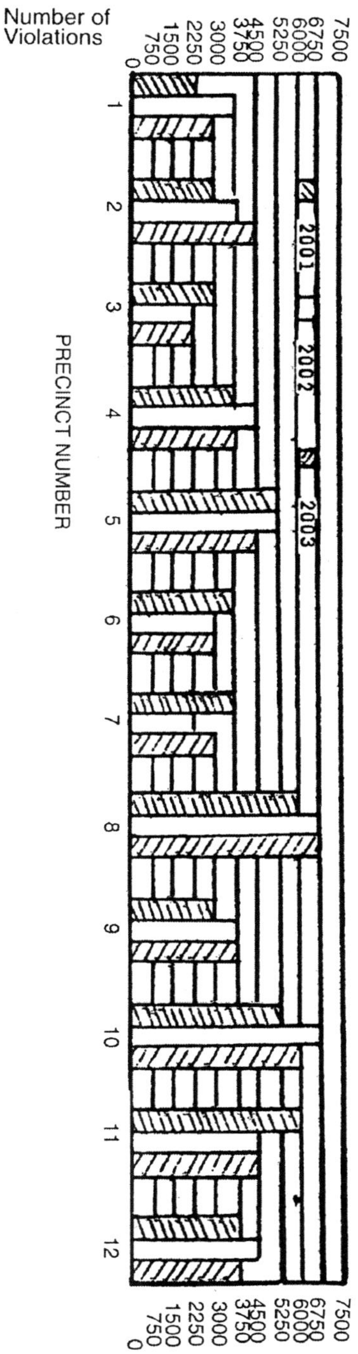

TABLE 2. TRAFFIC VIOLATION BY PRECINCT IN COMMUNITY Y- 2001 - 2003

1. Of the total number of traffic violations that occurred in Community Y during 2002, the percentage that occurred in Precinct 10 was MOST NEARLY 1.____

   A. 13.2% B. 14.8% C. 35.3% D. 132%

2. Of the following traffic violations, the one for which the number occurring in 2003 exceeded the average of the preceding two years by the GREATEST amount was 2.____

   A. speeding
   B. drunken driving
   C. ignoring signals
   D. weaving

3. According to these groups, the ratio of Class B violations to Class A violations showed 3.____

   A. the greatest increase from 2001 to 2002
   B. the greatest increase from 2002 to 2003
   C. the greatest increase from 2001 to 2003
   D. a decrease from 2001 to 2003

4. The one of the following traffic violations which showed the GREATEST percentage decrease from 2001 to 2003 was 4.____

   A. speeding
   B. failing to yield
   C. drunken driving
   D. ignoring signals

5. Assume that in 2004 there was a 10% increase in Class A violations and the same 10% increase in Class B violations over the preceding year, for each violation and in each precinct. Assume further that Precincts 11 and 12 were eliminated in 2004 and that their areas and number of violations were equally distributed among the 8th, 9th, and 10th Precincts. 5.____
   The number of violations of both classes that did occur in 2004 in Precinct 10 is MOST NEARLY

   A. 9,025 B. 350 C. 9,625 D. 15,075

KEY (CORRECT ANSWERS)

1. C
2. D
3. A
4. D
5. A

TEST 4

Questions 1-5.

DIRECTIONS: Questions 1 through 5 are to be answered SOLELY on the basis of the information contained in the graph on the following page.

MONTHLY INCIDENCE FOR ROBBERY AND BURGLARY FOR 2000
AND MONTHLY AVERAGES FOR THESE CRIMES FOR THE PRECEDING 5 YEARS

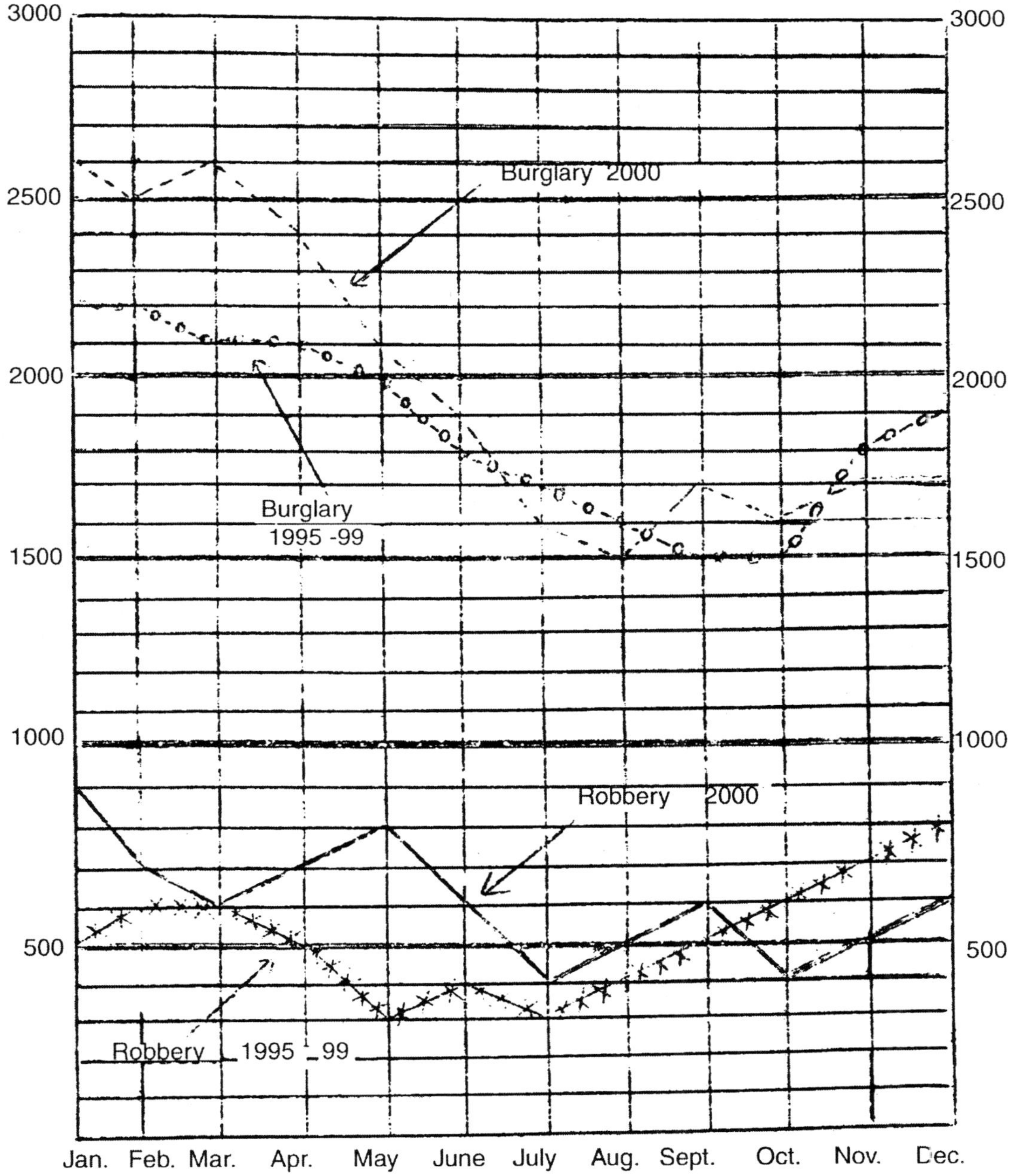

1. Of the total number of burglaries committed during the first half of 2000, the percentage which occurred during March was MOST NEARLY 1.____

   A. 15% B. 17% C. 18% D. 21%

2. The one of the following months for which the percentage increase in the 2000 incidence of crime over the previous five-year average incidence of crime for the same month is GREATEST is 2.____

   A. robbery during January
   B. burglary during March
   C. burglary during January
   D. robbery during May

3. A consideration of the data presented for robbery in the graph would justify the statement that the number of robberies committed during 3.____

   A. January of each of the years from 1995 through 1999 was less than the number of robberies committed during January 2000
   B. March of 2000 was the same as the number of robberies committed during March of 1999
   C. April of 2000 was 200 more than the total number of robberies committed during April of all of the preceding five years combined
   D. August of 2000 exceeded the average number of robberies committed during the months of August of the preceding 5 years

4. Assume that during December 1993 and December 1994 there was a combined total of 900 robberies committed. A seven-year average (1993-1999) can now be obtained. Of the following, it would be MOST correct to state that for the month of December, in connection with robberies, the 4.____

   A. 7-year average is less than the 5-year average by 100
   B. 7-year average is less than the 5-year average by 300
   C. difference between the 7-year average and the 2000 figure is greater than the difference between the 5-year average and the 1990 figure
   D. difference between the 7-year average and the 2000 figure is the same as the difference between the 5-year average and the 1990 figure

5. The month in 2000 during which the percentage decline from the preceding month in incidence of burglaries exceeded the percentage decline in average incidence of burglaries for the same period during the preceding 5 years by the GREATEST amount was 5.____

   A. May B. June C. July D. August

KEY (CORRECT ANSWERS)

1. C
2. D
3. D
4. A
5. C

TEST 5

Questions 1-5.

DIRECTIONS: Questions 1 through 5 are to be answered on the basis of the information given in the table below. The numbers which have been omitted can be calculated from the other numbers which are given.

NUMBER OF VEHICLE ACCIDENTS IN GREAT CITY
FOR THE PERIOD 1996 TO 2001

County	1996	1997	1998	1999	2000	2001	TOTAL
A	8,141	8,680	8,554	8,213	8,822	8,753	?
B	3,301	3,836	3,623	4,108	4,172	3 , 735	22,775
C	6,480	7,562	7,275	7,872	8,554	8,341	46,084
D	3,366	3,801	3,715	3,740	4,473	4,390	23,485
E	259	272	?	252	255	457	1,741
TOTAL	21,547	24,151	23,413	24,185	26,276	25,676	145,248

1. For the total period covered by the table, the average number of vehicle accidents per year in County A exceeded the average number per year in County D by APPROXIMATELY 1.____

A. 4,550 B. 5,450 C. 8,520 D. 27,000

2. In comparing the years 2000 and 2001, the one of the following statements which is MOST accurate is that the 2.____

A. number of accidents in County E and County B combined increased
B. number of accidents decreased in each of the five counties
C. number of accidents in County D and County E combined increased
D. decrease in the number of accidents in County C amounted to more than one-half of the decrease in the total number of accidents for the entire city

3. The percentage increase in 2001 over 1996 in vehicle accidents was LARGEST in County 3.____

A. A B. B C. C D. D

4. If the counties are ranked for each year according to the number of accidents (largest number to rank first), a county which will NOT have the same rank each year is County 4.____

A. A B. D C. C D. E

5. The LARGEST increase in the number of vehicle accidents from any one year to the next was in County 5.____

A. C B. B C. A D. D

KEY (CORRECT ANSWERS)

1. A
2. C
3. D
4. B
5. A

TEST 6

Questions 1-4.

DIRECTIONS: Questions 1 through 4 are to be answered on the basis of the following graph.

AVERAGE HOURLY INCIDENCE OF ARRESTS AND ACCIDENTS
FOR COMMUNITY X

(Hourly figures represent total number of occurrences in the immediately preceding hour)

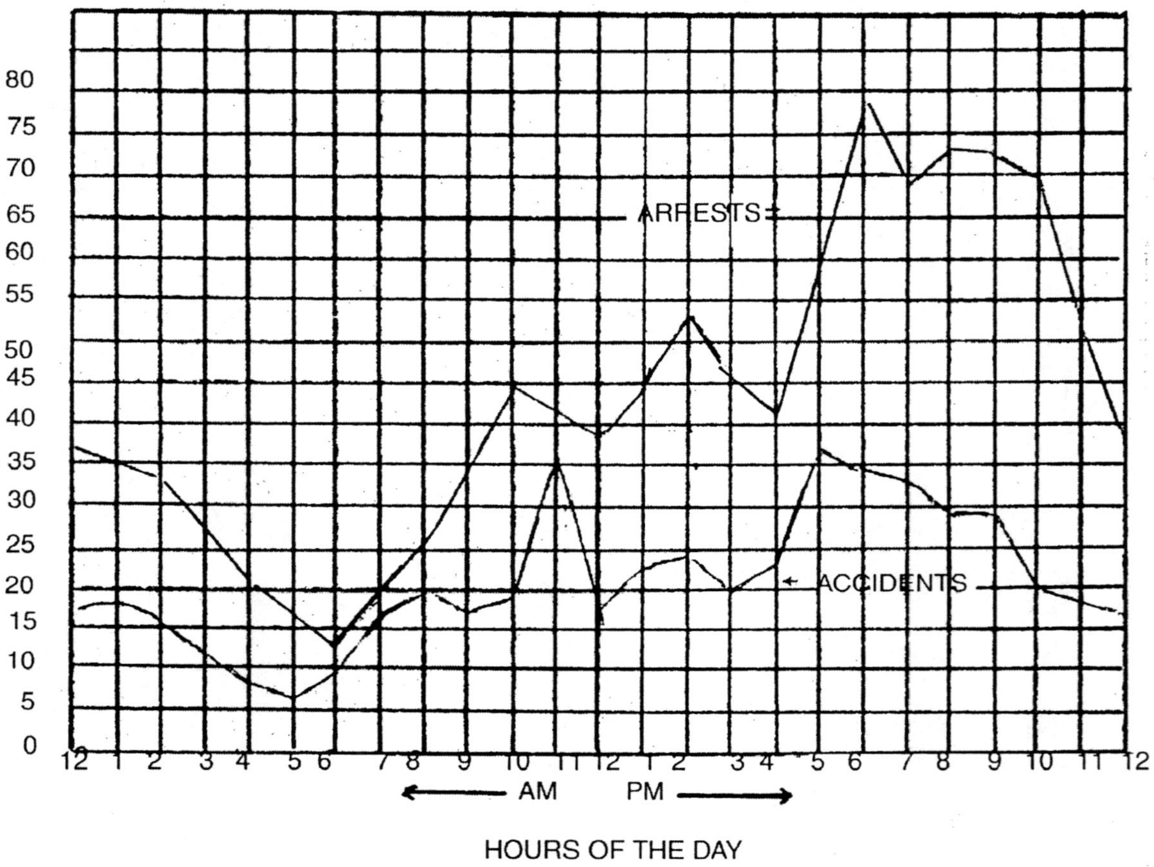

1. According to this graph, of the following hours of the day, the hour which shows the HIGHEST ratio of arrests to accidents is 1.____

   A. 2 P.M. B. 6 P.M. C. 8 P.M. D. 10 P.M.

2. According to the above graph, the LEAST average hour-to-hour variation, during the following time periods, was in the number of 2.____

A. arrests during the 4 P.M. through 8 P.M. period
B. accidents during the 12 Noon through 4 P.M. period
C. arrests during the 8 P.M. through 12 Midnight period
D. accidents during the 8 A.M. through 12 Noon period

3. According to the above graph, of all the accidents occurring from 12 Noon through Midnight, the percentage which occurred from 12 Noon through 4 P.M. was MOST NEARLY 3.____

A. 26% B. 30% C. 34% D. 38%

4. On the basis of the above graph, 4.____

A. an equal number of accidents was recorded daily at 8 A.M. and 3 P.M.
B. on any given day, during the year covered, there were more arrests recorded at 2 P.M. than at 10 A.M.
C. the number of accidents entered in the first 12 o'clock column must always equal the number of accidents in the last 12 o'clock column
D. the wide variation in the number of arrests makes statistical interpretation of the figures unreliable

---

KEY (CORRECT ANSWERS)

1. D
2. B
3. B
4. C

TEST 7

Questions 1-5.

DIRECTIONS: Questions 1 through 5 are to be answered on the basis of the following two statements and the diagram shown on the following page.

Statement 1: Room G will be the public intake room from which persons will be directed to Room F or Room H; under no circumstances are they to enter the wrong room, and they are not to move from Room F to Room H or vice-versa. A minimum of two officers must be in each room frequented by the public at all times, and they are to keep unauthorized individuals from going to the second floor or into restricted areas. All usable entrances or exits must be covered.

Statement 2: The senior officer can lock any door except the main entrance and stairway doors. He has a staff of five officers to carry out these operations.

NOTE: The senior officer is available for guard duty. Room J is an active office.

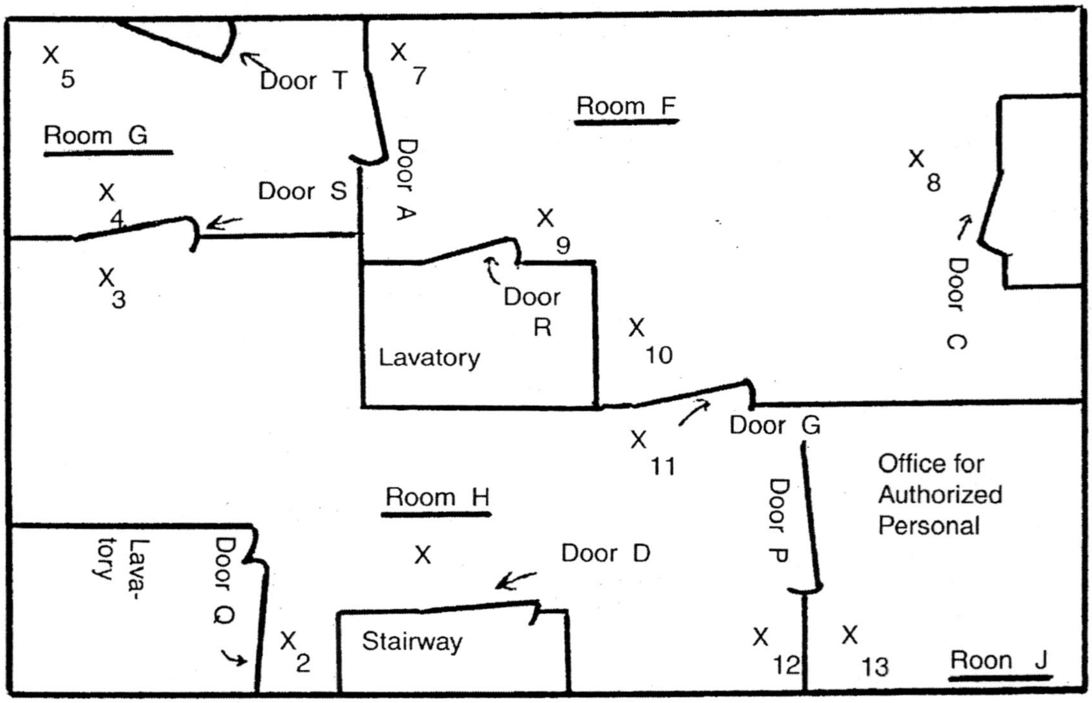

1. According to the instructions, how many officers should be assigned inside the office for authorized personnel (Room J)? 1.____

A. 0 B. 1 C. 2 D. 3

2. In order to keep the public from moving between Room F and Room H, which door(s) can be locked without interfering with normal office operations? Door(s) 2.____

   A. G B. P C. R and Q D. S

3. When placing officers in Room H, the only way the senior officer can satisfy the agency's objectives and his manpower limitations is by placing men at locations ______ and ______ . 3.____

   A. 1; 3 B. 1; 12 C. 3; 11 D. 11; 12

4. In accordance with the instructions, the LEAST effective locations to place officers in Room F are locations ______ and ______ . 4.____

   A. 7; 9 B. 7; 10 C. 8; 9 D. 9; 10

5. In which room is it MOST difficult for each of the officers to see all the movements of the public? Room 5.____

   A. G B. F C. H D. J

KEY (CORRECT ANSWERS)

1. A
2. A
3. B
4. D
5. C

TEST 8

Questions 1-4.

DIRECTIONS: Questions 1 through 4 are to be answered SOLELY on the basis of the following graph relating to the Burglary Rate in the City, 1993 to 1998, inclusive.

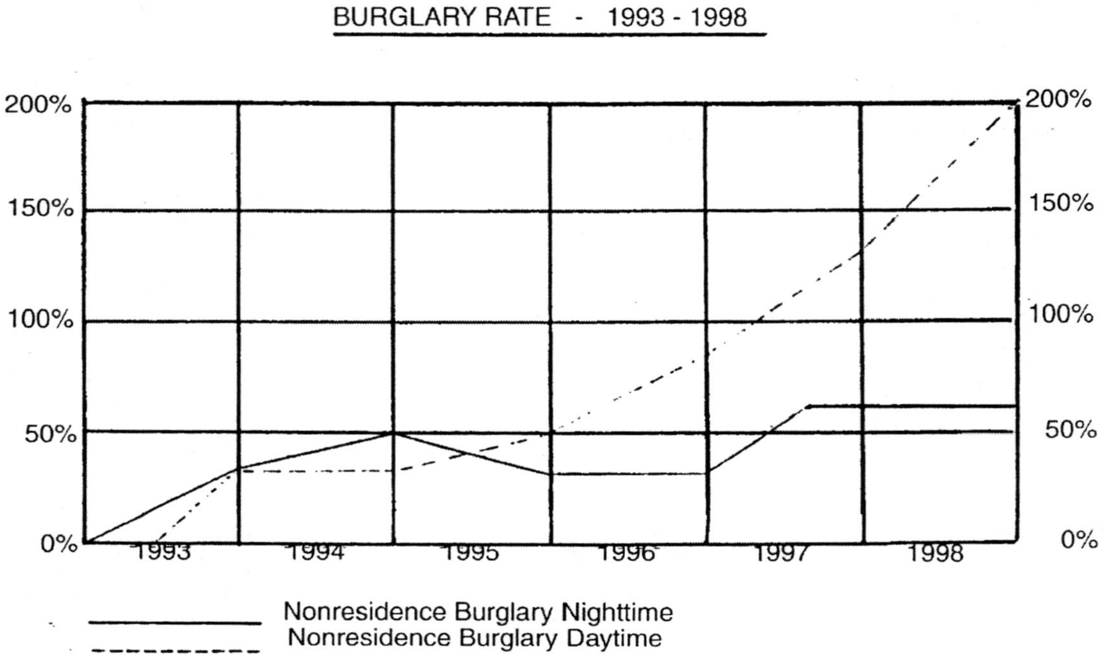

1. At the beginning of what year was the percentage increase in daytime and nighttime burglaries the SAME? 1.____

   A. 1993 B. 1995 C. 1996 D. 1998

2. In what year did the percentage of nighttime burglaries DECREASE? 2.____

   A. 1993 B. 1995 C. 1996 D. 1998

3. In what year was there the MOST rapid increase in the percentage of daytime non-residence burglaries? 3.____

   A. 1994 B. 1996 C. 1997 D. 1998

4. At the end of 1997, the actual number of nighttime burglaries committed 4.____

   A. was about 20%
   B. was 40%
   C. was 400
   D. cannot be determined from the information given

KEY (CORRECT ANSWERS)

1. A
2. B
3. D
4. D

TEST 9

Questions 1-4.

DIRECTIONS: Questions 1 through 4 are to be answered SOLELY on the basis of the following graphs.

BUDGETS FOR POLICE
IN MILLIONS OF DOLLARS
(ACTUAL DOLLARS)
1997-2001

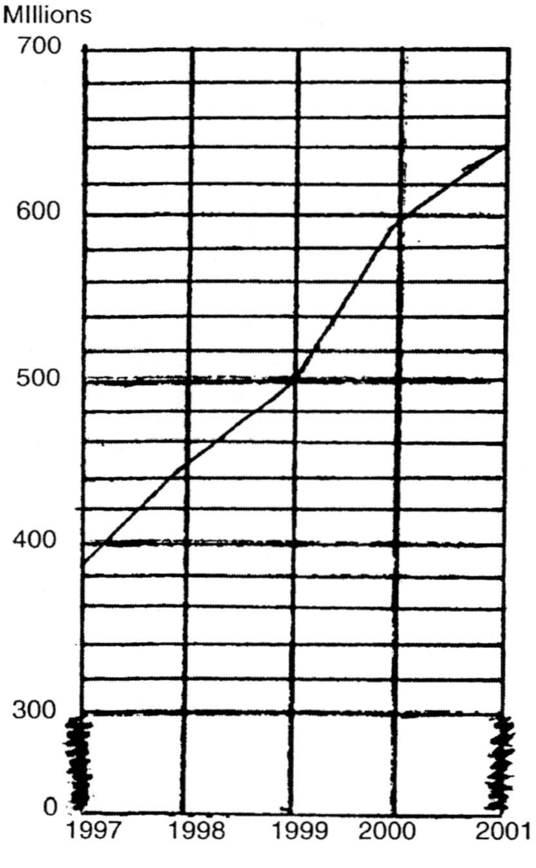

BUDGETS FOR OTHER
CRIMINAL JUSTICE EXPENDITURES
IN MILLIONS OF DOLLARS
ACTUAL DOLLARS)
1997-2001

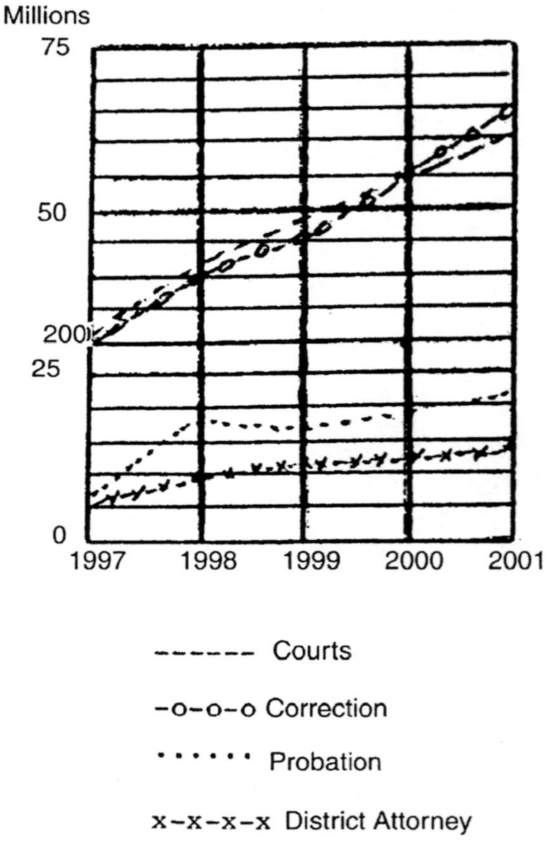

1. In 2001, the amount of money budgeted for courts amounted to APPROXIMATELY what percentage of the amount of money budgeted for police? 1.____

A. 10% B. 20% C. 30% D. 40%

2. In 2000, the police budget exceeded the sum of amounts budgeted for the four other criminal justice expenditures MOST NEARLY by 2.____

   A. $410,000,000 B. $459,000,000
   C. $475,000,000 D. $487,000,000

3. Between which of the following years did the amount of money budgeted for one category of criminal justice decrease by about one million dollars? 3.____

   A. 1997-1998 B. 1998-1999
   C. 1999-2000 D. 2000-2001

4. If the 1998 dollar was worth 96% of the 1997 dollar and the 1999 dollar was worth 90% of the 1997 dollar, the increase in the budget for Correction from 1998 to 1999, in terms of the 1997 dollar, amounted to 4.____

   A. $2,100,000 B. $4,200,000
   C. $4,320,000 D. $4,700,000

KEY (CORRECT ANSWERS)

1. A
2. B
3. B
4. A

TEST 10

Questions 1-4.

DIRECTIONS: Questions 1 through 4 are to be answered SOLELY on the basis of the following table.

STOLEN AND RECOVERED PROPERTY
IN COMMUNITY IN 2003 AND 2004

Type of Property	Value of Property Stolen		Value of Property Recovered	
	2003	2004	2003	2004
Currency	$ 264,925	$ 204,534	$ 10,579	$ 13,527
Jewelry	165,317	106,885	2-0,913	20,756
Furs	10,007	24,028	105	1,620
Clothing	62,265	49,219	4,322	15,821
Automobiles	740,719	606,062	736,701	558,442
Miscellaneous	356,901	351,064	62,077	103,117
TOTAL	$ 1,600,134	$1.341,792	$834,697	$713,283

5. Of the following types of property, the one which shows the HIGHEST ratio of *value of property recovered* to *value of property stolen* is 5.____

   A. clothing for 2003
   B. currency for 2003
   C. jewelry for 2004
   D. miscellaneous for 2004

6. Of the types of property which show a decrease from 2003 to 2004 in the value of property stolen, the one which shows the GREATEST percentage decrease in the value of the property recovered is 6.____

   A. automobiles
   B. currency
   C. furs
   D. jewelry

7. According to the above table, the total value of currency and jewelry stolen in 2004, as compared to 2003, decreased APPROXIMATELY by 7.____

   A. 3%
   B. 20%
   C. 28%
   D. 38%

8. According to the above table, the TOTAL value of all types of property recovered was 8.____

   A. a slightly lower percentage of the value of property stolen for 2003 than for 2004
   B. less for the year 2003 than the value of any individual type of property recovered for the year 2004
   C. approximately 60% of the value of all property stolen in 2003 and approximately 70% in 2004
   D. greater for the year 2004 than the value of any individual type of property recovered for the year 2003

KEY (CORRECT ANSWERS)

1. D
2. A
3. C
4. A

INTERPRETING STATISTICAL DATA GRAPHS, CHARTS AND TABLES

EXAMINATION SECTION

TEST 1

DIRECTIONS: Each question or incomplete statement is followed by several suggested answers or completions. Select the one that BEST answers the question or completes the statement. *PRINT THE LETTER OF THE CORRECT ANSWER IN THE SPACE AT THE RIGHT.*

Questions 1-4.

DIRECTIONS: Questions 1 through 4 are to be answered SOLELY on the basis of the following table.

STOLEN AND RECOVERED PROPERTY IN COMMUNITY X
1998-1999

Type of Property	Value of Property Stolen 1998	Value of Property Stolen 1999	Value of Property Recovered 1998	Value of Property Recovered 1999
Currency	$264,925	$204,534	$10,579	$13,527
Jewelry	165,317	106,885	20,913	20,756
Furs	10,007	24,028	105	1,620
Clothing	62,265	49,219	4,322 7	15,821
Automobiles	740,719	606,062	36,701	558,442
Miscellaneous	356,901	351,064	62,077	103,117
TOTAL	$1,600,134	$1,341,792	$834,697	$713,283

1. Of the following types of property, the one which shows the HIGHEST ratio of *value of property recovered* to *value of property stolen* is 1.____

   A. clothing for 1998
   B. currency for 1998
   C. jewelry for 1999
   D. miscellaneous for 1999

2. Of the types of property which show a decrease from 1998 to 1999 in the value of property stolen, the one which shows the GREATEST percentage decrease in the value of the property recovered is 2.____

   A. automobiles
   B. currency
   C. furs
   D. jewelry

3. According to the above table, the total value of currency and jewelry stolen in 1999, as compared to 1998, decreased APPROXIMATELY by 3.____

   A. 3%
   B. 20%
   C. 28%
   D. 38%

4. According to the above table, the TOTAL value of all types of property recovered was 4.___

A. a slightly lower percentage of the value of property stolen for 1998 than for 1999
B. less for the year 1998 than the value of any individual type of property recovered for the year 1999
C. approximately 60% of the value of all property stolen in 1998 and approximately 70% in 1999
D. greater for the year 1999 than the value of any individual type of property recovered for the year 1998

KEY (CORRECT ANSWERS)

1. D
2. A
3. C
4. A

TEST 2

Questions 1-6.

DIRECTIONS: Questions 1 through 6 are to be answered SOLELY on the basis of the information supplied in the chart below.

LAW ENFORCEMENT OFFICERS KILLED
(By Type of Activity)
1991-2000

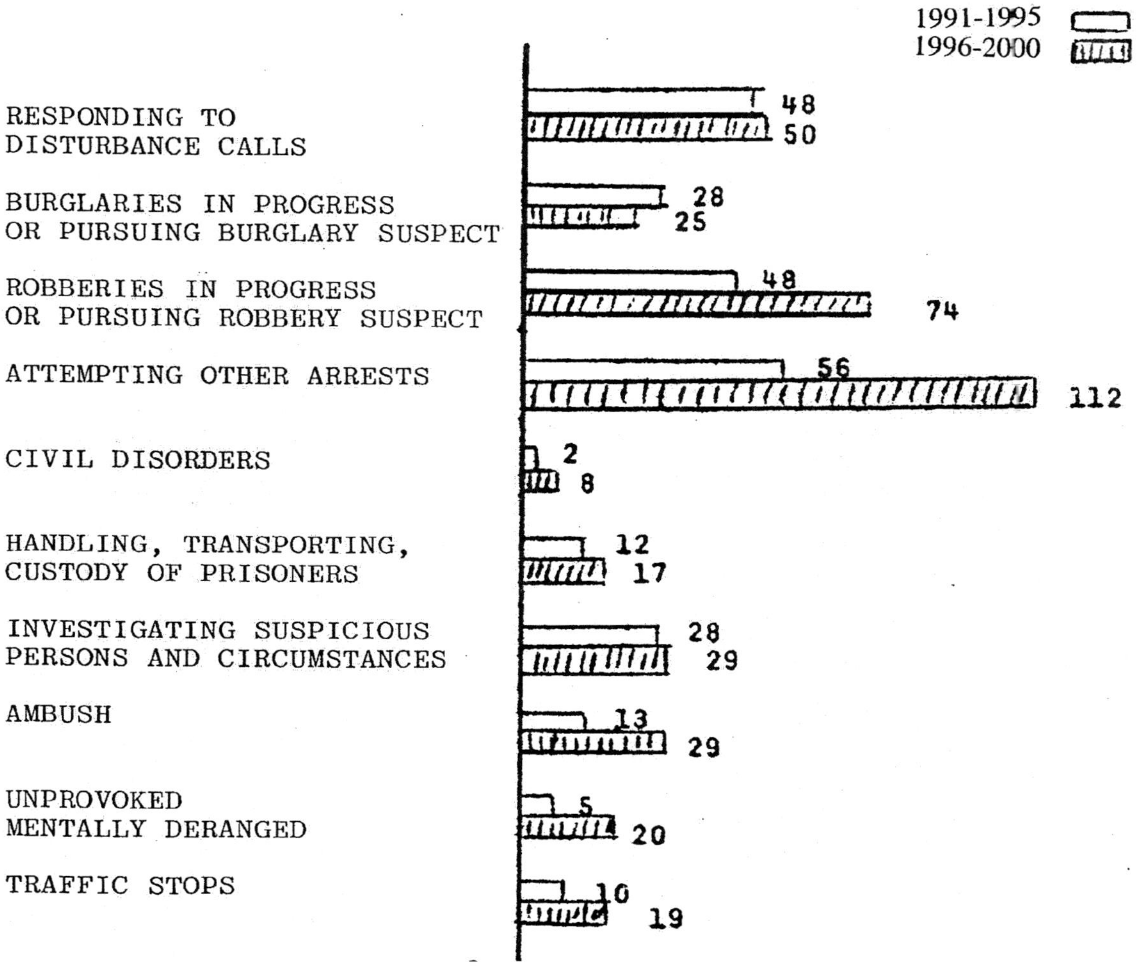

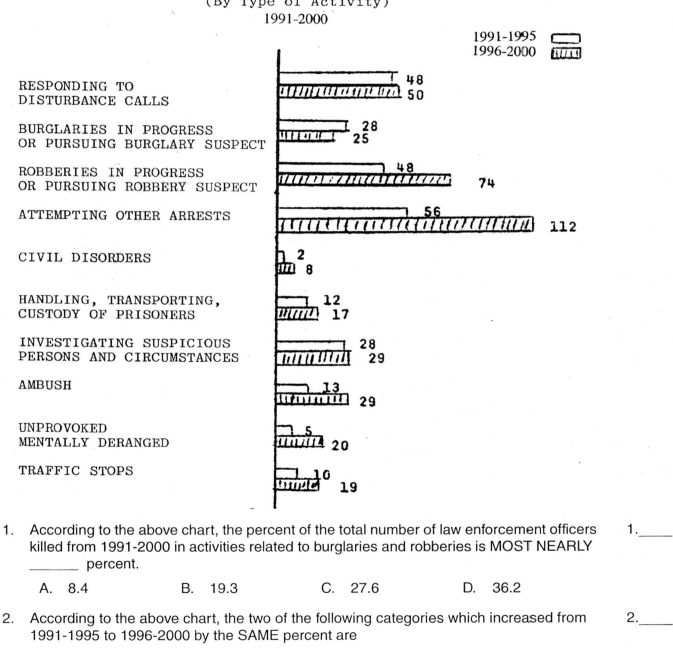

1. According to the above chart, the percent of the total number of law enforcement officers killed from 1991-2000 in activities related to burglaries and robberies is MOST NEARLY _______ percent. 1._____

   A. 8.4 B. 19.3 C. 27.6 D. 36.2

2. According to the above chart, the two of the following categories which increased from 1991-1995 to 1996-2000 by the SAME percent are 2._____

   A. ambush and traffic stops
   B. attempting other arrests and ambush

C. civil disorders and unprovoked mentally deranged
D. response to disturbance calls and investigating suspicious persons and circumstances

3. According to the above chart, the percentage increase in law enforcement officers killed from the 1991-1995 period to the 1996-2000 period is MOST NEARLY _______ percent. 3.___

A. 34 B. 53 C. 65 D. 100

4. According to the above chart, in which one of the following activities did the number of law enforcement officers killed increase by 100 percent? 4.___

A. Ambush
B. Attempting other arrests
C. Robberies in progress or pursuing robbery suspect
D. Traffic stops

5. According to the above chart, the two of the following activities during which the total number of law enforcement officers killed from 1991 to 2000 was the SAME are 5.___

A. burglaries in progress or pursuing burglary suspect and investigating suspicious persons and circumstances
B. handling, transporting, custody of prisoners and traffic stops
C. investigating suspicious persons and circumstances and ambush
D. responding to disturbance calls and robberies in progress or pursuing robbery suspect

6. According to the categories in the above chart, the one of the following statements which can be made about law enforcement officers killed from 1991 to 1995 is that 6.___

A. the number of law enforcement officers killed during civil disorders equals one-sixth of the number killed responding to disturbance calls
B. the number of law enforcement officers killed during robberies in progress or pursuing robbery suspect equals 25 percent of the number killed while handling or transporting prisoners
C. the number of law enforcement officers killed during traffic stops equals one-half the number killed for unprovoked reasons or by the mentally deranged
D. twice as many law enforcement officers were killed attempting other arrests as were killed during burglaries in progress or pursuing burglary suspect

---

KEY (CORRECT ANSWERS)

1. C
2. C
3. B
4. B
5. B
6. D

TEST 3

Questions 1-6.

DIRECTIONS: Questions 1 through 6 are to be answered SOLELY on the basis of the graph below.

YEARLY INCIDENCE OF MAJOR CRIMES FOR COMMUNITY Z
1997-1999

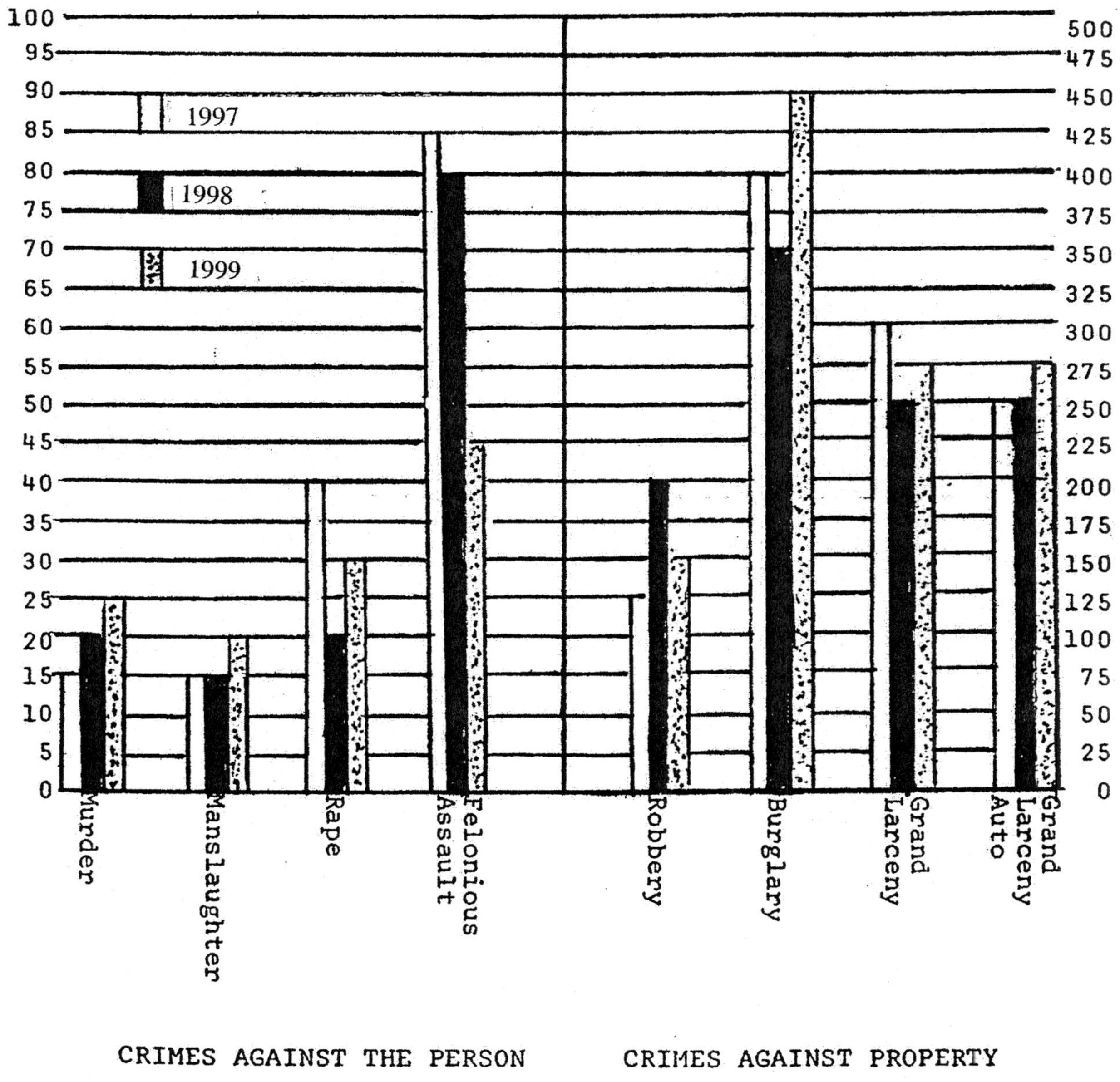

1. Of the following crimes, the one for which the 1999 figure was GREATER than the average of the previous two years was 1._

   A. grand larceny
   B. manslaughter
   C. rape
   D. robbery

2. If the incidence of burglary in 2000 were to increase over 1999 by the same number as it increased in 1999 over 1998, then the average for this crime for the four-year period from 1997 through 2000 would be MOST NEARLY 2._

   A. 100
   B. 400
   C. 415
   D. 440

3. The above graph indicates that the percentage INCREASE in grand larceny auto over the previous year was 3._

   A. greater in 1999 than in 1998
   B. greater in 1998 than in 1999
   C. greater in 1999 than in 1997
   D. the same in both 1998 and 1999

4. The one of the following which cannot be determined because there is not enough information in the above graph to do so is the 4._

   A. percentage of *Crimes Against Property* for the three-year period which were committed in 1997
   B. percentage of *Crimes Against the Person* for the three-year period which were murders committed in 1998
   C. percentage of *Major Crimes* for the three-year period which were committed in the first six months of 1998
   D. major crimes which were following a pattern of continuing yearly increases for the three-year period

5. According to this graph, the ratio of *Crimes Against Property* to *Crimes Against the Person* for 1999, as compared to the ratio for 1998, is 5._

   A. increasing
   B. decreasing
   C. about the same
   D. cannot be determined

6. Assume that it is desired to present information from the above graph to the public in a form most likely to gain their cooperation in a special police effort to reduce the incidence of grand larceny auto. 6._
   The one of the following which is MOST likely to result in such cooperation is a public statement that

   A. in 1999, approximately .75 of an automobile was stolen every day
   B. in 1999, one automobile was stolen, on the average, about,32 hours hours
   C. the number of automobiles stolen per year will increase from year to year
   D. there were more crimes of grand larceny auto than crimes of robbery committed during the past three years

---

KEY (CORRECT ANSWERS)

1. B	4. C
2. D	5. A
3. B	6. B

TEST 4

Questions 1-7.

DIRECTIONS: Questions 1 through 7 are to be answered SOLELY on the basis of the information contained in the following tables and chart.

TABLE 1

Number of Murders bv Region, United States: 1999 and 2000

Region	Year	
	1999	2000
Northeastern States	2,521	2,849
North Central States	3,427	3,697
Southern States	6,577	7,055
Western States	2,062	2,211

Number in each case for given year and region represents total number (100%) of murders in that region for that year.

TABLE 2

Murder by Circumstance, U.S. - 2000
(Percent distribution by category)

Region	Total	Spouse Killing spouse	Parent Killing child	Other family killings	Romantic triangle and lovers' quarrels	Other arguments	Known Felony type	Suspected felony type
Northeastern States	100.0	9.6	3.7	6.1	7.9	38.4	25.4	8.9
North Central States	100.0	11.3	3.0	8.9	5.0	39.5	22.4	9.9
Southern States	100.0	13.8	2.2	8.8	8.4	46.0	13.9	6.9
Western States	100.0	12.5	4.9	7.0	6.4	32.2	28.0	9.0

CHART 1

Murder by Type of Weapon Used, U.S. - 2000
(Percent Distribution)

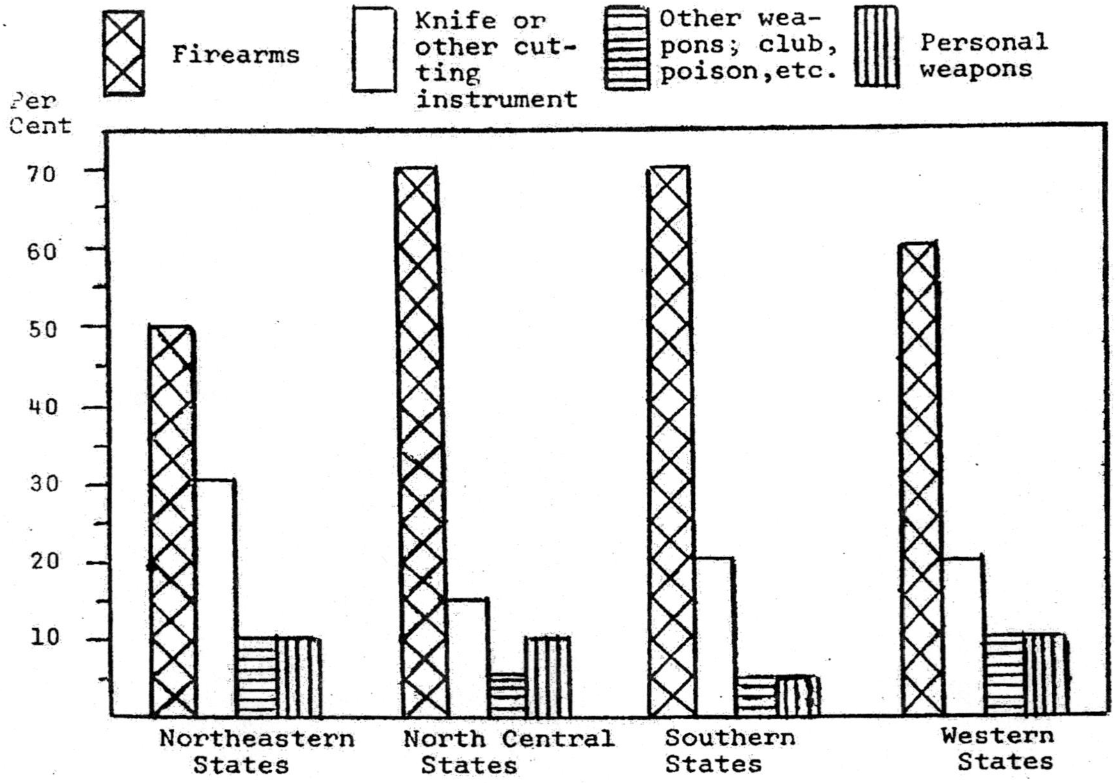

1. The number of persons murdered by firearms in the Western States in 2000 was MOST NEARLY 1.___

   A. 220 B. 445 C. 1235 D. 1325

2. In 2000, the number of murders in the category *Parent killing child* was GREATEST in the _______ States. 2.___

   A. Northeastern B. North Central
   C. Southern D. Western

3. The difference between the number of persons murdered with firearms and the number of persons murdered with other weapons (club, poison, etc.) in the North Central States in 2000 is MOST NEARLY 3.___

   A. 2200 B. 2400 C. 2600 D. 2800

4. In 1999, the ratio of the number of murders in the Western States to the total number of murders in the U.S. was MOST NEARLY 4.___

   A. 1 to 4 B. 1 to 5 C. 1 to 7 D. 1 to 9

5. The total number of murders in the U.S. in the category of *Romantic triangles and lovers' quarrels* in 2000 was MOST NEARLY 5.____

   A. 850 B. 950 C. 1050 D. 1150

6. Which of the following represents the GREATEST number of murders in 2000? Persons murdered by 6.____

   A. firearms in the Western States
   B. knives or other cutting instruments in the Southern States
   C. knives or other cutting instruments and persons murdered by other weapons (club, poison, etc.) in the Northeastern States
   D. knives or other cutting instruments, persons murdered by other weapons (club, poison, etc.) and persons murdered by personal weapons in the North Central States

7. From 1999 to 2000, the total number of murders increased by the GREATEST percentage in the ______ States. 7.____

   A. Northeastern
   B. North Central
   C. Southern
   D. Western

KEY (CORRECT ANSWERS)

1. D
2. C
3. B
4. C
5. D
6. B
7. A

TEST 5

Questions 1-5.

DIRECTIONS: Questions 1 through 5 are to be answered SOLELY on the basis of the following.

DISTRIBUTION OF CITIZENS' RESPONSES TO STATEMENTS
CONCERNING SHERIFFS' ARRESTS
(Number of citizens responding = 1171)

	CATEGORIES				
	(A) Strongly Agree	(B) Agree	(C) Disagree	(D) Strongly Disagree	(E) Don't Know
I. Sheriffs act improperly in arresting defendants, even when these persons are rude and ill-mannered	12%	37%	36%	9%	6%
II. Sheriffs frequently use more force than necessary when making arrests	9%	19%	46%	19%	7%
III. Any defendant who insults or physically abuses a sheriff has no complaint if he is sternly handled in return	13%	44%	32%	7%	4%

1. The total percentage of responses to Statement III OTHER THAN *Strongly Agree* and *Disagree* is 1.___

   A. 45% B. 46% C. 55% D. 59%

2. The number of *Disagree* responses to Statement II is MOST NEARLY ' 2.___

   A. 71 B. 114 C. 539 D. 820

3. Assume that for Statement II the (B) percentage of responses were doubled and the (A) percentage increased one and a half times. 3.____
If the (D) and (E) percentages remained the same, the (C) percentage would then MOST NEARLY be

A. 23% B. 26% C. 39% D. 52%

4. The total number of *Don't Know* responses is MOST NEARLY 4.____

A. 17
B. 188
C. 200
D. a figure which cannot be determined from the table

5. If the percentage of Disagree responses to Statement III were 35% less, the resulting percentage would MOST NEARLY be 5.____

A. 11% B. 14% C. 15% D. 21%

KEY (CORRECT ANSWERS)

1. C
2. C
3. A
4. C
5. D

TEST 6

Questions 1-3.

DIRECTIONS: Questions 1 through 3 are to be answered SOLELY on the basis of the statistical report given below.

The following is a statistical report of the activities of the bureau during the current year as compared with the previous year.

	Current Year	Previous Year
Memoranda of law prepared	68	83
Legal matters forwarded to Corporation Counsel	122	144
Letters requesting legal information	756	807
Letters requesting departmental records	139	111
Matters for publication	17	26
Court appearances of members of bureau	4,678	4,621
Conferences	94	103
Lectures at Police Academy	30	33
Reports on proposed legislation	194	255
Deciphering of codes	79	27
Expert testimony	31	16
Notices to court witnesses	55	81
Briefs prepared	22	18
Court papers prepared	258	--

1. According to the report, the percentage of bills prepared and sponsored by the Legal Bureau which were passed by the State Legislature and sent to the Governor for approval was APPROXIMATELY 1.___

   A. 3.1%
   B. 2.6%
   C. .5%
   D. not capable of determination from the data given

2. According to the statistical report, the activity showing the GREATEST percentage of *decrease* in the current year as compared with the previous year was 2.___

   A. matters for publication
   B. reports on proposed legislation

C. notices to court witnesses
D. memoranda of law prepared

3. According to the statistical report, the activity showing the GREATEST percentage of *increase* in the current year as compared with the previous year was 3.____

A. court appearances of members of the bureau
B. giving expert testimony
C. deciphering of codes
D. letters requesting departmental records

KEY (CORRECT ANSWERS)

1. D
2. A
3. C

TEST 7

Questions 1-5.

DIRECTIONS: Questions 1 through 5 are to be answered SOLELY on the basis of the information contained in Tables I and II that appear below and on the following page.

TABLE I
NUMBER OF ARRESTS FOR VARIOUS CRIMES AND DISPOSITION

OFFENSES	TOTAL ARRESTED	INVESTIGATED AND RELEASED	HELD FOR PROSECUTION	GUILTY AS CHARGED	GUILTY OF LESSER OFFENSES	DISPOSITION OTHER THAN CONVICTION
Murder	48	10	38	12	9	17
Rape	41	10	31	8	3	20
Aggravated assault	241	106	135	36	32	67
Robbery	351	177	174	98	35	41
Burglary	890	371	519	322	88	109
Larceny	1,665	466 78	1,199	929	58	212
Auto theft	464		386	278	46	62
TOTAL	3,700	1,218	2,482	1,683	271	528

TABLE II

ARRESTS FOR LARCENY - PERCENTAGE OF SUCH ARRESTS
BY AGE AND SEX

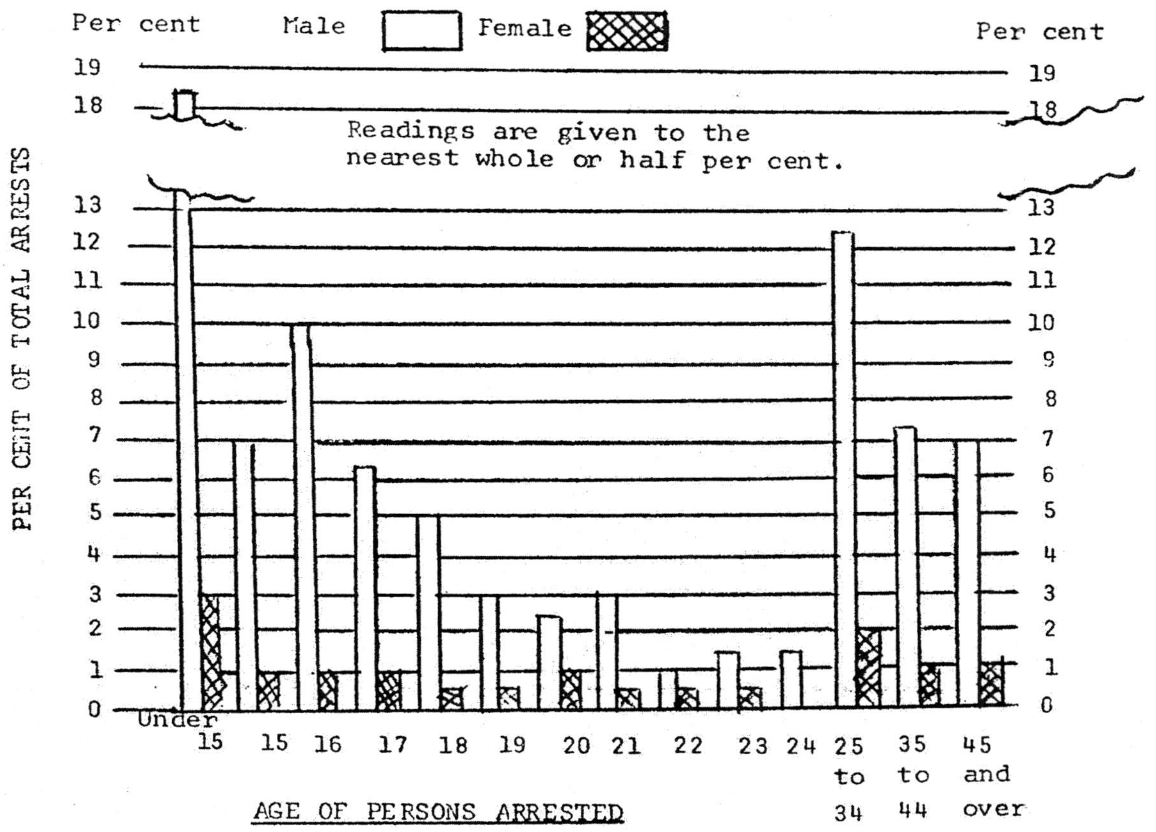

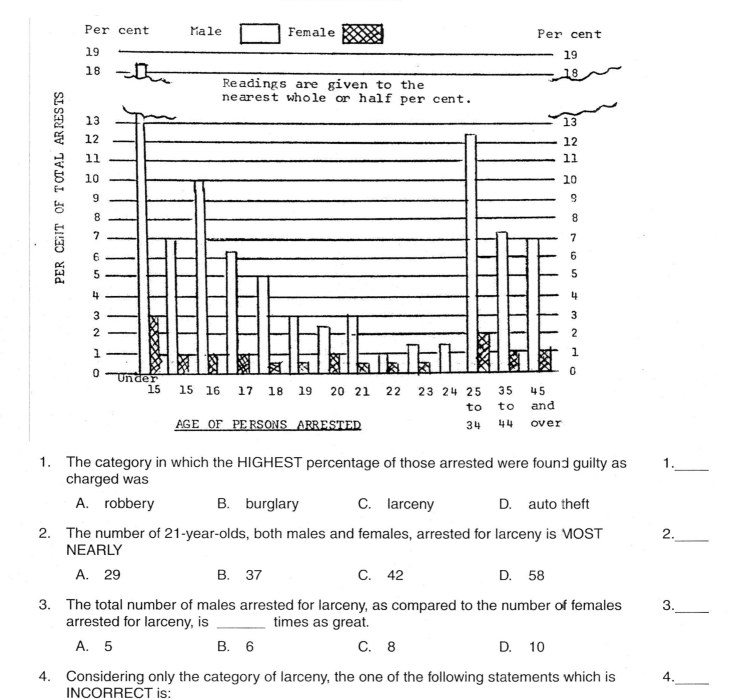

1. The category in which the HIGHEST percentage of those arrested were found guilty as charged was 1.____

   A. robbery B. burglary C. larceny D. auto theft

2. The number of 21-year-olds, both males and females, arrested for larceny is MOST NEARLY 2.____

   A. 29 B. 37 C. 42 D. 58

3. The total number of males arrested for larceny, as compared to the number of females arrested for larceny, is _______ times as great. 3.____

   A. 5 B. 6 C. 8 D. 10

4. Considering only the category of larceny, the one of the following statements which is INCORRECT is: 4.____

   A. The percentage of 25-year-old males arrested cannot be determined
   B. Twice as many 16-year-old males were arrested as 18-year-old males

C. The percentage of 16-year-old males arrested was twice as high as the percentage of 18-year-old males
D. Persons 19 years of age and younger accounted for exactly half of the total arrests for larceny

5. The one of the following which is the MOST accurate statement with respect to the disposition of arrests in each category is that in 5.___

A. no category was the number investigated and released greater than half the number arrested
B. no category was the number investigated and released less than one-fifth of those arrested
C. only two categories was the number found guilty of lesser offense greater than one-tenth of those arrested
D. only one category was the number found guilty as charged less than one-fourth of those arrested

---

KEY (CORRECT ANSWERS)

1. D
2. D
3. B
4. D
5. C

TEST 8

Questions 1-5.

DIRECTIONS: Questions 1 through 5 are to be answered SOLELY on the basis of the table below.

VALUE OF PROPERTY STOLEN - 2002 AND 2003
LARCENY

Category	2002		2003	
	Number of Offenses	Value of Stolen Property	Number of Offense	Value of Stolen Property
Pocket -picking	20	$1,950	10	$ 950
Purse- snatching	175	5,750	20	12,500
Shoplifting	155	7,950	225	17,350
Automobile thefts	1,040	127,050	860	108,000
Thefts of auto accessories	1,135	34,950	970	24,400
Bicycle thefts	355	8,250	240	6,350
All other thefts	1,375	187,150	1,300	153,150

1. Of the total number of larcenies reported for 2002, automobile thefts accounted for MOST NEARLY 1._____

   A. 5% B. 15% C. 25% D. 50%

2. The LARGEST percentage decrease in the value of the stolen property from 2002 to 2003 was in the category of 2._____

   A. pocket-picking
   B. automobile thefts
   C. thefts of automobile accessories
   D. bicycle thefts

3. In 2003, the average amount of each theft was LOWEST for the category of 3._____

   A. pocket-picking
   B. purse-snatching
   C. shoplifting
   D. thefts of auto accessories

4. The category which had the LARGEST numerical reduction in the number of offenses from 2002 to 2003 was 4._____

   A. pocket-picking
   B. automobile thefts
   C. thefts of auto accessories
   D. bicycle thefts

5. When the categories are ranked for each year according to the number of offenses committed in each category (largest number to rank first), the number of categories which will have the SAME rank in 2002 as in 2003 is 5.___

A. 3 B. 4 C. 5 D. 6

KEY (CORRECT ANSWERS)

1. C
2. A
3. D
4. B
5. C

TEST 9

Questions 1-5.

DIRECTIONS: Questions 1 through 5 are to be answered SOLELY on the basis of the graphs below.

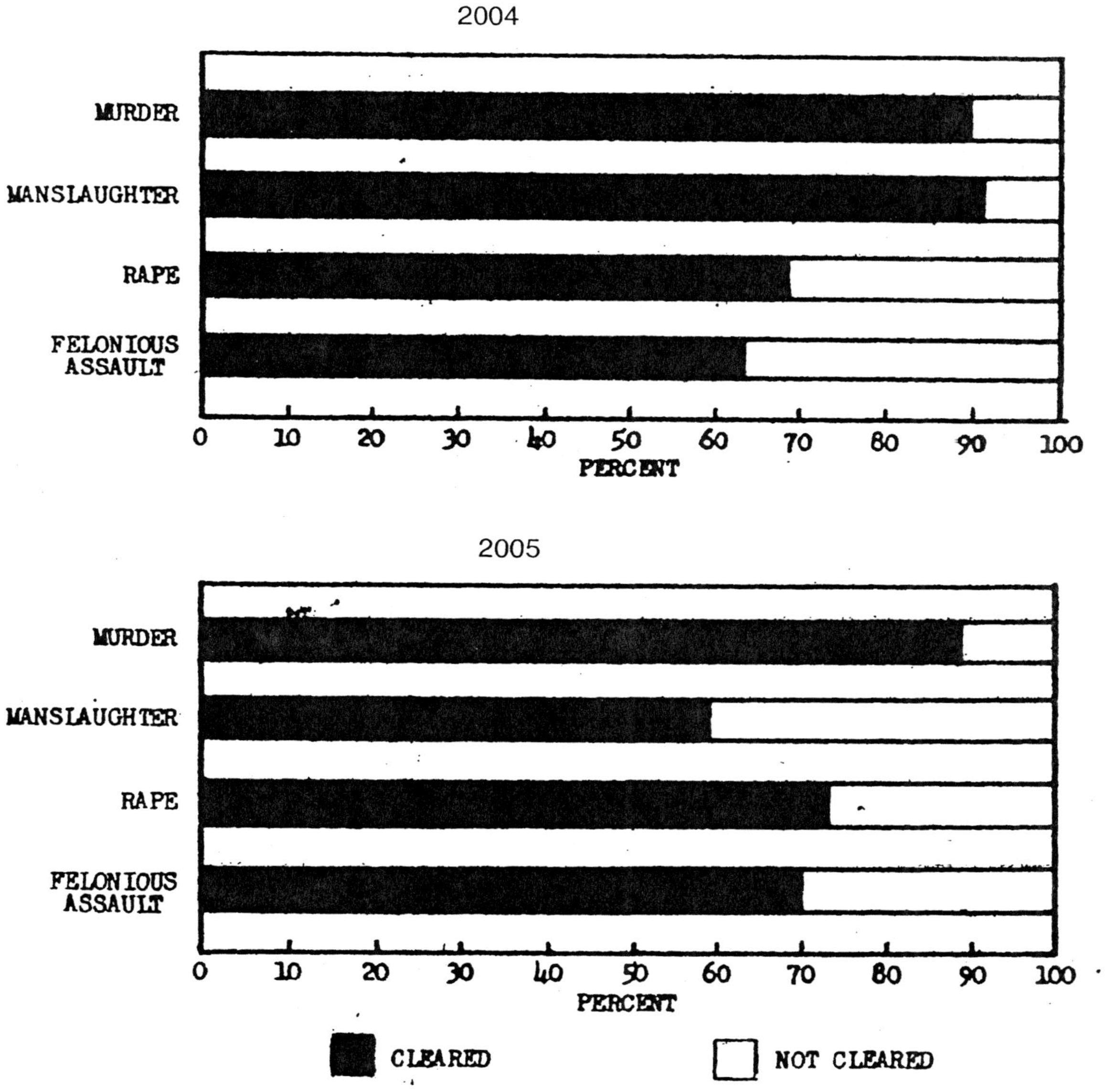

NOTE: The clearance rate is defined as the percentage of reported cases which were closed by the police through arrests or other means.

1. According to the above graphs, the AVERAGE clearance rate for all four crimes for 2005 1._____

   A. was greater than in 2004
   B. was less than in 2004

C. was the same as in 2004
D. cannot properly be compared to the 2004 figures

2. According to the above graphs, the crimes which did NOT show an increasing clearance rate from 2004 to 2005 were 2._

A. manslaughter and murder
B. rape and felonious assault
C. manslaughter and felonious assault
D. rape and murder

3. According to the above graphs, the average clearance rate for the two-year period 2004-2005 was SMALLEST for the crime of 3._

A. murder
B. manslaughter
C. rape
D. felonious assault

4. If, in 2005, 63 cases of reported felonious assault remained *not cleared,* then the total number of felonious assault cases reported that year was MOST NEARLY 4._

A. 90 B. 150 C. 210 D. 900

5. In comparing the graphs for 2004 and 2005, it would be MOST accurate to state that 5._

A. it is not possible to compare the total number of crimes cleared in 2004 with the total number cleared in 2005
B. the total number of crimes reported in 2004 is greater than the number in 2005
C. there were fewer manslaughter cases cleared during 2004 than in 2005
D. there were more rape cases cleared during 2005 than manslaughter cases cleared in the same year

KEY (CORRECT ANSWERS)

1. B
2. A
3. D
4. C
5. A

TEST 10

Questions 1-5.

DIRECTIONS: Questions 1 through 5 are to be answered SOLELY on the basis of the following chart.

FATAL HIGHWAY ACCIDENTS

	Drivers Over 18 Years of Age			Drivers 18 Years of Age And Under		
2003	Auto	Other Vehicles	Total	Auto	Other Vehicles	Total
January	43	0	43	4	0	4
February	52	0	52	10	0	10
March	36	0	36	8	0	8
April	50	0	50	17	0	17
May	40	2	42	5	0	5
June	26	0	26	8	0	8
July	29	0	29	6	0	6
August	29	1	30	3	0	3
September	36	0	36	4	0	4
October	45	1	46	2	1	3
November	54	1	55	3	0	3
December	66	1	67	3	0	6
TOTALS	506	6	512	76	1	77

1. The average number of fatal auto accidents per month during 2003 involving drivers older than eighteen was MOST NEARLY 1.____

   A. 42 B. 43 C. 44 D. 45

2. The TOTAL number of fatal highway accidents during 2003 was 2.____

   A. 506 B. 512 C. 582 D. 589

3. The month during which the LOWEST number of fatal highway accidents occurred was 3.____

   A. March B. June C. July D. August

4. Of the total number of fatal highway accidents during 2003 involving drivers older than eighteen, the percentage of accidents which took place during December is MOST NEARLY 4.___

A. 10 B. 13 C. 16 D. 19

5. The GREATEST percentage drop in fatal highway accidents occurred from 5.___

A. February to March
B. April to May
C. June to July
D. July to Augus

KEY (CORRECT ANSWERS)

1. A
2. D
3. D
4. B
5. B

BASIC FUNDAMENTALS OF WRITTEN COMMUNICATION

CONTENTS

INSTRUCTIONAL OBJECTIVES

1. Ability to write legibly.
2. Ability to fill out forms and applications correctly.
3. Ability to take messages and notes accurately.
4. Ability to write letters effectively.
5. Ability to write directions and instructions clearly.
6. Ability to outline written and spoken information.
7. Ability to persuade or teach others through written communication.
8. Ability to write effective overviews and summaries.
9. Ability to make smooth transitions within written communications.
10. Ability to use language forms appropriate for the reader.
11. Ability to prepare effective informational reports.

CONTENT

INTRODUCTION

Public-service employees are required to prepare written communications for a variety of purposes. Written communication is a fundamental tool, not only for the public-service occupations, but throughout the world of work. Many public-service occupations require written communication with ordinary citizens of diverse backgrounds, so the trainee should develop the ability to write in simple, nontechnical language that the ordinary citizen will understand.
This unit is designed to develop the student's ability to communicate effectively in writing for a number of different purposes and in a number of different formats. Whatever the particular purpose or format, however, effective writing will require the writer:

- to have a clear idea of his purpose and his audience;
- to organize his thoughts and information in an orderly way;
- to express himself concisely, accurately, and concretely;
- to report relevant facts;
- to explain and summarize ideas clearly; and
- to evaluate the effectiveness of his communication.

1. BUSINESS WRITING

Several forms of written communication tend to recur frequently in most public-service agencies, including:

- letters
- forms
- memoranda
- minutes of meetings
- short reports
- telegrams and cables
- news releases
- and many others

The public-service employee should be familiar with the principles of writing in these forms, and should be able to apply them in preparing effective communications.

Letters

Every letter sent from a public-service agency should be considered an ambassador of goodwill. The impression it creates may mean the difference between favorable public attitudes or unfavorable ones. It may mean the difference between creating a friend or an enemy for the agency. Every public-service employee has a responsibility to serve the public effectively and to provide services in an efficient and courteous manner. The letters an agency sends out reflect its attitudes toward the public.

The impression a letter creates depends upon both its appearance and its tone. A letter which shows erasures and pen written corrections gives an impression that the sending agency is slovenly. Similarly, a rude or impersonal letter creates the impression that the agency is insensitive or unfeeling. In preparing letters, the employee should apply principles of style and tone which will serve to create the most favorable impression.

Select the Letter Type. The two most common types of business letters are letters of inquiry and letters of response - that is, “asking” letters and “answering” letters. Whichever type of letter the employee is asked to write, the following guidelines will simplify the task and help to achieve a style and tone which will create a favorable impression on the reader.

Select the Right Format. Several styles of letter format are in common use today, including:

- the indented format,
- the block format, and
- the semi-block format.

Modified forms of these are also in use in some offices. The student should become familiar with the formats preferred for usage in his office, and be able to use whichever form the employer requests.

Know the Letter Elements. Every letter includes certain basic elements, such as:

- the letterhead, which identifies the name and address of the sender.
- the date on which the letter was transmitted.
- the inside address, with the name, street, city, and state of the addressee.
- the salutation, greeting the addressee.
- the body, containing the message.
- the complimentary close, the “good-bye” of the business letter.
- the signature, handwritten by the sender.
- the typed signature, the typewritten name and title of the sender.

In addition, several other elements are occasionally found in business letters:

- the *attention line,* directing the letter to the attention of a particular individual or his representative.
- the *subject line,* informing the reader at a glance of the subject of the letter.

- the *enclosure notation,* noting items enclosed with the letter.
- the *carbon-copy notation,* listing other persons who receive copies of the letter.
- the *postscript,* an afterthought sometimes (but not normally) added following the last typed line of the letter.

Be Brief. Use only the words which help to say what is needed in a clear and straightforward manner. Do not repeat information already known to the reader, or contained elsewhere in the letter. Likewise, do not repeat information contained in the letter being answered. Rather than repeat the content of a previous letter, one can say something like, "Please refer to our letter dated March 5."

An employee can shorten his letters by using single words that serve the same function as longer phrases. Many commonly used phrases can be replaced by single words. For example,

Phrase	Single word
in order to	to
in reference to	about
in the amount of	for, of
in a number of cases	some
in view of	because
with regard to	about, in

Similarly, avoid the use of adjectives and nouns that are formed from verbs. If the root verbs are used instead, the writing will be more concise and more vivid. For example,

Noun form	Verb form
We made an adjustment on our books	We adjusted our books
We are sorry we cannot make a replacement of	We are sorry we cannot replace
Please make a correction in our order	Please correct our order

Be on the lookout for unnecessary adjectives and adverbs which tend to clutter letters without adding information or improving style. Such unnecessary words tend to distract the reader and make it more difficult for him to grasp the main points. Observe how the superfluous words, italicized in the following example, obscure the meaning: "You may be *very much* disappointed to learn that the *excessively large* demand for our *highly popular recent* publication, 'Your Income Taxes,' has led to an *unexpected* shortage of this *attractive* publication and we *sadly* expect they will not be replenished until *quite* late this year."

Summarizing, then, *a good letter is simple and clear, with short, simple words, sentences, and paragraphs. Related parts of sentences and paragraphs are kept together and placed in an order which makes it easy for the reader to follow the main thoughts.*

Be Natural. Whenever possible, use a human touch. Use names and personal pronouns to let the reader know the letter was written by a person, not an institution. Instead of saying, "It is the policy of this agency to contact its clients once each year to confirm their status," try this: "Our policy, Mr. Jones, is to confirm your status once each year."

Use Concrete Nouns. Avoid using abstract words and generalizations. Use names of objects, places, and persons rather than abstractions.

Use Active verbs. The passive voice gives a motionless, weak tone to most writing. Instead of "The minutes were taken by Mrs. Smith," say, "Mrs. Smith took the minutes." Instead of "The plans were prepared by the banquet committee," say, "The banquet committee prepared the plans."

Use a Natural Tone. Many people tend to become hard, cold, and unnatural the moment they write a letter. *Communicating by letter should have the same natural tone of conversation used in everyday speech.* One way to achieve a natural and personal tone in the majority of letters is through the use of personal pronouns. Instead of saying, "Referring to your letter of March 5, reporting the non-receipt of goods ordered last February 15, please be advised that the goods were shipped as requested," say, "I am sorry to hear that you failed to receive the items you ordered last February 15. We shipped them the same day we received your letter."

Forms

In most businesses and public service agencies, repetitive work is simplified by the use of *forms.* Forms exist for nearly every purpose imaginable: for ordering supplies, preparing invoices, applying for jobs, applying for insurance, paying taxes, recording inventories, and so on. While the forms encountered in different agencies may differ widely, several principles should be applied in completing any form

- *Legibility.* Entries on forms should be clear and legible. Print or type wherever possible. When space provided is insufficient, attach a supplementary sheet to the form.

- *Completeness.* Make an entry in every space provided on the form. If a particular space does not apply to the applicant, enter there the term "N/A" (for "not applicable"). The reader of the completed form will then know that the applicant did not simply overlook that space.

- *Conciseness.* Forms are intended to elicit a maximum amount of information in the least possible space. When completing a form, it is usually not necessary to write complete sentences. Provide the necessary information in the least possible words.

- *Accuracy*. Be sure the information provided on the form is accurate. If the entry is a number, such as a social security number or an address, double-check the correctness of the number. Be sure of the spelling of names, No one appreciates receiving a communication in which his name is misspelled.

Memoranda

The written communications passing between offices or departments are usually transmitted in a form known as *"interoffice memorandum."* The headings most often used on such "memos" are:

- TO: identifying the addressee,
- FROM: identifying the sender or the originating office,
- SUBJECT: identifying briefly the subject of the memo,
- DATE: identifying the date the memo was prepared.

Larger agencies may also use headings such as FILE or REFERENCE NO. to aid in filing and retrieving memoranda.

In writing a memo, many of the same rules for letter-writing may be applied. Both the appearance and tone of the memo should create a pleasing impression. The format should be neat and follow the standards set by the originating office. The tone should be friendly, courteous, and considerate. The language should be clear, concise, and complete.

Memos usually dispense with salutations, complimentary closings, and signatures of the writers. In most other respects, however, the memorandum will follow the rules of good letter-writing.

Minutes of Meetings

Most formal public-service organization conduct meetings from time to time at which group decisions are made about agency policies, procedures, and work assignments. The records of such meetings are called *minutes*.

Minutes should be written as clearly and simply as possible, summarizing only the essential facts and decisions made at the meeting. While some issue may have been discussed at great length, only the final decision or resolution made of it should be recorded in the minutes. Information of this sort is usually included:

- Time and place of the call to order,
- Presiding officer and secretary,
- Voting members present (with names, if a small organization),

- Approval and corrections of previous minutes,
- Urgent business,
- Old business,
- New business,
- Time of adjournment,
- Signature of recorder.

Minutes should be written in a factual and objective style. The opinions of the recorder should not be in evidence. Every item of business coming up before a meeting should be included in the minutes, together with its disposition. For example:

- "M/S/P (Moved, seconded, passed) that Mr. Thomas Jones take responsibility for rewriting the personnel procedures manual."
- "Discussion of the summer vacation schedule was tabled until the next meeting."
- "M/S/P, a resolution that no client of the agency should be kept waiting more than 20 minutes for an interview."

Note that considerable discussion may have surrounded each of the above items in the minutes, but that only the topic and its resolution are recorded.

<u>Short Reports</u>

The public-service employee often is called upon to prepare a short report gathering and interpreting information on a single topic. Reports of this kind are sometimes prepared so that all the relevant information may be assembled in one place to aid the organization in making certain decisions. Such reports may be read primarily by the staff of the organization or by others closely related to the decision-making process.

Reports may be prepared at other times for distribution to the public or to other agencies and institutions. These reports may serve the purpose of informing public opinion or persuading others on matters of public policy.

Whatever the purpose of the short report, its physical appearance and style of presentation should be designed to create a favorable impression on the reader. Even if the report is distributed only within the writer's own unit, an attractive, clear, thorough report will reflect the writer's dedication to his assignment and the pride he takes in his work.

Some guidelines which will assist the trainee in preparation of effective short reports include use of the following:

- A good quality paper;
- Wide and even margins, allowing binding room;

- An accepted standard style of typing;
- A title page;
- A table of contents (for more lengthy reports only);
- A graphic numbering or outlining system, if needed for clarity;
- Graphics and photos to clarify meaning when useful;
- Footnotes, used sparingly, and only when they contribute to the report;
- A bibliography of sources, using a standard citation style.

A discussion of the organization of content for informational reports follows later in this document.

Telegrams and Cables

From time to time messages of special urgency must be sent by public telegraph wires, cables, and radio. With this service, written communications may be exchanged worldwide within minutes at a cost not greatly more than for a letter.

The public-service employee should be familiar with the telegraph service and able to prepare written messages for this medium. The student should be familiar with the classes of service available: "full-rate service," "day letter," and "night letter," since the class of service will affect the style of writing.

Skill in preparing telegraph messages rests largely on the writer's ability to summarize. The essential information must be presented in the fewest possible words. Good messages would follow these guidelines:

- Omission of articles and prepositions unless essential to meaning,
- Use of verb forms of the fewest words,
- Use of single words rather than phrases,
- Omission of unnecessary information and words.

For example:

> "I am taking American Airlines Flight 222 from Chicago at 8:15 Wednesday evening and will arrive at Los Angeles International Airport at 10:15. I would appreciate it if you would meet me."

Can be compressed to:

> "Arriving American 222 Los Angeles International Wednesday 10:15 PM. Please meet."

The minimum charge on a full-rate telegram is based upon 15 words. The student should develop skill in writing 15-word summaries in telegraph style.

<u>News Releases</u>

From time to time, the public-service employees may be called upon to prepare a news release for his agency. Whenever the activities of the agency are newsworthy or of interest to the public, the agency has an obligation to report such activities to the press. The most common means for such reporting is by using the press release. Most newspapers and broadcasting stations are initially informed of agencies' activities by news releases distributed by the agencies themselves. Thus, the news release is a basic tool for communicating with the public served by the agency.

The news release is written in news style, with these basic characteristics:

- Sentences are short and simple.
- Paragraphs are short (one or two sentences) and relate to a single item of information.
- Paragraphs are arranged in *inverted order*—the most important in information appears first.
- The first or *lead* paragraph summarizes the entire story. If the reader went no further, he would have the essential information.
- Subsequent paragraphs provide further details, the most important occurring first.
- Reported information is attributed to sources; that is, the source of the news is reported in the story.
- The expression of the writer's opinions is scrupulously avoided.
- The 5 W's (who, what, why, where, when) are included.

News releases should be typed double spaced on standard 8 1/2 x 11 paper, with generous margins and at least 2" of open space above the lead paragraph. Do not write headlines - that is the editor's job. At the top of the first page of the release include the name of the agency releasing the story and the name and phone number of the person to contact if more information is needed. If the release runs more than one page, end each page with the word "-more-" to indicate that more copy follows. End the release with the symbols "###" to indicate that the copy ends at that point.

Accuracy and physical appearance are essential characteristics of the news release. Typographical errors, or errors of fact, such as misspelled names, lead editors to doubt the reliability of the story. Great care should be taken to assure the accuracy and reliability of a news release.

2. REPORTING ON A TOPIC

At one time or another, most public-service employees will be asked to prepare a report on some topic. Usually the need for the report grows out of some policy decision contemplated by the agency for which full information must be considered. For example:

- Should the agency undertake some new project or service?
- Should working conditions be changed?
- Are new specialists needed on the staff?
- Or should a branch office be opened up?

Or any of a hundred other such decisions which the agency must make from time to time.

When called upon to prepare such a report, the employee should have a model to follow which will guide his collection of information and will help him to prepare an effective and useful report.

As with other forms of written communication, both the physical appearance and content of the report are important to create a favorable impression and to engender confidence. The physical appearance of such reports has been discussed earlier; additional suggestions for reports are given in Unit 3. Basic guidelines follow below for organizing and preparing the content.

Preparation for the Report

What is the Purpose of the Report? The preparer of the report should have clearly in mind why the report is needed:

- What is the decision being contemplated by the agency?
- To what use will the report be put?

Before beginning to prepare the report, the writer should discuss its purpose fully with the decision-making staff to articulate the purpose the report is intended to serve. If the employee is himself initiating the report, it would be well to discuss its purpose with colleagues to assure that its purpose is clear in his own mind.

What Questions Should the Report Answer? Once the purpose of the report is clear, the questions the report must answer may begin to become clear. For example, if the decision faced by the agency is whether or not to offer a new service, questions may be asked such as these:

- What persons would be served by the new service?

- What would the new service cost?
- What new staff would be needed?
- What new equipment and facilities would be needed?
- What alternative ways exist for offering the service?
- How might the new service be administered?

And so on. Unless the purpose of the report is clear, it is difficult to decide what specific questions need to be answered. Once the purpose is clear, these questions can be specified.

Where Can the Relevant Information be Obtained? Once the questions are clear in the writer's mind, he can identify the information he will need to answer them. Information may usually be obtained from two general sources:

- *Relevant documents.* Records, publications, and other reports are often useful in locating the information needed to answer particular questions. These may be in the files of the writer's own agency, in other agencies, or in libraries.

- *Personal contacts.* Persons in a position to know the needed information may be contacted in person, by phone, or by letter. Such contacts are especially important in obtaining firsthand accounts of previous experience.

The Text of the Report

What are the Answers to the Questions? Once the relevant in-formation is in hand, the answers to the questions may be assembled.

- What does the information reveal? This activity amounts to summarizing the information obtained. It often helps to organize this summary around the specific questions asked by the report. For example, if the report asks in one part, "What are the costs of the new service likely to be?" one section of the report should summarize the information gathered to answer this question.

Organizing the Report. The organization of a report into main and subsections depends upon the nature of the report. Reports will differ widely in their organization and treatment. In general, however, the report should generally follow the pattern previously discussed. That is, reports which generally include the following subjects in order will be found to be clear in their intent and to communicate effectively:

- *Description of problem or purpose.* Example: "One problem facing our agency is whether or not we should extend our hours of operation to better serve the public. This report is intended to examine the problem and make recommendations."

- *Questions to be answered.* Example: "In examining this problem, answers were sought to the following questions: What persons would be served? What would it cost? What staff would be needed?"

- *Information sources.* Example: "To answer these questions, letters of complaint for the past three years were examined. Interviews with clients were conducted by phone and in person, phone interviews were conducted with the agency directors in Memphis, Philadelphia, and Chicago,"

- *Summary of findings.* Example: "At least 25 percent of the agency's clients would be served better by evening or Saturday service. The costs of operating eight hours of extended service would be negligible, since the service could be provided by rescheduling work assignments. The present staff report they would be inconvenienced by evening and Saturday work assignments."

The Writer's Responsibilities. It is the writer's responsibility to address finally the original purpose of the report. Once the questions have been answered, an informed judgment can be made as to the decision facing the agency. It is at this stage that the writer attempts to draw conclusions from the information he has gathered and summarized. For example, if the original purpose of the report was to help make a decision about whether or not the agency should offer a new service, the writer should draw conclusions from the information and recommend either for or against the new service.

Conclusions and Recommendations. Example: "It appears that operating during extended hours would better serve a significant number of clients. The writer recommends that the agency offer this new service. The present staff should be given temporary assignments to cover the extended hours. As new staff are hired to replace separating persons, they should be hired specifically to cover the extended hours."

3. PERSUASIVE WRITING

Often in life, people are called upon to persuade individuals and groups to adopt ideas believed to be good, or attitudes favorable to ideas thought to be worthwhile or behavior believed to be beneficial. The public service employee may find he must persuade the staff of his own agency, his superiors, the clients of the agency, or the general public in his community.

Persuading others by means of written and other forms of communication is a difficult task and requires much practice. Some principles have emerged from the study of persuasion which may provide some guidelines for developing a model for persuasive writing.

General Guidelines for Writing Persuasively

Know the Credibility of the Source. People are more likely to be persuaded by a message they perceive originates from a trustworthy source. Their trust is enhanced if the source is seen as authoritative, or knowledgeable on the issue discussed in the message. Their trust is increased also if the source appears to have nothing to gain either way, has no vested interest in the final decision. Then, the assertions made in persuasive writing should be backed up by referencing trustworthy and disinterested information sources.

Avoid Overemotional Appeals. Appealing to the common emotions of man—love, hate, tear, sex, etc.—can have a favorable effect on the outcome of a persuasive message. But care should be taken because, if the appeal is too strong, it can lead to a reverse effect. For example, if an agency wanted to persuade the public to get chest X-rays, it would have much greater chance of success if it adopted a positive and helpful attitude rather than trying to frighten them into this action. For instance, appealing mildly to the sense of well-being which accompanies knowledge of one's own good health, instead of shocking the public by showing horror pictures of patients who died from lack of timely X-rays.

Consider the Other Man's Point of View. To persuade another to one's own point of view, should the writer include information and arguments contrary to his own position? Or should he argue only for his own side?

Generally, it depends on where most of the audience stand in the first place. If most of the audience already favor the position being advocated, then the writer will probably do better including only information favorable to his position. However, if the greater part of the audience are likely to oppose this position, then the writer would probably be better off including their arguments also. In this case, he may be helping his cause by rebutting the opposing arguments as he introduces them into the writing.

An example of this technique might occur in arguing for such an idea as a four-day, forty-hour workweek. Thus: "Many people feel that the ten-hour day is too long and that they would arrive home too late for their regular dinner hour. But think! If you have dinner a littler later each night, you'll have a three-day weekend every week. More days free to go fishing, or camping. More days with your wife and children." That is good persuasive writing!

Interpersonal Communications

The important role of interpersonal communication in persuading others—face-to-face and person-to-person communications—has been well documented. Mass mailings or printed messages will likely have less effect than personal letters and conversations between persons already known to each other. In any persuasion campaign the personal touch is very important.

An individual in persuading a large number of persons will likely be more effective if he can organize a letter-writing campaign of persuasive messages written by persons favorable to his position to their friends and acquaintances, than if his campaign is based upon sending out a mass mailing of a printed message.

Conditions for Persuading. In order for an audience of one or many to be persuaded in the manner desired, these conditions must be met:

- the audience must be *exposed* to the message,
- members of the audience must *perceive* the intent of the message,
- they must *remember* the message afterwards,
- each member must *decide* whether or not to adopt the ideas.

Each member of the audience will respond to a message differently. While every person may receive the message, not everyone will read it. Even among those who read it, not everyone will perceive it in the same way. Some will remember it longer than others. Not everyone will decide to adopt the ideas. These effects are called *selective exposure, selective perception, selective retention,* and *selective decision.*

The Persuasion Campaign. How can one counteract these selective effects in persuading others? One thing that is known is that *people tend to be influenced by persuasive messages which they are already predisposed to accept.* This means a person is more likely to persuade people a little than to persuade them a lot.

In planning a persuasion campaign, therefore, the messages should be tailored to the audiences. Success will be more likely if one starts with people who believe *almost* as the writer wants to persuade them to believe—people who are most likely to agree with the position advocated.

The writer also wants to use arguments based on values the particular audience already accepts. For example, in advocating a new teenage job program, he might argue with business men that the program will help business; with parents, that it will build character; with teachers, that it is educational; with taxpayers, that it will reduce future taxes; and so on.

The idea is to find some way to make sure that each member of the particular audiences reached can see an advantage for himself, and for the writer to then tailor the messages for those audiences.

4. INSTRUCTIONAL WRITING

Another task that the public-service employee may expect to face from time to time is the instruction of some other person in the performance of a task. This may sometimes involve preparing written instructions to other employees in the unit, or preparing a training manual for new employees.

It may sometimes involve preparing instructional manuals for clients of the unit, such as "How to Apply for a Real Estate License," "How to Bathe your Baby," or "How to Recognize the Symptoms of Heart Disease."

Whatever the purpose or the audience, certain principles of instruction may be applied which will help make more effective these instructional or training communications. These are: *advance organizers, practice, errorless learning,* and *feedback.*

Advance Organizers

At or near the beginning of an instructional communication, it helps the learner if he is provided with what can be called an "advance organizer." This element of the communication performs two functions:

- it provides a framework or "map" for the leader to organize the information he will encounter,
- it helps the learner perceive his purpose in learning the tasks which will follow.

The first paragraphs in this section, for example, serve together as an advance organizer. The trainee is informed that he may be called upon to perform these tasks in his job *(perceived purpose),* and that he will be instructed in advance organizers, practice, errorless learning, and feedback *(framework, or "map").*

Practice

The notion of *practice makes perfect* is a sound instructional principle. When trying to teach someone to perform a task by means of written communication, the writer should build in many opportunities for practicing the task, or parts of it. This built-in practice should be both appropriate and active:

- *Appropriate practice* is practice which is directly related to learning the tasks at hand.

- *Active practice* is practice in actually performing the task at hand or parts of it, rather than simply reading about the task, or thinking about it.

By inserting questions into the text of the communication, by giving practice quizzes, exercises, or field work, one can build into his instructional communication the kind of practice necessary for the reader to readily learn the task.

Errorless Learning

The practice given learners should be easy to do. That is, they should not be asked to practice a task if they are likely to make a lot of mistakes. When a mistake is practiced it is likely to recur again and again, like spelling "demons," which have been spelled wrong so often it's difficult to recall the way they should be spelled. Because it is better to practice a task right from the first, it is important that learners do not make errors in practice.

- One method for encouraging correct practice is to give the reader hints, or *prompts,* to help him practice correctly.

- Another method is to instruct him in a logical sequence a little bit at a time. Don't try to teach everything at once. Break the task down into small parts and teach each part of the task in order. Then give the learner practice in each part of the task before giving him practice in the whole thing.

- A third way of encouraging errorless learning is to build in practice and review throughout the communication. The learner may forget part of the task if the teacher doesn't review it with him from time to time.

Remember, people primarily learn from what they do, so build in to the instructional communication many opportunities for the learner to practice correctly all of the parts of the task required for learning, first separately and then all together.

Feedback

The reader, or learner, can't judge how well he is learning the task unless he is informed of it. In a classroom situation, the teacher usually confirms that the learner has been successful, or points out the errors he made, and provides additional instruction. An instructional communication can also help learners in the same way, by providing *feedback* to the learner.

Following practice, the writer should include in his instructional communication information which will let the reader know whether he performed the task correctly. In case he didn't, the writer should also include some further information which will help the reader perform it correctly next time. This feedback, then, performs two functions:

- it helps the learner confirm that his practice was done correctly, and

- it helps him correct his performance of the task in case he made any errors.

Feedback will be most helpful to the learner if it occurs immediately following practice. The learner should be brought to know of his success or his errors just as soon as possible after practice.

STUDENT LEARNING ACTIVITIES

- Write "asking" and "answering" letters, and answer a letter of complaint, using the format assigned by the teacher.
- Write memoranda to other "offices" in a fictitious organization. Plan a field trip using only memos to communicate with other students in the class.
- Take minutes of a small group meeting. Or attend a meeting of the school board and take minutes.
- Write a short report on a public service occupation of special interest to you.
- Write a 15-word telegram reserving a single room at a hotel and asking to be picked up at the airport.
- Write a news release announcing a new service offered to the public by your agency.
- Based upon hearing a reading or pretaping of a report, summarize the report in news style.
- View films on effective communication, for example, *Getting the Facts, Words that Don't Inform,* and *A Message to No One.*
- For a given problem or purpose, compile a list of specific questions you would need to answer to write a report on the topic.
- For a given list of questions, discuss and compile a list of information sources relevant to the questions.
- As a member of a group, consider the problem of "What field trip should the class take to help students learn how to write an effective news release?" What questions will you need to answer? Where will you obtain your information?
- As a member of a group, gather the information and prepare a short report based on it for presentation to the class.
- Write a report on a problem assigned by your teacher.
- Write a brief persuasive letter to a friend on a given topic. Assume he does not already agree with you. Apply principles of source credibility, emotional appeals, and one or both sides of the issue to persuade him.

- Plan a persuasive campaign to persuade a given segment of your community to take some given action.
- Write a short instructional communication on a verbal learning task assigned by your teacher.
- Write a short instructional communication on a learning task which involves the operation of equipment.
- Try your instructional communications with a fellow student to check for errors during practice.

TEACHER MANAGEMENT ACTIVITIES

- Have students practice letter writing. Assign letters of "asking" and "answering." Read them a letter of complaint and ask them to write an answering letter. Establish common rules of format and style for each assignment. Change the rules from time to time to give practice in several styles.
- Have small groups plan an event, such as a field trip, assigning the various tasks to one another using only memoranda. Evaluate the effectiveness of each group's memo writing by the speed and completeness of their planning.
- Have the class attend a public meeting. Assign each the task of taking the minutes. Evaluate the minutes for brevity and completeness.
- Encourage each student to prepare a short report on a public service occupation of special interest to himself.
- Give the students practice in writing 15-word telegrams.
- Have the students prepare a news release announcing some new service offered to the public, such as "Taxpayers can now obtain help from the Internal Revenue Service in completing their income tax forms as a result of a new service now being offered by the agency."
- Give the students practice in summarizing and writing leads by giving them the facts of a news event and asking them to write a one or two-sentence lead summarizing the significant facts of the event.
- Read a speech or a story. Have students write a summary and a report of the speech or story in news style.
- Show films on effective communication, for example, *Getting the Facts, Words that Don't Inform,* and *A Message to No One.*
- State a general problem and have each student prepare a list of the specific questions implied by the problem.

- State a list of specific questions and discuss with the class the sources of information which might bear upon each of the questions.

- Have small groups consider and write short reports jointly on the general problem, "What field trip should the class take to help students learn how to write an effective news release?" Have each group identify the specific questions to be answered, with sources for needed information.

- Have each student identify and prepare a short report on a general problem of interest.

- Assign students to work in groups of three or four to draft a letter to a friend to persuade him to make a contribution to establish a new city art museum.

- Assign the students to groups of five or six, each group to map out a persuasive campaign on a given topic. Some topics are "Give Blood," "Get Chest X-Ray," "Quit Smoking," "Don't Litter," "Inspect Your House Wiring," etc.

- Have each student identify a simple verbal learning task and prepare an instructional communication to teach that task to another student not familiar with the task.

- Have each student prepare an instructional manual designed to train someone to operate some simple piece of equipment, such as an adding machine, a slide projector, a tape recorder, or something of similar complexity.

- Have each student try his instructional communication out on another student, unfamiliar with the task. He should observe the activities and responses of the trial student to identify errors made in practice. He should revise the communication, adding practice, review, and prompts wherever needed to reduce errors in practice.

EVALUATION QUESTIONS

Written Communications

1. Which type of letter would be correct for a public service worker to send? 1.___

    A. A letter containing erasures
    B. A letter reflecting goodwill
    C. A rude letter
    D. An impersonal letter

2. Memos usually leave out: 2.___

    A. Complimentary closings
    B. The name of the sender
    C. The name of the addressee
    D. The date the memo was sent

3. A good business letter would not contain: 3.___

    A. Short, simple words, sentences, and paragraphs
    B. Information contained in the letter being answered
    C. Concrete nouns and active verbs
    D. Orderly placed paragraphs

4. In writing business letters it is important to: 4.___

    A. Use a conversational tone
    B. Use a hard, cold tone
    C. Use abstract words
    D. Use a passive tone

5. Messages between departments in an agency are usually sent by: 5.___

    A. Letter
    B. Memo
    C. Telegram
    D. Long reports

6. Repetitive work can be simplified by the use of: 6.___

    A. Memos
    B. Telegrams
    C. Forms
    D. Reports

7. In filling out forms and applications, it is important to be: 7.___

    A. Legible
    B. Complete
    C. Accurate
    D. All of the above

8. Memos should be: 8.____

A. Clear
B. Brief
C. Complete
D. All of the above

9. Minutes of meetings should not include: 9.____

A. The opinions of the recorder
B. The approval of previous minutes
C. The corrections of previous minutes
D. The voting members present

10. Reports are written by public service workers to: 10.____

A. Assemble information in one place
B. Aid the organization in making decisions
C. Inform the public and other agencies
D. All of the above

11. News releases should include: 11.____

A. A lead paragraph summarizing the story
B. Long paragraphs about many topics
C. The writer's opinion
D. All of the above

12. Readers of news releases and reports are influenced by the: 12.____

A. Content of the material
B. Accuracy of the material
C. Physical appearance of the material
D. All of the above

13. The contents of a report should include: 13.____

A. A description of the problem
B. The questions to be answered
C. Unimportant information
D. A summary of findings

14. People tend to be influenced easier if: 14.____

A. They can see something in the position that would be advantageous to them
B. They are almost ready to agree anyhow
C. The appeal to the emotions is not overly strong
D. All of the above

KEY (CORRECT ANSWERS)

1. B
2. A
3. B
4. A
5. B

6. C
7. D
8. D
9. A
10. D

11. A
12. D
13. C
14. D

BASIC FUNDAMENTALS OF ORAL COMMUNICATION

TABLE OF CONTENTS

BASIC FUNDAMENTALS OF ORAL COMMUNICATION

Instructional Objectives

1. Ability to speak fluently, with correct articulation and pronunciation;
2. Ability to group words into meaningful phrases;
3. Ability to stress words and phrases to enhance communication;
4. Ability to control voice volume and tone according to needs;
5. Ability to use speech forms appropriate for the audience;
6. Ability to use body control and visual aids to enhance communication;
7. Ability to participate effectively in informal conversation and group discussion;
8. Ability to speak effectively and confidently before a group;
9. Ability to persuade or convince listeners; and
10. Ability to value the importance of oral communication as an essential skill for working in public service occupations.

Content

Introduction

Oral communication is one of the more basic processes underlying human relationships. The use of speech to transmit ideas, to probe the ideas of others, to teach, to persuade, to entertain, to motivate, and to otherwise influence and affect others is a uniquely human activity. Speech is used in the most casual and informal of human interactions, as well as in formal settings involving many persons. Through the mass media, the sounds and forms of speech may reach millions of persons simultaneously. Thus the ability to speak effectively in a variety of settings is an essential skill in all activities in which human beings interact with one another.

A basis is provided herein for the development of the student's ability to communicate effectively through speech for a variety of purposes and in a variety of settings, particularly those common to public-service occupational settings. Whatever the particular purpose or setting, however, effective speech will require the speaker to have a clear idea of his purpose and his audience, to organize his thoughts and information in an orderly way, to express himself effectively through his delivery and his knowledge of human relations, to report relevant facts, to explain and summarize clearly, and to evaluate the effectiveness of his communication.

This unit provides a framework for organizing instruction in basic speech skills, while providing practice in speaking for several purposes in several settings.

General Principles

Whatever the particular purpose or setting for oral communication, the speaker can add to his effectiveness by applying certain general principles. In general, these principles can be considered under two broad categories:

- principles affecting delivery, and
- principles affecting human relations.

These two categories are perhaps the most important aspects of oral communication. The principles of delivery and human relations must be applied in a variety of speaking situations.

Principles Affecting Delivery

The delivery of oral communications may be considered under two general categories of:

- *physical delivery,* which includes voice control, articulation, pronunciation, body control, and visual aids; and
- *verbal delivery,* including choice of words and style of delivery.

Physical Delivery

Voice Control: The effectiveness of oral communication depends in large measure upon the physical delivery of speech symbols, one major aspect which is voice control. Voice control has several distinguishing characteristics: pitch, volume, duration, and quality:

- *Pitch* is the characteristic of sound as it relates to the musical scale. Each person's voice has a certain pitch level that may be considered as high, low, or medium. Certain conditions of pitch can cause communication to suffer:
    - when the voice is pitched too high
    - when it is pitched too low
    - when it lacks variety of pitch and is monotonous

- *Volume,* or loudness, is another characteristic of voice. Speakers may be troubled when the voice volume is:
    - too great
    - too weak, or
    - lacking variety, or monotonous.

- *Duration* refers to the length of time a sound lasts, particularly the vowel sounds. There are two chief problems related to this control:
    - over-lengthening of vowels, resulting in a drawl
    - eliminating or clipping of vowels, resulting in erratic and staccato speech patterns.

- *Quality of voice* refers to that characteristic which distinguishes one person's voice from another's, the voice's "fingerprint," so to speak. The student should strive to achieve a pleasing and harmonious quality. Common quality faults include:
    - nasality (too much nasal resonance)
    - denasality (too little nasal resonance)
    - harshness, hoarseness and breathiness.

Articulation: To make himself understood, the speaker must produce speech in such a way that the audience is able to recognize the individual words he speaks. This is dependent upon the elements of:

- *Articulation,* or the joining together of consonants and vowels that go to make up the word, and

- *pronunciation,* or the fitting together of these sounds according to commonly accepted standards.

These concepts are often confused. *Articulation has to do with the clarity or distinctness of utterance,* while *pronunciation has to do with regional or dictionary standards.* It may be said, "We mispronounce words when we don't know how to pronounce them; we misarticulate words when we know how to pronounce them but fail to do so." Through habit, carelessness, and indifference, individuals may acquire such articulation problems as:

- *substitution of one sound for another,* in such words as:
    - "dat" for that
    - "winduh" for window
    - "git" for get
    - “yur” for your
    - "liddle" for little

- *insertion of extra sounds,* as:
    - ath-uh-lete for athlete
    - ekscape for escape
    - acrosst for across
    - fil-um for film.

- *omission of certain sounds,* such as:
    - at for that
    - probly for probably
    - em for them
    - slep for slept
    - pitcher for picture

- *misplacement of accent,* for example:
    - com-PAIR-a-ble for COM-par-a-ble
    - pre-FER-a-ble for PREF-er-a-ble
    - the-A-ter for THE-a-ter

Pronunciation: A person may be able to form all the speech sounds in a word accurately without saying the word correctly. The letters of words do not always represent the same sounds. When the person can form the sounds of a word correctly but does not know the acceptable way to form them, he has a pronunciation problem. The way to achieve acceptable pronunciation is to check new words in the dictionary and to be sensitive to the pronunciations heard in the speech of others. If others pronounce a word differently, the word should be looked up at the very next opportunity before using it again. The teacher must play a central role in identifying words misarticulated and mispronounced by students.

Body Language as Communication: In addition to voice and articulation-pronunciation controls, a speaker's whole body acts as an important tool in the physical delivery of speech. Through the judicious use of eye contact, facial expression, and body activity the speaker can supplement and reinforce his spoken communication by means of visual symbols.

Eye Contact: It is important for effective oral communication that the listeners feel that the speaker is speaking directly to them. No matter if the speaker is addressing one person or many, each listener should gain a feeling that the speaker is addressing him. Thus, *eye contact* between the speaker and his audience is essential in virtually every speaking situation. No matter what the setting, therefore, the speaker should make every attempt to meet the eyes of all members of the audience to achieve a feeling of directness and all-inclusiveness. The eyes of the speaker should meet those of members of the audience, not look past them or avoid them, nor over their heads, out of the window, down at the floor, or up at the ceiling. Eye contact with members of the audience will also help the speaker watch for audience reactions, for signs of misunderstanding, doubt, or question which may help him modify his communication in response to audience reactions.

Facial Expression: Another form of body control is the use of *facial expression* to clarify and enliven oral communication. The speaker's face, used effectively, can reflect his interest in his own message, the intensity of his feelings, his sincerity and purposefulness. Hiding behind a mask of blankness and composure can deny the speaker an important tool in the communication of his ideas. To develop this facility with facial expression, the learner should try always to communicate ideas in which he has a high interest and in which he has a sense of competence and concern. It is difficult to generate facial liveliness when speaking on a topic of little personal concern.

Body Activity: The use of gestures and general *body activity* provides another means for supplementing speech. The use of motor activity involving the head, torso, arms, hands, or gross body movement to emphasize the spoken word is a skill that may be cultivated. A shrug of the shoulders, a nod of the head, a straightening of the torso, a lift of the chin, or a step toward the audience can indicate indifference, emphasis, firmness of purpose, a questioning attitude, or determination.

Body activity can, however, be overdone to the point where too much activity may distract from the message. The use of body activity must be judicious if it is to have a controlled and desired effect on the listeners.

Another fault in this area involves the unconscious use of distracting mannerisms that may result from habit, nervousness, or preoccupation. Such mannerisms usually are unrelated to the content of the message, such as shifting weight from foot to foot, finger or foot tapping, nose or head fiddling, generalized arm waving, lint picking, and the like. The student should learn to normally use body movement only for specific purposes, while trying to eliminate all mannerisms and overuses that distract from the message.

Visual Aids Help Oral Communication: The physical delivery of speech may be enhanced also through the use of visual aids. Visual aids may be useful for several purposes:

- *for getting attention and interest.* Well-chosen and relevant aids command attention through their shape, color, texture, or movement. A speaker can capture attention by using materials that appeal directly to the senses.
- *for clarifying.* When words are insufficient to communicate an idea, a visual aid may help make an idea clearer. A sketch or drawing, a photograph or model, often can clarify in an instant what may be impossible to describe verbally.

- *for impressing on memory.* Aside from getting attention and clarifying an idea, the speaker may wish to affect the listener's memory. A well-chosen visual aid may help etch an idea on the memory far more effectively than a well-turned phrase.
- *for increasing poise.* The use of visual aids may provide a framework for the speaker's activity, giving him something to do that may serve to increase confidence. The use of visual aids as a "crutch" should not be encouraged in the long run; however, their use in this way may serve to aid the self-confidence of the learner in the initial stages of speech training.

Many types of visual aids may be found useful to supplement oral communications. These include charts, graphs, maps, globes, chalkboard sketches, flip charts, models, moving pictures, projected slides and illustrations, photographs, or television enlargements. In using visual aids, the speaker should follow several basic guidelines:

- He should use the visual material purposefully;
- He should be certain that the entire audience can see the aid;
- He should maintain eye contact while using the aid; and
- He should avoid dividing attention with the aid when it is not in use.

Verbal Delivery

The effectiveness of oral communication depends also upon the speaker's choice of language and his style of delivery. The words he uses, the phrasing by which he assembles them, and the manner in which he delivers them, are the elements of *verbal delivery.*

Choice of Language: Good language in oral communication is language adapted to the audience and to the occasion. In choosing language, the speaker must consider himself, the ideas he wants to express, the characteristics of the audience, and the nature of the setting. Thus he must ask himself, "Is this expression suitable for me to use in communicating this thought to this audience on this occasion?"

Use clear language: To accomplish this, the speaker should use language that clarifies his thoughts. Language should be simple and not pompous. Unnecessarily complex expressions or technical terms should be avoided. Too many words, too ornate words, too pretentious words, can hamper communication. The criteria of clarity in speaking are directness, economy, and aptness. For example,

- Instead of “prevarication”, say “lie”;
- Instead of “domicile”, say “home”;
- Instead of “this moment is one of great joy to my heart,” say “I'm glad to be here.”

Seek precise words: It is also a good idea to use precise language. Words and expressions which are specific to the intended meaning are more likely to communicate that meaning than more general and abstract words. In this vein:

- Instead of “car,” try hardtop, sedan, Ford, or 1973 hatch-back Pinto;
- Instead of “said,” try replied, stated, cried, commented, uttered.

Avoid imprecise wording: Avoid roundabout expressions, or *euphemisms,* which create special problems in lack of precision. "Soft-pedaling" an idea now and then may be justified if the speaker does not sacrifice his overall credibility. But care must be taken that the use of euphemisms does not act to call into question the speaker's ideas or intent. Therefore,

- Instead of "he passed to his just reward," try → "he died"
- "he received his termination notice" → "he was fired"
- "the effects were not inconsiderable" → "the effects were great"

Use appealing language: The speaker should also seek to use language that will enliven his thoughts. One way to achieve this is to use language that appeals to the senses. Thus language that appeals to movement, color, light, texture, form, taste, smell, sound, and the like will tend to put life in the speaking. Thus,

- Instead of "a difficult peace", try → "a hard and bitter peace"
- "an old ship" → "a splintery, creaking old ship"

Animate abstract ideas: Figurative language, too, can enliven speech by animating an abstract idea. The use of simile, metaphor, personification, and irony (look up the meanings in your dictionary) are especially useful. For example,

- Instead of "her arrival silenced everyone", try → "her arrival was like a chill winter wind"
- "he paced to and fro" → "he was like a caged lion"
- "the winds rustled the trees" → "the trees whispered in the winds"
- "we worked a lot of overtime" → "oh, we twiddled away our time and often left early!"

Use varied techniques: The speaker should develop ways to vary his choice of language. Variety in expression can help to sustain interest and attention, while often clarifying meaning. Students should practice changing their language by use of techniques such as:

- varying the shaping of sentences (use of questions, use of imperatives, varying order of phrases, etc.);
- building climax within passages;
- using parallelisms (recurring similarities of phrase or word arrangements);
- using alliteration (repeating first syllables, or consonants in consecutive words)
- using repetition of phraseology;
- using fresh language, i.e. avoiding the ordinary and the hackneyed, or shopworn, cliché-type phrases.

Use appropriate language: The speaker should always take special pains to use language appropriate to the occasion, and language which is standard. The speaker can be too formal or too informal, either of which will reduce, for particular occasions, the effectiveness of his communication. While the formality of language may be adjusted to the occasion, rarely will it be appropriate to use common slang or the language of the streets in any formal communication setting. Similarly, the use of standard speech will usually be appropriate and aid in communicating ideas, whereas the use of substandard language forms may inhibit understanding and reduce the speaker's credibility among many segments of his audience.

Use natural language: Further, it is important on all occasions that the speaker use language that is his own, language that is familiar and comfortable. Each student should work toward developing broader vocabulary and a greater variety of language skills, but should be discouraged from trying to achieve these in large steps. Language skills are developed over long periods of time, and at any given stage of development the student should use the language with which he is most comfortable and natural. In this way each student, over time, may develop uniqueness and effectiveness of style – that characteristic of one's speech which brands it distinctly as his own.

Develop a Good Style of Delivery: Finally, *control of delivery rate, rhythm* and *phrasing* will be essential to achieving clarity and effectiveness in oral communication. *Rate* may be controlled by the number and duration of the silent spaces between words and phrases, as well as by the time taken in the production of individual sounds, particularly the vowel sounds. Faster rates may be called for at times; at other times, slower rates. Variations in rate can affect the clarity of communication as well as the mood. A slow and ponderous rate may create a mood of solemnity; a rapid rate, one of lightness and joyfulness. One should vary his rate within speech to achieve variety as he varies other aspects of verbal delivery.

These variations, together with the individual's use of pauses and techniques of sound production act to generate a *rhythm of speech* that is part of the individual's style. Care should be taken that the use of pauses aids rather than hinders meaning – that pauses occur in appropriate places.

Also, special care should be taken that irrelevant sounds, such as "ah," "uh," and "um" do not creep into the individual's speech to fill up the spaces and to break up the flow of ideas. The rate and rhythm of speaking should compare favorably to a musical composition in which the breaks, accelerations, slow-downs, and repetitions add interest and clarity to the composer's purpose.

Principles Affecting Human Relations

In addition to those principles of oral communication which affect delivery, a number of principles of oral communication affect the relationship between the speaker and his audience. It should be self-evident that a listener will be more receptive to a speaker's ideas if a positive relationship exists between them. The speaker can apply certain principles which will tend to create and to maintain this type of positive relationship.

Respect the Dignity of Others

Every human being desires self-respect, a sense of personal worth, and dignity. In dealing with others it is basic to honestly nourish this desire. If we do or say anything which will injure another's dignity, if we humiliate or demean him in any way, we create resentment and antagonism which can obstruct effective communication. To implement this principle, try the following techniques in both formal and informal communications:

- *Make the other person right in something.* Even though you may disagree with him, start your search for agreement by pinpointing something in which he is right and go on from there.
- *Avoid complaining or finding fault.* The complainer and the faultfinder destroy all reasonable relations with others. Follow the maxim, "fix the error, not the blame." Protect the dignity of others by showing your respect for them personally, even while you may disagree with their ideas or criticize their work.

- *Avoid arguments.* Arguing with another implies that he is ignorant or mistaken and thereby diminishes his dignity. Antagonism can easily form around argument and obstruct effective communication. By being modest in advancing ideas and by avoiding telling others they are wrong, a speaker can reduce the possibility of damaging arguments. Rather than saying, "It is obvious that.. ..," or "Any right-thinking person can see that.. ..," try saying, "It appears to me that ....," or "Let us consider the possibility that ...."
- *Admit personal mistakes.* If one is willing to admit that he is human enough to make an error, others find their own self-image taking on increased stature.

Develop An Honest Interest in Other People

This second principle challenges us to develop an attitude of curiosity about others and to pursue this curiosity rather than to tell others about ourselves. Rather than a "Here I am" attitude, develop a "There you are" attitude. Such an attitude creates respect in others, and enables one to know those with whom he deals, to understand them, and to treat them as individuals. To cultivate an attitude of interest in others, try the following techniques:

- *Be an interested listener.* One cannot possibly respect another's point of view unless he hears it out.
- *Smile honestly and often.* A person need not agree with, approve of, or like another's point of view; understanding, recognition, and interest are sufficient to stimulate an honest smile which will reflect one's appreciation and respect for the other's point of view.
- *Ask questions frequently to understand others.* Questions are valuable because they require people to take specific actions in the direction of others. A good question reveals that one has really been listening and further, that he has an interest in what was said. And it gives another an opportunity to further reveal himself, thus providing a mechanism for getting better acquainted.

Recognize Individual Uniqueness and Worth

This third principle asks us to see people as individuals, to respond positively to their better qualities, and to understand their weaknesses. To develop ability in this area, try such methods as:

- *Get names right and use them often.* One's use of it reveals recognition of his uniqueness. Using names correctly and frequently not only satisfies the natural desire of another for recognition, but also aids a person to identify another as an individual.
- *Be appreciative and quick to give approval.* Being ready and generous with appreciation builds good human relations in two ways. It nourishes the receiver's feeling of self-esteem and worth, and it trains the giver to be observant of the strong or desirable traits and behavior of others.
- *Assume that people will behave in a good manner.* If we ascribe the best of motives and intentions to others, they will be inclined to live up to them. Assume the best of every person and you will rarely be disappointed. Assuming the best of them gives implied recognition to their worth as individuals.
- *Respect the rights and opinions of others.* A person need not always agree with the opinions of others, but he must respect the right of others to hold opinions different from his own and refrain from belittling or contradicting them.

The opinions of others are very much a part of their psychological and intellectual makeup, and to refuse respect for an opinion is to deny respect to the person himself. *Effective communication cannot occur between persons without mutual respect for their rights and opinions.*

Cooperate With the Wants of Others

This fourth principle emphasizes that behavior is directed from within a person as he attempts to satisfy his own wants or to solve his own problems. If a person seeks to communicate with others and to direct their behavior in a particular direction, he must cooperate with the wants which motivate them. That is, he must align his purposes with their wants and avoid the appearance of denying or frustrating those wants. Nevertheless, there is a difference between cooperating with the wants of others and giving in to them. Cooperation simply implies that one should present his case in a way which will reveal how the listener will benefit. Some techniques for implementing this principle follow:

- *Encourage initiative.* Great energy can be released by encouraging and tactfully guiding the initiative of others. Challenging the creative imagination of others in proposing solutions to problems; in developing plans, in organizing for action, and the like reveals the speaker's respect for the ideas of others, and can go a long way to assure their cooperation and participation in the final activity. When one's own initiative and imagination has been challenged, he is more likely to align himself with the decisions that are finally reached.
- *Help the other person get what he wants.* When another sees a person willing to help him satisfy his wants, an atmosphere conducive to effective communication and cooperation has been established. Try to recognize what others want and address the issues from their point of view.
- *Present problems and ask for solutions.* When one must ask another for help, when he must assign work, or when he wants to enlist cooperation, then he will often find it more productive to present the problem and ask for help in its solution than to make a direct demand. Instead of saying, "George, move those boxes out of the aisle," try saying, "George, these boxes are dangerous where they are; someone may injure themselves. Is there some other handy place for them where they will be out of the way?" By involving George in solving the problem you show respect for his ideas, and he will likely WANT to help solve the problem.
- *Present doubts, opinions or objections in question form.* Sometimes we must necessarily disagree with another. When it is necessary, we can make our disagreement more objective and more acceptable to others if we avoid over-positive or challenging statements. One technique for achieving this is to voice our concerns in the form of questions, which may minimize the possibility of arousing resentment or starting an argument.

Person-to-Person Communications

Not only in the public-service occupations, but also in business, industry, and everyday life, the form of communication most often used is *person-to-person speaking.* Any human activity which requires the interaction of two or more persons will rely heavily on person-to-person speaking to establish and maintain social relationships, to plan, coordinate, and carry out cooperative tasks. *Effectiveness in person-to-person communication is essential for effectiveness in most jobs.*

Informal Conversation: The major difference between conversation and public speaking is that in conversation there is give-and-take, while in public speaking the speaker does all the talking. Yet even this difference may be more apparent than actual, for in real life conversants may hold the floor for long periods of time, and public speakers may be seeking two-way communication with their audiences.

There are few firm rules of conversation that will hold true in all situations because conversational situations may vary so widely. Not only do topics vary, but the makeup of the conversants in age, occupation, interest, education may also vary. So may the time, place, and purpose of the gathering. So many situations are possible that the conversationalist who tries to meet them all in the same manner is doomed to failure. *The good conversationalist will try to develop a wise adaptability.* Some guidelines that may prove helpful are:

- Pursue only those subjects of interest to all the conversants;
- Avoid saying about another what you might resent being said about yourself;
- Avoid statements which you would be embarrassed to have repeated with your name cited as the source;
- Maintain a conversational tone: good-humored, alert, and vigorous, without being rancorous;
- Express opinions, but avoid being opinionated; contend without being contentious;
- In general, adhere to the principles of good human relations discussed in the previous section.

Interviewing: Most persons, at one time or another, have been interviewed. Public service employees, at one time or another, may be expected to conduct interviews. While interviews have many characteristics in common with conversation, there are important differences. An interview is a planned conversation – it is arranged in advance by the parties and is intended to accomplish some purpose. Interviews may be *structured* (directive) or *unstructured* (non-directive) in form. The former is likely to be task- or subject-centered and is most common in work situations. The latter are likely to be person-centered and are used for counseling, analysis, and therapy. Thus, they usually require that the interviewer have substantial professional training. There are many kinds of, and purposes for, interviews. For example:

- *Employment interviews:* for securing, developing, and training employees;
- *Induction interviews:* for orienting new employees;
- *Performance review interviews:* for training, and developing employees;
- *Counseling interviews*: for personal and personnel matters;
- *Correction interviews:* for disciplining and guidance of staff;
- *Grievance interviews:* reverse correction interviews;
- *Data gathering interviews:* to obtain special information;
- *Consulting interviews:* exchange of information and problem-solving with an expert;
- *Sales interviews:* for persuading another;
- *Order-giving interviews:* to assign tasks and procedures;
- *Exit interviews:* a debriefing of an employee upon separation.

From the above it can be seen that interviews are directed toward serving three basic goals:

- to increase understanding through information-giving and information-getting;

- to persuade; and
- to solve problems.

To be effective, interviews should be carefully planned. Objectives should be determined in advance, and thought should be given to major obstacles likely to arise. The strategy and tactics of the interview should be planned beforehand, and consideration should be given to some contingency plans in the event that certain events occur during the interview.

The beginning of the interview should establish a workable arrangement between the parties by establishing an appropriate atmosphere, stimulating interest and attention, and presenting the problem or goal of the interview. The body of the interview should pursue the above objectives.

The close of the interview should round out and gracefully terminate the interview. The gist of the interview should be reviewed or summarized; the bases for further conversations should be established if necessary; and appreciations should be expressed.

Group Discussions: The term "group discussion" describes an activity that enables a number of cooperative people to talk freely about a problem under the leadership of a member of the group. They have the common purpose of interchanging ideas for specific needs. Group discussion is sometimes confused with debate, but the two activities differ in purpose, in format, and in the attitude of the participants. *The purpose of debate is advocacy; the purpose of discussion is inquiry.*

In group discussion, the participants deliberate seriously with minimum restraints. They work in cooperation with one another in discussion at least until the group as a unit has reached a solution to a problem. Their purpose is to inquire in order to learn all aspects of a problem, and then to solve it. Although participants may disagree, their purpose is to sort out the areas of agreement in arriving at answers.

Techniques of Group Discussion: The techniques and formats of group discussion may vary, but the underlying purpose remains the same – to inquire into the essential aspects of a problem and to solve it. Some types of discussions, such as the *meeting,* or *round-table,* are not intended for audiences; others, such as the *panel,* the *symposium,* and the *forum,* are planned for audiences. Whatever the format, the participants should remember that they are acting as a group studying a question. It requires real skill on the part of all participants to pool relevant information, to move the discussion forward, to limit heated cross talk, and to stress areas of agreements.

Criteria for group discussion: Group discussion is useful only if the group has a real problem to solve and if its members all agree on what that is. Thus, stating the question in an effective way is important to promote fruitful discussion. Here are some criteria for worthwhile discussions:

- The problem should deserve a solution.
- The problem should be worth the time spent on it.
- The problem should be either timely or timeless.
- The problem should be able to be solved in the time available.
- The group should be competent to solve the problem.
- The problem should be stated in question form.

- The question for discussion should not be stated in a form demanding a "yes" or "no" answer, but in a form indicating a need for discussion. (Instead of: "Should the federal government control the press?" try: "What should be the role of the federal government in regulating the press?")

Leading a discussion requires some special skills. The discussion leader must insure the orderly, systematic, and cooperative consideration of the question. He tries to direct the course of the discussion without manipulating the group to accept any particular conclusion. He assures that every member of the group has an opportunity to participate, and that no one monopolizes the floor. He provides needed facts or calls upon others to provide them. He summarizes when needed and restates the issues under discussion. He strives to keep the emphasis upon agreement and cooperative thinking in order to avoid conflict.

A simple functional plan for discussion leadership might include the following steps for a problem-solving discussion:

- Introduction of the problem by the leader
- Defining potentially confusing terms
- Presentation of relevant facts by group members
- Specifying criteria for judging a good solution
- Presentation by members of possible solutions
- Analysis of solutions in relation to criteria
- Decision: which solution is preferred, or what additional information is needed before a decision can be made

Forms of group discussion: Several forms of group discussion are in common use. Each occasion for group discussion implies its own format for discussion that will best serve its own specific needs, purposes, and interests. The common formats include:

- The *round table* (or informal) group discussion is usually not observed by an audience. The preferred number of participants is from four to seven, although good discussions may be held with as many as fifteen or as few as three participants. The discussants should cooperate courteously in reaching a decision. Formal recognition to speak is not necessary. The outstanding characteristic of the round-table discussion is its informality.
- The *panel* is similar except for the presence of an audience. With an audience, the members are more formal in their presentations, speaking not only for themselves, but for the audience as well. If the audience participates by asking questions after the solution has been reached, the activity is called a *panel forum.*
- A *symposium* differs from the panel or round-table because all participants, perhaps three or four, are experts on phases of the question. The speakers give set speeches in order and are provided little opportunity for interchanging ideas with their fellow participants. The symposium is typically presented for the benefit of an audience. Often a panel follows a symposium, offering the participants an opportunity, after their individual presentations, to exchange ideas in a discussion format. When the audience is invited to ask questions of the participants, the activity is called a *symposium-forum.*
- The *forum* is an activity distinguished by audience participation. The forum may be used in combination with a panel, a symposium, a lecture, a debate, or any other form that may be useful to communicate basic information to the

audience prior to its participation. The leader, in conducting a forum, should explain the procedures to be followed by members of the audience in asking questions or making comments, including how to be recognized, how much time will be allowed, and the like.

Group discussion is an excellent means of pooling knowledge, reaching decisions, and informing the public. The public-service employee will find himself participating in group discussion both within his organization, at staff meetings and other groups, and for audiences as a means of informing public opinion.

Speaking Before Groups

The distinction between speaking IN a group and speaking BEFORE a group is not always apparent. If, as a member of a group, one speaks his piece for five full minutes without interruption, or if he rises and speaks from a standing position, is he speaking in the group or before it? While it is a popular notion that group speaking, or public speaking is characterized by a much higher degree of formality, and by one-way communication from the speaker to his audience, it is well to consider speaking before a group as simply dignified, amplified conversation. *Public speaking, at its best, seeks to establish a carefully planned conversational relationship with a group of persons.*

The public-service employee will find many occasions in which he will be called upon to speak before a group. The group may be his co-workers, as at a staff or committee meeting; his colleagues, as at a professional conference; or members of the public, as at a public meeting, or a meeting of a citizens' group. Whatever the particular occasion, the employee may be called upon to speak before a group for any of several purposes. The general principles of effective oral communication apply to public or group speaking, as well as to person-to-person speaking, and attention to these principles will aid in developing effectiveness in speaking before groups. Public-service employees commonly participate in speaking before groups for the purposes of informing, instructing, persuading, motivating, or entertaining.

Speaking to Inform

The primary purpose of the speech to inform is to convey information to listeners to clarify a point of view, a process, a method, an idea, a problem, or a proposed solution. By far the greatest amount of speaking before a group is done to convey information. The content may vary from relatively simple, concrete topics, such as how to complete a personnel form, to highly abstract topics, such as how a client-centered program will affect relations with clients.

Three general types of informing speeches are commonly used in public-service work:

- reports
- briefings
- informational talks

An *oral report* summarizes in orderly fashion a body of information, usually assembled by the person making the report.

A *briefing* is similar to a report, except that it usually occurs as a prelude to some imminent action. All the facts needed for decision-making actions are assembled immediately before the action, and conveyed to those who will be making the decisions.

The *informational talk* is less formal, usually delivered by a knowledgeable person without need for much formal preparation. An informational talk might be presented by the head of an agency about the agency's work to a group of new employees. A simple and typical four-part outline for information speeches consists of the following parts:

- Introduction – tell them what you are going to tell them
- Key Idea – tell them the main or central idea
- Body – tell them the details
- Conclusion – tell them what you told them

Speaking to Instruct

Almost every employee in a public agency at one time or another will be expected to teach or train others. This teaching will often occur in a group situation, and the employee will function as a teacher, speaking to the group, assigning practice, evaluating student work, and similar activities. Speaking for this purpose should generally follow the rules of good human relations, of course, but additionally should use certain principles of learning which will increase the effectiveness of teaching.

When speaking to instruct or train a group, the instructor should employ the following principles:

- *Include an advance organizer:* A summary of the tasks that will be learned, and a reason for learning them
- *Provide active practice:* Give the learners, or listeners, plenty of opportunity to practice what you want them to learn. Ask a lot of questions; hand out worksheets; break the group into "buzz" groups for discussion; get them actively involved.
- *Help them succeed:* Don't assign them work or ask them questions which they are likely to fail. Give them hints if necessary during practice, but help them succeed.
- *Give them plenty of feedback:* If they answer a question correctly, or turn in a correct worksheet, or make a correct contribution in some other way, let them know it right away. Not tomorrow, or next week, but let them know immediately.

If these principles can be incorporated into instructional talks and training sessions, they are likely to be more effective.

Speaking to Persuade

The public-service employee may find himself speaking to persuade a group from time to time. In ordinary work situations, he may wish to persuade his fellow workers to adopt a new policy, or a certain attitude toward their work. On other occasions, he may be speaking to members of the public, trying to persuade them favorably toward his agency, or to avail themselves of the agency's program.

Basically, there are three types of appeals that the speaker can make to his audience:

- *Logical Appeals:* Through the use of deductive reasoning (from general ideas to specific conclusion) and inductive reasoning (from specific data to a general conclusion), and the presenting of factual evidence to support this reasoning, the speaker appeals mainly to the listener's intellect and reason.

- *Psychological Appeals:* Through appeals to the listener's motivations, feelings and values, the speaker tries to get his listeners to WANT to adopt the idea being presented.
- *Personal Appeals:* Through his own personal effect, the speaker tries to influence his listeners – by characterizing his own reputation, appearance, personality and character in a way that will create a favorable and receptive climate for his ideas.

Beyond these types of appeals, the persuasive speaker will do well to attend carefully to the principles of good human relations discussed earlier.

Speaking to Motivate

Another occasion for speaking before a group is to motivate them – to excite, arouse, or spur them on. Usually such speaking is occasioned by some strong feelings in the speaker about his subject. He may, for example, feel that the staff of the agency is simply not attaching sufficient importance to certain areas of their work. At a staff meeting he might address the group and try to get them "fired up" about that work.

Speaking of this type generally follows the patterns of the persuasive speech, since we often are seeking to influence the listeners in a particular direction. Typically, however, its appeal tends to focus upon the psychological, since the speaker is usually more interested in affecting attitudes, motivations, and values than he is in affecting beliefs.

Speaking to Entertain

While not normally central to the duties of public-service employees, the entertaining speech is an occasional responsibility that may fall to almost anyone. At an annual dinner, a staff party, an agency picnic, one may be called upon to speak briefly to a group in a light and casual tone. When called upon on such an occasion, one should be especially aware that he need not be uproariously funny to be entertaining. *To entertain means simply to amuse or to divert.*

It is well to recognize that few persons have the practiced skills of a professional comedian to keep an audience laughing from start to finish. The occasional speaker who seeks to entertain an audience, to amuse and divert them for a few brief moments, does well to adapt his humor to the local and familiar experiences of his audience.

In general, the entertaining speech should attend to the principles of good human relations. The speaker should not develop humor at the expense of any person's dignity. While he may poke gentle fun at himself, rarely can one poke fun at others without injuring their dignity and self-esteem. As with other purposeful speeches, speeches to entertain may be organized around the four-part outline discussed earlier.

STUDENT LEARNING ACTIVITIES

- Prepare a list of principles affecting delivery, and a list of principles affecting human relations. Develop checklists for evaluating the speech of others based upon these principles.
- Participate in informal conversation with two others before the class. No topic should be decided in advance. Following the conversation, participate in a class critique of the conversation.
- Participate in two interview situations set up by your teacher. In one, function as the interviewer; in the other, as the interviewee.

- Participate in a round-table discussion on a problem assigned by your teacher.
- Participate in a panel-forum on a problem assigned by your teacher.
- Participate as a member of a symposium-forum on a problem assigned by your teacher.
- Prepare and present a 5-minute oral report on a topic assigned by your teacher.
- Prepare and present a 5-minute lesson on a subject assigned by your teacher.
- Prepare and present a 5-minute persuasive or motivational speech on a subject assigned by your teacher.
- Prepare and present a 5-minute speech to entertain the class.
- Participate in critiques of the speeches and discussions involving other students. Use principles of delivery and human relations as the basis for your criticism.

TEACHER MANAGEMENT ACTIVITIES

- Have each student develop checklists for critiquing oral communications based upon the principles of delivery and human relations discussed in the first topic. Through class discussion, develop a checklist evaluation form that will be used by the class for evaluating speech performance.
- Have students in groups of three participate in informal conversations. Topics should not be decided in advance. The setting should be informal as possible. But the conversation should be observed and evaluated by members of the class. "Buzz" groups may be formed, with teams of "evaluators" dropping into the groups.
- Assign interview situations to pairs of students, designating the interviews and the interviewees. Students should be given ten or fifteen minutes to prepare for their part of the interview. Interviews should be critiqued by the class.
- Assign students to round-table panel and symposium groups. Assign each a problem to discuss. Have each group discuss its problem before the class. Critique the discussions.
- Have each student prepare a five-minute report, a five-minute lesson on some subject, a five-minute persuasive speech, a five-minute entertainment speech, on topics you approve. Presentations should be evaluated by the class using the critique forms developed by the class.

EVALUATION QUESTIONS

1. Effective speakers have voices that: 1.______
   - A. Have a pleasant pitch and volume
   - B. Lack variety of pitch
   - C. Have great volume
   - D. Have a very high pitch

2. A competent speaker would: 2.______
   - A. Look at the people in the front row
   - B. Look at the people in the back row
   - C. Look at all the people in the group
   - D. Look at the people in the middle of the group

3. Looking at the audience is helpful to the speaker because: 3.______
   A. It helps the speaker watch for audience reaction
   B. It helps the speaker watch for signs of misunderstanding
   C. It enables the speaker to pick out signs of doubt
   D. All of the above

4. An effective speaker would: 4.______
   A. Look lively and sincere
   B. Keep his face as blank as possible
   C. Look overly composed;
   D. Look disinterested about the subject

5. Body language can indicate: 5.______
   A. Emphasis
   B. Firmness of purpose
   C. Indifference
   D. All of the above

6. These items would be included in a group of visual aids: 6.______
   A. Phonograph records and record player
   B. Charts, graphs, and maps
   C. Tape decks and cassettes
   D. All of the above

7. It is preferable for a speaker to use: 7.______
   A. Many abstract and general words
   B. Precise words
   C. Fancy words
   D. Round-about expressions

8. As a speaker, you should: 8.______
   A. Use your own language
   B. Pattern your language after someone else
   C. Imitate highly educated people
   D. Use the occasion to try out big words you are learning

9. Accomplished speakers: 9.______
   A. Deliver their speeches as fast as they can to economize time
   B. Deliver their speeches at a very slow rate
   C. Give very solemn speeches at a rapid rate
   D. Vary the rate within the speech to achieve variety

10. An effective speaker would: 10.______
   A. Speak rapidly without leaving any break between sentences
   B. Fill up the spaces by saying "ah"
   C. Pause occasionally
   D. Use "you know" to fill in

11. A good technique in human relations is to: 11.______
   A. Tell others they are wrong about everything
   B. Point out the other person's faults
   C. Admit your own mistakes
   D. Attack others personally

12. The most sought after people are those who: 12.______
   A. Tell others all about themselves
   B. Are good listeners
   C. Smile only when necessary
   D. Let others know how they feel about every subject

13. For a person who has recently been hired, it is preferable to: 13.______
   A. Be quick to show what others are doing wrong
   B. Be suspicious of others until they prove themselves
   C. Try to convince others to think as you do on every subject
   D. None of the above

14. A good technique in human relations is to: 14.______
   A. Ask the opinions of others
   B. Help other people get what they want
   C. Present your doubts in the form of a question
   D. All of the above

Answer Key

1. A	4. A	7. B	10. C	13. D
2. C	5. D	8. A	11. C	14. D
3. D	6. B	9. D	12. B	

BASIC FUNDAMENTALS OF INTERPERSONAL RELATIONSHIPS

TABLE OF CONTENTS

BASIC FUNDAMENTALS OF INTERPERSONAL RELATIONSHIPS

INSTRUCTIONAL OBJECTIVES

1. Ability to distinguish between formal and informal behavior.
2. Ability to identify the important factors in communicating with people.
3. Ability to understand how defense mechanisms affect communication with others.
4. Ability to identify the roles played in effective person-to-person communication.
5. Ability to acquire the human relations skills needed for getting along with others both on and off the job.
6. Ability to establish greater personal effectiveness with others so as to develop better cooperation and superior-subordinate relationships in public-service working situations.
7. Ability to recognize the mutual dependence of individuals on each other.
8. Ability to form positive attitudes toward the worth and dignity of every human being.
9. Ability to become aware of how feelings affect one's own behavior, as well as one's relationships with other people.
10. Ability to use an understanding of human relationships to effectively work with people.
11. Ability to improve communications with others by developing greater effectiveness in dealing with people in the world of public service.

CONTENT

INTRODUCTION

Perhaps the single most important skill that a public-service worker. or anyone for that matter, needs, is the ability to get along with other people. "Person-to-person" relationships are the building blocks of all social interactions between two-individuals. If there is one essential ingredient for success in life, both on and off the job, it is developing greater effectiveness in dealing with people.

The skill of the teacher is critical to the success of this unit. He should establish a permissive and non-threatening group climate in which free communication and behavior can take place. The importance of this unit cannot be over stated. The overall objective is to establish greater personal effectiveness with others and to develop better co-operative and superior-subordinate relationships in the public-service occupations. Obtaining greater "self-awareness" is a large part of this goal. Because interpersonal relations are affected by a variety of factors, some attention should be given initially to basic rules of conduct and behavior on the job.

1. INTERPERSONAL CONDUCT AND BEHAVIOR ON THE JOB

Most public-service agencies have clearly defined rules and regulations. The behavior of the public-service worker is often guided by the established procedures and directives of that individual agency. In many cases, even individual departments or units will have procedures manuals, which regulate conduct and office work.

Formal Organization of the Office

At one point or another, most public-service employees either work directly in an office, or come in frequent contact with other people working in an administrative or staff office. Students should become familiar with the organizational structure of the occupational groups in which they are planning on working. A park worker, for example, must know about the organization of the Parks Department–what kinds of staff or administrative services are provided, what about training, what are the safety rules, what goes into personnel records, etc. Preparing a flow chart of the relationships between different positions in a particular agency is one way of learning about the organization of that office or agency.

Office as a Setting for formal and Informal Relations

It is necessary to become aware of the different kinds of social relations shared with co-workers and the public. Some co-workers, for example, are seen only at work, and others are seen socially after work and/or on weekends. Factors that determine which co-workers become *personal* friends and which are just *work* friends should be considered and discussed.

On the other hand, a public-service worker usually has more formal relationships with the public with whom he comes into contact. Consider the relationships of the preschool teacher's aide and his students, the library helper and his library patrons, the police cadet and the general public, etc. In each of these cases, the public expects the public-service worker to help them with a particular service.

Although the distinction between formal and informal social relationships is not always clear, one should be sensitive to the fact that both kinds of relationships affect the behavior of the public and the public-service employee, Normally, the very organization of the public-service office helps to create a social climate for developing working relationships of a formal nature, and personal relationships with co-workers and the public which are of a more impersonal nature.

Office Behavior

Specific kinds of behavior relate to these formal and informal relationships with other people. Typically, the formal relationship is well prescribed and regulated by procedures or directives. The license interviewer, as an example, has specific questions to ask, and specific information to obtain from the applicant. Their relationship can be described as formal or prescribed by regulation. On the other hand, other office behavior can best be described as informal and non-prescribed (or *free*). Interpersonal relations in this case are often more personal and relaxed by their very nature.

2. INTERPERSONAL COMMUNICATION - THE MEANING

Interpersonal communication can be defined as a two-way flow of information from person-to-person. One cannot Study human relations without examining the constant relationships that man has with other people; the individual does not exist in a vacuum. Most of man's psychological and social needs are met through dealings with other people. In fact, one psychiatrist (Harry Stark Sullivan) has developed a theory of personality based upon interpersonal situations. This viewpoint, known as the *Interpersonal Theory of Psychiatry,* claims that personality is essentially the enduring pattern of continued interpersonal relationships between people. This interpersonal behavior is all that can be observed as personality.

Importance of Face-to-Face Contacts

The very phrase. *Public Service Occupations,* suggests frequent face-to-face contacts with not only the general public, but with co-workers as well. With possibly a few exceptions, practically every public-service employee encounters frequent person-to-person contacts both on and off the job. The ability to get along with people is a very important part of public-service work.

Listening Techniques

Effective listening is a critical part of interpersonal communications. Listening is an active process, requiring not only that one must *pay attention* to what is being said, but that one must also *listen* for the meaning of what is being said. Almost one-half of the total time spent communicating, (reading, writing, speaking, or listening) is spent in listening.

Even though people get considerable practice at listening, they don't do too well at it. Many studies have shown that, on the average, a person retains only about 25 percent of a given speech after only 10 minutes have elapsed. Most people forget three quarters of what they hear in a relatively short period of time. Clearly, people need to improve their listening skills if they are to become more effective in their relations with other people.

3. FACTORS IN INTERPERSONAL COMMUNICATION

There are a number of components that affect the person-to-person relationship. Some of the factors common to both the sender and the receiver in a person-to-person communication are:

The Attitudes and Emotions of the Individuals

For example - two people are shouting and screaming at each other - how effective is their interpersonal communication?

- *The Needs and Wants of the People Communicating*

Both the sender and receiver have unique desires, some open, and some hidden from the other person. These needs can and do strongly influence interpersonal relationships.

- *The Implied Demands of the Sender and Receiver*

  An important factor in interpersonal communications involves requests or demands. How are these demands handled? What are some typical responses to demands? These factors are common to both the sender and the receiver in interpersonal relations and affect the individual behavior of the people communicating.

The Choice of Words of the Conversant

One's choice of words can have a direct bearing on the interpersonal communication. The vocabulary one uses in interpersonal relationships should be appropriate for the occasion. For example, a preschool teacher's aide would not use the same vocabulary in talking to a three-year-old, as she would in talking to the preschool teacher.

How Each Sees the Other

The process of communicating from person-to-person is greatly influenced by the perception that the sender and receiver have of each other. The feelings that a person has toward the other person are reflected in his tone of voice, choice of words, and even in his *body language.* A reference book mentioned in the resource section of this unit, *How to Read a Person Like a Book,* deals with the importance of body language in person-to-person relationships.

The Right Time and Place

Another factor that may be important in interpersonal relationships is the timing of the communication. For example, one of the first things a supervisor should do if he wants to talk over a problem with his subordinate, is ask the question: "Is this the right time and place?" Problems should not generally be discussed in the middle of an office, where other employees, or the public, can hear the discussion. Personal problems should be discussed only in private.

The Effect of Past Experience

In general, the quality of the person-to-person transaction will depend upon the past experience of the individuals. Human beings have acquired most of their opinions, assumptions, and value judgments through their relationships with other people. Past experience not only helps to teach people about effective interpersonal relationships, it is also often responsible for the irrational prejadices that a person displays. A strong bias usually blocks the interpersonal relationship if the subject of the communication concerns that particular bias.

The Effect of Personal Differences

An additional factor in interpersonal communications involves the intelligence and other personal differences of the people communicating. An example of such a personal difference is the *objectivity* of the people involved, as compared with their *subjectivity*. One person may try to be very fair and objective in discussing a point with another person, yet this other person is, at the same time, taking everything personally and being very subjective in his viewpoint. It is almost as if an adult was talking to an angry child.

Such differences can impede the communications flow between two people. In fact, all the factors mentioned in communications should be examined as to whether they block or facilitate interpersonal relationships. *The most effective interpersonal relationships are those that are adult-like in their character.*

4. DEFENSE MECHANISMS IN INTERPERSONAL RELATIONS

Defense mechanisms are attempts to defend the individual from anxiety. They are essentially a reaction to frustration - a self-deception.

Causes for Defense Mechanisms

In order to help understand some of the causes for defense mechanisms, remember the basic human needs:

- *Biological or physiological needs* - hunger, water, rest, etc.
- *Psychological or social needs* - status, security, affection, justice etc.

Fear of failure in any of these basic needs appears to be related to the development of defense mechanisms; attitudes toward failure, in turn, originate out of the fabric of childhood experience. The social and cultural conditions encountered during childhood determine the rewards and controls which fill one's later life. These childhood experiences, and their resultant consequences, affect personality development, the individual's value system, and his definition of acceptable goals.

Individuals who are dominated by the fear of failure may react by using one of these defense mechanisms:

- *Rationalization* - making an impulsive action seem logical.

- *Projection* - assigning one's traits to others.

- *Identification* - assuming someone else's favorite qualities are their own.

Results of Use of Defense Mechanisms

A common factor to all defense mechanisms is their quality of *self-deception.* People cling to their impulses and actions, perhaps disguising them so that they become socially acceptable. Their defense mechanisms can be found in the everyday behavior of most normal people and, of course, have *direct influences* on interpersonal relationships.

A person, for example, who is responsible for a particular job makes a mistake, and the work doesn't get done. When confronted with the problem by his supervisor, the individual puts the blame on someone or something else. This is a very common form of a defense mechanism.

Defense mechanisms can sometimes have *negative influences* on interpersonal communications. They can contribute to the individual forming erroneous opinions about the other person's motives. These mechanisms can alter the perceptions and evaluations made about the individual by other people, Ways to understand these mechanisms must be sought; one solution is to become more aware of the common defense mechanisms, and to become less defensive through greater acceptance of others.

5. THE INFLUENCES OF ROLE-PLAYING IN INTERPERSONAL RELATIONS

Everyone wears a mask and plays a certain role or roles in life. Even if the role one plays is to be himself, that particular form of behavior can still be considered a role. As a public-service employee, one's role is to serve the public. This can be done in a number of ways. Some of the factors involved in public-service roles will be mentioned below:

Exploring Superior-Subordinate Relations

Public-service employees are accountable for their actions. From the entry-level public administrative analysis trainee, to the President of the United States, every public servant must be accountable to either an immediate supervisor, a governing body, or to the public itself. Entry-level public-service employees gain experience and get promoted, but they continue to be subordinates and responsible for their actions, even though they also become supervisors and have people working for them.

Simulation exercises can be developed which will examine the perceptions of the superior by the subordinate. *Authority* and *power* factors may enter in here, as the superior also perceives the subordinate in a particular way. *Dominance* and *need* factors are at work in superior-subordinate relationships, and the style of leadership used *(autocratic, democratic,* or *lassiez-faire)* is a form of leadership role.

Peer relationships can be explored through simulation exercises. The ways in which co-workers perceive each other and the resultant effect on cooperation is one area to be examined. Ways to establish a climate or environment for effective, cooperative relations should be sought.

It is desirable also to simulate, for better comprehension, interpersonal communications with the general public. Role-playing techniques, which permit the exploration of person-to-person relationships, are highlighted in the following section on simulation exercises.

Interpersonal Relations Achieved Through Simulation

The preparation of students for entry-level public-service occupations must include an opportunity to experience meaningful interpersonal relations. Public-service employees, whether office or field workers, experience personal relationships with other people every day. The initial success of the public-service worker will depend in large measure upon his ability to interact effectively with others in the office or field. Accordingly, a principle objective of simulation exercises for entry-level public-service education is to have the student acquire the necessary interpersonal relations skills that make for success in all public-service occupations.

When developing a model public-service simulation with the principal objective being to improve favorable interpersonal relations, certain criteria must be established. These criteria may be stated as follows:

- *Interpersonal relations must be the principal component of the simulation*. Provision must be made for students to interact with others in an office interpersonal setting so that they may work and communicate effectively with one another.

- *The simulation must be as realistic as possible*. Realism can best be accomplished by simulating an actual public-service operation in as many areas as possible.

- *Originality must play an important part*. Model simulations, currently in use, must not be copied in an effort to maintain simplicity.

- *The simulation must be interesting*. Students must be motivated to participate in the simulation and to be enthusiastic about its operation.

- *The simulation must be unstructured*. Provision must be made to allow for an awareness of events as they take place. Students must learn to cope with a situation without prior knowledge that the situation will occur.

In order for the teacher to determine if the model public-service simulation developed has, in fact, improved interpersonal relations, the simulation must be evaluated in terms of meeting the established objectives.

6. MEASURING INTERPERSONAL RELATIONS

Survey of Interpersonal Values

A valid and reliable instrument for measuring interpersonal relations, such as the *Survey of Interpersonal Values,* may be used for this purpose. This instrument is intended for grades 9-12, and is designed to measure the relative importance of the major factored interpersonal value dimensions. These values include both the subject's relations with others and others with himself. The value dimensions considered are:

- *Support*--being treated with understanding, encouragement, kindness, and consideration.

- *Conformity*--doing what is socially correct, accepted, and proper.

- *Recognition*--being admired, looked up to, considered important, and attracting favorable notice.
- *Independence*--being able to do what one wants to do, making one's own decisions, doing things in one's own way.
- *Benevolence*--doing things for other people, sharing, and helping.
- *Leadership*--being in charge of others, having authority or power.

A pretest on interpersonal values is administered before the model public-service simulation actually begins, and the same test is administerd as a post-test after a stipulated period of time. By comparison of results, and through the use of applicable statistics, the gain in behavior modification in interpersonal relations can be determined, as a result of using the model public-service simulation.

Analysis of Interpersonal Behavior

Public-service employees should be aware of their own needs, and of the needs of other people. They should be able to recognize situations or behavior calling for professional help, and be able to refer people to such appropriate help. New employees must be able to use their knowledge of person-to-person relationships to effectively work with people.

In order to become more effective in interpersonal relationships, students must gain an understanding of:

- *Self-evaluation* - to be able to assess their own strengths and weaknesses.
- *Group Evaluation* - as a class to be able to evaluate other individuals' competencies in interpersonal communications.
- *Correction of own self-perception* - to be able to do something about the knowledge and attitudes formed by adjusting their individual behavior.

STUDENT LEARNING ACTIVITIES

- Define formal and informal social behavior.
- List the important factors in interpersonal communication.
- View and discuss the film strip, *Your Educational Goals, No. 2: Human Relationships.*
- Role play in alternate supervisor-subordinate relationships practicing effective interpersonal communication.
- Write an essay on "Defense mechanisms affect interpersonal relationships."
- View the film, *The Unanswered Question,* and discuss human relationships afterwards.
- Listen to a discussion of structured interpersonal communications and evaluate the effectiveness of the person-to-person relationship.

- In small groups, discuss the ways in which people are mutually dependent on each other,
- Use simulation exercises to practice interpersonal relations.
- List the different kinds of roles and games played in interpersonal communications.
- Debate the statement: *Understanding person-to-person relations is one of the most important skills a person can acquire for success in life.*
- Discuss how understanding interpersonal relationships can help a person to effectively work with people.
- Define the role of recognizing one's own feelings in relation to others.

TEACHER MANAGEMENT ACTIVITIES

- Have the students define formal and informal social behavior.
- Show transparencies on interpersonal relations, *(Social Sensitivity lour Relationship with Others)* and discuss concepts afterwards.
- Assign written exercises on the important factors in interpersonal communication.
- Set up role-playing exercises on subordinate-supervisor roles in effective interpersonal communication.
- Encourage small-group discussions of the ways people are mutually dependent on each other.
- Show a movie on human relationships *(The Unanswered Question)* and discuss key points afterwards.
- Separate the class into teams to debate such statements as: Understanding interpersonal relations is one of the most important skills a person can acquire for success in life.
- Encourage individual study and reading in interpersonal relationships.
- Assign an essay on the worth and dignity of man in interpersonal relations.
- Bring in public-service workers who deal with others to talk to the class about the value of effective interpersonal communications.

Evaluation Questions

Fill in the crossword puzzle below.

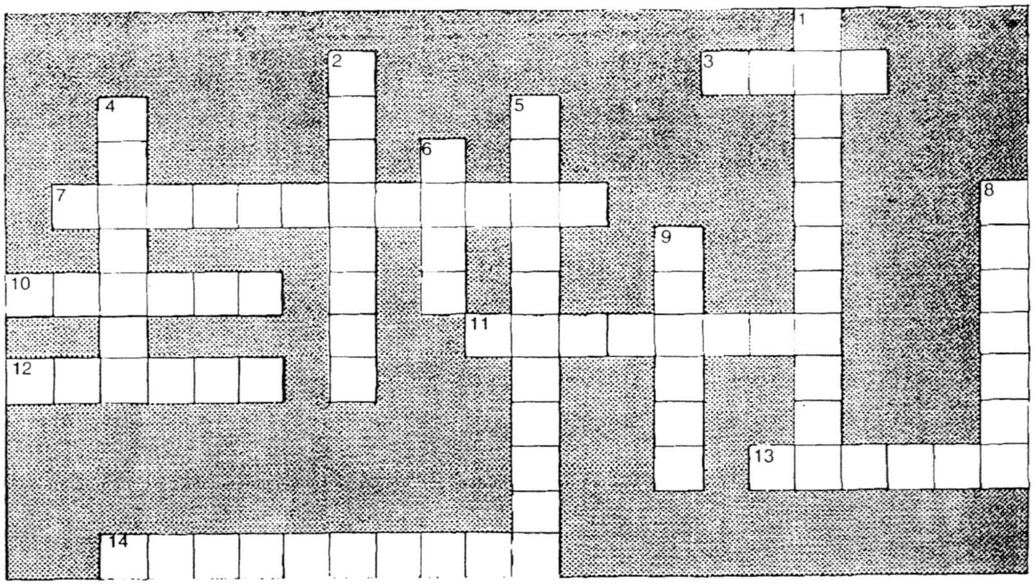

ACROSS:

3. A strong prejudice or ______ can block good relationships.
7. Being abie to do what one wants to do satisfies the need tor ______.
10. One's _______ of words should be correct for the occasion.
11. Friends usually have an ______ relationship.
12. In talking over problems with others, is important.
13. Everyone needs to feel ______.
14. ______ is assigning one's traits to others.

DOWN:

1. We ______ when we try to make our actions seem logical.
2. When we assume someone's qualities as our own we ______ with that person.
4. Individuals ______ when they do what is socially proper.
5. When we attract favorable attention, we gain ______
6. Some people have a strong ______ of failure.
8. ______ mechanics help to protect a person from anxiety.
9. A public service worker usually has a ______ relationship with the public.

Answer Key

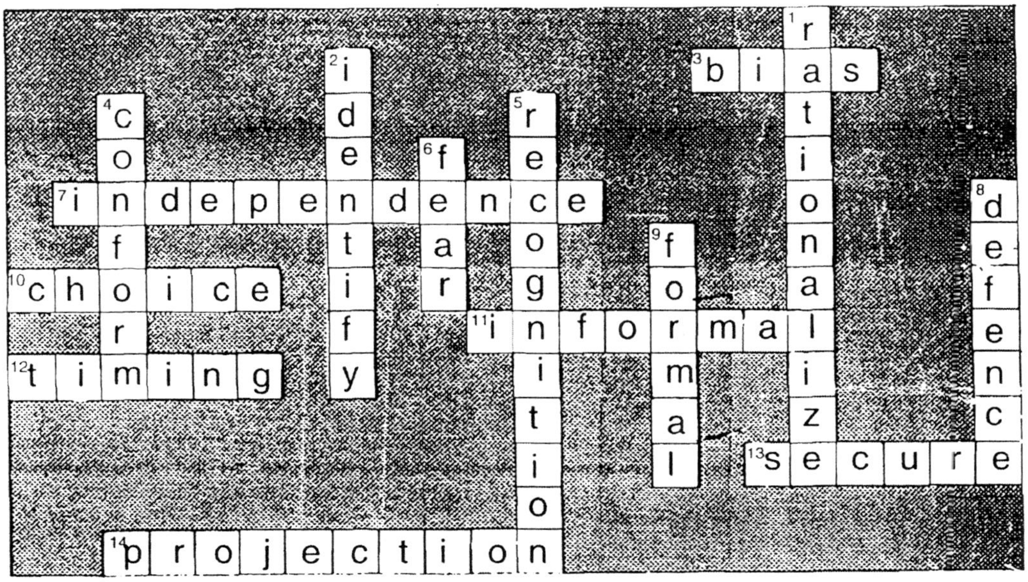
1 rationalize
2 identify
3 bias
4 conformity
5 recognition
6 fear
7 independence
8 defence
9 formal
10 choice
11 informal
12 timing
13 secure
14 projection

TECHNIQUES OF DECISION MAKING

CONTENTS

TECHNIQUES OF DECISION MAKING

INSTRUCTIONAL OBJECTIVES

1. Ability to define decision making.
2. Ability to learn the decision-making formula.
3. Ability to learn how to state problems simply and accurately.
4. Ability to determine the difference between a symptom and a cause.
5. Ability to determine which facts are most important to a decision.
6. Ability to be able to qualify information according to importance and subject classification.
7. Ability to learn to identify two or more alternative solutions for a problem.
8. Ability to develop an openness to creative ideas.
9. Ability to learn to weigh the consequences of alternative decisions.
10. Ability to select and justify the most appropriate decision.

CONTENT

<u>INTRODUCTION</u>

Every person, each day, is faced by numerous situations which require the making of many decisions throughout the course of the day. It is necessary to answer such questions as: *When do I get up in the morning? What clothes will I wear? What will I have for breakfast? Which route will I take to school?*

Working in the field of public service, an individual is constantly faced with a series of situations which require him to take some particular course of action. Many such actions may not require special decision making on his part, because his particular organization has provided ways for him to make these decisions rather automatically. For example, there are department policies, and standard ways of performing certain jobs. A person also has his own past experiences of success which enable him to easily make certain decisions for such things as: the hours he should work, his rate of pay, and the required forms which must be completed for certain kinds of activities. All of these things are handled rather automatically on the job, because people have methods of handling certain things in certain ways. These become habit. They fit within a regular pattern.

There are many situations faced by a decision maker where the consequences of his action are so minor that it doesn't really matter which way he decides to solve a given problem as long as it is resolved: for example, what pencil to choose; the color of the paper on a final report; the diverting of automobiles during a traffic jam.

However, there are also other situations where the way a manager or supervisor solves a problem has great impact on an organization. Sometimes a person doesn't have a chance to actually know what is right and what is wrong. Judgment might have no well established basis. The opportunity to select between two alternatives of equal value does not exist. The situation is not clearcut. It requires thought and careful judgment; it has far-reaching consequences on the organization-affecting the quality of service, costs, schedules, the relationships between people in a working unit. Appropriate action must be taken in such assorted areas as overtime, employee dismissal, grievances, types of equipment to purchase, ways to reduce waste. The effectiveness and efficiency of the decision-making process of one individual can have far-reaching impact on a public-service organization.

Good decisions allow individuals to control and monitor their operations. Bad ones can cause worse problems and hinder the effectiveness of an organization. Things just don't happen by chance. They are made to happen. They are arranged. They can quite often be developed over a period of time which has been required by the nature of the problem or activity.

1. <u>WHAT IS DECISION MAKING?</u>

Decision making involves a conscious choice or selection of one behavior alternative from a group of two or more behavior alternatives.

Thus, there are two basic elements in a decision-making process: one, the matter of conscious choice, and the other of alternatives. *To decide, then, really means to cut off, to come to a conclusion, to end.*

2. <u>*A FORMULA FOR DECISION MAKING*</u>

Decision-making is a skill that can be developed. One way in which it can be developed is through a formula, a procedure which provides a formal process or system involving the basic rules of decision-making. There are no born decision makers, but some people appear to act very efficiently on the basis of hunches. These people may never be seen with charts and graphs, or performing a lot of analytical tasks. However, they've probably developed their own way of sifting facts and of solving problems. Good decision makers usually know their personnel; have prior experience; they can put together difficult possibilities quickly. They have their own personal *formulas* of decision making.

An effective technique to help make decisions is through the aid of a formula –a kind of check-off list to help find answers to difficult situations, to resolve problems, to handle unique situations. Such a formula enables one to take advantage of his past experiences, to see the whole picture, and to utilize all the facts he can find which are applicable to the solution.

A decision-making formula worthy of our consideration has six steps:

- *Isolate* - State the apparent problem or situation with which you plan to deal.
- *Analyze* - Gather the facts.
- *Diagnose* - Organize and interpret the facts.
- *Prescribe procedures* - State the real problem or situation.
- *Implement procedures* - Develop alternative solutions.
- *Evaluate* - Select the most appropriate alternative. Decide.

We will consider each of these steps separately. However, it should be kept in mind that these separate steps are really all related and part of the whole process of decision making.

A. *Isolate the Problem*. A problem can be a situation, question, matter, or person that is perplexing or difficult, that obstructs the way to achieving a goal or objective.

Almost everyone has problems: students have study problems when they don't know answers to test questions; people have money problems when they can't pay all of their bills. Individuals have problems with people who are unfriendly; problems with their girlfriends or boyfriends; growth problems; health problems; psychological problems.

There are professionals and specialists to whom people can go with their problems. A person takes his malfunctioning car to a mechanic, he calls on the plumber to fix leaky pipes, contacts the doctor when he doesn't feel well. These specialists are skilled problem solvers in a particular area. They have had special training and experience. They may even have had to pass examinations to obtain certificates or licenses.

In decision making, one must recognize problems as well as symptoms of problems. It is particularly important to be able to separate symptoms from causes.

What is the Real Problem? Problems are often presented in very broad terms: "Gee, John, they've really fouled up in accounting. Go straighten them out." "Boy, do we have a morale problem." "We have to introduce that new system right away." "Those two managers just don't get along."

Consider the question of morale, for example. Is morale really the problem, or is it more accurately the symptom of another problem? Chances are that it is a symptom of a problem rather than the real problem itself. The problem situation might be poor organizational structure, bad working conditions, an unfriendly supervisor, unfair treatment, or a number of other difficulties.

To help in determining what is a symptom and what is a cause, several questions must be asked:

- *"How else might the problem be stated?"* The placement of accountants in one isolated department, without the opportunity to discuss actual income and outgo with supervisors, has given us unrealistic budget figures.

  The lack of adding machines, a broken calculator, dim light, uncomfortable room temperatures, and individual working spaces has caused a greater number of absences.

  The accounting manager has openly criticized senior staff members in front of their fellow workers.

  The department secretaries were all forced to work overtime for staying five minutes past their lunch hours.

- *"What else is involved?"*

  If there are no communications between accountants and supervisors, neither group will know the reasons behind the requests or needs of the others.

  There has been talk about a computer eliminating some of the accounting jobs.

  The senior accountants have been slow to pick up the new accounting procedures.

  This is the tenth time this month that the financial unit has been unable to take care of the people in line because the secretaries were not here.

- *"Are there similar problems in other departments?"*

  The people in supplies have been ordering the wrong equipment.

  There have been layoffs in several departments.

  Several department managers are competing for the job of assistant director of our organization.

  None of the other departments have problems with secretaries.

- *"Is this a problem or a symptom?"*

  The real problem is that the accountants have not been properly informed of the organizational structure, and thus have very poor understanding of the departments which comprise the organization.

  Another organization nearby has announced opportunities for accountants at higher pay, and in new offices.

  The accounting manager and his senior staff do not plan departmental modifications together.

  Only one of the secretaries has a watch and it is five minutes slow. They play bridge at lunch time several days each month.

- *"How do others perceive the problem?"*

  Talk to all the accountants and managers individually.

  Talk to personnel about accounting re-classification.

  Interview the senior staff.

Visit with the secretaries.

<u>*What are the Problems? What are the Symptoms?*</u> If your automobile won't start, it might not be because it's old, the engine is dirty, or your windshield wipers don't work the car may be out of gas. It might, however, be time to give it some other attention, too. If you can recognize the symptoms, you can avoid a lot of problems.

B. <u>Analyze the Facts.</u> When the problem is recognized, then all the facts required for a successful decision can, and should be accumulated. Too often, people think they have all the facts, but they don't. It's like trying to put together a jigsaw puzzle, and recognizing, after many frustrating hours, that six pieces are missing.

Frequently, the decision maker feels that because he is in a particular situation, he knows it better than anyone else can know it. The issue may, therefore, be somewhat clouded. This cloudiness may prevent him from seeing what is actually there.

How many times have individuals had to make a decision and found that they didn't have the right facts or sufficient quantities of facts to insure a good decision? Both the quality and effectiveness of most decisions can be seriously reduced without good facts.

When gathering facts, one should write them down, and gather them into one comprehensive list. The decision maker can then visualize them all at the same time, and is much less likely to overlook or forget any of them. In dealing with large amounts of information, he can grade sub-topics and keep track of them in a systematic way.

How many facts should be gathered? The number usually depends on the nature and complexity of the situation.

Basically it means that the amount of information accumulated depends upon such factors as:

- The amount of time available.
- Is it an emergency situation or not?
- The seriousness of the situation.
- The availability of information, etc.

Where are the Needed Facts Obtained?

- First, he might turn to available records. He usually has financial records, personal records, records of transactions, and records of activities.
- Second, he may have references: newspapers, journals, old letters, the like.
- Third, and very importantly, he has other people, or he has a staff. There is a great deal of expertise within most public-service organizations: specialists in economics, human relations, law, health, safety, and other areas; all responsive to the request of the decision-maker. An outside expert, or consultant, may be required in difficult situations.
- Finally, look at other organizational units which have been confronted with similar problems. Quite often, through investigation, the decision-maker finds that precedents have been set which he may have to follow. In law, for example, he may have to base a decis.ion on the verdict of a case held on the same issue, long ago in a distant place.

Sources of information are unlimited. It takes a great deal of initiative to uncover them.

How should the facts be obtained? Here again, there are questions we must ask ourselves:

- What kinds of facts are available?
- What information is available?
- Is there enough?

- Is help needed, and where can it be obtained?

- Who else might have the information needed?

Going back to the morale problem, which was found to be the result of a basic lack of communication between accountants and departmental managers, how might the decision-maker proceed?

In gathering the facts, he would have to obtain both the accountant's records and the manager's records. The decision-maker might call upon organizations of similar size and activity, to see how they handle difficulties of this nature. He might talk to one or more senior accountants in a large public accounting firm or contact the governmental auditors. He might even write letters to colleagues seeking their advice.

The decision-maker might hold a meeting of selected members of his staff, or assign a task force of accountants and managers to look into the matter.

As he begins to gather his facts, the decision-maker will discover that other information is required. Additionally, he will uncover sources of other facts. The quality of the facts he gathers ultimately affects the quality of his decisions. The better the data, the better the opportunity to make a good decision.

C. Organizing the Facts. Once the facts have been collected, it becomes very important that they be organized to help the decision-maker interpret what they really mean. To do this, it's helpful to set them up in categories -- to pull like items together.

This procedure helps people to know whether certain facts are more important than others, and thus deserve special consideration.

Grouping the Facts. There are several categories into which information can be grouped, such as: cost, time, past precedent, procedures, leadership, quality, and productivity:

Cost. In cost considerations, one must look at unit costs, personnel costs, material costs, equipment costs, mailing costs, etc. If, for example, an individual is attempting to determine the cost of mailing out new contracts to several hundred vendors with whom the agency deals, the following costs may have to be considered, among others:

- *Duplication costs per duplicated copy.*

- *Salary costs of writing new contract.*

- *Salary costs of typing contracts.*

- *Costs of new contract forms.*

- *Costs of envelopes.*

- *Costs of writing departmental letters.*

Time. Time is usually calculated in terms of the personnel costs or salaries paid. The basic periods of time hours, days, weeks, months, years are quite often combined in terms of man-hours, man-weeks, man-years, etc., to enable the numbers of hour units to be multiplied by salary allocations. Equipment time, particularly in this age of computers, can be quite expensive.

Past Precedent. This is a category relating together data on similar situations in the past, and to consider the decisions arrived at in those situations for their bearing on the decision to be made in the present.

Procedures. These are also important. Most public-service organizations have certain ways of accomplishing functions or providing services. They have been proven over a period of time to be most appropriate to particular situations. Here, too, is where organizational policy making may be involved and possibly changed and modified.

Leadership. This would include the directions and decisions which brought about a particular situation, and permit review of the factors which were present when prior decisions were made.

Quality. The quality of facts is important. There must be an assurance that the right data, and the most applicable figures and information, are available.

Productivity. This category would enable a comparison between various activities which would bring about particular results. It would provide an opportunity to look at the output of a department or project team.

In pulling together like items, one can see trends, certain facts which may be more important than others, and areas where there are gaps in the information.

In organizing facts, the following questions should be asked:

- Which facts are related to each other?

- Are these facts related to any not listed?

- What is the extent of their relationship?

- Are they relevant to this situation?

- What is the level of reliability of the facts?

- Can the problem be more clearly defined with the information listed?

- How can it be done?
- How much time is there for further organization?
- Are these facts recurring or one time events?

D. <u>Stating the Real Problem</u>. Having examined the data, the decision-maker is now in a position to state the *real* problem or situation with which he has to deal. He now knows whether he has a problem, or just a misunderstanding. Was the original statement just a symptom, or was it a real situation? It might be that there are several problems. Whatever the situation, it must be stated in clear and simple terms. It should be written down.

A problem is a situation which deviates from an expected standard, or norm of desired performance. In decision making, one starts with an *apparent* problem. The decision maker gathers more information in order to more accurately identify the situation with which he is going to deal.

<u>Is there a real problem? or just symptoms?</u> The data have been gathered and organized. Now it is necessary to zero in on the actual situation, and to see whether there is a real problem. Was the initial identification a symptom of a problem, or was it a real cause? Is there one problem, or several?

If the decision-maker neglected to gather the facts, and then to organize, analyze, and categorize them, he might find himself working on the wrong situation. He could spend a great deal of time and effort on symptoms, and could actually be working on the wrong problem. Certainly, he could overlook a number of relevant factors.

If a medical doctor spent all of his time studying symptoms, he might be too late to address an actual problem and his patient could die. Similarly, in a public-service organization, *if too much time and energy is spent in chasing symptoms instead of causes, problems can become crises.*

<u>What objective is to be achieved?</u> Remember, one must still think about decision making in terms of fulfilling objectives.

When it is known what kind of performance should be achieved, and what kind of performance has been received, the necessary effort is simple merely to measure the difference between those two points. The decision-maker must identify the deviation and its extent. He will also have to specifically state the standard, or *norm,* toward which he is trying to return.

In other words, not only does he have to state the problem to which he is going to address himself, but he must specifically state the objective he wants to achieve.

In the previous illustration of the public-service organization and the communication problems between the accountants and managers, the objectives could, perhaps, be restated in this manner: *it is necessary to design a realistic and accurate budget for costs.*

This stage would complete the problem identification part of the decision-making process. Now, he can get on with decision-making itself.

E. <u>*Developing Alternative Solutions*</u>. With the *real* problem determined and stated, the decision-maker is now in a position to begin the development of alternative solutions. Notice that there is an "s" on the end of "solution." Decision-makers should be interested in as many solutions to a problem as can be developed.

This particular phase of the decision making process should be very free-wheeling. It should produce a number of ideas. The decision-maker should keep his mind open. He should not be too judgmental, but should avoid premature criticism. *Criticism given too early can destroy new ideas that could be beneficial.*

Picture a staff meeting, where the assistant director of the agency presents an entirely new approach to providing recreational opportunities for senior citizens. He is interrupted by his superior, the director, who tells him that his idea is ridiculous. It is unlikely that he would ever bring up the subject again unless he were extremely persistent and unafraid of the director. *Creative thinking can be squelched by a superior who criticizes without having much of a basis for criticism.*

The number of alternatives that can be developed at any one point in time is a function of how much time is spent in developing these alternatives. It's always helpful to stop and ask: "If I didn't have any rules to follow in this organization, would I handle the situation any differently?" Or, "What else could I do?" Perhaps it is desirable to modify several previously stated alternatives to produce one better alternative.

<u>*Present all alternatives for consideration.*</u> By considering all ideas as initially feasible, they can be brought out into the open. Such occasions are often called brain storming sessions. Regardless of how silly an idea might seem at first, perhaps when it is considered in the light of other possibilities it may turn out to be a fairly useable solution; or maybe a portion of that idea might be able to be combined with another idea and thereby produce the ultimate solution.

What, for example, would have happened if someone stifled the idea of the paper clip? "Isn't that stupid, who'd want to hold pieces of paper together with bent up wire?" Evidently, people laughed at Columbus, and his idea of a round world; they laughed at John Fulton and his steamship; and even at a young man named Fosbury, who high-jumped backwards. Regardless of ridicule, however, each of these men, in his solution to the problem at hand, succeeded in his particular project.

How many people have been shot-down in creative projects, by comments such as these: "We've tried it and it didn't work," "That's against policy," "It would cost too much," "He hasn't got the experience," "He"'s too young."

<u>List the Alternatives.</u> Looking at the positive side of the argument, there should be positive consideration of all methods, objects, and persons available, to satisfy the needs of decision-making. Once again, write down all of the alternatives, so that they can be comprehensively considered.

To do this, one can list all of the alternatives across the top of a chart and then systematically consider all the factors under each alternative. This chart, or *matrix,* as it is called, can then be used to evaluate the best solution.

As an example, let us assume legislation is passed in each state to award home and business loans and educational benefits to veterans of the Vietnam war. Then a matrix somewhat like this can be made:

	ALTERNATIVES				
	#1	#2	#3	#4	#5
Staff involved					
Labor costs					
Material costs					
Equipment costs					
Services included					
Services excluded					
facilities needed					
Number of veterans processed per day					
Publicity requirements					
Applicable policy					
New policies needed,					
etc.					

The list can be long, but it is well worth it. If, for example, one is considering attending a community college or university, but can't make up his mind. He can develop a chart with all of the things that are important to him on the side of the chart, and the schools under consideration acros the top. Then a five-point scale can *be* applied to each item, with five being the highest mark and zero the lowest. The school with the most points might be the most likely alternative under all the prevailing circumstances. Still, one cannot be completely definite on this basis alone, so it is necessary to move to the next step in the decision-making process, that of selection.

F. <u>Selecting the Best Alternative Solution.</u> The most important part of the decision-making process is the selection of the most appropriate alternative: *deciding.* This is the stage during which criticism is appropriate. Judgment must be made on all facets of the problem and the alternative solutions. The effectiveness of each of the solutions must be evaluated in terms of the objectives towards which the decision-maker is oriented. He must look carefully at, and criticize severely, such items as cost, timeliness, workability, acceptability, and implementation.

- Can the solution be made to work?
- Will the staff cooperate?
- Will those who are served make the necessary adjustments?
- Are there the skills in the organization to carry out the program?

List the Consequences of the Decision. As these and other items are considered, it is desirable to write down all of the consequences of each of the decisions. List the pro's and con's. It is not enough to add them together and make a decision on that basis, such as in the selection of a college, in the previous section. Not only does one use some type of scale, but he assigns different weights to different items. Using the previous college selection chart, the decision-maker might have to weight costs higher than the availability of co-educational dormitories, or the scholastic reputation of the school over the strength of its football team.

Be a Devil's Advocate. The more desirable alternatives should be scrutinized in a negative way. Take the opposite position, that is, play the *devil's advocate.* Mentally implement the plan and consider the adverse consequences.

Take one of the most favorable-looking alternatives. Ask:

- "Will it affect other departments?"
- "What could go wrong?"
- "What are the potential sources of breakdown?"
- "What new problem might it create?"
- "Where would the resistance be?"

Consider the extent to which these consequences will probably come about and the degree of seriousness of each one. Select second and even third choices in order to plan for contingencies.

Scrutinize the Final Alternative Thoroughly . Once the alternatives have been narrowed to only one, which appears to fill the need, then this one alternative should be subjected to one final round of positive questions:

- Will this decision fulfill the original goal?
- Can the agency live with the decision permanently?
- Is the timing of the decision right?
- Does the decision bring about the greatest benefit for the greatest number?

Involve Your Superiors. It is often necessary and desirable to go to the superiors with the decision. Ordinarily, the problem would be presented, with the attendant factors affecting it, and the alternative solutions which could resolve it. Then the decision-maker would indicate his reasons, with their consequences, for selection of the particular alternative.

G. Implement the Decision. After a decision is made, it must be implemented. The necessary steps must be initiated to carry it out. The whole management cycle of planning, organizing, and controlling must be brought into action, as well as other available management tools.

3. SUMMATION

No phase of the management cycle or any other organizational function could be carried out if decisions were not made. Planning, organizing, controlling, as well as motivating, communicating, and setting standards; these all require endless strings of decisions or choices. This is why the final process of decision making is so important.

Good decisions are the result of understanding responsibilities, involving others, knowing the organization, understanding one's own strengths and weaknesses, and being accountable for decisions made.

In understanding the responsibilities involved, one must know where to get information and be cognizant of the extent to which people can take action.

Through involving others, they gain a sense of ownership in the decision, and become more committed. They remove their defense mechanisms.

Knowing an organization requires an awareness of its organizational history and objectives, where the power centers lie, the limits of one's authority, and the way in which work is actually accomplished.

One's understanding of himself and his own shortcomings insures that he will seek out expertise he does not possess himself, and will develop ways to improve his own skills.

The individual should have this motto: *Remember, when you get right down to it, one person may have to decide – YOU!*

STUDENT LEARNING ACTIVITIES

- Prepare a definition of *decision making,*
- Write a brief paper on the decision-making formula.
- Participate in a class discussion about decision making in a selected public-service agency. Try to identify top, middle, and low-level decisions.
- Prepare a definition of the term *problem.*
- Interview a public-service official to identify a problem within his organization. Follow with a class discussion.
- Prepare a brief paper describing three examples of symptoms and their causes.
- Participate in a problem-solving case study.
- Write a brief paper on why facts must be gathered to aid in the decision-making process.
- Identify the kinds of facts and resources you must use to prepare for making decisions about a teacher-assigned topic.
- Participate in a discussion about fact finding.
- Develop with the class, and have at least 20 students complete, a survey questionnaire with open-ended questions on ways in which your school can be improved. Organize responses according to subject and year ranking of importance.
- Participate in a class discussion on the results of the questionnaire survey.
- After the class has decided on one or more ways in which the school can be improved, prepare a report on one of the objectives including:

  statement of an objective,

  facts needed and how obtained,

  categorizing the facts.
- Deliver an oral version of your report. Respond to questions and comments from the class,
- Choose five articles from the newspaper on five different topics: sports, politics, crime, etc. State the actual problem being addressed.

- Participate in a class discussion about problem identification, and problem statements. Sharpen your problem statements if necessary.

- Participate in a class discussion about problems identified and possible alternative solutions.

- Using the example of the State legislature passing a bill awarding home and business loans and educational benefits to veterans of the Gulf War, develop a set of alternative plans as to how the legislation may be carried out.

TEACHER MANAGEMENT ACTIVITIES

- Have students define *decision making.*

- Assign students a paper on the decision-making formula.

- Conduct a class discussion about decision-making in a selected public service agency.

- Have students prepare their own definitions of the term *problem.*

- Assign students interviews with public-service officials to identify selected organizational problems.

- Conduct a class discussion on problems in public-service organizations.

- Have students develop and discuss reports and three examples of symptoms and their causes.

- Select and assign a case study to the class in problem solving.

- Assign a paper on why facts must be gathered to aid in the decision-making process.

- Prepare a list of considerations in several public-service agencies. Have each student select one consideration around which he will gather essential facts to make a decision.

- Conduct a discussion on fact finding.

- Assign the class a survey project, entitled "How Can Our School be Improved?" Have students develop their own questionnaire and administer it to at least 20 students. Ask them to organize their results according to subject and rank of importance.

- Organize a class discussion on the results of the surveys.

- Once one or more items of possible school improvement have been agreed upon, assign the students a report to contain the following:

statement of an objective,

facts needed and how obtained,

categorizing of facts.

- Organize oral presentations of student reports.

- Assign students the reading of five articles from a newspaper on five different topics: sports, polttfcs, crime, etc. Have them state the actual problem being discussed.

- Conduct a class discussion on problem identification and problem statements.

- Assign a brief paper on the symptoms of five problems and the causes in a public service agency selected by each student.

- Conduct a class discussion on the problems and solutions identified.

- Using the example of the new bill for veterans of the Gulf War, have students develop a set of alternatives.

- Insure that the students are open to new and abstract suggestions.

- Direct oral presentations of students in which they review their original problems, the sources and categories of facts, the alternatives available for solution, their respective consequences, and their ultimate decisions. Have students challenge one another's decisions.

Evaluation Questions
Techniques of Decision Making

Read the problem carefully, and answer each of the following questions.

You are a library assistant. Mrs. Smith, the librarian, has two high school aides, Susan and Mary. Mrs.Smith has told you that she may fire Susan if her attitude does not improve. She complained about Susan's laziness and stated that Susan's work was never finished. Mrs. Smith asked you to talk to Susan about improving her attitude. When you tried to talk to Susan about this, she got upset and went home.

After observing the aides' workload for a few days, you notice that Susan has much more work than Mary.

1. What is the problem? ______________________________

2. Name one solution. ______________________________

3. What are the consequences of this solution? ______________________________

4. List another solution. ______________________________

5. What are the consequences of this solution? ______________________________

6. Which do you think is the best solution? ______________________________

Read the problem carefully, and answer each of the following questions.

You are in charge of the recreation program at the community center. Your job is to keep activities running smoothly. On the daily schedule, one-half hour has been set aside for basketball. While you have stepped out for a moment, ten of the Green Hornets and ten of the Purple Dragons arrived to play basketball. As each group has two teams set up, neither group would give in. Unfortunately, a fight began. The fight ended just as you returned. Each group plans to play tomorrow. You must make a decision.

1. What is the problem? ______________________________

2. Name one solution. ______________________________

3. What are the consequences of this solution? ______________________________

4. List another solution. ______________________________

5. What are the consequences of this solution? ______________________________

6. Which do you think is the best solution? ______________________________

Answer Key

Answers will vary on this test. The instructor may wish to have a discussion after the test, with students justifying their selections. Students may be evaluated on the soundness of their judgement.

BASIC FUNDAMENTALS OF INTERVIEWING

TABLE OF CONTENTS

BASIC FUNDAMENTALS OF INTERVIEWING

INSTRUCTIONAL OBJECTIVES

1. Ability of the public-service employee to work toward becoming a good interviewer or interviewee on his job and in his life
2. Ability to conduct referral or other interviews to obtain and verify information
3. Ability to observe interviewees skillfully
4. Ability to evaluate the effectiveness of an interview
5. Ability to cope with problems that come up during an interview
6. Ability to check an applicant's references

CONTENT

INTRODUCTION

This unit is designed to develop the student's ability to interview people, and to obtain and verify information. It will also give trainees practice in special-purpose interviews, such as making referrals, classifying prohibited behavior, protective intervention, employment, financial eligibility, etc.

Public-service workers will be required to give different kinds of interviews on various occasions. They may be required to interview other professional personnel in their major occupational group and to grant interviews to official personnel. They will certainly be interviewed at some time for such things as jobs, raises, credit ratings, and opening bank accounts. Certain public-service workers will also be required to interview clients, patients, pupils, families, etc.

For the majority of the students, the role of an interviewer will be a new one. In the past, some of them have been the unwilling, nervous, perhaps hostile recipients of interviews by welfare workers, police, and employers. Practice interviews, relative to their future jobs, can serve as a base for proficiency in interviewing skills.

Students should acquire necessary theory and skills to become aware of the various kinds of interviews and the people who conduct them. Various types of interviews include: employment, counseling, newspaper reporting and police interrogation. Interviews are performed by a wide variety of people: psychologists, social-service workers, lawyers, salesmen, policemen, tax inspectors, immigration officers, journalists, and many more.

1. BEFORE THE INTERVIEW STARTS

Reasons for Interviews: The kind of interview depends basically on its reason – some give advice, some seek information, some give information. Here are some of the major reasons for conducting an interview:

- To obtain information
- To evaluate a person's background
- To evaluate the interviewee's character and/or personality
- To provide information
- To maintain good public or employee relations

Completing Applications or Forms: Another major reason for conducting an interview is to help the public or coworkers in filling out applications or forms. In this kind of interview one needs to assist the interviewee in clarifying needed information or in filling in the form correctly. Since needed information can easily be omitted, the forms must be checked for completeness.

If a form is to be used for a later interview, the interviewer may want to prepare questions from the information furnished. Areas to look for in this case include:

- Identifying factors needing elaboration
- Identifying factors that will bring out more information
- Identifying factors that are not clear

In reviewing applications or forms, there are certain critical areas to watch for, such as an interviewee's work experience. The applicant's work experience should contain sufficient details in these areas:

- Amounts of time
- Types of work experience
- Financial levels of compensation

These three factors are usually given great weight in evaluating the applicant. Other important areas to watch include the applicant's financial ability, and his prior credit references. Age should be taken into account when checking credit references. A young man or woman, for example, should not be expected to have established an extensive credit rating.

2. CONDUCTING INTERVIEWS

An interview is essentially an interaction between people through words and acts. During this process, knowledge is acquired by both interviewer and interviewee.

It is important to note that the information sought should be purposeful and related to the reason for the interview. A license interviewer should not be primarily concerned with attempting to classify whether the interviewee's behavior requires intervention from the law enforcement agencies. Common sense should dictate that the kinds of questions asked should be determined by the "role" of the agency, and the immediate concerns of the person being interviewed.

Starting the Interview: One of the first tasks in the beginning of an interview is the establishment of rapport, or mutual liking or respect. After a friendly atmosphere has been created by putting the applicant at ease, the interviewer can ask the first question. If the interview has to do with a specific application, the interviewer should pick non-controversial matter from the form to discuss first. Use of these techniques is designed to get the applicant talking. An atmosphere should be created that will encourage the interviewee to discuss freely what is on his mind.

Importance of Understanding People: The interviewer should have a good knowledge of human behavior and interpersonal relationships. He should realize that people often behave in an inconsistent way. They may give themselves away in an interview by saying one thing orally, and by expressing the opposite meaning in body movements.

The interviewer should be able to observe applicants skillfully. The responsibility of utilizing all the senses to obtain and mentally verify information received during the interview occurs daily on the job. The successful social-service worker, for example, must master these techniques quickly in order to improve his effectiveness.

<u>Guiding the Body of the Interview:</u> Ask questions to get information. There are basically two kinds of questions: *directive and nondirective.*

The *directive question,* as its name implies, guides or directs the interviewee in a specific area. Directive questions can usually be answered with a few words, such as "yes" or "no." A typical directive question might be, "How long have you worked at the XYZ Company?"

Nondirective questions, on the other hand, give the interviewee a chance to say what is on his mind. Words such as *what, how,* and *why are* often used in nondirective questioning. A typical nondirective question might be, "Why did you leave the XYZ Company, Mr. Rean?"

A good technique to use to encourage the applicant to talk is to begin with a nondirective question. If the applicant does not respond appropriately to a nondirective question, then use a more directive question. An example of this technique could be:

Interviewer: *What did you dislike most about your last job?*
Interviewee: *Oh, not much.*
Interviewer: *Did you feel as though your supervisor treated you fairly?*
Interviewee: *My supervisor! That guy was definitely not fair—let me tell you...*

In the above simplified example one can see how the interviewer began with a general question about the job, and when he felt that the applicant didn't respond appropriately, he used a more specific directive question, which in this case triggered a response from the applicant. By alternating between directive and nondirective questions, an interviewer can skillfully guide the discussion and obtain the necessary information from the interviewee.

<u>Related Factors:</u> Factors that will affect the relationship in the interview can either help or hinder the process. These will strengthen the relationship: interest, demonstrated concern, attentiveness, willingness to listen, and questioning for fuller understanding of issues at hand. On the other hand, there are some factors which obstruct relationships, such as indifference, judgmental attitudes, insensitivity, being aloof, inactivity, or being late for appointments.

<u>Purpose of Interview:</u> If the purpose of the interview is to help the interviewee, the interviewer should be *supportive,* and exhibit a positive and active understanding of feelings which are given expression by his behavior. However, if the interview is designed to be an interrogation of a prisoner, the method of its conduct is determined by many factors: suspect, crime, time element, and location (field, home, or headquarters).

Techniques and methods of police interrogation have had to change in recent years, and the police must now be more aware of protecting each citizen's private rights. Each suspect should be advised of his rights before his statement will be considered admissible for evidence. Citizens must not be arbitrarily subjected to interrogation; the officer must have more than just a hunch, and must be able to substantiate his reason for an interrogation. However, if an officer has good reason to be suspicious, whatever the reasons may be, he has a duty to make the inquiry or interrogation.

As can be seen, the purpose of the interview can have a drastic effect on guiding the body of the interview.

<u>Closing the Interview:</u> In terminating the interview, the interviewee should be told when he can expect a decision or obtain the necessary information he needs. If possible, the interviewer should answer any final questions the applicant may have.

If the applicant has to be rejected, the interviewer should accomplish this diplomatically. Courtesy and tact are especially important at this point in the interview, if a good image of the interviewer's agency is to be projected to the public.

<u>Remembering Key Points:</u> An effective technique for the interviewer to use during the interview is to take notes. This will help him to remember the main points of the conversation. On some occasions, however, taking notes during the course of an interview can be distracting to the applicant, or can sometimes inhibit the interviewee's responsiveness. In such cases, the interviewer should write his notes immediately after the interview. The applicant will not then be distracted, and the interviewer can remember the key points of the discussion while they are still fresh in his mind.

<u>Problems in Interviewing:</u> A major difficulty in interviewing involves dealing with *ambivalence* (feelings of simultaneous attraction and repulsion) and sometimes, open conflict. The interviewer should become aware of these types of applicant behavior:

- The pers*on asks for advice, but doesn't use it*
- The person agrees to a plan, but doesn't carry it out
- *The perso*n says one thing, and does another

Does this ambivalence exist in only the interviewee, or does it also exist in the interviewer? In fact, the degree to which the interviewer understands himself and is aware of his own feelings has a direct effect on the conduct of the interview. Problem areas to explore include:

- *The feelings of the Interviewer* - Do they interfere in an interview? What forms of expression do they take? Is control of one's own feelings important? Why?
- *Over-involvement by the Interviewer* - Is this helpful or harmful? What kinds of behavior might result from a non-professional approach to interviewing?

Prejudice: If the interviewer is rigid and inflexible in his thinking, this could have a harmful impact on the interview. The goal of the interviewer should be to become aware of his personal biases, and honestly try to control them, so that the interview can be conducted in a fair and honest way.

Confidentiality: A public office is, in many ways, a public trust. As an interviewer, one should become familiar with the extent to which confidential information is shared by other people in his agency. The procedures for sharing confidential information should be known, and a clear definition should be given at each agency as to what constitutes confidential information. Whenever information of a confidential nature must be shared with others, it should be on a need-to-know basis, and its confidentiality should be carefully explained to the person receiving the information.

Dependence, Interdependence and Independence:

- How are the qualities of dependence, interdependence and independence manifested in the interview? To some extent, these characteristics exist in all people.
- Are these qualities good or bad, or does it depend upon the circumstances?

For example, a positive aspect of dependence is the ability to trust and form deep personal relationships. A negative aspect of being overly dependent is the resultant lack of self-reliance and initiative. People who are independent are usually self-confident; however, too much independence could be a problem in the interviewing process. Interdependence among individuals can be seen in marriages, working relationships, and in interviewing. Examples of group interdependences include:

- Between agencies
- Between agencies and the community, and
- Between local, state and federal governmental agencies

Undue Hurry When Questioning Applicants:

- Don't anticipate what the interviewee is going to say. It's easy to jump to conclusions; much harder to hold one's judgment.
- Another habit to avoid is putting words in the applicant's mouth.
- Don't let the applicant lead you astray in the interview.
- Get the interviewee back on the track by acknowledging his remark, and asking a directive question back on the main point of the discussion.

Controlling the Interview: The extent to which the interviewer feels a need to control the interview will, of course, be determined by the purpose of the interview. Much less control would be exerted on an interviewee in a social-service agency than in a law enforcement agency while interrogating a suspect.

Shy applicants should be encouraged to open up by asking them non-directive or open-ended questions. An overly talkative applicant can be controlled by asking more directive questions, and by watching for digressions during the discussion.

Common Weaknesses of Interviewers: Here are some of the more common faults of interviewers:

- *Talking too much* - especially in those interviews that are designed to get information from the interviewee.
- *Guiding applicant too much* - particularly in those interviews that are designed to allow the interviewee to express whatever is troubling him.
- *Dominating the interview* - it should be a process of give and take.
- *Talking down to the applicant*- this condescending attitude can usually be spotted pretty easily.
- *Failing to listen* - a common fault, however, inexcusable for an interviewer.

3. AFTER THE INTERVIEW

<u>Evaluating the Interview</u>

- What information was learned about the applicant?
- Was it sufficient?

- What was not learned that should have been?
- If problems came up in the interview, who made the decisions?
- What was the role of the interviewer and interviewee?

Some of the factors involved in decision-making are:

- Facts involved - how are they maintained?
- Availability of acceptable alternatives
- Readiness to take action

There are definite dangers to be aware of when making decisions or evaluating an interviewee. One such danger is irrational prejudice. Each of us is biased to a certain extent, either for or against certain ethnic, racial, or religious groups. The better the interviewer understands himself, and In particular the more he is aware of his personal beliefs towards certain individuals and groups, the better off he will be for having recognized them. He can then compensate for any prejudicial bias.

This bias could work in the opposite manner. For example, an interviewer could be so blinded by an applicant's good traits, that he would not see his faults because of this *halo effect.*

<u>Checking References:</u> A part of the process of many interviews involves the actual checking of personal references for these purposes:

- To verify information obtained from the application and interview
- To obtain an evaluation by people who know the interviewee's work history
- To obtain additional information not disclosed on the application or during the interview

Additional verifying information may be obtained from letters of reference supplied by the applicant. There are some disadvantages to letters of reference. They may be vague or even dishonest. Sometimes, such letters may not contain the information sought. Quite often, information supplied directly by the applicant's past employers is the best source to use. When evaluating replies, consider these factors:

- They may not be complete
- They may be vague to cover negative factors
- They may contain information taken from records which may not tell the complete story

<u>Obtaining Information from References:</u> Letter writing is a standard way of obtaining information about an individual. However, since a letter may take too much time, or cost too much, it is recommended that the telephone should be used whenever possible. One reason for the telephone's effectiveness is that a direct contact with the reference is possible. This makes for better communication, since specific questions and follow-up answers can be obtained. In addition, doubts and omissions can be picked up from the person's voice.

Before making a telephone call to a reference, a checklist of questions should first be prepared. In talking to the reference, the following guidelines should be utilized:

- Establish rapport
- Be businesslike
- Let reference talk freely
- Don't put words in respondent's mouth
- Probe for strengths and weaknesses

A personal visit is sometimes advantageous, and can often be more effective in bringing out more information about the applicant. In such cases, arrange to meet the reference and use the same principles as in the telephone checks.

Finally, information may be obtained concerning references by the hiring of outside investigators. This method has the advantages of getting more personal and more objective information. There are, however, certain disadvantages: the outside investigator may not obtain the best available information, and there may be considerable expense involved.

STUDENT LEARNING ACTIVITIES

- Participate in role-playing exercises after being given a brief introduction to the basic techniques of interviewing.
- Role-play in a wide variety of interviews, such as employment, welfare eligibility, and license application, and gain experience as both an interviewer and interviewee.
- Observe interviews during role-playing exercises, evaluating what the interviewee is communicating.
- Listen to examples of interviews on tape, and be prepared to discuss the techniques used to overcome problems that developed during the interview.
- Interview public-service workers in your community about their jobs to learn more about careers, and practice newly acquired interviewing skills.
- Write a short essay on how to conduct an interview. Include the start, guidance, conclusion, and evaluation of the results.
- Talk to public-service employees who do a great deal of interviewing in their jobs. Be prepared to discuss questions with them.
- Talk to your school guidance counselor or psychologist about interviewing skills.

TEACHER MANAGEMENT ACTIVITIES

- Plan on utilizing role-playing exercises to practice knowledge learned.
- Have students play both the interviewer and interviewee in various types of interviews, such as eligibility, employment, license interviews, etc.
- Prepare tapes of different types of interviews, and play them for the class to discuss and evaluate.
- Encourage students to use all their senses as interviewers to carefully observe what is being communicated by the interviewee.
- Encourage individual practice of interviewing skills whenever possible, such as with local public-service employees.
- Assign short essays on the process of interviewing: starting, guiding, concluding, and evaluating.
- Obtain specialized interviewing materials, such as public-safety techniques from neighboring police departments.

- Arrange to have public service workers come into the class to talk about interviewing techniques.
- Provide opportunities for the school guidance counselor or psychologist to discuss interviewing skills.
- Approach the theory of interviewing through practice situations whenever possible.
- Borrow interviewing films from the local library or educational resource center.

Evaluation Questions
Interviewing Skills

1. The purpose of an interview could be: 1.____

   A. To obtain information
   B. To give information
   C. To evaluate a person's background
   D. All of the above

2. The first job of the interview is to: 2.____

   A. Get to the subject quickly
   B. Put the applicant at ease
   C. Tell the applicant about the boss
   D. Tell the applicant about the job that is open

3. A skillful interview will: 3.____

   A. Watch the applicant's body language
   B. Listen to the applicant
   C. Ask questions to get information
   D. All of the above

4. Questions that are specific and can be answered "yes" or "no" are: 4.____

   A. Directive
   B. Non-directive
   C. Indirective
   D. None of the above

5. If the applicant cannot be hired, the interview should: 5.____

   A. Avoid telling the applicant
   B. Tell the applicant as bluntly as possible
   C. Tell the applicant tactfully
   D. Give the applicant another chance

6. Taking notes during an interview can: 6.____

   A. Help the interviewer remember the main points
   B. Be distracting to the interviewee
   C. Make the interviewee reluctant to talk
   D. All of the above

7. An interviewer with personal likes and dislikes should: 7.____

   A. Try to control them in order to be flexible
   B. Try to find people with the same likes and dislikes
   C. Try to get rid of all personal likes and dislikes
   D. None of the above

8. The telephone is an effective way of finding information because 8.____

A. Doubts can be picked up from a person's voice
B. The person called can talk freely
C. It doesn't take much time
D. All of the above

9. Interviewers should: 9.___

A. Reach conclusions about the applicant as soon as possible
B. Keep applicants on track by asking directive questions
C. Let applicants talk on any subject comfortable to them
D. Help with words when the applicant is unable to think

10. Shy applicants may talk more if the interviewer: 10.___

A. Looks bored
B. Asks open-ended questions
C. Asks directive questions
D. Does most of the talking

11. Interviewers should: 11.___

A. Talk down to the applicant
B. Make sure they dominate the interview
C. Listen as well as talk
D. Guide the applicant's words

12. After interviews, interviewers should ask themselves: 12.___

A. What was learned about the applicant?
B. What was not learned?
C. What problems came up and if they were solved?
D. All of the above

13. Which one is not a reason for asking for personal references? 13.___

A. To find out information about the applicant's family
B. To find what people who know the applicant think of their work
C. To find out if the information on the application is true
D. To get more information

14. Letters of reference may be: 14.___

A. Incomplete
B. Vague
C. Dishonest
D. All of the above

15. Information told in confidence should: 15.___

A. Not be kept from all office personnel
B. Not be told to anyone
C. Be told to those who need-to-know
D. None of the above

KEY (CORRECT ANSWERS)

1. D
2. B
3. D
4. A
5. C
6. D
7. A
8. D
9. B
10. B
11. C
12. D
13. A
14. D
15. C

Planning, Conducting, and Recording an Interview

"Talk is cheap because supply exceeds demand."

The above statement may be true in many situations, but when it comes to an investigator trying to get answers out of a witness, the opposite will probably happen. One of the most important skills investigators can develop is the ability to get people to open up and talk to them. In this chapter, you will learn about the "art" of interviewing. Yes, it is an art because those who do it well are more successful than those who shrug interviewing off as just "asking questions and writing down answers."

An interview is more than just going to someone's house, knocking on the door, and then asking questions. It takes planning. If you come across in a threatening manner or can't adequately explain why you need to interview a witness, you'll never get any voluntary cooperation. If you ask complex questions or don't allow witnesses to tell their story in their own words, you're not going to get what it is you are after. And finally, if you cannot adequately convey to others what you found out during the interview, it may as well not have taken place. The "art" of interviewing consists of three phases— planning, conducting, and recording— all of which are discussed in this chapter.

- State the purpose of a financial interview.
- List the objectives of a financial interview.

- Describe the elements that must be considered when planning an interview.
- Describe techniques used when conducting an interview.
- Identify and describe methods used to record an interview.

"Just the facts." Remember Sergeant Joe Friday's famous phrase from the television show Dragnet? For years, every week like clockwork, Joe had the uncanny ability to detect, investigate, and resolve criminal matters in 30 minutes or less.

Television makes it look easy. Unfortunately it isn't. Detecting and investigating a financial crime can take weeks, months, and even years. So, while reality significantly differs from what happens on television, one thing remains the same— financial investigators, just like Joe Friday, search for facts by interviewing people.

Few skills are as important to the financial investigator as the ability to talk to people and successfully gather information from them. Yet, law enforcement officers are not empowered to force people to talk to them. These powers are granted only to courts, grand juries, and certain judicial and legislative bodies. Consequently, investigators face the double duty of convincing the interviewee (hereafter called the **witness**) to agree to be interviewed and then getting the witness to talk after getting inside the door.

What is an Interview?

An Interview
- *Face-to-face*
- *Task related purpose*

Phone interviews. Employment interviews. Counseling interviews. Investigatory interviews. As you can see, there are many types of interviews. And though they all serve different purposes, they are founded on the same definition: an **interview** is a specialized form of oral, face-to-face communication between people that is entered into for a specific task-related purpose associated with a particular subject matter.[1]

For the financial investigator, two aspects of this definition should be noted. The first one is that an interview is a face-to-face communication. Not only will investigators listen to what witnesses say, they will be able to see what the witnesses do. The visual and non-verbal aspects of an interview are very important and should not be overlooked. Secondly, the interview has a specific task-related purpose. This task-related purpose is what makes an interview different from mere conversation. A conversation can take off in many directions; an interview must be focused on relevant content.

Introduction to the Financial Interview

Before we get into a general discussion of the interview process, we should look at some specifics of the financial interview. The purpose of a financial interview, its objectives, and the type of question to be asked during a financial interview are discussed below.

Purpose and Objectives

For the financial investigator, the interview is a tool used to determine what knowledge a witness has concerning an investigation. Knowledge in this context includes information about the allegation or crime in question, and any relevant records in a witness's possession. The information and documents provided to the investigator form the basis of the **witness's testimony.**

A financial interview is different from a financial interrogation. Financial interviews are conducted to obtain information and documentation from witnesses. Financial interrogations are conducted with suspects and hostile witnesses to elicit confessions or admissions of culpability. An investigator may plan on conducting an interview and have it turn into an interrogation. Conversely, interrogation can commence only to discover that the witness appears to be innocent, and with that, an interrogation turns into an interview.

The financial interview is not something that investigators undertake haphazardly. Prior to each interview, they must decide what they hope to accomplish by interviewing a particular witness. In other words, they must determine the interview's objective(s).

The objectives of a financial interview are:[2]

- To obtain information that establishes or refutes the allegation or crime under investigation
- To obtain leads for further development of the case
- To obtain all information and documents in the witness's possession relative to the financial investigation
- To obtain the cooperation of the witness for any subsequent legal proceeding
- To obtain background and personal information about the witness and motivation for involvement in the crime

Type of Question Asked

A financial interview is a special type of investigatory interview. During most investigations, people are interviewed to obtain their recollections of events. For example:

"Can you describe the person who came into the bank?"

"Do you remember if anyone was with him?"

"What color was the car she purchased?"

Ask questions *related to specifics, not just general recollections*

Financial interviews go beyond recollection questions. Like the financial investigation itself, they are concerned with specific details of financial transactions and the movement of money. For example:

"Why did you have this check cashed?"

"You notarized two signatures on this document. One is the suspect's. Who is the other individual?"

"How did she pay for the car?"

The Three Phases of an Interview

For any investigator, an interview is more than just asking a witness some questions. Who should be interviewed? What questions should be asked? In what order should the questions be asked? Where should the interview take place? How can the witness be put at ease so that he or she cooperates? What happens to the information collected? These are just some of the questions an investigator must ask before, during, and after the interview.

A good interview requires a lot of forethought, skillful execution, and an ability to convey what happened during the interview to others. The interview process is comprised of the following three phases:

- Planning
- Conducting
- Recording

Planning an Interview

Prior to planning any interview, the investigator is usually faced with one or more of the following conditions:[3]

- A crime has been alleged or committed, but the facts relating to the situation have not yet been established
- A complainant or victim has been identified. This could be an individual, business, or governmental entity
- Records or documents reflecting financial transactions relating to the suspected criminal activity have surfaced
- Rumors, innuendo, or factual information pointing to a specific suspect have emerged

The investigator uses the interview to develop information about these existing conditions. The information collected will be used to support or dispel the allegations.

Selecting Witnesses

When an investigation begins, investigators must determine who they want to interview and in what order. Traditional criminal cases are generally investigated by first contacting the outer circle of honest, disinterested witnesses and then working inward to the co-conspirators and ultimately to the target. Law enforcement normally starts the interview process with the complaining witness and after exhausting his or her knowledge of the facts and reasons for suspicion, proceeds in a similar manner around the outer circle of witnesses.[4]

In a financial investigation this traditional sequence is often altered. Following the movement of money dictates talking to witnesses that have knowledge of financial transactions. Accordingly, the hierarchy of interviews is determined by the degree of knowledge or participation in financial activities created by the alleged criminal event or crime at issue. For example, in a political corruption investigation, documents showing the movement of money from the payer of the bribe to the taker of the bribe would be of paramount importance to the investigator. People with documents (bankers, money couriers, business associates) would be priority contacts. In an embezzlement or tax evasion investigation, the key interviews would be with custodians of accounting records and internal audit files, and tax return preparers. Even in a drug case, financial transactions decide the order of contacts for the investigator. The priority witnesses will have records reflecting the suspect's use of proceeds from the drug trade. While each investigation offers a different set of interview options and priorities, the bottom line in a financial investigation is that every person who has documents pertaining to financial transactions, or knowledge about them, should be interviewed.

Types of Witnesses

One of the things an investigator must consider prior to contacting an individual for an interview is what type of witness will that person be. Will he or she be cooperative, hostile, or have no feelings one way or the other? Prospective witnesses can be categorized into three general types:[5]

Types of Witnesses

Neutral	This is an uninterested third party such as a custodian of public or financial records. This person has no interest in the outcome of the investigation and provides documents and/or unbiased information.
Friendly	A friendly witness is one who cooperates. Witnesses are friendly for a variety of reasons. Certain people naturally tell anybody everything. Others realize that they stand to benefit from providing information about the suspect to authorities. Also, many people seem to enjoy "playing detective" and get caught up in the excitement of being a part of an important investigation.
Reluctant or hostile	This is an uncooperative party who is typically a friend or associate of the suspect. This witness may also be hostile due to his or her own culpability in the criminal activity under investigation.

Neutral and friendly witnesses usually agree to interviews upon request. No more than proper identification and introduction by the investigator opens the door. Interviewing hostile witnesses often presents greater challenges. Most likely, these witnesses will not voluntarily submit to an interview. They refuse to provide information and documents.

Since law enforcement cannot, on its own, compel any witness to say or do anything, investigators need assistance from the legal system. With approval from a government attorney (i.e. city or district attorney, or U.S. Attorney) the investigator can be issued a document (i.e., summons, subpoena) which commands a witness to appear and submit to an interview. The investigator serves this document on the witness and, if the witness disregards the document, contempt charges and incarceration possibly could result. But even an investigative tool that can command appearance before the investigator does not override a witness's constitutional guarantees. So, while a hostile witness can be ordered to open the door and submit to an interview, he or she cannot be compelled to say anything incriminating.

Contacting the Suspect

In Chapter 4, we stated that the suspect was a valuable source of information. It follows then that deciding when to interview the suspect is an important decision. Should he or she be contacted at the start of the investigation or confronted upon its completion? Should the investigator contact the suspect at all? The decision is determined by the investigator and is different for each investigation. Interviewing the suspect during the early stages of the investigation makes good sense if it is feared that records in his or her possession may be destroyed or an alibi may be concocted. Often, catching the suspect off guard results in a more responsive interview filled with more answers and more documents. Also, early interviews have resulted in quick confessions and/or early indications of innocence.

On the other hand, delaying contact with the suspect may be advantageous if information and documents gathered from other witnesses can be used to refute the suspect's alibis and lies. Additionally, confessions sometimes occur when the suspect is confronted face to face with the evidence of guilt.

In certain situations, the suspect may not be interviewed at all. He or she may be beyond the reach of law enforcement (i.e. out of the country) or may be represented by an attorney who refuses to allow his or her client to be interviewed on constitutional grounds.

Method of Questioning

While planning an interview, the investigator must determine the method of questioning to use. Questioning can be organized in a number of ways:

- **Chronological method.** The witness is questioned about the events in the order that they occurred from beginning to end. This is the usual organization of questioning.

- **Questioning according to documents.** In this type of interview format a particular document (financial statement, canceled check, tax return) is the focus. The witness may be the legal custodian of the record and have no other involvement in the investigation.

- **Questioning according to transactions or events.** The witness may have sold the subject a house or delivered a package for him or her. The questions in this situation would center on the event and radiate from there.

During the planning phase, the investigator should prepare a written outline that lists main topics to be covered in the interview. An outline allows the investigator to concentrate on important ideas and areas to be covered. However, writing down every specific question to be asked and in a specified order should be avoided as this has the tendency to make the investigator inflexible and tied to the next question. The investigator unwittingly becomes guided by what is written on the sheet of paper instead of what is being said by the witness. Also, the witness may catch a glimpse of the upcoming questions and prepare responses in advance. The following page contains a simplified example of an interview outline. The outline used for an actual interview would be more extensive.

Sample Interview Outline

Ray Austin Interview

Introduction:	Identify Self State Purpose
Background:	DOB SSN Address Married Wife (Maiden Name) Children Source of income Parents Education Military Prior Arrest, Convictions

Assets	Liabilities	Cash-on-Hand

Associates:	Adkins HTB Inc. Allen Cleveland Massey TB Trust Massey Cemetery Rosemary Westbury Tony Idaho Toni Boise Marc Fresno

Conducting an Interview

Once an investigator is finished with the planning phase, he or she is ready to conduct the interview. The interview itself is composed of three distinct parts:

- Introduction
- Body
- Close

Introduction

The introduction is critical as it sets the tone for the whole interview. It serves the following two purposes:

- Allows the investigator to identify himself or herself to the witness
- Allows the investigator to state the purpose of the contact

The following shows right and wrong ways for an investigator to introduce himself or herself.[6]

Wrong

"Mr. Smith, my name is John Jones and this is Mary Adams. We're with the government. We're investigating Jim Dealer and we need to talk to you."

Right

"Mr. Smith, my name is John Jones. I am a Special Agent with the Internal Revenue Service's Criminal Investigation Division. This is Special Agent Mary Adams from the Drug Enforcement Administration. We are currently conducting an investigation involving alleged violations of money laundering laws by Jim Dealer. May we speak to you for a few moments?"

The objective of the introduction is to put witnesses at ease and to get them to agree to answer questions. However, once the investigator identifies himself or herself, the next question normally is asked by the witness.

Witness:	"Why are you contacting me?"
Investigator:	"We would like to ask some questions about your financial dealings with Jim Dealer and his associates."

Since the investigator's goal is to put the witness in a frame-of-mind to answer questions, he or she must supply a reason which leads the witness to perceive that he or she will benefit from cooperating with the investigator. If the witness believes that the investigator represents a threat, voluntary cooperation is generally lost. The next page shows some right and wrong ways to gain the cooperation of a hesitant witness.

During the introduction, the investigator should ask general, almost generic, questions such as name, address, telephone number, and date of birth. Since many witnesses are apprehensive, the investigator needs to be patient and avoid rushing into important questions. Through reassuring the witness that his or her cooperation will not cause any undue hardships, inconveniences, or embarrassment, a rapport can be established that will assist both the witness and the investigator during the interview process. When the introduction has been completed and the witness is ready to talk, the investigator moves on to the second part of the actual interview— the body.

Right and Wrong Ways to Gain the Cooperation of a Witness

Wrong

Witness:	"Why should I talk to you? I don't want to get involved."
Investigator:	"You should have thought of that sooner— it's too late now. We can talk here or we can talk downtown. It's your choice."

Right

Witness:	"Why should I talk to you? I don't want to get involved."
Investigator:	"You certainly are not required to talk to me. I am just seeking some information on a serious matter which may or may not result in legal action. By speaking informally with me now, it may save you the trouble of having to testify later, depending on the information you have. Is that o.k.?"

or

Witness:	"I don't want to answer any questions at this time without first talking to my lawyer."
Investigator:	"You certainly don't have to talk to me, with or without your lawyer. Let's do it this way. Let me ask you a few questions and if you don't want to answer them, just say so. I'm not trying to get you into trouble, I'm just trying to do my job and get some answers. Is that o.k.?"

The Body

The body of the interview is the fact finding part of the interview process. Questions are asked and answers are provided. The structure of the interview is determined by the method of questioning (chronological, by document, or by transaction or event) which should have been pre-determined and outlined by the investigator.

In this stage of the interview, witnesses should be allowed to tell their story in their own words. Recognizing that a witness's story will usually be disjointed and rambling, the investigator must be prepared to put order to the material— find the details, focus for clarity, and ensure the accuracy. For the investigator, conducting an interview is much more than just asking questions and writing down answers. This process requires concentration and active participation by the investigator if his or her objectives are going to be achieved.

The time-honored questioning devices of *who, what, where, when, why,* and *how* allow investigators to push witnesses for details. Investigators should continue the questions until they are convinced that a witness's knowledge of a topic is exhausted. Details, details, details! Whether recollections or records, it is the detail provided by the witness that lays the foundation for a successful financial investigation. The following exchange between an investigator and a witness illustrates how to pursue the detail in a line of questioning.

Investigator: "How was the kickback payment made?"

Witness "At a meeting."

Investigator: "Where did this meeting take place?"

Witness: "In Mr. X's office."

Investigator: "How many people were there?"

Witness: "There were three of us."

Investigator: "Who were they?"

Witness: "Mr. X, Bill Baker, and me."

Investigator: "How was the kickback divided?"

Witness: "Mr X split it into three piles."

Investigator: "How much did each of you get?"

Witness: "I don't know. Mr. X didn't count the money. He just estimated the size of each pile."

Investigator: "Did you all get the same size piles?"

Witness: "Yes. I counted it at my office. I had just a little over $100,000."

Investigator: "Would you say that Mr. X received about $100,000 also?"

Witness: "That would seem about right."

A witness's opinion of events often clouds the facts. Although there is nothing wrong with requesting an opinion from a witness, the investigator, through proper questioning, needs to separate the facts (what was said) from the opinions (what was talked about). The goal is a verbatim recollection from the witness. For example:

Wrong

"What did you and Jim Dealer talk about?"

Right

"What did Jim Dealer say to you?
What did you say to him?"

As was stated earlier, an investigator must actively participate in the interview process. It's not as simple as ask a question, write down a response. The investigator must constantly analyze responses, and continually check for inconsistencies, inaccuracies, and incompleteness. For example:

Investigator:	"How long did your meeting with Mr. Grey last?"
Witness:	"It lasted all day."
Investigator:	"What did Mr. Grey say?"
Witness:	"Not much."

An all day meeting with not much said should raise a red flag in the investigator's mind. This line of questioning needs to be pursued.

During an interview, investigators have a multitude of tasks to handle simultaneously. From listening to a response and recording it, to formulating the next question, they have a lot to do. There are some general "do's and don'ts" that investigators should consider when performing an interview. They are found on the next page.

Interview Do's and Don'ts

- *Do* interviews as a team. One investigator listens and controls the questioning while the second records the responses.

- *Do* interview witnesses individually. Attempting to interview two witnesses in the same room at the same time results in one of two things—one witness influences the other's responses or one witness becomes mute thereby allowing the second witness to answer all the questions. Always separate witnesses and conduct their interviews simultaneously.

- *Do* control the interview. Don't let, for example, an attorney who is present disrupt the interview. Before beginning the interview, advise each participant of their role in the process. This should help eliminate any control problems.

- *Do* provide the witness with an out. If a witness has previously denied knowledge, or has supplied false information, there is often reluctance to admit it. The investigator should provide this witness an "out". It normally will be taken. For example:

  "Mr. Smith, I know when we talked before you denied knowing Mr. Dealer. You probably forgot about meeting him. Can we start over?"

- *Don't* ask compound/complex or negatively phrased questions, (i.e. "you didn't see the money, did you?"). Questions should be simple, to the point, and positively phrased.

- *Don't* make threats and avoid threatening remarks. Threats rarely work, so overbearing tactics should be avoided. The "good cop/bad cop" interview technique looks good on television but is usually inappropriate in financial investigations.

As was discussed in Chapter 3, in our legal system, documents cannot speak for themselves, either figuratively or literally. A witness must identify, explain, and introduce every financial document to give it meaning in any legal proceeding or court action. So what does interviewing have to do with the introduction of documents into a legal proceeding. Plenty! Successful interviewing creates cooperative witnesses who breathe life into financial records involving the movement of money.

Technical areas such as accounting procedures or business specialties should be covered in detail during the body of an interview. The investigator should ask questions concerning the document's entries, meanings, and purposes. The investigator should also determine the identity of the document's custodian and solicit the authenticity of the document. Investigators should not be afraid to ask questions and should keep that old saying, "There is no such thing as a stupid question" in mind. Any question can lead to a surprising answer.

The investigator's job during the interview process is not complete until he or she has exhausted the witness's knowledge on the important topics relative to the ongoing investigation. Successful interviews obtain information and financial leads, as opposed to solving the case. If enough interviews are conducted and enough information is uncovered, the case will solve itself.[7]

The Close

After the witness has provided information, the investigator should review the key points gathered during the body of the interview. This process of summing up the important facts serves the following two purposes:

- It allows the investigator to clarify the facts
- It provides an opportunity for the investigator and witness to agree with the investigator's summation

Once the summation has been agreed on, the investigator should ask the following three questions:[8]

- **"Is there anything that I have forgotten to ask?"** Probably the number one reason investigators fail to get the answers they seek is that they simply fail to ask the question. Using this "catch-all" question allows the witness the opportunity to play detective.

- **"Is there anyone else you think I should speak with?"** This question is designed to find more leads. If the witness is hesitant, it's ok to say that his or her name will not be revealed to the person(s) suggested.
- **"Is there anything else that you would like to say?"** This should be the investigator's last question. It gives the witness one final chance to say anything that he or she wishes.

Exit gracefully, even after encounters with hostile witnesses. Soothe the apprehensive witness by mentioning that all the information that he or she provided will be held in confidence and/or for official purposes only. If the witness was cooperative, thank him or her for the cooperation; if nothing was said, express regrets and leave the door open for future contacts.

Recording an Interview

Investigators conduct interviews to obtain information and documents in an attempt to resolve financial crimes. It is also necessary to prepare a permanent record of each interview for future reference and use. Often in a financial investigation, persons interviewed become trial witnesses. The record of the financial interview as prepared by the investigator can be used to refresh the witness's memory and assist the witness in the identification process relative to a financial document.

The complexity and investigative importance of an interview determines the best method to record it. In situations where no information is secured, a limited report or record of interview is acceptable. However, in situations where "case critical questions" are answered, or denials are made by an important witness, a more formal record becomes necessary. The only constraint in the recordation process is the requirement for **accuracy** and **completeness** by the investigator preparing the written summary.

When an investigator plays the role of an interviewer, he or she must be accurate, fair and just. The prosecuting attorney relies on the investigator's written notes taken during an interview. The investigator's portrayal of the interview process should accurately and completely reflect the witness's testimony.

Informal Notes

The **"informal notes"** taken by investigators during the course of the interview, in conjunction with their recollections, provide the basis for the written record. Informal notes should contain sufficient detail to permit investigators to refresh their memories as to what transpired during the interview. Any method of recording the details is sufficient if it shows the date, time, place, persons present, and what occurred. The following is an example of the informal notes taken by Special Agent John Jones during an interview with Richard Smith. Special Agents Jones and Adams interviewed Smith concerning a financial transaction (the purchase of a car) he had with the suspect, Jim Dealer.

Example of Informal Notes

John Jones, IRS
Mary Adams, DEA
July 25, 1991
10am - 10:47am

Re: Jim Dealer

Talked w/Richard Smith
123 A. Street

Dealer called Smith about truck Smith advertised. Dealer came to see truck about ½ hour after call. Test drove truck around block then paid $25,000 in cash, in $100 bills, for truck.

1990 truck, serial # 1173945

Memorandum

A second way to record interviews is to "formalize" the investigator's informal notes into a **"memorandum of interview"**. A memorandum should be prepared when details of an interview are too numerous to be fully and properly related through informal notes. It should state what occurred during the interview and show the date, time, place, and persons present. If the person interviewed was advised of his or her constitutional rights during the interview, this fact should also be noted in the memorandum. The final typed memorandum should be prepared as soon as possible, and promptly signed and dated by the investigators present during the interview. The actual date of preparation should be shown at the bottom of the memorandum. If it becomes necessary to correct or supplement a memorandum after it has been finalized, the supplemental memorandum should clearly state the date and reason for such action, and the previous memorandum should be attached.

Handwritten notes made during an interview and used as the basis for a more detailed memorandum may be subject to inspection by a court and should be retained in the case file. Investigators should confine memorandums to the facts developed in the interviews and should avoid opinions, conclusions, and other extraneous matters.

When deciding whether or not to use a memorandum as a means of recording interview notes, an investigator should consider the following advantages and disadvantages:

Advantages and Disadvantages of the Memorandum

Advantages	Disadvantages
Informal	Does not contain the exact words of the interviewee
Contains all pertinent testimony obtained in the interview	Since information was not mechanically recorded, there is a chance for some information to be forgotten
Memorandums can be prepared by topic and therefore are easy to follow	
Does not require an oath or affirmation	

An example of a memorandum appears on the following page.

Example of Memorandum of Interview

In re: James Dealer
115 South Street
Miami, Florida

Present: Richard Smith, Witness
Special Agent, Mary Adams
Special Agent, John Jones

Place: Office of Richard Smith
117 Elm Street
North Miami, Florida

Date: July 25, 1991

Time: 10:00 a.m. to 10:47 a.m.

1. S/A Adams and I made a field call to a travel agency located at 117 Elm Street, the known employer of Richard Smith. Records obtained from State vehicle registration files reveal that Smith transferred the title of a truck (serial number 1173945) to Dealer in May, 1990.

2. After proper introduction and identification (by displaying our credentials and badges), I asked Mr. Smith if he would answer a few questions about the sale of his truck. Mr. Smith agreed and when asked, stated the following:

   a. He advertised his truck for sale in a newspaper at $25,000.

   b. Dealer responded to the ad and bought the truck by paying $25,000 in currency, composed of one hundred dollar bills.

   c. The sale was completed on May 29, 1990, when the currency was exchanged for the truck and registration paperwork.

3. Mr. Smith further stated that he would agree to reducing the information to a written affidavit and swear to it's accuracy.

4. I suggested that we meet again tomorrow at his home to prepare the affidavit. Mr. Smith agreed.

5. This interview concluded at 10:47 a.m. when we left Mr. Smith's office.

I (prepared/dictated) this memorandum on July 26, 1991, after refreshing my memory from notes made during and immediately after the interview with Richard Smith.

John Jones
Special Agent

I certify that this memorandum has recorded in it a summary of all pertinent matters discussed with Richard Smith on July 25, 1991.

Mary Adams
Witness

Question and Answer Statement

A question and answer statement is a complete transcript of the questions, answers, and statements made by each participant during an interview. It may be prepared from a stenographer's notes or from a mechanical recording device. The source used to prepare the transcript should be preserved and associated with the case file as it may be needed in court to establish what was said.

A question and answer statement should contain:

- When and where the testimony was obtained
- The name and address of the person giving the testimony
- The matter the testimony relates to, including the purpose of the interview
- The name and title of the investigator asking questions and the name and title of the person giving answers
- The names and titles of all persons present during the testimony and the reason for each person being present, if not obvious
- The consent of the person being interviewed to use a tape recorder if a mechanical recording is being made
- Information given to the person being interviewed concerning his or her rights to counsel and against self-incrimination, if appropriate
- Administration of an oath if given
- Questions and answers establishing that the statement was made freely and voluntarily, without duress, and that no promises or commitments were made by the investigators
- Signatures of the investigators who conducted the interview and the person being interviewed
- Signature and the certification of the person transcribing the statement, showing the source of the original information used
- Information that the person being interviewed was given the opportunity to examine the statement, correct any errors, and sign it

The following is a format that can be used for question and answer statements.

Question and Answer Statement Format

Testimony of (name, address) given at (location including address) at (time) on (date) about (subject of investigation and their address).

Present at this interview are (names and titles of all persons present).

Questions were asked by (name and title of person asking the questions) and answers given by (person being interviewed).

This interview is being recorded, as agreed upon, by means of (method of recording).

1. **Q.** You were requested to appear at (location) to answer questions concerning (subject matter). (If appropriate, advise the person being interviewed of his or her rights to counsel, etc..)

2. **Q.** Please stand and raise your right hand. Do you (person being interviewed) solemnly swear that the answers you are about to give to the questions asked will be the truth, so help you God?

3. **Q.** Did you sell a truck that you owned to Mr. Jim Dealer?

 A. (answer)

4. **Q.** How much did he pay you for the truck?

 A. (answer)

• Note: The interview is brought to a close with the following questions.

120. **Q.** Have I, or has any other investigator or officer, threatened or intimidated you in any manner?

 A. (answer)

121. **Q.** Have I, or any other investigator or officer, offered you any rewards, promises or immunity, in return for this statement?

 A. (answer)

122. **Q.** Have you given this statement freely and voluntarily?

 A. (answer)

123. **Q.** Is there anything further you care to add for the record?

 A. (answer)

After this statement has been transcribed, you will be given an opportunity to read it, correct any errors, and sign it.

• Note: When transcribing the statement include the following:

I have carefully read the foregoing statement consisting of page 1 to (last page number), inclusive, which is a correct transcript of my answers to questions asked me on (date of statement) at (location where statement was given), relative to (subject of investigation and their address). I hereby certify that the foregoing answers are true and correct, that I have made the corrections shown, have placed my initials opposite each correction, and that I have initialed each page of the statement.

(signature of person giving statement)

Subscribed and sworn to before me at (time), on (date) at (present location).

(signature and title of investigator)

(signature and title of witnessing investigator)

I (name of person transcribing statement), do hereby certify that I took the foregoing statement of (person giving statement) from (method of recording) and personally transcribed it and have initialed each page.

(signature and title of transcriber)

Normally people will review and sign a question and answer statement after it has been put in its final form. Sometimes, for various reasons, the person may change his or her position and refuse to sign the statement. When an investigator is faced with such a refusal, he or she should request that the statement be read and verified for correctness. In such situations, the following can be inserted at the end of the statement:

> *This statement was read by (name) on (date) who stated that it was true and correct, but refused to be placed under oath or to sign it.*

Just as there are advantages and disadvantages to using a memorandum as a recording device, so there are for the use of a question and answer statement.

Advantages and Disadvantages of the Question and Answer Statement

Advantages	**Disadvantages**
Reflects both <u>questions</u> and <u>answers</u>	Usually contains unnecessary material
Questions are generally asked in a logical sequence	Is often very long and involved
Is difficult to dispute with claims of misunderstanding	It is unedited; therefore, it picks up incorrect grammar, etc
Is preferred when the issues are complicated	Tape recorder will pick up outside noises which can disrupt recording
	Unable to make voice distinction
Is useful when the person testifying under oath is illiterate or below average intelligence	Mechanical failure (if tape recorder used)
Can be used to challenge or discredit a witness	Can be viewed as intimidating by deponent; therefore, witnesses are often not willing to participate

Affidavit

An **affidavit** is a written declaration of facts made voluntarily and confirmed by oath or affirmation. The text of an affidavit may be prepared extemporaneously or composed by agreement between the **affiant**, the person making the statement, and the investigator. An affidavit can be either typed or handwritten, and prepared either by the affiant or investigator. There are certain advantages to allowing the affiant to compose and write an affidavit. These advantages are :

- The affidavit will be in the affiant's own words
- The affidavit will be more credible because it is in the affiant's own handwriting. It would be difficult for the affiant to later deny the affidavit was his or hers

One advantage to having the investigator prepare the affidavit is that the investigator will ensure that only relevant information will be covered and that the information will appear in an orderly fashion. In cases where the affiant is unable to either read or write, a witness other than the affiant or the investigator must read the affidavit to the affiant before he or she signs it. The affidavit must also be signed by both the investigator and witness.

No particular form of affidavit is required by common law. It is customary that affidavits have a caption or title, the judicial district in which given, the signature of the affiant, and the jurat. A **jurat** is the certification on an affidavit declaring when, where, and before whom it was sworn.

The affidavit is one of the most commonly used forms of recording testimony. It can be used during trial to impeach a witness, refresh memory, or it can be introduced as evidence. An affidavit should not contain hearsay or information about which the witness has no direct knowledge. If the person being interviewed was advised of his or her constitutional rights, this should be included in the affidavit.

A sample affidavit is found on the next page.

Sample Affidavit

United States of America Southern)
Judicial, District of Florida)

I, Richard L. Smith, state that:
I reside at 123 A Street, Miami, Florida
I am currently employed as a travel agent at Miami Travel, located at 117 Elm Street, Miami, Florida. On May 28, 1990, I placed a newspaper advertisement in the Miami Herald classified ads offering my 1989 truck for sale. I listed the asking price as $25,000. On May 29, I received a phone call from a man who said that he read the ad and would like to see my truck. He stated that he would like to look at it that afternoon. I gave him my address and he came over about 30 minutes later. I gave him the keys and we took a ride around the block. He said that he would buy the truck for $25,000. He opened the trunk of the car he was driving and pulled out a briefcase. We went into my house where he took $25,000 in one hundred dollar bills from the briefcase to pay for the truck. I was surprised at being paid in currency, but the man stated that he wanted the truck today and knew that it would take time for a check to clear the bank, so he brought cash. I gave him the ownership papers for the truck. I said thanks for buying the truck and gave him my business card requesting that he give me a call if he needed any travel planning. He gave me his business card and said he was in the import-export business. Jim went to his car and made a telephone call and a couple of minutes later two guys arrived and one drove Jim's car while Jim drove the truck away. I have not seen or heard from Jim since that day. On today's date, I gave Special Agent John Jones a copy of the truck registration, serial number 1173945, that I sold to Jim Dealer on May 29, 1990, and the business card I received from Jim Dealer on that same date. I have received a receipt for both of these items from Special Agent Jones.

I have read the foregoing statement consisting of 1 page(s), and have signed it. I fully understand this statement and it is true, accurate, and complete to the best of my knowledge and belief.

I made this statement freely and voluntarily without any threats or rewards, or promises of reward having been made to me in return for it.

Richard L. Smith
(Signature of affiant)
Subscribed and sworn to me before this 29th
day of July, 1991,
at Miami, Florida

John Jones
(Signature)

Special Agent
(Title)

Mary Adams
(Signature of witness, if any)

The affidavit, like the memorandum and the question and answer statement, has advantages and disadvantages to its use. Prior to using an affidavit, the items listed below should be considered.

Advantages and Disadvantages of an Affidavit

Advantages	Disadvantages
Preserves probable testimony	Does not reflect questions asked
Frequently used in requiring testimony from: Hostile witnesses Witnesses who have changed allegiance	May contain non-related information if prepared by affiant May not contain all pertinent information when prepared by affiant
May be used as grounds to impeach witness	May not be well written or clear if prepared by affiant
Usually is easier to write than other types	
Valuable in developing an investigation	
May be written or typed and prepared on the spot	
May be concise and brief	

Sworn Statement

A sworn statement is, in a general sense, a declaration of matters of fact. It may be prepared in any form and should be signed and dated by the person preparing it. A sworn statement has the same judicial bearing as an affidavit. The investigator taking the statement administers an oath prior to the witness signing the statement. The following is an example of an oath that can be administered:

Do you (name of person giving statement) solemnly swear that everything contained in this statement is true and correct.

Mechanical Recordings

A mechanical recording device may be used to record statements when a stenographer is not readily available— if all parties to the conversation consent. A recording device also may be used in conjunction with a stenographer, when necessary, again provided that all parties consent. When mechanical recording devices are used, the following guidelines are suggested:

- Identify, on tape, the individuals engaged in the conversation, any other persons present, and the time, date, and location
- Immediately after the original has been made, make a copy of the tape for use in transcribing the conversation. If the recording was made during an undercover operation, seal and store the original after a transcribed copy has been made
- Keep a written record of the tape's custodians and storage arrangements from the time it was recorded to the time it is submitted as evidence
- When tape recordings are going to be used in taking a confession, advise the suspect of his or her rights and have the suspect state at the start of the tape recording that he or she is aware that a recording is being made
- Off the record discussions between the investigator and the suspect should not be permitted during a recorded interview and should be kept to a minimum during a recorded interview with anyone else

Form Letter

A form letter can be used to request information of a similar nature from several third parties. An example of a form letter is found on the next page.

Prosecuting Attorney's Office
Glynn County
300 South Main Street, 4th Floor
Brunswick, GA 31523
Telephone: (912) 555-5982

June 4, 1992

Ms. Michelle Tallmadge
1111 B Street
Glynco, GA 31520

Dear Ms. Tallmadge,

This office is conducting an investigation concerning Rosemary Westbury for the years 1989, 1990, and 1991. Ms. Westbury is a corporate officer of Massey TB, Inc. She is also the trustee for Massey TB Trust. We have reviewed the bank records of Massey TB, Inc., and Massey TB Trust. We found several checks made payable to you. Please answer the questions below which relate to the checks we found. We have included copies of the checks for your review.

Should you have any questions, please call investigator Dennis S. Paul at the telephone number listed above.

1. Did you receive checks number 1521, 1571, 1681, 1952, 1991?

____

2. Did you endorse these checks?

____

3. Please explain why these checks were deposited into Massey TB Trust's bank account.

____

____

____

____

____

4. We would like to talk to you about these checks. Please call us, or provide your daytime telephone number so we can schedule an appointment.

____

Sincerely, Dennis S. Paul

Grand Jury Transcript

A complete grand jury transcript will contain the questions, answers, and statements made by each participant before the grand jury. This transcript can be used as basis for a charge of perjury if the witness gives false information before the grand jury.

The Art of Interviewing

Through practice, an investigator can improve his or her interview skills. But, equally important is practicing the art of critical self-analysis when dealing with others. This starts by stripping away the prejudices and other self-imposed barriers to impartiality that surface when communicating with people. It continues by learning to converse in different styles of language. Interviewing a college graduate and a fifth grade drop-out require different communication skills. How something is said is just as important as what is said. Everyone communicates through speech patterns and non-spoken behavior patterns. Witnesses sense the presence of the investigator's questions, not only with their ears, but by watching his or her gestures, making or avoiding eye contact, and feeling the stress in the room.

The interview process should flow naturally. The investigator should enter into the interview with general questions in mind. After the first question is asked, the investigator assumes a new role— the listener. Contingent upon what is heard the investigator leads the interview toward the next question and then listens. This asking and listening process, controlled by the investigator, continues until the objectives of the interview have been achieved.

A successful interviewer has empathy for others. No one likes the thought of appearing foolish. Many witnesses are actually victims of fraudulent actions committed against them by the subject of the investigation and are embarrassed about being victimized. For example, businesses victimized by insiders are often reluctant to let the public know that they were vulnerable to fraud. A business may have more than money at stake. It becomes a matter of confidence and prestige in the public or industry's eye. An investigator who can become sensitive to a witness's situation quickly improves his or her interviewing techniques.

Summary

The goal of an investigator is to conduct each interview in such a manner as to gather all available information and documents pertaining to the investigation and then make a permanent record of each witness's testimony for further reference.

The planning phase of the interview process is the foundation of an interview. Poor planning will have the same effect on an interview as a weak foundation has on a building. Proper planning enhances the probability of a successful interview. A successful interview can create a cooperative witness who can breathe life into financial records. It could also provide additional leads for the investigator to solve the case.

Once the investigator has decided on who, when, where, and how to interview the witness, the investigator should prepare a topical outline of the questions to be asked. Just as planning is the foundation of the interview process, the opening of an interview sets its tone. The body of the interview is the fact finding part of the process. The closing summarizes the key facts and provides an opportunity for the witness and the investigator to agree with the summation.

The medium used to record an interview should be reflective of the significance of the witness and the information and records provided by the witness.

Interviewing is a skill that can be developed and improved upon through practice. Few skills are as important to the financial investigator as the ability to talk to people and successfully gather information from them.

Questions and Exercises

Answer the following questions and then check your responses with those provided on pages at the back of the book.

1. How does an interview differ from an interrogation?

2. How do questions asked in a financial interview differ from those asked in other types of investigative interviews?

3. What are some things an investigator should consider when planning financial interviews during the course of an investigation?

4. Identify and describe the three methods of questioning that can be used in a financial interview.

5. Why is the introduction critical to a successful interview?

6. How can an investigator gain the cooperation of a hesitant witness?

7. Explain the following statement:

The interview process is more than just asking questions and writing down responses.

8. What is wrong with the following question?

He didn't have anyone with him when he came into the bank did he, but if he did, do you remember if the person was male or female and can you give a description of the person?

9. What is the last question an investigator should ask during an interview?

10. You are preparing to record an interview and you can't decide which method of recordation to use. You are torn between the memorandum and the question and answer statement. Describe the pros and cons of each.

11. What advantages are there to having a witness compose and write his or her own affidavit?

Endnotes

1 Cal W. Downs, G. Paul Smeyak, and Ernest Martin, *Professional Interviewing,* (New York: Harper and Row Publishers, 1980), p. 5

2 Joseph T. Wells, W. Steve Albrecht, Jack Bologna, Gilbert Geis, and Jack Robertson, *Fraud Examiner's Manual,* (National Association of Certified Fraud Examiner's, 1989), Section 1, p. 15

3 *Fraud Examiner's Manual,* Section 1, p. 14

4 *Fraud Examiner's Manual,* Section 1, p. 7

5 *Fraud Examiner's Manual,* Section 11, pp. 15, 16

6 Format for examples adopted from *Fraud Examiner's Manual,* Section 1, pp. 20 - 23

7 *Fraud Examiner's Manual,* Section 1, p. 31

8 *Fraud Examiner's Manual,* Section 1, p. 23, 24

KEY (CORRECT ANSWERS)

1 A financial interview is conducted to obtain information and documentation from a witness. A financial interrogation is conducted for a different purpose. Its purpose is to elicit confessions or admissions of culpability from suspects or hostile witnesses.

2 Many investigative interviews focus on the recollection of witnesses. Questions such as "Do you remember seeing any suspicious cars in the neighborhood? or What color jacket was he wearing? are asked. Financial interviews go beyond recollection questions and deal with the specific details of financial transactions and the movement of money.

3 When planning interviews, an investigator should consider the following:

- Who should I interview?
- In what order should I interview the witnesses?
- What type of witness is this person going to be?
- Should I contact the suspect?
- When should I contact the suspect?
- What method of questioning should I use?

4 There are three general methods of questioning an investigator can use during a financial interview:

- The chronological method
- Questioning according to documents
- Questioning according to transactions or events

With the chronological method of questioning, a witness is questioned about the events in the order that they occurred, from beginning to end. With questioning according to documents, a particular document (financial statement, canceled check, tax return) is the focus of the interview. When questioning according to transaction or event, questions focus on a particular situation.

5 The introduction is critical as it sets the tone for the whole interview. Its primary objective is to put the witness at ease and get him or her to agree to answer questions.

6 To get hesitant witnesses to agree to cooperate, and investigator must avoid coming across as a threat. He or she should try to lead witnesses to believe that they will benefit from cooperating with the investigator.

7 An investigator must actively participate in the interview process. He or she must constantly analyze responses, and continually check for inconsistencies, inaccuracies, and incompleteness. Also, investigators must attend to what witnesses do during an interview. The visual and non-verbal aspects of an interview are very important.

8 The sentence is negatively phrased, and so long and complex that no one is going to understand it. Investigators should avoid asking complex and negatively phrased questions. All questions should be simple, to the point, and positively phrased.

9 The final question an investigator should ask is: "Is there anything else that you would like to say?" It gives the witness one final chance to say anything that he or she wishes.

10 The major advantage of the question and answer statement is that it contains all of the questions asked and answers provided during an interview. Of course, this could be viewed as a disadvantage also. The statement will be long, unedited, and could contain unnecessary material. On the other hand, the memorandum is more informal and it contains all pertinent testimony obtained during the interview. However, the testimony is recorded as the investigator recalls after refreshing his or her memory through informal notes. The memorandum does not contain the exact words of the witness. Both the memorandum and question and answer statement are good methods for recording an interview. The choice the investigator makes should be based on the complexity and investigative importance of the interview.

11 By allowing the affiant to create the affidavit, the investigator ensures that the affidavit will be in the affiant's own words and the credibility of the affidavit will increase because it is in the affiant's own handwriting. It would be difficult for the affiant to later deny the affidavit was his or hers.

Evidence

In this chapter we will discuss various concepts related to evidence. We will look at the differences between direct and circumstantial evidence. We will discuss various standards of proof and see how the standard of proof for a criminal case differs from the standards for a civil case. Selected "rules of evidence" also will be presented. The chapter begins with a discussion of the grand jury process, for it is here that initial evidence gathering efforts help determine whether a suspect in a criminal case goes to trial.

- Describe the grand jury process.
- Describe the "investigative tools" used by the grand jury.
- Define evidence.
- Distinguish among the five standards of proof.
- Describe different classifications of evidence.
- Determine the admissibility of evidence by applying selected rules of evidence.

One of the major responsibilities of a financial investigator is to gather evidence. But there are many things the investigator must consider in his or her quest for evidence. Does the evidence hear directly upon a fact the prosecution wants to prove or must inferences be made to link the evidence to a fact? Is the person who supplied some relevant fact able to testify to that fact or are the communications between that person and the accused privileged? This chapter provides an introduction to many concepts surrounding the collection, strength, and admissibility of evidence. But before we get into a discussion of evidence, we will look at the grand jury process. It is here that the determination is made to charge someone with a violation of criminal law. The evidence an investigator collects plays a large role in determining whether there is sufficient cause to believe that the accused committed a crime.

The Grand Jury

The American system of justice is **adversarial** in nature. This means that both parties involved in the litigation (prosecution and accused) present evidence to a third party (judge or jury) for a determination of who is right or wrong (guilt or innocence). This differs dramatically from other systems of justice. For example, in an **inquisitional system,** defendants are presumed guilty and the evidence to convict them is extracted from their mouths.

One of the many legal concepts that the American colonists brought with them from England was that an individual accused of a high crime or major criminal violation should stand accountable to that accusation in front of his or her peers. Under our Constitution, a person cannot be **indicted,** receive a formal written complaint of criminal charges, without first having the facts and the reasons leading up to and contained within the indictment reviewed and approved by a jury of his or her peers - **a grand jury.**

At the federal level, a grand jury consists of 16 to 23 people chosen from the general population in a judicial district. The jurors investigate accusations against people and other entities. Upon a finding of probable cause, a grand jury returns an indictment which requires the accused to stand trial for a criminal violation.

Normally a grand jury "sits," or deliberates, for a period of eighteen months to perform its function. Grand jury proceedings are held in secrecy, and as such, only the jurors, government attorney, witness, and stenographer are present while the jury is in session. When the jury is deliberating or voting, no one else is allowed in the jury room.

The role of the grand jury is that of fact finder. The jury meets to gather information and documents, and to listen to witness testimony concerning alleged criminal violations. After the information, documents and testimony have been gathered, the grand jury decides, by voting, whether or not to return a criminal indictment. It takes 12 jurors to return an indictment, no matter how large the jury.

Tools of the Grand Jury

To accomplish their fact finding, the grand jury has the power to call witnesses to provide testimony, to issue orders that require the production of records, and to impose legal sanctions to ensure compliance with its powers. The primary investigative tool of the grand jury is the **subpoena** which requires a witness to appear before the grand jury. A subpoena can also require a witness to produce records and documents. A subpoena details the testimony or records to be supplied and the place and time for the witness' appearance before the grand jury. Subpoenaed witnesses that fail to comply can be cited for contempt of court and those that are dishonest while providing testimony may face perjury charges. Witnesses may not have their attorneys present with them during the grand jury proceeding, however, witnesses can confer with their attorneys outside the grand jury proceedings before answering questions.

Another grand jury investigative tool is the **grant of immunity.** Immunity is granted to convince or compel a witness to provide testimony or produce documents. By guaranteeing that the witness will not be prosecuted, the grand jury can obtain important information otherwise unavailable. There are two types of immunity grants: transactional and use.

Transactional Immunity

Transactional immunity completely protects the witness from prosecution for any criminal offenses about which he or she testifies during the grand jury proceedings. If a witness states that she has laundered money for a drug dealer, she cannot be charged for the offense if she has been provided transactional immunity. This form of immunity is rarely used.

Use Immunity

Use immunity protects witnesses from the prosecution's "use" of their testimony against them. Let's look at that same witness who laundered drug money. If she is granted use immunity, she cannot be prosecuted for money laundering unless the prosecuting attorney can develop independent information and evidence from a completely separate source of the witness' criminal wrongdoing.

Immunity can be given either formally or informally. **Formal immunity** is granted by the court. As part of a grand jury proceeding, the prosecuting attorney makes an application to a court (i.e. federal judge) requesting a grant of formal immunity for the witness. The court official reviews the application and bases his or her findings on:

- The importance of the information to the success of the investigation

- The availability of the information from other sources

- The culpability of the witness

If the court approves the application, a grant of formal immunity is issued to the witness.

Informal immunity is offered to grand jury witnesses by the prosecuting attorney via issuance of a "letter of immunity." Such a letter assures witnesses that their grand jury testimony will not be used against them in any subsequent criminal legal proceeding.

Immunity is a powerful tool and the investigator and prosecuting attorney must use it wisely. They must weigh the evidence they will receive from a witness against that witness' criminal wrong doings. The prosecutor will usually ask for a proffer. This is a statement from the witness which details his involvement and cannot be used against him. It is used to determine if immunity should be offered.

Role of the Financial Investigator in the Grand Jury Process

Financial investigators routinely work with grand juries. They serve subpoenas, gather information, take testimony from witnesses, and report their investigative findings to the grand jury. The cloak of secrecy applies to all information gathered by the agent during the grand jury proceedings.

The financial investigator also assists the prosecution in the investigative decision-making process. The investigator who has talked to witnesses and analyzed the financial information can advise the attorney on issues such as order of witness appearance, questions to ask the witness, and even whom to offer immunity grants.

A major advantage in conducting financial investigations through the grand jury process is the ability for various law enforcement agencies to work together. Allegations of criminal violations often impact various statutes for which numerous agencies hold investigative authority. Under the auspices of the grand jury, multiple violations can be simultaneously investigated and ultimately charged through a coordinated multi-agency effort.

One disadvantage to conducting an investigation through the grand jury process is related to the secrecy requirements of the grand jury. Grand jury information may not be used in non-grand jury investigations unless a court order is obtained permitting the release of the grand jury information. If a suspect is not indicted by the grand jury, the grand jury's investigative findings cannot be used in other investigative activities (i.e. intelligence sharing or other ongoing investigations) unless so authorized by a court order.

What Is Evidence?

From the discussion on the grand jury proceeding, you can see that the financial investigator's role as a gatherer of evidence is a vital one. In its simplest terms, **evidence** is anything that can make a person believe that a fact or proposition is true or false. Both parties involved in a lawsuit can submit evidence to prove their points. In a criminal case, the prosecution must present evidence to prove the commission of a crime. They do so by gathering information, documents, and other items that prove the elements of a crime. The defense presents evidence to show that allegations are invalid.

Standards of Proof

Evidence is collected to establish **proof.** In the world of law enforcement, the concept of proof varies according to the situation. In a criminal case, evidence must establish proof of a crime "beyond a reasonable doubt." In most civil cases, evidence must be strong enough to incline a person to believe one side over the other. Discussions concerning five standards of proof follow.

Beyond a Reasonable Doubt

A defendant charged with a criminal violation is presumed innocent until proven guilty. In a *criminal proceeding,* the government bears the burden of proving that the accused is guilty of the charges - the accused does not have to prove his or her innocence. To receive a guilty verdict, the government must prove each and every element of a crime beyond a reasonable doubt.

The concept of **beyond a reasonable doubt** is something that many of us talk about and, perhaps, struggle with. We do not have to be sitting on a jury to give our personal opinions about a case. We can read about a case in the newspaper. Some, we can watch on television. So, when we get ready to give our personal verdicts of guilt or innocence, we must measure the evidence presented and determine if the prosecution has proven its case beyond a reasonable doubt. And then we ask ourselves "What is meant by 'reasonable doubt'?"

Video Spectral Comparator's are new technological tools used to clarify images and differentiate inks on documents. This technology was used to show conclusive proof that a check originally made payable to the IRS was altered through the use of different inks.

Reasonable doubt is the degree of certainty that you have in accomplishing or transacting the more important concerns of your everyday life. For example, you are out for your nightly walk around the neighborhood and you stop at an intersection. At the same time, a car happens to pull up to a stop sign at the same intersection. You and the driver make eye contact and the driver waves at you to cross the street. You cross because you are convinced, beyond a reasonable doubt, that the car will not pull out and run over you.

We just described "reasonable doubt" in lay person's terms. Let's see how the court defines "reasonable doubt?" A recent court decision (U.S. v. Sunderland) defines the concept as follows:

> *A reasonable doubt, is a doubt founded upon a consideration of all the evidence and must be based on reason. Beyond a reasonable doubt does not mean to moral certainty or beyond a mere possible doubt or an imaginary doubt. It is such a doubt as would deter a reasonably prudent man or woman from acting or deciding in the more important matters involved in his or her own affairs. Doubts which are not based upon a reasonable and careful consideration of all the evidence, what are purely imaginary, or borne of sympathy alone, should not be considered and should not influence your verdict. It is only necessary that you should have certainty with which you transact the more important concerns in life. If you have that certainty, then you are convinced beyond a reasonable doubt.*

A defendant may not be convicted upon mere suspicion or conjecture. A defendant should be acquitted if the evidence is equally consistent with innocence as with guilt.[1]

Preponderance of Evidence

The degree of proof required in many *civil matters* is a **preponderance of evidence.** Let's say you are sitting on a jury in a case involving a lawsuit where one person is suing the other. You listen to the evidence presented by the defendant and then you listen to the evidence presented by the plaintiff. When it comes time to deliberate, you find that you happen to believe the plaintiff. Both sides presented evidence but the evidence presented by the plaintiff made you believe that person. This is proof by preponderance of evidence - evidence that inclines an impartial mind to one side rather than the other. And with preponderance of evidence, it is not the quantity of evidence that matters, it's the quality. For example:

> *...when it is said that the burden rest upon either party to establish any particular fact or proposition by preponderance or greater weight of evidence, it is meant that the evidence offered and introduced in support thereof to entitle said party to a verdict, should, when fully and thoroughly considered, produce the stronger impression upon the mind and be more convincing when weighed against the evidence introduced in opposition thereto. Such preponderances are not always to be determined by the number of witnesses on the respective sides, although it may be thus determined all of the things being equal.*[2]

Clear and Convincing Evidence

Another standard of proof used in certain *civil cases* where fraud may be involved is **clear and convincing evidence.** This type of proof is not proof beyond a reasonable doubt as required in a criminal case, but is stronger than a mere preponderance of evidence as normally required in a civil matter. For example:

> *A mere preponderance of the evidence, meaning merely the greater weight of the evidence, is not sufficient to prove fraud. This does not mean that you must be convinced of fraud beyond a reasonable doubt, because this is not a criminal case. However, an allegation of fraud does require a greater degree of proof than is required in most civil cases, and a mere preponderance of the evidence while enough to incline the mind of an impartial juror to one side of the issue rather than the other, is not enough to prove fraud. Fraud must be established by evidence which is clear, cogent, and convincing.*[3]

Probable Cause

The three standards of proof just presented can be distinguished from **probable cause** which serves as the basis for arrest and search warrants. Probable cause is all the facts and circumstances within the knowledge of an investigator about a criminal activity that can be considered reasonable and trustworthy. For an arrest warrant to be issued, probable cause must be sufficient to cause a person of reasonable caution to believe that a crime has been committed and that the accused has committed it. To have a search warrant issued, probable cause must be sufficient to make a reasonable person believe that a crime has been or will be committed and that the evidence sought exists in the place to be searched. Probable cause requires more than mere suspicion or hunches but less than a preponderance of evidence.

Suspicious Situation

At the opposite end of the spectrum from "beyond a reasonable doubt" in the continuum of standards of proof is the **suspicious situation.** In Terry v. Ohio, 392 U.S. 1 (1968), the Supreme Court established case law stating that police may briefly detain and question a person for investigative purposes if there exists specific "articulable suspicions." Such a valid detainment of a suspect may yield evidence to effect arrest or provide evidence in support of a crime.

Classifications of Evidence

Now that you are familiar with the standards of proof, let's look at the types of evidence that can be presented. In legal terminology, evidence has various classifications. Evidence may be classified according to its proof results (direct or circumstantial) or according to its source (real, documentary, or testimonial). The following paragraphs describe the different classifications of evidence. Evidence admitted through a process called "judicial notice" is also discussed.

Direct Evidence

A person under investigation is suspected of accepting a $5,000 bribe. Another person states that he was with the suspect on November 12, and saw the suspect accept the bribe. This person has provided **direct evidence** of the crime. Direct evidence is evidence to the precise point at issue.[4] A person is suspected of accepting a bribe; another person says he saw the suspect accept a bribe. Nothing needs to be inferred or presumed.

Circumstantial Evidence

Now let's look at the same suspect, only this time let's look at some evidence that is not directly related to the point at issue. An investigator states that the suspect's bank statement reveals that the suspect deposited $5,000 on November 12. Another person testifies that on November 12, she saw the suspect having breakfast with the person suspected of offering the bribe. When looked at individually, neither of these pieces of evidence prove that the suspect accepted a bribe. However, viewed together, you get the feeling that the suspect could have accepted the bribe at breakfast and then deposited it in his bank.

The evidence presented in the previous paragraph is **circumstantial evidence.** Circumstantial evidence is evidence relating to a series of facts other than those at issue that tend, by inference, to establish the fact at issue.[5] Circumstantial evidence proves the existence of the fact indirectly and depends on the strength of the inferences raised by the evidence. The use of circumstantial evidence is recognized by the courts as a legitimate means of proof when it involves proving several material facts which, when considered in a relationship to each other, tend to establish the existence of the principle or ultimate fact.

Circumstantial evidence is the only type of evidence generally available to show certain elements of a crime, such as malice, willfulness, intent, or legal concepts which exist only in the mind of the perpetrator of the deed. Accordingly, the proof of most financial violations is based upon circumstantial evidence.

Real Evidence

Real evidence is evidence that is tangible; it can be presented to the jury for inspection. Material objects such as knives, bullets, guns, and jewelry are examples of real evidence.

Documentary Evidence

Documentary evidence consists of writings and documents, such as judicial or official records, contracts, deeds, and the less formal writings such as letters, memorandums, books, and records of private persons and organizations. Documentary evidence is primarily circumstantial in nature and must be introduced by a witness who can testify to the existence and authenticity of the evidence.

Testimonial Evidence

Testimonial evidence is evidence given by word of mouth. Witnesses under oath and affirmation provide testimonial evidence. A **witness** is a person who can testify as to what he or she knows from having seen, heard, or otherwise observed.

Judicial Notice

Not everything presented during a trial must be proved. There are matters so well known to the court that it would be a waste of time to compel a party to offer evidence of their truth. For example, it is a well known fact that the formula for water is H_2O. There's no reason for a lawyer to call a witness to the stand to attest to that fact. The judge can allow the court to accept certain facts as evidence through a legal process known as **judicial notice.** However, if there is evidence which reasonably puts a fact in dispute, judicial notice will not be taken.

Rules of Evidence

The investigator is the one who gathers evidence during the investigative process. For the investigator, evidence of financial crimes includes the following:

- Admissions and confessions freely given by the suspect
- Statements made by witnesses who either observed the criminal event or were victimized by it
- Physical things which relate to the criminal activity (i.e. books and records, currency, bank account information, etc.)
- Analysis completed by the investigator

But even the best of evidence, that which would result in overwhelming indications of guilt, will mean nothing and will be inadmissible at trial if the investigator ignores the rules and procedures regarding the admissibility of evidence at trial. These rules directly impact on the financial investigator during the investigative process.

At the federal level, the rules governing criminal procedures and evidence have been codified and represent the benchmark to follow when gathering information during the investigative process. The following rules are relevant to financial investigations:

- Rule 401, Relevancy and Competency
- Rule 501, Privileged Communications
- Rule 801, Hearsay
- Rule 901 (a), Chain of Custody
- Rules 1001 and 1002, Best Evidence and Requirement of Original

Relevancy and Competency (Rule 401)

To be admissible, evidence must be relevant and competent. These terms are not synonymous. If a fact offered in evidence relates in some logical way to the principle fact it is considered to be **relevant.** The **competency** of evidence means that the fact offered into evidence is adequately sufficient, reliable, and relevant to the case and is presented by a qualified and capable witness.

Relevancy implies a traceable and significant connection. A fact may not bear directly on the principle fact but it is considered relevant if it constitutes one link in a chain of evidence or if it relates to facts that would constitute circumstantial evidence. Some evidentiary matters that are considered relevant and therefore admissible are:[6]

- The motive for a crime
- The ability of the defendant to commit this specific crime
- The opportunity to commit the crime
- Threats or expressions of ill will by the suspect
- The means of committing the offense
- Physical evidence at the scene linking the accused to the crime
- The suspect's conduct and comments at the time of arrest
- The attempt to conceal and/or destroy evidence
- Valid confessions

Evidence, even if logically relevant, may be excluded by the Court if that evidence is likely to inflame or confuse a jury, or consume too much time. For example, testimony as to the statistical probability of guilt of the defendant, while logically relevant when based on prior testimony, may be considered too prejudicial and unreliable to be accepted by the Court.[7]

The issue of competency can relate to the witness presenting the evidence or the evidence itself. If a person is called to testify and does not understand the nature of the oath or is unable to narrate with understanding the facts that he or she is to testify to, that witness' competency will be questioned. Examples of incompetent evidence include confessions involuntarily obtained or unsigned carbon copies of a document which are offered into evidence without any explanation for the failure to produce the original.

Privileged Communications (Rule 501)
This rule is based on the belief that it is necessary to maintain the confidentiality of certain communications. However, it covers only those communications that are a "unique product" of a protective relationship. The one to whom the information has been given cannot divulge that information without the consent of the other party. Some of the more prevalent claims to privileged relationships are:

- Attorney/Client
- Husband/Wife
- Clergyman/Penitent
- Physician/Patient

- Accountant/Client
- Law Enforcement Officer/Informant

Attorney/Client

The attorney/client privilege must be strictly adhered to. However, this privileged relationship does not make every communication between a client to his attorney confidential. It applies only to those communications meant to be confidential and made to the attorney in his or her capacity as an attorney. When it does apply, the privilege covers corporate as well as individual clients.

For the investigator, the attorney/client privilege does not apply when a suspect's attorney is merely a conduit for handling funds or is involved in something like researching or recording the transfer of title to real estate (without consultation for legal advice). Similarly, if the attorney is acting as an accountant or tax return preparer, this privilege may not be applicable.

Husband/Wife

Communications between a husband and wife, privately made, are generally assumed to have been intended to be of a confidential nature, and therefore held to be privileged. These communications remain privileged even after a marriage terminates. However, if it is obvious from the circumstances or nature of a communication that no confidence was intended, there is no privilege. For example, communications between a husband and wife made in the presence of a friend are not privileged.

In addition to the confidential communication privilege, there exists an independent privilege—a testimonial privilege. A married person may refuse to testify against his or her spouse, at least when the latter is a defendant in a criminal prosecution.

Clergyman/Penitent

The privilege between clergyman and penitent has been recognized in the Federal courts, but this privilege has not been extended to financial matters, such as contributions made through a clergyman.

Physician/Patient

Many state courts recognize the physician/patient privilege, although Federal courts generally have not approved it.[8]

Accountant/Client

The accountant/client communication privilege is *not recognized* under common or Federal law. Workpapers belonging to an accountant are not privileged and must be produced if required.

Similarly, a suspect may be required to produce an accountant's workpapers if they are in his or her possession.

An accountant employed by an attorney, or retained by a person at the attorney's request to perform services essential to the attorney/client relationship, may be covered by the attorney/client privilege.

Law Enforcement Officer/Informant

This privilege allows law enforcement agencies to withhold from disclosure the *identity* of persons who furnish information concerning violations of law. Unlike other privileges, it is the identity of the informant that is privileged, not the communication.

This privilege also differs from the others in that it can be waived only by the government, whereas the others are for the benefit of, and can be waived by, the accused individual. Where disclosure of an informant's identity or the content of the communication is relevant to a fair trial, the court may order disclosure. If the government withholds the information, the court could dismiss the charges.

Conversations in the known presence of third parties do not fall within the purview of privileged communications. The protected communications are those that are, in fact, intended to be confidential. Exceptions are recognized for those situations where third parties are indispensable to the communication itself (i.e., legal secretary, stenographer, or transcriber).

Hearsay (Rule 801)

Hearsay is evidence that does not come from the personal knowledge of the declarant but from the repetition of what the declarant has heard others say. For example, an investigator says that the suspect's business manager told him that checks written by the suspect were for personal expenses, not business expenses. This information would be considered hearsay and inadmissible in court. The information would be admissible if the business manager provided the testimony.

The major reason hearsay is inadmissible is the potential unreliability of the witness providing the hearsay. Witnesses must tell what they themselves know, not what they have heard from others. Testimony that merely repeats what another person said is not admitted as evidence because of the possibility of distortion or misunderstanding.[9]

The justice system recognizes that there are occasions when exceptions to the hearsay rule must be made. From a financial investigative standpoint, exceptions to the hearsay rule include the following:[10]

- Valid confession/tacit admission
- Prior statements
- Statement against interest
- *Res gestae* statement/excited utterance
- Dying declaration
- Official records rule
- Shop book rule
- Expert testimony

Valid Confession/Tacit Admission

A valid confession is a statement by the suspect acknowledging the facts and validity of those facts upon which a criminal conviction rests. Perhaps during an interview with the suspect, the suspect tells the investigator: "Yeah, I took the money. I got sick of my boss living the easy life off of all the hard work that I do so I forged his name to a couple of checks and tried to take off for South America." A **tacit admission** is less than a full acknowledgment by the suspect but is a statement of facts relative to his or her criminal activity. An investigator can offer into evidence a valid confession or tacit admission only if it was legally obtained during the course of an investigation.

Prior Statements

If a defendant takes the stand in his or her own defense, the prosecution can introduce, during cross-examination, statements made by the defendant at prior trials or hearings. This is done to show inconsistencies with the defendant's current testimony, or to reflect expressed or implied charges against the defendant relating to the current trial.

Statement Against Interest

A **statement against interest** is a prior acknowledgment of a material fact relevant to an issue now being litigated but this prior acknowledgment differs from what is now being claimed. For example, in a tax evasion prosecution, evidence in the form of a financial statement submitted for life insurance shows a defendant's net worth to be higher than she now claims. This prior statement can be used as evidence against the defendant.

Res Gestae Statement (Excited Utterance)

A **res gestae statement** is a spontaneous comment made at a time of great emotional strain (i.e., at the time of arrest or at the scene of an accident). The theory to allow this exception to the hearsay rule is that it is very likely that a statement made at such a time is a truthful response. For example, during a raid of a bookmaking establishment, one of the persons in the establishment, upon seeing the raiding officers enter the room says: "Burn the betting slips!" Even though the speaker is never identified and is not available as a witness, an investigator who heard the statement may be permitted to testify about it to prove that betting slips existed.

Dying Declarations

Dying declarations, either orally or in writing, are presumed to be forthright and honest statements. Since the witness is unavailable, an exception to the hearsay rule is made and the person who heard the dying declaration can testify to its validity.

Official Records Rule

The official records rule allows for the introduction of books, records, reports, and compilations kept as a regular and routine duty by a public official. Custodians of those records, even though they did not make the record per se, may introduce and act as witnesses for this type of official record at trial.

Shop Book Rule

The shop book rule states that books of original entry kept in the regular course of business can be introduced in court by the person who has custody of the books even though this person may not be the person who made the original entries to the books. In this instance, the "custodian" must authenticate the records, testify that he or she is the custodian, that the entries are original (not copies), and finally, that the entries were made contemporaneously with the transactions transcribed therein. For example, in attempting to prove a sales transaction between the defendant and Company ABC, the prosecution would call as a witness an employee of Company ABC who would bring the business' bookkeeping records to court. This employee, who is not the person who made the original entries into the books, would prove the sales transaction by showing how the funds paid to Company ABC by the defendant were recorded in the business's bookkeeping system.

Expert Testimony

In cases where the subject matter is too difficult or too technical for jurors to understand without assistance, expert testimony is permitted.

Chain of Custody (Rule 901 (a))

This rule requires that when evidence is obtained during the course of an investigation, it should be marked, identified, inventoried, and preserved to maintain its original condition and to establish a clear chain of custody until it is introduced at trial. This rule applies to documentary evidence and any other objects acquired by the investigator. The term "acquired" means that the evidence was obtained as a result of a subpoena, search warrant, voluntary submission, or discovery during the course of the financial investigation. If gaps in possession or custody occur, the evidence itself may be challenged at trial on the theory that the document or object introduced may not be the original or is not in its original condition, and therefore is of doubtful authenticity.

For a document to be considered admissible as evidence, it is necessary to prove that it is the same document that was secured by the investigator and that it is in the same condition as it was when it was secured. An investigator who obtains original documents should immediately identify them by some type of marking so that he or she can later testify that they are the documents that were obtained and that they are in the same condition as they were when first obtained. Markings include an investigator's initials and the date the information was obtained, and could be placed in the margin, in the corner, or in some other inconspicuous place on the front or back of each document secured. If circumstances dictate that such markings would render the document subject to attack on the grounds that it has been defaced or that the document is not in the same condition as when it was obtained, the investigator may place the document into an envelope and write a description or any other identifying information relating to the document on the face of the envelope.

Best Evidence and Requirement of Original (Rules 1001 and 1002)

The Best Evidence Rule applies only to documentary evidence. It states that the best proof of the contents of a document is the document itself. However, if an original has been destroyed or is in the hands of another party *and* it is not subject to legal process by search warrant or subpoena, an authenticated copy of that original may be substituted as evidence.

Facts about a document, other than its contents, are provable without its production. For example, the fact that a sales contract was made is a fact separate from the actual terms of the contract and may be proved by testimony alone.

Certain documents such as leases, contracts, or even letters, which are signed in more than one copy are all considered originals and any one of the copies may be produced as an original. Production consists of either making the written document available to the judge and counsel for the adversary, or having it read aloud in open court.

All evidence falling short of the standard for best evidence is classified as **secondary evidence.** Secondary evidence may be either the testimony of witnesses or a copy of the writing. Before secondary evidence can be admitted, there must be satisfactory evidence showing the present or former existence of an original document. It must be established that the original has been destroyed, lost, stolen or otherwise unavailable. Further, it must be established that the party offering the document into evidence attempted all reasonable means to obtain the original. In each case, the sufficiency of the search for the original is a matter to be determined by the court. If a document is offered as secondary evidence, it must be shown to be a correct copy of the original.

For federal purposes, secondary evidence may be either a copy of the document or testimony of witnesses relating to the contents of the document itself. For example, the testimony of an investigator as to the contents of a sales invoice that is unavailable would be secondary evidence. The investigator's testimony is admissible even though the person who prepared the invoice is available to testify. The Best Evidence Rule will not be invoked to exclude oral testimony of one witness merely because another witness could give more conclusive testimony. However, in other jurisdictions, testimony will not be allowed to prove the contents of a document if there exists a secondary evidence to prove its contents. This is known as the **majority rule.**

If an original document is destroyed by the party attempting to prove its contents and who is offering it for evidence, secondary evidence will be admitted if the destruction was in the ordinary course of business or by mistake, or even intentionally, provided it was not done for any fraudulent purpose

Summary

The rules of evidence and procedure establish the legal framework within which the financial investigator works. A full confession of guilt by the suspect becomes worthless if it was illegally obtained and therefore inadmissible in court. The investigative process requires the gathering of information, documents, and testimony from witnesses, victims, and subjects involved in criminal activities. Though the legal statutes institute the benchmarks of right and wrong, and the elements and degrees of proof necessary for criminal conviction, it is the rules of evidence and criminal procedure that control both the investigative process and the resultant judicial proceeding.

Questions and Exercises

Answer the following questions then check your responses with those provided at the back of the book.

1. a. How many jurors usually "sit" on a federal grand jury?

b. How many jurors does it take to return an indictment?

2. Differentiate between transactional immunity and use immunity.

3. What is evidence?

4. What is the relationship between evidence and proof?

5. Differentiate between the following standards of proof: "beyond a reasonable doubt" and "preponderance of evidence."

6. You are investigating a mail fraud scheme. One of the elements of the crime is the use of mails to further the scheme. Provide an example of direct and circumstantial evidence that you could collect to prove this element of the crime.

7. What is judicial notice? Provide an example.

8. When an investigator gathers evidence, why is it important that he or she keep the terms "relevancy" and "competency" in mind?

9. Todd White is on trial in Federal court for drug trafficking and money laundering offenses. Read the following descriptions of proposed testimony and, based on the privileged communications rule, answer the following questions for each description: 1) Is the testimony admissible in court? and 2) Why or why not?

a. Todd White's wife, Kay, says that before they were married, Todd told her that he made a lot of money selling drugs.

1)

2)

b. While they were married, Kay White saw Todd measuring white powder on a set of scales. She saw him put the white powder into bags.

1)

2)

c. While they were married, Todd told Kay that the powder in the bags was cocaine. Kay was not involved in the distribution of drugs.

1)

2)

d. Todd's son, Joey, says his father asked him to sell some cocaine at school.

1)

2)

e. Leon Norton, Todd's accountant says that Todd told him that he had $25,000 in income from his auto repair business and $250,000 in income from an inheritance.

1)

2)

f. Kent Parks, Todd's attorney, says that he handled a real estate closing for a house Todd bought. Todd paid $250,000 for the house.

1)

2)

10. Why is hearsay evidence inadmissible?

11. What is the shop book rule?

12. What do the terms "best evidence" and "secondary evidence" mean to an investigator?

Endnotes

1 U.S. v. Sutherland, 56-2 USTC 9651 (D.D. Colo.)

2 Wissler v. U.S. 58-1 USTC par 9414 (So. Dist. of A)

3 Gladden v. Self, 55-1 USTC 9227 (E.D. Ark.), Add'd 224 F2d 282 (CA-8)

4 John Evarts Tracy, *Handbook of the Law of Evidence,* (New York: Prentice-Hall, Inc., 1952), p. 6

5 *Handbook of the Law of Evidence,* p. 6

6 Jack T. Wells, W. Steve Albrecht, Jack Bologna, and Gilbert Geis, *Fraud Examiners Manual,* (National Association of Certified Fraud Examiners, 1989), Section 11, p. 45

7 *Fraud Examiner's Manual,* Section 11, p. 44

8 Stephen A. Saltzburg and Michael M. Martin, *Federal Rules of Evidence Manual: A Complete Guide to the Federal Rules of Evidence, 5th Edition, Volume 1,* (Charlottesville, VA: The Michie Company, 1990), p. 423

9 *Fraud Examiners Manual,* Section 11, p. 49
10 *Fraud Examiner's Manual,* Section 11, pp. 49, 50

U.S.C. 1343, fraud by wire, radio, or television. Elements of the crime include the following:

- Intent
- Scheme to defraud
- Use of interstate communications to further scheme

d. David Stevens is a bank employee who is using his position with the bank to commit embezzlement and bank fraud. The statutes violated and their corresponding elements are as follows:

1) Title 18 U.S.C. § 656. Theft, embezzlement, or misapplication by bank officer or employee

- Intent
- The suspect is a bank employee or officer
- The suspect attempted to defraud the bank

2) Title 18 U.S.C. § 1344. Bank fraud

- Intent

- Scheme to defraud a financial institution

e. Linda Carson is threatening to use the fact that her competitor is involved in a criminal activity to get that person to do something against his or her will. Linda is committing blackmail in violation of Title 18 U.S.C. § 873. Elements of the crime include the following:

- Intent
- The suspect made threats

f. Susan Tompkins is in violation of Title 26 U.S.C. § 7203, Willful failure to file return, supply information, or pay tax. Elements of the crime include the following:

- Duty to pay
- Failure to pay
- Willfulness

5 Lance Gordon is intentionally structuring his financial transactions so that the financial institutions he is dealing with do not file Currency Transaction Reports. The money involved happens to be from an illegal activity, therefore, Lance is in violation of Title 31 U.S.C. 5324, Structuring transactions to evade reporting requirement prohibited.

6 Use of mails to further scheme–Direct evidence could be an item of mail received by a victim of the fraud that was sent by the suspect to perpetuate the fraud. Circumstantial evidence could be testimony from a postal employee who assisted the suspect in matters related to the mailing.

7 Judicial notice is when a judge allows a known fact to be admitted as evidence. Examples of judicial notice include: George Washington was our first president; May 2, 1993 fell on a Saturday; and a financial depression occurred in America in 1931.

8 According to Rule 401, evidence must be relevant and competent. A fact presented as evidence must, in some logical way, relate to proving the case. If you are trying to prove that the suspect committed bank fraud, you're not going to submit as evidence testimony stating that the suspect washed his car every Sunday morning. It's not relevant. And you've got to make sure that the relevant evidence is provided by a competent person. Testimony provided by a former spouse with an ax to grind may not come off as very convincing.

9 a. Kay White can, if she chooses to (she has testimonial privilege), provide the testimony because it is not a confidential communication since it occurred before she and Todd were married.

b. Again, Kay can, if she chooses, provide the testimony. In this instance she'd testify to something she saw, not something that was said.

c. This testimony is covered by the confidential communication privilege. Kay can provide it only if Todd consents to the testimony.

d. Joey can provide the testimony since there is no parent/child communications privilege.

e. Leon Norton can provide the testimony since the Federal courts do not recognize an accountant/client communications privilege.

f. Kent Parks can provide the testimony since it deals with an event rather than a communication.

10 Hearsay evidence is inadmissible because when one person repeats what another has said, there is room for distortion and misunderstanding.

11 The shop book rule allows that a person who currently is the "custodian" of a business's books can introduce the books and provide testimony about them even though that person did not make the original entries.

12 The terms "best evidence" and "secondary evidence" apply to documentary evidence. If evidence concerning a document is needed, the "best evidence" is the document itself. If the original has been destroyed or is not attainable even through the use of a search warrant or subpoena, an authenticated copy of the document can be used. "Secondary evidence" is used when an original of the document in question is unavailable. A witness can testify to the contents of the document or a copy of the document.

Appendix

This appendix contains a listing of selected sources of business information and government records available to the financial investigator.

Business Records

Abstract and Title Company Records

- Maps and tract books.
- Escrow index of purchasers and sellers of real estate (primary source of information)
- Escrow files (number obtained from index)
- Escrow file containing escrow instructions, agreements, and settlements
- Abstracts and title policies
- Special purpose newspapers published for use by attorneys, real estate brokers, insurance companies, and financial institutions. These newspapers contain complete reports on transfers of properties, locations of properties transferred, amounts of mortgages, and releases of mortgages.

Agriculture Records

- County veterinarians
- Commission merchants
- Insurance companies (insure shipments)
- Transportation companies
- Storage companies
- County and state fair boards
- County farm agents
- State cattle control boards (some states maintain records of all cattle brought in and taken out of state)

Automobile Manufacturer and Agency Record

- Franchise agreements
- Financial statements of dealers
- New car sales and deliveries (used car purchases, trade-ins, and sales)

• Service department (mileage, order, and delivery signature to indicate presence in area)

Bonding Company Records

• Investigative and other records on persons and firms bonded

• Financial statements and date

• Address of person on bond

Specialized Commercial Credit Organizations

• United Beverage Bureau

• National Fuel Credit Association

• Jewelers Board of Trade

• Lumbermen's Credit Association

• Produce Reporter Company

• Packer Produce Mercantile Agency

• Paper and Allied Trade Mercantile Agency

• Lyon Furniture Mercantile Agency

• American Monument Association

Credit Reporting Agencies

The Fair Credit Reporting Act of 1971 restricts the availability of information from credit reporting agencies to governmental investigative agencies. Credit reports may only be furnished:

—In response to the order of a court having the jurisdiction to issue such an order;

—Upon written request of the consumer; or

—To a person who has a legitimate business need for the information in regard to a business transaction involving the consumer, including but not limited to credit, insurance, and employment purposes.

There is no specific exception provided in the act that will allow law enforcement agencies to obtain credit reports for investigative purposes. The act provides criminal penalties for obtaining information under false pretenses and for unauthorized disclosures by officers or employees of consumer reporting agencies.

The identifying information which is available under the act is limited to a consumer's name, address, former addresses, place(s) of employment, and former place(s) of employment.

If identifying information is needed for investigative purposes the following credit reporting agencies can be checked:

• Local credit rating and collection agencies

• Local office of National Association of Retail Credit Men

—Insurance applicants

—American Service Bureau

—Hooper Holmes Agency

—Retail Credit Company

• Mortgage Loans

—Loan exchange (clearing house loan information)

—Retailer's Commercial Agency (performs credit investigations for credit cards, banking, and mortgages)

• Transportation

—TRINC (furnishes statistics on the trucking industry).

—Motor Carrier Directory (lists motor carriers with revenues totaling $50,000 or more).

• Manufacturers

—The "Census File of Manufacturers" contains a census of manufacturing plants in the United States.

• Marketing Services

—Dun and Bradstreet, Inc.

—Market Service Bureau

—Middle Market Director (business guide of firms with a net worth between $500,00 and $1,000,000)

—Million Dollar Directory (business guide firms with a net worth of $1,000,000 or more)

—Metal Working Directory (marketing director of metal working plants in the United States)

—Vendor Account Services (used by retail stores in processing accounts payable, buying, and merchandise control)

• International

—International Credit Reports (a division of Dun and Bradstreet which furnishes credit reports on overseas credit)

—International Market Guides (Middle and South America only)

—Continental Europe (lists European businesses in 39 countries)

—Guide to Key British Enterprises (lists prominent firms throughout the United Kingdom)

—Synopsis of Dun– Mexico

—Synopsis of Dun– Brazil

—Reference book– Argentina

—Bradstreet Register

International Mercantile Claims Division

Department Store Records

- Charge accounts
- Credit files

Detective Agency Records

- Investigative files

—Civil

—Criminal

—Commercial

—Industrial

- Character checks
- Fraud and blackmail investigations
- Divorce evidence
- Missing persons search
- Security patrols and guards
- Undercover agents
- Shadow work
- Lie detector tests
- Personnel screening and fingerprinting
- Service checking
- Restaurants
- Public transportation
- Stores

Distributors' Records

- Wholesale toiletry (cash rebates are paid by toiletry manufacturers). Details of available contracts which pay rebates to wholesale toiletry distributors are contained in publications issued by the Toiletry Merchandisers Association, Inc., 230 Park Avenue, New York, N.Y. 10017, and the Druggist Service Council, Inc., 1290 Avenue of the Americas, New York., N.Y. 10019
- Gambling equipment
- Wire service
- Factory, farm, home, office equipment, etc.

Drug Store Records

- Prescription records (name, address, date, and physician issuing prescription)

Fraternal, Veterans, Labor, Social, and Political Organization Records

- Membership and attendance records
- Dues, contributions, and payments
- Locations and history of members

Hospital Records

- Entry and release dates
- Payments made

Hotel Records

- Identity of guest
- Payments made by guest
- Credit record
- Forwarding address
- Reservations for travel (transportation companies and other hotels)
- Telephone calls made to and from room
- Freight shipments and luggage (in and out)

Insurance Company Records (Life, accident, fire, burglary, automobile, and annuity policies)

- Applications (background and financial information, insurance carried with other companies)
- Fur and jewelry floaters (appraised value and description)
- Customers' ledger cards
- Policy and mortgage loan accounts
- Dividend payment records
- Cash value and other net worth data
- Correspondence files
- Payment records on termination, losses, or refunds on cancellations
- Payments to doctors, lawyers, appraisers, and photographers hired directly by the insurance company to act for the company or as an independent expert

Laundry and Dry Cleaning Records

- Marks and tags (marks are sometimes invisible and are brought out by use of ultraviolet rays)
- Files of laundry marks

—Local or State police departments
—National Institute of Dry Cleaning, Inc., Washington, D.C.

Lenders Exchange or Consumer Loan Exchange

An organization known as the Consumer Loan Exchange or Lenders Exchange exists in all of the large cities in the United States, as well as in some of the smaller cities. It is a nonprofit organization supported by and for its members. Most the lending institutions are members of the exchange. It can supply information concerning open and closed loan accounts with member companies, and is a good source of general background information. These organizations are not listed in directories or telephone books. Their location in a city may be obtained through local lending agencies.

National Charge Plan Records
National agencies, such American Express, Diners Club, and Carte Blanche, which provide credit cards for use in charging travel, entertainment, goods and services, can determine whether an individual or business has an account from their central index files. If details of the account are needed, information requests should indicate whether only copies of the monthly statements or copies of both the statements and charge slips are desired, name, social security number, the time period to be covered, the subject's address, and the name and address of the subject's employer or business. Requests should be directed to:

American Express Company, 770 Broadway, New York, N.Y. 10003, and Diners Club/Carte Blanche, Adjustment Department, 180 Inverness Drive West, Englewood, CO 80111.

Newspaper Records (from a newspaper's morgue)

- Relatives, associates, and friends
- Previous places of employment (employee or company publications)
- Police and FBI files
- Schools (yearbooks, school papers, etc.)
- License bureaus (drivers, chauffeurs, taxis, etc.)
- Military departments
- Fraternal organizations
- Church groups
- Race tracks
- Nightclub or sidewalk photographers and photography studios

Public Utility Company Records

- Present and previous address of subscriber
- Payments made for service and "major" purchases

Publications

- *Who's Who in America* and various States
- Tax services
- City directories
- *Billboard* (amusements, coin-machines, burlesque, drive-ins, fairs, state, radio, TV, magic,

music machines, circuses, rinks, vending machines, movies, letter lists, and obituaries)

- *Variety* (literature, radio, TV, music, state, movies, obituaries, etc.)

- *American Racing Manual* (published by Triangle Publications, Inc., 10 Lake Drive, P.O. Box 1015, Highstown, New Jersey 08520). Records showing amounts paid to owners of winning horses by each race track in the United States, Canada, and Mexico

- Professional, trade, and agriculture directories and magazines

- *Moody's Investors Service Inc.*

- *Standard and Poor's Corporation*

Real Estate Agency or Savings and Loan Association Records

- Property transactions

- Financial statements

- Payments made and received (settlement sheets)

- Credit files

- Loan applications. These do not contain quite the same information as loan applications given to a bank. A savings and loan association depends primarily upon real estate security rather than upon other assets and liabilities of a borrower.

Telephone Company Records

- Local directories, library of "out of city" directories

- Message unit detail sheets (in some areas) which list numbers called by a particular telephone

- Investigative reports on telephones used for illegal purposes

- Payments for service

- Toll calls. Because of the existence of more than one long distance carrier, toll records of a local phone company may be an incomplete listing of such calls. There may be a second telephone bill from another company, such as GT&E or MCI.

Transportation Company Records

- Passenger lists, reservations

- Destinations

- Fares paid

- Freight carrier-shippers, destinations, and storage points

- Departure and arrival times

Government Records

State Police (Central Records Section)

- Criminal cases

- Criminal intelligence

- Inflammable liquid installations
- Firearms registrations
- Investigations conducted for other departments
- Traffic arrests and motor vehicle accident investigations
- Noncriminal and criminal fingerprint records
- "Rogues gallery"
- Investigation of aviation rules and non-carrier civilian aircraft accidents
- Police training school files

City Police

- Criminal identification

—Records of arrests, accidents, and general information

—Alphabetical indexes of every complainant or suspect

—"Aided" cards (citizen assistance)

—Gun permits or applications and registrations

—Lost or stolen articles

—Pawn shop files

—Towed or repossessed autos

—Ambulance files

—Business information files

—"Scofflaw files" (consistent violator of minor offense– primarily traffic)

- Other divisions

—Criminal division files

—Forgery squad (check squad)

—Juvenile division

—Morals or vice squad files

—Narcotics bureau

—Organized crime division

—Police force personal history files

—Public relations office (press file)

—Traffic division files

Small Town Police

- Criminal index cards
- Criminal arrest cards
- Accident reports
- Complaint forms
- Offense reports

County Police (Sheriff)

- Criminal records

—Crimes involving bodily violence

—Crimes involving theft

—Crimes involving worthless checks

—Personal history sheets on people connected with the crimes

—Juvenile division records

—County business owners

- Traffic records

—Name, address, license plate number, driver's license number, arrest number, date and place of birth, sex, color, age, occupation, height, weight, complexion, color of hair, eyes, marks, and facts of arrest

National Sheriffs Association Directory

- List of State institutions and their superintendents

- State and Federal enforcement agencies and territorial jurisdictions

- Associate members of National Sheriffs Association

- County sheriffs

- Address of National Auto Theft Bureau

Other State and Local Law Enforcement and Quasi-Law Enforcement Organizations

- Specialized police organizations

- Public, semi-public, and private organizations

- The industrial security officer

- International Association of Chiefs of Police

- The monthly police administration review list of police publications

State and Local Court Records

Typically, there are three levels of courts within the State system. There is a Trial Court, where most litigation begins, an Appellate Court, which is the first level of appeal, and Court of Final Appeal. Sometimes you will find a court below the Trial Court which works much like the magistrate does in the Federal system.

Most litigation, such as divorce or breach of contract, takes place in the State and local system. Documents submitted to the court in connection with a divorce are particularly helpful in financial investigations. It is not unusual for detailed asset and liability information to be present in a divorce file.

Probate records describing estates and distribution of estates are also found in the State and local court system. These may be particularly helpful in negating nontaxable sources of cash.

Anytime a person is involved in a civil action, whether it be for breach of contract or some type of negligence action, a wealth of background information on the individual is usually provided to the opposing party through the court. A record of this information will be kept in the case files of the court and is available to an investigator.

Federal Government Records

Bureau of Alcohol, Tobacco, and Firearms (ATF)

• Distillers, brewers, and persons or firms who manufacture or handle alcohol, as a sideline or main product

• Inventory or retail liquor dealers and names of suppliers as well as amounts of liquor purchased by brand

• Names and records of known bootleggers

• Names of subjects of investigations by ATF

• Processors, manufacturers, and wholesalers of tobacco products

• List of all Federal firearms license holders, including manufacturers, importers, and dealers

• List of all Federal explosives license holders, including manufacturers, importers and dealers

• For weapons manufactured or imported after 1986, capability of tracing any firearm from manufacturer or importer to retailer

Bureau of the Public Debt

• U.S. savings bonds purchased and redeemed

• Requests for information must be addressed to:

Bureau of the Public Debt
Division of Transactions and Rulings
200 Third Street
Parkersburg, West Virginia
26101

Federal Aviation Agency (FAA)

This agency maintains records which reflect the chain of ownership of all civil aircraft in the United States. These records include documents relative to their manufacture and sale (sales contracts, bills of sale, mortgages, liens, transfers, inspections, and modifications). They also maintain licensing and medical information on pilots.

Federal Aviation Administration
Civil Aviation Security Division
AAC– 90, P.O. Box 25082
Oklahoma City, Oklahoma
73125

Department of Agriculture

- Licensed meat packers and food canners
- Inspections made under Pure Food and Drug Act
- Transactions with individuals and businesses (subsidies and adjustments)

Department of Defense

The Department of Defense maintains data concerning pay, dependents, allotment accounts, deposits, withholding statements (Forms W-2), and any other financial information relative to military personnel. This information is available at one the following offices, depending upon the branch of the Armed Forces to which the individual was or is presently attached:

United States Army Finance Center
Indianapolis, Indiana 46249
Request must include the complete name and Army serial number

Air Force Finance Center
RPTP
Denver, Colorado 80279

Director, Bureau of Supplies and Accounts
Department of the Navy
13th and Euclid Streets
Cleveland, Ohio 44115

Department of the State

- Import and export licenses
- Foreign information
- Passport records (date and place of birth required). Recent data may be obtained from the local district court.

Drug Enforcement Administration (DEA)

- Licensed handlers of narcotics
- Criminal records of users, pushers, and suppliers of narcotics

Federal Bureau of Investigation (FBI)

- Criminal records and fingerprints
- Anonymous Letter Index
- National Stolen Property Index (stolen Government property, including military property)
- Nonrestricted information pertaining to criminal offenses and subversive activities
- National Fraudulent Check Index

U.S. Customs Service

- Record of importers and exporters
- Record of custom house brokers

- Record of custom house truckers (cartage licenses)

- List of suspects

- Records of persons who transport or cause to be transported currency of more than $10,000, or certain monetary instruments at one time into or out of the United States

U.S. Secret Service

- Records pertaining to counterfeit, forgery, and United States' security violation cases

- Records pertaining to anonymous letters and background files on persons who write "crank" letters

- Secret Service's central files in Washington, D.C., contain an estimated 100,000 handwriting specimens of known forgers. An electronic information retrieval system facilitates comparison of questioned handwriting with the specimens on file for identification purposes.

U.S. Postal Service

- Mail watch or cover

- Current or forwarding addresses of subjects and third parties

- Photostats of postal money orders. Requests for such records must be addressed to:

Money Order Division
Postal Data Center
P.O. Box 14965
St. Louis, Missouri 63182

- Addresses of post office box holders. These requests should be made only when efforts to obtain the information from other sources are unsuccessful. Information can be obtained from the Inspector-in-Charge or Postal Inspector. Check with the local post office to learn the identity of the inspector who can furnish the information.

Immigration and Naturalization Service (INS)

- Records of all immigrants and aliens

- Deportation proceedings

- Passenger manifests and declarations (ship, date, and point of entry required)

- Naturalization records (names of witnesses to naturalization proceedings and people who know the suspect)

- Lists of passengers and crews on vessels from foreign ports

- Financial statements of aliens and persons sponsoring their entry

Interstate Commerce Commission (ICC)

The ICC has information concerning individuals who are or have been officers of transportation firms engaged in interstate commerce. This information includes the officer's employment and financial affiliations.

In addition to the record information available from the ICC, most safety inspectors of the ICC are good sources of "reference" information because they have personal knowledge of supervisory employees of the various carriers in their region.

IRS National Computer Center

The National Computer Center is located in Martinsburg, West Virginia and it maintains the Master File, a tax record of all known taxpayers. The Master File is designed to accumulate all data pertaining to the tax liabilities of all taxpayers, regardless of location. The Master File is separated into several categories. Two of the categories are the Business Master File and the Individual Master File.

Securities and Exchange Commission (SEC)

• Records of corporate registrants of securities offered for public sale, which usually show:

—A description of registrant's properties and business

—A description of the significant provisions of the security to be offered for sale and its relationship to the registrant's other capital securities

—Information as to the management of the registrant

—Certified financial statements of the registrants

• Securities and Exchange Commission News Digest (a daily publication giving a brief summary of financial proposals files and the actions taken by the SEC)

• The SEC Bulletin is issued quarterly and contains information of official actions with respect to the preceding month. It also contains a supplement which lists the names of individuals reported as being wanted on charges of violations of the law in connection with securities transactions. It is available upon request at any of the SEC regional or branch offices in the following cities:

Atlanta, GA
Miami, FL
Boston, MA
New York, NY
Chicago, IL
Philadelphia, PA
Cleveland, OH
Salt Lake City, UT

Denver, CO
San Francisco, CA
Detroit, MI
Seattle, WA
Fort Worth, TX
St. Louis, MO
Los Angeles, CA
Washington, D.C.

- The SEC's Securities Violations Section maintains comprehensive files on individuals and firms who have been reported to the Commission as having violated Federal or State securities laws. The information pertains to official actions taken against such persons, including denials, refusals, suspensions, and revocations of registrations; injunctions, fraud orders, stop order, cease and desist orders; and arrests, indictments, convictions, sentences, and other official actions.

Social Security Administration

The Social Security Administration, headquartered in Baltimore, is responsible for the issuance of social security numbers. Records on social security paid by an individual or business are not available for review by the public.

If a social security number is known, it might lead to helpful information regarding the location in which the card was issued. Since many people apply for a social security number at a young age, this in turn can lead to locating the place of birth of an individual. There are nine digits in the social security number. With the exception of the 700 series, the first three digits reflect the state of issue. The last six digits are individual identifiers. The table on the next page contains a listing of the states of issue of the first three digits.

Initial Numbers	State of Issuance	Initial Numbers	State of Issuance
001 - 003	New Hampshire	449 - 467 627 - 645	Texas
004 - 007	Maine	468 - 477	Minnesota
008 - 009	Vermont	478 - 485	Iowa
010 - 034	Massachusetts	486 - 500	Missouri
035 - 039	Rhode Island	501 - 502	North Dakota
040 - 049	Connecticut	503 - 504	South Dakota
050 - 134	New York	505 - 508	Nebraska
135 - 158	New Jersey	509 - 515	Kansas
159 - 211	Pennsylvania	516 - 517	Montana
212 - 220	Maryland	518 - 519	Idaho
221 - 222	Delaware	520	Wyoming
223 - 231	Virginia	521 - 524	Colorado
232 - 236	West Virginia	525, 585, 648 - 649 allocated,not in use	New Mexico
237 - 246, 232 with middle digits 30	North Carolina	526 - 527 600 - 601	Arizona
247 - 251	South Carolina	528 - 529 646 - 647 allocated, not in use	Utah
252 - 260	Georgia	530	Nevada
261 - 267 589 - 595	Florida	531 - 539	Washington
268 - 302	Ohio	540 - 544	Oregon
303 - 317	Indiana	545 - 573 602 - 626	California
318 - 361	Illinois	574	Alaska
362 - 386	Michigan	575 - 576	Hawaii
387 - 399	Wisconsin	577 - 579	Washington, DC
400 - 407	Kentucky	580 groups 01 - 18	Virgin Islands
408 - 415	Tennessee	580 (groups above 20) - 584, 596 - 599	Puerto Rico
416 - 424	Alabama	586	Guam, American Samoa, Northern Mariana Islands, Philippine Islands
425 - 428, 587 588 allocated, not in use	Mississippi	700 - 728	Railroad employees with special retirement act
429 - 432	Arkansas		
433 - 439	Louisiana		
440 - 448	Oklahoma		

Veterans Administration (VA)

• Records of loans, tuition payments, insurance payments, and nonrestrictive medical data related to disability pensions are available at regional offices. This information, including photostats, may be obtained by writing the appropriate regional office. All requests should include a statement covering the need and intended use of the information. The veteran should be identified clearly and, if available, the following information should be furnished:

—VA claim number

—Date of birth

—Branch of service

—Dates of enlistment and discharge

Federal Reserve Bank (FRB)

• Records of issue of United States Treasury Bonds

United States Coast Guard

• Records of persons serving on United States ships in any capacity

• Records of vessels equipped with permanently installed motors

• Records of vessels over 16 feet long equipped with detachable motors

Treasurer of the United States

Checks paid by the U.S. Treasury are processed through the Office of the Treasurer of the United States. Photostats of the canceled checks may be obtained by initiating a request through the U.S. government agency which authorized the check.

National Crime Information Center (NCIC)

The National Crime Information Center is a repository of data relating to crime and criminals gathered by local, State, and Federal law enforcement agencies. The NCIC's computer equipment is located at FBI Headquarters in Washington, D.C. The present equipment is capable of accommodating nearly 2 million records on criminal activities. In a matter of seconds, stored information can be retrieved through equipment in the telecommunications network. Connecting terminals are located throughout the country in police departments, sheriff's offices, State police facilities, and Federal law enforcement agencies. Dispatchers can respond quickly to requests. NCIC, as well as operating statewide systems, furnishes computerized data in a matter of seconds to all agencies participating in the centralized State systems. The goal of NCIC is to serve as a national index to fifty statewide computer systems and heavily populated metropolitan area systems.

NCIC Headquarters might be compared to a large automated "file cabinet" with each file having its own label or classification. Such a cabinet of data contains information concerning:

Stolen, missing, or recovered guns

Stolen articles

Wanted persons

Stolen/wanted vehicles

Stolen license plates

Stolen/wanted boats

Stolen/embezzled/missing securities

National Law Enforcement Telecommunications System (NLETS)

NLETS is a computerized communication network linking State and local enforcement agencies in all 50 States. It can provide information such as criminal history, driver's licenses, and vehicle registration.

El Paso Intelligence Center (EPIC)

EPIC is a multi-agency operation that collects, processes, and disseminates information on narcotics traffickers, gun smugglers, and alien smugglers in support of ongoing field investigations.

If a suspect is or has been engaged in any of the previously mentioned activities, it is possible that EPIC will have intelligence information on him or her. This information might include the name of the individual, his or her known activities, significant events, associations among individuals or activities, aircraft or vessels used by the subject, observations of both foreign and domestic movements of the subject, and his or her associates and their aircraft or vessels. EPIC also provides the name, agency, and telephone number of each investigator having expressed an interest in or having data regarding a subject. EPIC records often contain substantial *financial* information relative to the subject.

International Criminal Police Organization (Interpol)

Interpol is an international police agency with bureaus set up in member countries. In the

United States, the National Central Bureau is under the direction and control of the Departments of Justice and Treasury.

The National Central Bureau can assist in such things as criminal history checks, license plate and driver's license checks, and the location of suspects, fugitives, and witnesses.

The Federal Courts

This system is basically a three step process. The first step is the U.S. District Court;, the second, the U.S. Court of Appeals; and the third, the U.S. Supreme Court. Since most court records are similar, we will only deal with the U.S. District Court in this appendix.

- U.S. District Courts

There are U.S. District Courts in every State (the larger States have several) and in the District of Columbia, Guam, Puerto Rico, the Canal Zone, and the Virgin Islands.

The U.S. District Court has exclusive jurisdiction in bankruptcy, maritime and admiralty, patents, copyright penalties, fines under Federal law, and proceedings against consul and vice consuls of foreign states. In addition, it has jurisdiction when the United States or a national bank is a party, and in cases where the law specifically states that the U.S. District Court has original jurisdiction.

The U.S. District Courts have concurrent jurisdictions with State courts on "Federal questions" when the dispute arises under the Constitution, laws, or treaties of the United States; disputes between citizens of different States; one U.S. citizen and one citizen of a foreign state; or a citizen and a foreign state.

The U.S. District Court has broad criminal jurisdiction over all offenses against the laws of the United States. When both Federal and State laws are violated by one committing a crime, the offender is subject to prosecution in both the Federal and State courts for the separate crimes.

The files of the clerk's office of a U.S. District Court are not as complex as those of a State court of original jurisdiction. For the investigator, **the most important records in the custody of a clerk of a U.S. District Court are the case records.** These records consist of the files (case papers), the minutes, and the dockets.

—The files consist of pleadings, processes, and written

orders and judgments of the court, and such other papers as pertain directly to the case.

—The minutes record, in summary form, of what happened during the proceedings. In some courts, the minutes are an integral part of the file.

—The docket sheet on each case is a chronological summary, not only of what takes place in court, but also of the papers in the file. The docket sheet can be very valuable to an investigator who is looking for only one item in a huge file. In most U.S. District Courts there are separate sets of dockets for bankruptcy, and civil and criminal cases. Some clerks have found it to their advantage to keep a set of miscellaneous dockets, and most clerks keep the docket sheets for closed cases in a separate area.

The clerk of a district court will have a record of banking institutions that have been designated as depositories for money of estates in bankruptcy.

The United States District Courts have jurisdiction to naturalize aliens and maintain copies of the certificates of naturalization as well as a name index of the individuals naturalized. If an alien elects to change his or her name at naturalization, both the old and new name appears in the index. In addition, a copy of the subject's Application to File Petition for Naturalization appears in the court records. This form (N-400) contains considerable information about the alien being naturalized.

- Other Federal Courts

To handle particular types of cases, Congress has established special courts. They are described in the *Guide to Court Systems* as follows:

—Court of Claims— The U.S. Government permits certain claims to be brought against itself in the U.S. Court of Claims.

—U.S. Customs Court— When certain merchandise is imported into the United States, customs duties have to be paid to the U.S. Government. Customs collectors at various ports in the United States classify merchandise and appraise it. When an importer complains on the rate, or that the merchandise was improperly excluded, the U.S. Customs Court is the court to which the case must be brought. Appeals from the U.S. Customs Courts are taken to the Court of Customs and Patent Appeals. This court also reviews certain decisions of the Patent Office and the U.S. Tariff Commission.

This appendix contains information regarding the American Bankers Association prefix numbers of cities and states and a listing of Federal Reserve Districts.

Federal Reserve Districts

1 - Boston
2 - New York
3 - Philadelphia
4 - Cleveland
5 - Richmond
6 - Atlanta
7 - Chicago
8 - St. Louis
9 - Minneapolis
10 - Kansas City
11 - Dallas
12 - San Francisco

THE NUMERICAL SYSTEM
of The American Bankers Association
Index to Prefix Numbers of Cities and States

Numbers 1 to 49 inclusive are Prefixes for Cities
Numbers 50 to 99 inclusive are Prefixes for States
Prefix Numbers 50 to 58 are Eastern States
Prefix Number 59 is Hawaii
Prefix Numbers 60 to 69 are Southeastern States
Prefix Numbers 70 to 79 are Central States
Prefix Numbers 80 to 88 are Southwestern States
Prefix Number 89 is Alaska

Prefix Numbers of Cities in Numerical Order

1 New York, N.Y.
2 Chicago, Il.
3 Philadelphia, Pa.
4 St Louis, Mo.
5 Boston, Mass.
6 Cleveland, Ohio
7 Baltimore, Md.
8 Pittsburgh, Pa.
9 Detroit, Mich.
10 Buffalo, N.Y.
11 San Francisco, Ca.
12 Milwaukee, Wis.
13 Cincinnati, Ohio
14 New Orleans, La.
15 Washington, D.C.
16 Los Angeles, Ca.
17 Minneapolis, Minn.
18 Kansas City, Mo.
19 Seattle, Wash.
20 Indianapolis, Ind.
21 Louisville, Ky.
22 St. Paul, Minn.
23 Denver, Colo.
24 Portland, Ore.
25 Columbus, Ohio
26 Memphis, Tenn.
27 Omaha, Neb.
28 Spokane, Wash.
29 Albany, N.Y.
30 San Antonio, Tx.
31 Salt Lake City, Ut
32 Dallas, Tx.
33 Des Moines, Iowa
34 Tacoma, Wash.
35 Houston, Tx.
36 St. Joseph, Mo.
37 Fort Worth, Tx.
38 Savannah, Ga.
39 Oklahoma City, Ok.
40 Wichita, Kan.
41 Sioux City, Iowa
42 Pueblo, Co.
43 Lincoln, Neb.
44 Topeka, Kan.
45 Dubuque, Iowa
46 Galveston, Tx.
47 Cedar Rapids, Iowa
48 Waco, Tx.
49 Muskogee, Ok.

Prefix Numbers of States in Numerical Order

50 New York
51 Connecticut
52 Maine
53 Massachusetts
54 New Hampshire
55 New Jersey
56 Ohio
57 Rhode Island
58 Vermont
59 Hawaii
60 Pennsylvania
61 Alabama
62 Delaware
63 Florida
64 Georgia
65 Maryland
66 North Carolina
67 South Carolina
68 Virginia
69 West Virginia
70 Illinois
71 Indiana
72 Iowa
73 Kentucky
74 Michigan
75 Minnesota
76 Nebraska
77 North Dakota
78 South Dakota
79 Wisconsin
80 Missouri
81 Arkansas
82 Colorado
83 Kansas
84 Louisiana
85 Mississippi
86 Oklahoma
87 Tennessee
88 Texas
89 Alaska
90 California
91 Arizona
92 Idaho
93 Montana
94 Nevada
95 New Mexico
96 Oregon
97 Utah
98 Washington
99 Wyoming
101 Territories

ANSWER SHEET

TEST NO. ______________ PART ______ TITLE OF POSITION ______________________________
(AS GIVEN IN EXAMINATION ANNOUNCEMENT - INCLUDE OPTION, IF ANY)

PLACE OF EXAMINATION ______________________________ ______________________ DATE ______________
(CITY OR TOWN) (STATE)

RATING

USE THE SPECIAL PENCIL. MAKE GLOSSY BLACK MARKS.

1 A B C D E	26 A B C D E	51 A B C D E	76 A B C D E	101 A B C D E
2 A B C D E	27 A B C D E	52 A B C D E	77 A B C D E	102 A B C D E
3 A B C D E	28 A B C D E	53 A B C D E	78 A B C D E	103 A B C D E
4 A B C D E	29 A B C D E	54 A B C D E	79 A B C D E	104 A B C D E
5 A B C D E	30 A B C D E	55 A B C D E	80 A B C D E	105 A B C D E
6 A B C D E	31 A B C D E	56 A B C D E	81 A B C D E	106 A B C D E
7 A B C D E	32 A B C D E	57 A B C D E	82 A B C D E	107 A B C D E
8 A B C D E	33 A B C D E	58 A B C D E	83 A B C D E	108 A B C D E
9 A B C D E	34 A B C D E	59 A B C D E	84 A B C D E	109 A B C D E
10 A B C D E	35 A B C D E	60 A B C D E	85 A B C D E	110 A B C D E

Make only ONE mark for each answer. Additional and stray marks may be counted as mistakes. In making corrections, erase errors COMPLETELY.

11 A B C D E	36 A B C D E	61 A B C D E	86 A B C D E	111 A B C D E
12 A B C D E	37 A B C D E	62 A B C D E	87 A B C D E	112 A B C D E
13 A B C D E	38 A B C D E	63 A B C D E	88 A B C D E	113 A B C D E
14 A B C D E	39 A B C D E	64 A B C D E	89 A B C D E	114 A B C D E
15 A B C D E	40 A B C D E	65 A B C D E	90 A B C D E	115 A B C D E
16 A B C D E	41 A B C D E	66 A B C D E	91 A B C D E	116 A B C D E
17 A B C D E	42 A B C D E	67 A B C D E	92 A B C D E	117 A B C D E
18 A B C D E	43 A B C D E	68 A B C D E	93 A B C D E	118 A B C D E
19 A B C D E	44 A B C D E	69 A B C D E	94 A B C D E	119 A B C D E
20 A B C D E	45 A B C D E	70 A B C D E	95 A B C D E	120 A B C D E
21 A B C D E	46 A B C D E	71 A B C D E	96 A B C D E	121 A B C D E
22 A B C D E	47 A B C D E	72 A B C D E	97 A B C D E	122 A B C D E
23 A B C D E	48 A B C D E	73 A B C D E	98 A B C D E	123 A B C D E
24 A B C D E	49 A B C D E	74 A B C D E	99 A B C D E	124 A B C D E
25 A B C D E	50 A B C D E	75 A B C D E	100 A B C D E	125 A B C D E

ANSWER SHEET

TEST NO. ______________ PART ______ TITLE OF POSITION ______________________________
(AS GIVEN IN EXAMINATION ANNOUNCEMENT - INCLUDE OPTION, IF ANY)

PLACE OF EXAMINATION ______________________________ (CITY OR TOWN) ______________ (STATE) DATE ______________

RATING

USE THE SPECIAL PENCIL. MAKE GLOSSY BLACK MARKS.

1 A B C D E	26 A B C D E	51 A B C D E	76 A B C D E	101 A B C D E
2 A B C D E	27 A B C D E	52 A B C D E	77 A B C D E	102 A B C D E
3 A B C D E	28 A B C D E	53 A B C D E	78 A B C D E	103 A B C D E
4 A B C D E	29 A B C D E	54 A B C D E	79 A B C D E	104 A B C D E
5 A B C D E	30 A B C D E	55 A B C D E	80 A B C D E	105 A B C D E
6 A B C D E	31 A B C D E	56 A B C D E	81 A B C D E	106 A B C D E
7 A B C D E	32 A B C D E	57 A B C D E	82 A B C D E	107 A B C D E
8 A B C D E	33 A B C D E	58 A B C D E	83 A B C D E	108 A B C D E
9 A B C D E	34 A B C D E	59 A B C D E	84 A B C D E	109 A B C D E
10 A B C D E	35 A B C D E	60 A B C D E	85 A B C D E	110 A B C D E

Make only ONE mark for each answer. Additional and stray marks may be counted as mistakes. In making corrections, erase errors COMPLETELY.

11 A B C D E	36 A B C D E	61 A B C D E	86 A B C D E	111 A B C D E
12 A B C D E	37 A B C D E	62 A B C D E	87 A B C D E	112 A B C D E
13 A B C D E	38 A B C D E	63 A B C D E	88 A B C D E	113 A B C D E
14 A B C D E	39 A B C D E	64 A B C D E	89 A B C D E	114 A B C D E
15 A B C D E	40 A B C D E	65 A B C D E	90 A B C D E	115 A B C D E
16 A B C D E	41 A B C D E	66 A B C D E	91 A B C D E	116 A B C D E
17 A B C D E	42 A B C D E	67 A B C D E	92 A B C D E	117 A B C D E
18 A B C D E	43 A B C D E	68 A B C D E	93 A B C D E	118 A B C D E
19 A B C D E	44 A B C D E	69 A B C D E	94 A B C D E	119 A B C D E
20 A B C D E	45 A B C D E	70 A B C D E	95 A B C D E	120 A B C D E
21 A B C D E	46 A B C D E	71 A B C D E	96 A B C D E	121 A B C D E
22 A B C D E	47 A B C D E	72 A B C D E	97 A B C D E	122 A B C D E
23 A B C D E	48 A B C D E	73 A B C D E	98 A B C D E	123 A B C D E
24 A B C D E	49 A B C D E	74 A B C D E	99 A B C D E	124 A B C D E
25 A B C D E	50 A B C D E	75 A B C D E	100 A B C D E	125 A B C D E